MERLEAU-P

The Arguments of the Philosophers

The purpose of this series is to provide a contemporary assessment and history of the entire course of philosophical thought. Each book contains a detailed, critical introduction to the work of a philosopher or school of major influence and significance.

Also available in the series:

Aquinas	Eleonore Stump
*Descartes	Margaret D. Wilson
*Hegel	M.J. Inwood
*Hume	Barry Stroud
*Kant	Ralph C.S. Walker
*Kierkegaard	Alastair Hannay
*Locke	Michael Ayers
*Karl Marx	Allen Wood
Malebranche	Andrew Pyle
*Merleau-Ponty	Stephen Priest
*Nietzsche	Richard Schacht
*Plato	Justin Gosling
*Plotinus	Lloyd P. Gerson
*Rousseau	Timothy O'Hagan
*The Presocratic Philosophers	Jonathan Barnes
*Santayana	Timothy L.S. Sprigge
*Sceptics	R.J. Hankinson
*Wittgenstein, 2nd edition	Robert Fogelin

*also available in paperback

MERLEAU-PONTY

Stephen Priest

Routledge
Taylor & Francis Group

LONDON AND NEW YORK

First published 1998
by Routledge
11 New Fetter Lane, London EC4P 4EE

First published in paperback 2003

Simultaneously published in the USA and Canada
by Routledge
29 West 35th Street, New York, NY 10001

Typeset in Times by
Graphicraft Limited, Hong Kong
Printed and bound in Great Britain by
TJ International Ltd, Padstow, Cornwall

British Library Cataloguing in Publication Data
A catalogue record for this book is available from the British Library

Library of Congress Cataloging in Publication Data
A catalog record for this book has been requested

ISBN 0–415–06263–2 (hbk)
ISBN 0–415–30864–X (pbk)

To Kerry

'Etre corps, c'est être noué à un certain monde . . .'
Maurice Merleau-Ponty *Phénoménologie de la Perception* (p. 173)

'To be a body, is to be tied to a certain world . . .'
Maurice Merleau-Ponty *Phenomenology of Perception* (p. 148)

Contents

CONTENTS

CONTENTS

Preface

Even though logical positivism is officially defunct, Western philosophy retains an optimistic faith in the procedures of the natural sciences to solve problems that are really philosophical. This faith is nearly always misplaced and Merleau-Ponty's thought provides a most valuable antidote to it. Merleau-Ponty shows us how to make room for human subjectivity in a world of science.

At the time of writing, Anglo-American philosophy is still in the grip of a putative distinction between something called 'analytical philosophy' and something else called 'modern continental philosophy'. The distinction does not withstand historical, geographical and philosophical scrutiny. Despite the conspicuous methodological and stylistic distinctions between phenomenology, existentialism, logical atomism, logical positivism, linguistic analysis, structuralism, post-structuralism, hermeneutics and others, all these movements operate (consciously or not) within a fundamentally Kantian anti-metaphysical framework. Historically and geographically they are all German and Austrian in their modern genesis.

On the other hand, there is a genuine and valuable distinction between using logical arguments to try to solve philosophical problems and doing anything else. In this book I have tried to show respect for Merleau-Ponty's work by arguing for and against what he says, even when he provides no arguments of his own.

Merleau-Ponty is an existential-phenomenologist. In Chapter II, I provide an understanding of his phenomenology and its derivation from Husserl. In Chapter III, I provide an understanding of his existentialism and its derivation from Hegel (whose patterns of thinking Merleau-Ponty thinks he never escapes). In Chapters IV–XIV, I engage Merleau-Ponty's existential phenomenology with problems about the body, perception, space, time, subjectivity, freedom, language, other minds, physical objects, art and being. In the last chapter, in briefest outline,

I sketch how we have to be even more subjectivist in our ontology than Merleau-Ponty if we wish to solve these problems. The first chapter is historical.

Most of this book was written during my period at Wolfson College Oxford during 1993. I am most grateful to Dr T.D.J. Chappell for proposing, and to Sir Isaiah Berlin for seconding, my election to a Visiting Scholarship at Wolfson and to the Governing Body for that election. I thank the President and the Fellowships and Membership Committee for my continued membership of the college and use of its excellent research facilities.

I am also grateful to Dr Fergus Kerr OP, Dr Richard Finn OP and my other colleagues at Blackfriars Hall, Oxford for providing such a stimulating environment in which to think, teach and write.

I also thank the University of Rhode Island for my appointment as Visiting Distinguished Professor during 1994 and the Rhode Island Committee for the Humanities for their sponsorship. I am grateful to Professor Cheryl Foster and Professor Galen Johnson of the University of Rhode Island Philosophy Department for valuable discussion of Merleau-Ponty's ideas.

Dr T.D.J. Chappell and Professor Timothy Williamson kindly gave of their time to discuss the content of the manuscript. I thank Maeve O'Donaghue, Anne Gerber and Eleanor Rivers for assistance with the manuscript and Professor Ted Honderich, Kerry Smallman and Peggy Priest for their various kindnesses.

Stephen Priest
Oxford

Abbreviations

Works of Merleau-Ponty

AD   *Les Aventures de la Dialectique* (Paris, Gallimard, 1955)
ADT   *Adventures of the Dialectic*, trans. Joseph Bien (Evanston, Northwestern University Press, 1973)
OE   *L'Oeil et l'Esprit* (Paris, Gallimard, 1964)
OET   'Eye and mind' in *The Primary of Perception*, trans. Y.M. Edie (Evanston, Northwestern University Press, 1964)
PP   *Phénoménologie de la Perception* (Paris, Gallimard, 1945)
PPT   *Phenomenology of Perception*, trans. Colin Smith (London, Routledge, 1962)
PM   *La Prose du Monde* (Paris, Gallimard, 1969)
PW   *The Prose of the World*, trans. John O'Neill (Evanston, Northwestern University Press, 1973)
S   *Signes* (Paris, Gallimard, 1960)
ST   *Signs*, trans. Richard C. McCleary (Evanston, Northwestern University Press, 1964)
SB   *The Structure of Behaviour*, trans. A.L. Fisher (Methuen, London, 1965)
SC   *La Structure du Comportement* (Presses Universitaires de France, Paris, 1942)
SNS   *Sens et Non-Sens* (Paris, Nagel, 1966)
SNST *Sense and Non-Sense*, trans. Hubert L. Dreyfus and Patricia Allen Dreyfus (Evanston, Northwestern University Press, 1964)
VI   *Le Visible et l'Invisible* (Paris, Gallimard, 1964)
VIT   *The Visible and the Invisible*, trans. Alphonso Lingis (Evanston, Northwestern University Press, 1968)

Works of Husserl

Ideas I *Ideas Pertaining to a Pure Phenomenology and to a Phenomeno-logical Philosophy* First Book trans. F. Kersten (Martinus Nijhoff, The Hague, 1982)

Ideas II *Ideas Pertaining to a Pure Phenomenology and to a Phenomeno-logical Philosophy* Second Book trans. R. Rojcewicz and A. Schuwer (Kluwer, Dordrecht, 1989)

Ideen I *Ideen zu einer reinen Phänomenologie und phänomenologischen Philosophie*, I Buch (Max Niemeyer, Halle, 1913)

Ideen II *Ideen zu einer reinen Phänomenologie und phänomenologischen Philosophie*, II Buch (Martinus Nijhoff, The Hague, 1952)

PV *Pariser Vorträger* in *Husseriana – Edmund Husserl, Gesam-melte Werke*, Vol. 1 (Martinus Nijhoff, The Hague, 1950)

PL *The Paris Lectures* trans. Peter Koestenbaum (Martinus Nojhoff, The Hague, 1975)

I

Life and Works

1 *Student and intellectual*

Maurice Merleau-Ponty was born on 14 March 1908 at Rochefort sur Mer (Charente Maritime). His father was killed in action in the First World War and he remained very close to his mother until her death in 1952. Despite his early bereavement he described his childhood as 'incomparable'.

He had the privilege of a first class education at two Paris *lycées*; Janson-de-Sailly and Louis-le-Grande and studied at the Ecole Normale Supérieure from 1926, graduating with the *agrégation de philosophie* in 1930. It was during his time at the Ecole Normale that he made the acquaintance of Jean-Paul Sartre. His at times tempestuous relationship with Sartre would change his life, personally, philosophically and politically.

Immediately after graduating Merleau-Ponty did his 'Service Militaire Légal' then worked as a school teacher at the Lycée de Beauvais from 1931 to 1933. After a year as *Boursier* at the Centre National de la Recherche Scientifique he taught again, this time at the Lycée de Chartres (1934–5). In 1935 he returned to the Ecole Normale to pursue graduate research as Agrégé Répétiteur de Philosophie.

Merleau-Ponty attended two sets of lectures in Paris which were important to his intellectual development: Husserl's 1929 Pariser Vorträger and Alexandre Kojève's series 'La Philosophie Religieuse de Hegel' which ran from January 1933 to May 1939. Despite the title, Kojève's lectures were really a humanist commentary on Hegel's *Phäno-menologie des Geistes* (1807) and were partly published in 1947 as *Intro-duction à la Lecture de Hegel*. Although Merleau-Ponty's German was at best rudimentary in 1929, the content of Husserl's lectures was discussed at informal meetings at which Merleau-Ponty was present. Besides, a French translation of their expanded version, *Cartesianische Meditationen*, was available from 1931.[1]

1

It is hard to establish degrees of influence in the history of ideas but it is clear that the existentialism and the phenomenology that Merleau-Ponty fused into his 'existential phenomenology' in his mature work are partly isomorphic with Kojève's Hegel and Husserl's summary of his transcendental phenomenology. Merleau-Ponty reads existentialism through the lens of the non-theological Hegel of Kojève and the other great twentieth century scholar of Hegel, Jean Hyppolite.[2] Merleau-Ponty endorses phenomenology only through a repudiation of what Husserl would regard as two of its central tenets emphasised in the *Pariser Vorträger*: the *epoché* and the transcendental ego. Husserl's *epoché* is a methodological agnosticism about the existence of the external world which facilitates the phenomenological description of consciousness. The transcendental ego is the irreducibly subjective source of consciousness revealed by the *epoché*.

Kojève's lectures were also attended by Raymond Aron, Georges Bataille, Jacques Lacan, Eric Weill and André Breton. During the 1930s Merleau-Ponty was part of a stimulating Parisian literary and philosophical milieu which was a heady mix of surrealism, psychoanalysis and nascent existentialism. Claude Lévi-Strauss tells us that it was about 1930 that he and Simone de Beauvoir met Merleau-Ponty.[3] Although he did not talk with him again until the winter of 1944–5 they met frequently from 1948, Merleau-Ponty absorbing structuralist ideas into his later phenomenology under Lévi-Strauss' influence.

The research Merleau-Ponty pursued at the Ecole Normale from 1935 was for the manuscript which became his *thèse complémentaire* in 1938 and his first book, *La Structure du Comportement*, published in 1942.[4]

2 The Structure of Behaviour

This book is a sustained critique of behaviourism in psychology. Although its targets are now rather dated, it is still useful as an antidote to contemporary neo-positivist and reductionist philosophies of mind (for example, at the time of writing, 'physicalism' and 'eliminative materialism'). Merleau-Ponty's strategy is to argue that putative denials of the reality of consciousness in fact presuppose consciousness. Reductionist philosophies of mind are therefore self-refuting. He also denies the determinist thesis that there are causally sufficient conditions for the obtaining of mental states. Rather, it is consciousness which (in a quasi-Humean way) constitutes some relations as causal. Although Merleau-Ponty accepts that human action can be studied by physics, biology and psychology he refuses to construe these as inquiries into ontologically separable domains between which causal relations could hold. Nor are psychology 'reducible' to biology and biology 'reducible' to physics, although he is enough of a naturalist to accept that the facts of physics are necessary for the facts of biology and the facts of biology are necessary for the facts of psychology and *a fortiori*, the facts of physics are necessary for the facts of psychology. Clearly, his endorsement of this hierarchy of necessary conditions is consistent with his repudiation of causal determinism.

Although *La Structure du Comportement* is anti reductionist and anti positivist, it eschews Cartesian dualism. It entails a naturalism which takes seriously the reality of conscious states but postulates no immaterial mind. In a partial anticipation of Peter Strawson's 1959 work *Individuals*,[5] Merleau-Ponty argues that the ability to draw a conceptual distinction between mental and physical substances presupposes a capacity to use what he calls 'human predicates' ('prédicats humains'). These are used to ascribe activities which are not clearly only mental or only physical to the whole human being. The concept of the human being is primordial with regard to the concept of mind and the concept of a human body. In this way Merleau-Ponty hopes to 'go beyond' 'mentalism' and 'materialism'.

By the time he wrote the book, Merleau-Ponty had not fully integrated the lessons of Husserl's phenomenology. That was to come in the 1945 work *Phénoménologie de la Perception*. In *La Structure du Comportement* he deploys Gestalt psychology against behaviourism. Indeed, the 'Structure' of his work's title is the word usually used to translate the German 'Gestalt' into French. 'Gestalt' means 'shape' or 'form' and the Gestalt psychologists held that the way in which an object presents itself to a perceiver is ambiguous depending on the perceiver's own conscious or unconscious preconceptions. It presents alternative *Gestalten*.

Merleau-Ponty argues that behaviour is ambiguous in a similar way. Any human action may be given various interpretations from the perspective of the agent or from the perspective of a third person observer. What someone is doing in performing an action cannot be simply read off from the physiology of the action and does not admit of causally sufficient mechanistic explanation.

For this reason, no piece of behaviour may be reduced to its alleged parts. What it is as a whole is always open to conscious interpretation. We can never rule out a priori the possibility of further possible interpretations of a single action.

In *La Structure du Comportement* several themes are introduced that will be conspicuous in his later philosophy.

Merleau-Ponty is a valuable critic of positivism: the doctrine that any problem may, in principle, be resolved using the experimental and mathematical techniques of the natural sciences. In the 1942 book he argues that consciousness and behaviour resist reductivist explanation, but by 1945, perception, the body, freedom, space, time and subjectivity are all deployed as obstacles to scientific progress.

The second edition of *La Structure du Comportement* appeared with a Preface by Alphonse de Waelhens taken from his 1951 book *Une Philosophie de L'Ambiguïté: L'Existentialisme de M. Merleau-Ponty.*[6] Merleau-Ponty did not readily endorse the expression 'philosophy of ambiguity' as a title for his entire philosophy up to 1951 but it is true that the ambiguity ascribed to behaviour in *La Structure du Comportement* is given new applications in *Phénoménologie de la Perception*. There the perceived is ambiguous, the body is ambiguous and the world is ambiguous.

The naturalised Cartesianism of *La Structure du Comportement* develops into the phenomenology of the body in *Phénoménologie de la Perception*. Until well into the 1950s Merleau-Ponty is trying to do justice to subjectivity, the reality of one's own existence, without commitment to Cartesian dualism.

Merleau-Ponty was called up into the 5-ième Régiment d'Infanterie de Ligne in August 1939, just prior to the outbreak of war in September. He was quickly transferred to the General Staff of the 59-ième Division Légère d'Infanterie and remained with that unit until, after the defeat of France in May–June 1940, he was captured and tortured by the Germans and discharged in the September.

He then joined the resistance group *Socialisme et Liberté* in which Sartre and Albert Camus were active. It was during the war that these three became close friends and Merleau-Ponty became imbued with existentialist ideas; Sartre's seminal fusion of existentialism and phenomenology, *L'Etre et le Néant* (1943)[7] predating the publication of his own *Phénoménologie de la Perception* by two years. Both Sartre and Camus had already published their early existentialist novels, Sartre's semi-phenomenological *La Nausée* appearing in 1938 and Camus' absurdist allegorical tale of a *pied noir*, *L'Etranger*, in 1942. Both writers were composing their major literary contributions to existentialism; Sartre *Les Chemins de la Liberté* (1945–9) and Camus *La Peste* (1947).

Existentialism is the attempt to solve fundamental problems of human existence such as: how to live in the face of certain death, the ethics of the exercise of freedom, the meaning of existence, including human existence, the appropriateness of political, religious and sexual commitments. It may be understood as a concrete reaction against two earlier philosophies. The early Danish existentialist, Søren Kierkegaard (1813–55) rejected the completable holism of Hegel's dialectic of consciousness in that philosopher's 1807 *Phänomenologie des Geistes*. Martin Heidegger (1889–1976) eschewed Husserl's phenomenological vocabulary (which remained rather mentalistic despite that philosopher's repudiation of psychologism) and replaced his transcendental

4

phenomenology with a new 'fundamental ontology'. Instead of inquiring into the essence of consciousness, Heidegger interrogated being; asked what it is to be. The existentialism of Sartre, de Beauvoir and Merleau-Ponty is also a reaction against all forms of 'essentialism', including Husserl's.

Existentialists divide into atheists, theists and Heidegger. The theists include not only Kierkegaard, who was a protestant theologian, but also the French Catholic Gabriel Marcel (1889–1973). Friedrich Nietzsche (1844–1900) is a vitriolic atheist and critic of Christianity. Sartre was an atheist as was Merleau-Ponty, despite a flirtation with the circle around the left wing French Catholic journal *L'Esprit* during the 1930s. Although Heidegger undertook an early theological training, overtly theistic themes are conspicuously absent from his mature philosophy, including *Sein und Zeit* (1927). Nevertheless, the thoroughness and profundity of his inquiry into being is of great theological interest.

The central themes of existentialism are taken up by Merleau-Ponty in *Phénoménologie de la Perception*: the critique of scientific empiricism, the concern with what it is like to exist, the lived body, a Cartesian concern with the first-person singular that nevertheless eschews mind–body dualism, the subjectivity of space and time, the reality of freedom.

For the remainder of the war Merleau-Ponty again worked as a school teacher, at the Lycée Carnot (1940–4) and Lycée Condorcet (1944–5). After the Liberation of August 1944 he joined the editorial committee of Sartre's newly founded review *Les Temps Modernes*. He functioned as political editor until 1953 publishing several papers in it on political and aesthetic themes. It was during the last two years of the war that he wrote his most influential work, the massive synthesis of existentialism and phenomenology, *Phénoménologie de la Perception*, which was published in 1945.

3 *The Phenomenology of Perception*

Phénoménologie de la Perception is divided into an introduction and three large parts. The introduction is subtitled 'Traditional Prejudices and the Return to Phenomena'.[8] It is an attack on the philosophical assumptions of empirical psychology. In particular, Merleau-Ponty offers a critique of 'the sensation' as a content of experience. Drawing partly on Gestalt psychology and partly on the later Husserl, Merleau-Ponty argues that there are no uninterpreted sensations or sensory 'data'. Rather, the pragmatic preconceptions of the perceiving subject, and the perceived context of the object of perception, make a difference to what that object is to that perceiver. In perception we are always

presented with interpreted objects and never with 'pure' sensations. It
follows from his account that the phenomenalist project of translating
sentences about the perceived world into sentences about sense data
without loss of meaning is impossible. It follows that that empiricist
theory of perception is false.

In his attack on empirical psychology Merleau-Ponty is at pains to
avoid philosophical rationalism: the doctrine that the nature of reality
may be discerned through thought, rather than through experience.
A *Leitmotif* of *Phénoménologie de la Perception* is the devising of a phenomenology that will eschew both empiricism and rationalism. Rationalism fails, in his view, partly because the existence and the detail of an
object cannot be fully grasped in thought and partly because rational
reflection on an object, again, involves interpretation and so changing the
object from its unreflected state.

Merleau-Ponty thinks that rationalism and empiricism both embody
a single mistake. This mistake is called 'objective thought' or 'objective
thinking'.[9] Empiricism includes the view that what is realistically the case
may be discovered through experience. Rationalism essentially includes
the view that what is the case may be discovered through thought.[10]
'Objective thought' is the thought that what is realistically the case may
be accessed by a subject in a way that is unaffected by the interpretations
and pragmatic concerns of that subject. Merleau-Ponty argues that this
is false because our subjective embodiment, our sensory and cognitive
apparatus and our practical purposes inescapably struc-ture the way the
world strikes us. It follows on Merleau-Ponty's view that if we wish
to understand the world it is not enough to study the world. We have to
study ourselves.

Part One of *Phénoménologie de la Perception* is called 'The Body'.[11]
It is a discussion of a concept crucial to an understanding of Merleau-
Ponty's existential phenomenolgy: incarnate subjectivity. He thinks
subjectivity is physical, or, to put it another way: I am my body ('Je suis
mon corps' PP, 175). His phenomenological descriptions steer a careful
course between mind–body dualism and materialism. Like the Cartesian
dualist he accepts the reality of consciousness and subjectivity. Like the
materialist he accepts that we are essentially physical beings. However,
as in *La Structure du Comportement*, he rejects the idea that we are
immaterial minds, and he rejects the idea that we are physical objects.
We are in fact *physical subjects.*

The fact of one's embodiment may be described phenomenologically.
It shows up in the peculiarly partial visual perspectives one has on the
one body that is one's own ('le corps propre' PP, 528), but not on any
other bodies, and in kinaesthetic experience. These odd but striking
phenomenological facts are regarded by Merleau-Ponty as more fundamental than the putative findings of philosophical and psychological

theory. They are presupposed by such theory, whether or not they are acknowledged or noticed.

Following Heidegger, Merleau-Ponty describes our mode of being as being-in-the-world.[12] The hyphenation of this expression is designed to denote the inseparability of human existence, the world, and the existential relations between them. The terms of the relationship may be abstractly separated in thought, but not in reality.

Part Two of *Phénoménologie de la Perception* is called 'The World as Perceived'.[13] It is a description of the ways in which our bodily subjectivity structures our experience of the world. Merleau-Ponty argues that scientific understandings of the world are abstract and presuppose phenomenological facts. For example, the depiction of space through geometry and physics depends upon space presented to us as we live in it. As science or positivist philosophies deny or repress the existence of subjective space, intersubjective or 'human' space and phenomenologically objective space, they deny or repress some of their own pre-suppositions and so lapse into incoherence. In the final part of the book Merleau-Ponty makes similar claims about time.

In Part Three 'Being-For-Itself and Being-in-the-World'[14] Merleau-Ponty discusses the cogito, temporality and freedom. He situates his thought *vis-à-vis* Sartre's *L'Etre et le Néant*, arguing that Sartre's libertarianism is exaggerated and that Sartre's bifurcation of being into being-in-itself and being-for-itself is antithetical in a way that is inimical to the adequate description of the dependencies between subjective and objective reality.

Phénoménologie de la Perception as a whole may be read in different ways. It is a defence of and an extrapolation of some of the ideas of the later Husserl, the Husserl of the *Lebenswelt* and the *Krisis der europäischen Wissenschaften*.[15] It is an attack on the earlier Husserl of *Ideen*, the Husserl of the transcendental reduction and the transcendental ego.[16] Husserl thought that a certain methodological agnosticism about the existence of the external world could facilitate the phenomenological description of the essence of consciousness. Merleau-Ponty argues in an 'externalist' way that consciousness cannot be made intelligible in abstraction from its contents or intentional objects and these are paradigmatically to be found in the world. It follows that Husserl's *epoché*, or suspension of the question of belief in an external world, is at best incompletable and possibly incoherent.

Rather like Sartre in his 1936 work *La Transcendance de L'Ego*, Merleau-Ponty rejects Husserl's transcendental ego as phenomenologically illegitimate.[17] This putative source of consciousness cannot appear to consciousness. Phenomenology cannot postulate what does not appear to consciousness, so phenomenology cannot rightly postulate the transcendental ego.

4 *Professor and man of letters*

He was made *Docteur ès Lettres* in July 1945 on the merits of his two books and took a number of university posts: *Maître de Conférences* and then professor at the Faculté des Lettres de Lyon (1945–8), *Maître de Conférences* then '*Professeur sans chaire*' at the Faculté de Lettres de Paris (1949–51) and *Chargé de Conférences* at the Ecole Normale (1946–9). In 1948–9 in a 'congé d'inactivité' he took the opportunity to visit the University of Mexico. From 1947–50 he was a member of the *Jury du Concours d'Entrée* at the Ecole Normale.

1952 was a crucial year in Merleau-Ponty's life. His mother died. He was elected to the Chair at the Collège de France and he fell out with Sartre, resigning from the editorial committee of *Les Temps Modernes* the next year.

On his election to the Chair *Le Figaro* of 3 March asked 'Is existentialism going to officially enter the Collège de France?'. *L'Aurore* of the next day suggested cynically about philosophical systems: 'existentialism offers over all the others the enormous advantage of having no morality' and added 'It is only a cerebral way of dancing the boogie-woogie'. Also on 4 March, Sartre and Camus' old resistance paper *Combat* sprang to Merleau-Ponty's defence: 'With M. Merleau-Ponty it is atheistic existentialism, the most original and most attractive current of French philosophy since the Liberation that will enter the Collège de France'.[18]

The Chair had been vacant since the death of Louis Lavelle and was held before him by Henri Bergson. Both were counted 'traditionalists' by the French literary and philosophical establishment and Merleau-Ponty's appointment was regarded as risqué in the extreme. In retrospect it seems less so. Merleau-Ponty was the most academic of the French existentialists and his thought is not more opaque than Bergson's 'philosophy of consciousness' which had enjoyed a vogue after the First World War comparable to that enjoyed by Sartre after the Second.

Nevertheless, Merleau-Ponty shared some of Sartre's left-wing political radicalism. During the Second World War the communists in France had borne the brunt of the resistance to the Nazi occupation and Merleau-Ponty, like Sartre, de Beauvoir and many other European intellectuals, was optimistic about Marxism as a means of not only resisting Nazism but overthrowing the inequalities of capitalism. However, Merleau-Ponty swiftly because disillusioned with Marxism in the 1950s, especially with Sartre's version of it. We are able to see this in the difference between the critique of Arthur Koestler's attack on Marxist totalitarianism in Merleau-Ponty's *Humanisme et Terreur* and the savage attack on Sartre in 'Sartre et L'Ultrabolchevisme' in the 1955 *Les Aventures de la Dialectique*.[19]

It is usually assumed that Merleau-Ponty and Sartre quarrelled in 1952–3 only for political reasons: over the theory of Marxism and the actuality of the Korean War. In fact the basis of disagreement was much wider and more philosophical. Bernard Pingaud, writing in *L'Arc*[20] rightly points out that Merleau-Ponty's resignation from the editorial committee of *Les Temps Modernes* was a departure from 'la "philosophie de la conscience"' and refers us to the closing pages of the chapter 'Sartre et l'Ultrabolchevisme' as evidence. Pingaud is correct to see a radical transition in Merleau-Ponty's thought in the 1950s. His synthesis of existentialism and phenomenology was essentially complete by the publication of *Phénoménologie de la Perception* in 1945 and the ruptures with Husserl over the *epoché* and the transcendental ego established. His writing in the 1950s was dominated by a Heideggerian concern with Being. We should not understand Merleau-Ponty as simply repudiating his early work: the critique of science and the phenomenology of the body. Rather, he is involved in a quasi-Heideggerian rewriting of it.[21] Rather as Heidegger in *Sein and Zeit* is in a sense still doing phenomenology but a phenomenology as fundamental ontology that appalled Husserl, so Merleau-Ponty is providing a rereading of his own existential phenomenology. At his death in 1961 this work was still incomplete. He had tentatively entitled it at different times *Etre et Sens*, *Généalogie du Vrai*, *L'Origine de la Verité*, *Le Visible et L'Invisible*. It was this last title that his friend Claude Lefort used for its posthumous publication in 1964. It is by far the most interesting, profound and original of Merleau-Ponty's works.

5 *The Visible and the Invisible*

Le Visible et L'Invisible is to *Phénoménologie de la Perception* as Heidegger's fundamental ontology is to Husserl's transcendental phenomenology. It effects a transition from a phenomenology of consciousness to a phenomenology of being.

Although *Phénoménologie de la Perception* departed from Husserlian phenomenology in its endorsement of the Heideggerian category being-in-the-world, Merleau-Ponty nevertheless came to think it took subject–object dualism as phenomenologically primitive and still made use of a comparatively superficial psychologistic vocabulary.

For this reason, Merleau-Ponty hoped in *Le Visible et L'Invisible* to renounce the vocabulary of 'concept', 'idée' ('idea'), 'esprit' ('spirit', 'mind'), and 'représentation' and deploy a new ontological vocabulary of 'dimensions': 'articulation', 'niveau' ('level'), 'charnières' ('hinges'), 'pivots' ('pivots'), 'configuration' ('configuration'), 'écart' ('separation'). In particular, no ontologically primordial commitment would be made to things possessing properties perceived by a conscious subject.

Because only six chapters of *Le Visible et L'Invisible* had been written by the time Merleau-Ponty died this radical project was never completed. Nevertheless, the most interesting section of the book: '*L'Entrelacs – Le Chiasme*' does show how it might have been implemented. 'Entrelacs' means 'intertwining' and 'chiasme' means 'chiasmus'. Merleau-Ponty does not simply deploy a new vocabulary to redenote the old dependencies between subject and object described in *Phénoménologie de la Perception*. Rather, the new ontological category of 'le chair' ('flesh') is used in a way that is primitive to the subject–object distinction. The choice of 'flesh' suggests that part of the phenomenology of the body to denote the totality of being so far as it is disclosed. 'Flesh' denotes everything that is surface, everything that in the old phenomenology we might wish to put on the *content* side of perception. The relationship between the visible and the invisible is more fundamental than the relationship between perceiver and perceived. It is one of 'intertwining' and 'chiasmus'. It is an intertwining because the flesh of the world is an inextricable mix of the visible and the invisible. It is chiasmic because visible and invisible are an isomorphic reversal of one another.

In their frequent meetings from 1948, Merleau-Ponty urged Lévi-Strauss to make explicit the philosophical presuppositions of his structural anthropology and Lévi-Strauss helped Merleau-Ponty to embed his existential phenomenology in historical and cultural 'situations'.

Indeed, it would be a gross oversimplification to take at face value the structuralist 'reaction' against phenomenology in the 1960s' work of Gilles Deleuze, Michel Foucault and Lévi-Strauss himself. Although prima facie structuralism is a philosophy of form and phenomenology a philosophy of content (despite all the talk about the *eidos* and the eidetic reduction in Husserl), although structuralism is an exposing of a priori quasi-linguistic rules and phenomenology is a description of experience, there are structuralist elements in Merleau-Ponty's writing which he consciously or unconsciously endorsed. For example, his distinction of signs into signals and symbols in *La Structure du Comportement* warrants a new reading of 'structure' in the title. His 1960 collection *Signes* engages with Lévi-Strauss not unsympathetically and Merleau-Ponty's posthumously published *La Prose du Monde* (1969) overtly integrates the essentials of Ferdinand de Saussure's structural linguistics into his own phenomenology of linguistic expression. This book appeared too late to be read in print by his structuralist critics, Deleuze's *Logique du Sens* also appearing in 1969, for example. Nevertheless, a 'structural phenomenology' could be reconstructed from the Merleau-Ponty corpus. Of course, such a synthesis might not be to the pure structuralist's taste. Lévi-Strauss reports:

> If the structuralist enterprise had awakened his interest and his sympathy despite everything that we know to separate him from it, this is without doubt because as he put it in the course of a colloquium on the sense and usage of the term 'structure' in which we were participating, he consented to find in it 'a new way of seeing being'.[22]

Lévi-Strauss is right however to find in Merleau-Ponty's account of music in *Le Visible et L'Invisible* a fusion of structuralism and phenomenology, of a priori form and phenomenological content.

Although Pingaud correctly identifies Merleau-Ponty's break with Sartre as essentially Heideggerian he could not see that it is also an anticipation of Derrida's deconstruction of the metaphysics of presence. Merleau-Ponty says in criticism of Sartre,

> if [. . .] one definitely admits of open, incomplete meanings, the subject must not be pure presence to itself and to the object[23]

and makes this suggestion about the subject,

> its signifying activity is rather the perception of a difference between two or several meanings.[24]

Although Merleau-Ponty has anticipated Derrida's deconstruction of Husserl in *Le Voix et la Phénomène*, this is because both Merleau-Ponty and Derrida are using a partial and uncomfortable synthesis of the structural linguistics of Ferdinand de Saussure and the 'Destruktion' of metaphysical thought by Heidegger in their critical furthering of phenomenology.[25]

Some of Merleau-Ponty's most interesting thoughts are expressed through his essays, which have been collected together as the volumes: *Sens et Non-Sens* (1948), *Signes* (1960), and *La Prose du Monde* (1969). Perhaps his two most insightful pieces are 'Le Doute de Cézanne' which appeared in *Sens et Non-Sens* and 'L'Œil et L'Esprit' which was published as a slim volume by Gallimard in 1964. 'Le Doute de Cézanne' includes a moving description of Cézanne's dedication to painting and the suggestion that Cézanne is painting the primordial phenomenological world that is presupposed by science. The idea that the painted world is more fundamental than the world according to science is taken up in 'L'Œil et L'Esprit'. There Merleau-Ponty also tries to ground his aesthetics in the phenomenology of the body, arguing that it is inconceivable that a mind could paint.

Merleau-Ponty died suddenly in the evening of Wednesday 3 May 1961. He collapsed while rereading Descartes in preparation for a class he was to deliver the next day.

II

Phenomenology

Phénoménologie de la Perception opens with the question 'What is phenomenology?' (PPT, vii).[1] In this chapter I shall answer the question by evaluating Merleau-Ponty's own answer to it. His answer largely consists in a critical appraisal of some tenets of Husserl's phenomenology.

1 *Existence and essence*

Merleau-Ponty defines 'phenomenology' as a kind of essentialism. He says 'Phenomenology is the study of essences' (PPT, vii).[2] Different conceptions of 'essence' are possible but, minimally, if P states the essence of x then P states what x is. This could prima facie take the form of defining 'x', or of stating the necessary and sufficient conditions for being x or for falling under the concept 'x'. Phenomenology is at least the attempt to specify both the properties something must have in order to belong to a certain class, and those properties such that if something possesses them it follows logically that it falls into that class.

Merleau-Ponty has so far provided a necessary but not a sufficient condition for some procedure's being phenomenological because some essentialism may be non-phenomenological even if Husserl's phenomenology is essentialist.[3]

Phenomenological essentialism is distinguished from essentialism in general by its concept of essence. The notion of *essence* is contrasted with that of an *individual* ('individuelle') and the criterion for distinguishing essences from (spatio-temporal) individuals is the conjunction of:

1   i is an individual if and only if i may exist only in one place at any one time;

and

13

2   e is an essence if and only if e may exist in more than one place at
    any one time.

To see this intuitively, a physical object is an individual because a physical object cannot occupy more than one place at one time but redness is
an essence because redness may be in different places at the same time.[4]
The essence/individual distinction approximates to the type/token or
universal/particular distinction so long as we allow that it makes sense
for universals or types to be spatio-temporally located, and for one and
the same type or universal to be located at numerically distinct places at
one and the same time. It is redness that exists at those places, not
simply tokens of redness.

The definition of 'phenomenology' must proceed at the level of meta-
essentialism and for two reasons: 'What is phenomenology?' is about
the essence of phenomenology, (and phenomenology is a kind of essentialism); and 'What is an essence?' is a request for the essence of an
essence.

Husserl (for example at *Ideen* I, §2–3) distinguishes the properties
putatively constitutive of any essence: those properties all and only
essences have in common in virtue of which they are essences.

Any particular spatio-temporal location of what the essence is the
essence of is (usually) irrelevant to what that essence is. This entails that
the specification of where and when something is is not a contribution
to specifying what it is.

A thing possesses its essence and each part of its essence with 'eidetic
necessity' (*Ideen* I, §2).[5] Some individual, i, is F with eidetic necessity if
and only if i could not fail to be F and yet be i. 'Being i' is ambiguous
between being the *sort* i is and being the *one* i is, but both senses are
intended. The obtaining of eidetic necessities is essentially constitutive
of essences.

Essences exhibit 'eidetic universality' (*Ideen* I, §2).[6] Some essence 'e'
exhibits eidetic universality if and only if; if i has F as part of e with
eidetic necessity then any individual numerically distinct from i, i*, that
has e is also F. If one thing has a property with eidetic necessity then
anything that is not that thing but is of the same sort has that property.
That this principle holds is also constitutive of essences.

If an individual, i, has an essence, e, then there is no reason in principle why some numerically distinct individual, i*, should not have e.
Nevertheless, an essence is paradigmatically (but not essentially) constituted by properties an individual has irrespective of its relations to
other individuals.

What further distinguishes phenomenological essentialism from other
essentialisms is the way in which essences come to be known. Essences
are intuited. 'Intuition' ('Anschauung') is Husserl's name for the mental

act by which some intellectual or perceptual content is directly appre-hended. In the intuition of essences ('Wesensanschauung') the essence of an individual is directly presented to consciousness. The procedure by which an essence is intuited is known as the 'eidetic reduction'[7] and essentially has two phases.[8] The essence is first intuited in the individual itself and then 'put into an idea'. Husserl describes these two phases as follows:

1   At first 'essence' designated what is to be found in the very own being of an individuum as the What of an individuum. (*Ideen* I, §3)

2   Any such what can, however, be 'put into an idea'. (*Ideen* I, §3)

In experiencing an object what the object is is intuited, or experienced directly. Then the essence ('Wesen', 'eidos') of the object is extracted and intuited as an idea: in abstraction from the object *qua* individual.

Not only any physical thing but also any act of consciousness and any abstract (for example mathematical or political) object may be subjected to the eidetic reduction. Indeed, for Husserl these are all in radically different ways possible objects of experience and any possible object of experience may be intuited eidetically.

The intuition of essences generates a set of propositions which are truths about essences. Such propositions are 'judgements having eidetic universal validity' (*Ideen* I, §5).[9] Some truth-valued item has universal eidetic validity if and only if: it has the truth value 'true', it could not have been false (i.e. it is a necessary truth), it is a report about the con-stitution of an essence, and there is no contradiction in the supposition that more than one individual shares the essence it denotes.

Merleau-Ponty says that according to phenomenology 'all problems amount to finding definitions of essences' (PPT, vii).[10] The eidetic reduc-tion is essential to the method of Husserlian phenomenology, so phe-nomenology is itself essentially an essentialism, but there is a more profound sense to Merleau-Ponty's remark. It is the ambition of phe-nomenology to leave on one side all the traditional disputes of meta-physics and make instead a fresh start in philosophy; engage in a kind of phenomenological description that will show how it is possible for metaphysical questions to be formulated.

The scope of the quantifier 'all' ('tous') is not explicitly stated but Merleau-Ponty means at least all the traditional problems of meta-physics. By using 'reviennent à' ('return to') Merleau-Ponty means: for any problem within the scope of 'tous' solving a problem about essence is a necessary condition for solving that problem. It is one of the central claims of phenomenology that phenomenology is prior to philosophy in this sense: without the phenomenological intuition of essences it is not possible to solve the problems of philosophy.

Eidetic language, then, putatively eschews metaphysical assumptions but is rather deployed in the passive reporting of intuited essences. Merleau-Ponty provides two examples of objects of the phenomenological search for essences; 'the essence of perception, the essence of consciousness' (PPT, vii)[11] which may be usefully contrasted with the example of physical objects.

It is part of the essence of a physical object not to be presented in its entirety in visual perception so physical objects necessarily only present some of their sides at a time. It is physical objects which Husserl has in mind when he writes:

> The specific character of certain categories of essences is such that essences belonging to them can be given only 'onesidedly', in a sequence 'many-sidedly', yet never 'all sidedly'. (*Ideen* I, §3)[12]

Acts of consciousness are phenomenologically contrasted with physical objects in at least two ways. Although acts of consciousness have parts they have no sides or 'profiles' ('Abschattungen'). Also, acts of consciousness are not presented perspectivally or from a point of view. It is this kind of eidetic fact that Merleau-Ponty has in mind when he says that phenomenology is the study of essences. It is a fundamental aim of Husserl's phenomenology to distinguish essences.

It is not too misleading to think of the phenomenological concept of the essence of x as the set of necessary and sufficient conditions for x being of some sort 'S' so long as the Husserlian notion of essence is borne strongly in mind. Then we can say that x belongs to S if and only if there exists a set of properties such that if x possesses those properties then it follows that x belongs to S and such that if x does not possess those properties then x does not belong to S. For example, if it is of the essence of x, because x is a physical object, that x be presented 'perspectivally' if visually perceived, then if x lacks this property then it necessarily follows that x is not a physical object and if x possesses this property then it follows that x is a physical object.

The intuition of an essence is made possible by the process of 'imaginative variation'[13] which allows the distinction between the contingent and the essential properties of an object to be drawn. Eidetic variation is the imaginary addition and subtraction of the properties of an object with the aim of disclosing its essence. For example, it turns out to be part of the essence of phenomenological red to be extended because phenomenological red cannot be thought in abstraction from a red extension through eidetic variation.

In case this account of eidetic variation be thought unduly psycho-logistic, it should be borne in mind that Husserl and Merleau-Ponty are describing a process whereby essences are intuited. They are not saying that the essence consists in the inconceivability of something's being otherwise; an object's lacking a property. Rather, the essence consists in the impossibility of the object lacking certain properties and the incon-ceivability rests on that. Husserl and Merleau-Ponty should be thought of as making explicit the psychological procedure that is the deciding that something is a necessity. Clearly, the repudiation of psychologism is consistent with holding that there is such a process.[14]

Phenomenological red is essentially extended because colour is 'founded' or 'grounded'[15] on extension. Founding or grounding is to be understood this way: a grounds b if and only if if not a then not b. In other words, a grounds b if and only if the existence or nature (or both) of a is a necessary condition for the existence or nature (or both) of b and, as is implied by this, b is sufficient for a.

Merleau-Ponty sometimes speaks of 'defining essences' (PPT, vii) ('definir des essences' PP, 1). This is loose because only linguistic items may be defined and essences are not linguistic items in phenomenology (even though linguistic items, as possible objects of experience have essences and there exists a phenomenology of language). We may refor-mulate Merleau-Ponty's expression more precisely in quasi-Husserlian terms and say that an essence is 'defined' if and only if some set of propositions exhibiting eidetic universality and necessity comes to be known through eidetic intuition such that that set truly reports the properties common and peculiar to a type.

To understand both what Merleau-Ponty endorses of Husserl and one of his most radical breaks with Husserl, a sharp distinction is required between questions of essence and questions of existence. Questions of essence have the form *What is x?* but questions of existence have the form *Is x?* or *Does x exist?* As we shall see in the next section, one of the most important procedures of Husserlian phenomenology is the attempt to answer questions of essence in abstraction from questions of existence. Intuitively, Husserl tries to find out *what things are* without deciding *whether they are*. Merleau-Ponty on the other hand argues that it is not possible to fully specify what something is without stating whether it is, even though something's *being* is not the same as its *being what it is*.

Phenomenology is a sustained attempt to answer essentialist ques-tions, but Merleau-Ponty claims this cannot be done without answering existentialist questions. This fusion of essentialism and existentialism is his 'existential phenomenology'.

2 *The natural attitude and its suspension*

Merleau-Ponty says phenomenology is a 'philosophy which places in abeyance the assertions arising out of the natural attitude, the better to understand them' (PPT, vii).[16] To understand this we need to understand Husserl's notion of the natural attitude and its phenomenological reduction or *epoché*.

'The natural attitude' ('natürliche Einstellung') is Husserl's expression for the set of mainly commonsensical beliefs a person holds before engaging in his phenomenology.

The world of the natural attitude ('die Welt der natürlichen Einstellung') is the set of truth conditions for those beliefs. It is 'I and my surrounding world' (*Ideen* I, §27).[17] It is spatio-temporal, contains physical objects, animate beings and conscious beings. Although it is presented to me from my own subjective first person singular point of view I am myself a member of this world. The physical objects and other conscious beings within it exist whether I am conscious of them or not. Sometimes they are directly present to my consciousness, sometimes only peripherally, sometimes not at all.

Husserl says 'I am conscious of a world endlessly spread out in space, endlessly becoming and having endlessly become in time' (*Ideen* I, §27).[18] These are not intended as metaphysical theses by Husserl but as reports of the way in which the world strikes one pre-phenomenologically, or commonsensically. He thinks the world *appears* infinite.

The world of the natural attitude is 'mitgegenwärtig' ('co-present') and the things in it are 'vorhanden' ('on hand') for me (*Ideen* I, §27). I am perceptually presented with objects as means to my ends. A table is there to place books on. Some books are there to be read, a glass to drink from. For this reason Husserl says the world of the natural attitude contains 'value characteristics' ('Wert-charaktere') and 'these value characteristics and practical characteristics also belong constitutively to the objects 'on hand' as objects' (*Ideen* I, §27).[19] People too are presented as friends, servants, relations. Within the natural attitude the world already strikes us as value laden and practical. Again, this is not a metaphysical thesis about values but a report of how the world naturally strikes us before we do phenomenology.

In a partial substantiation of Merleau-Ponty's claim that phenomenology is 'the study of essences' (PPT, vii) ('l'étude des essences' PP, i) Husserl attempts to isolate an essential feature of the natural attitude; a feature necessary and sufficient for the existence of the natural attitude. His scrutiny yields 'a general positing which characterises the natural attitude' (*Ideen* I, §30).[20] This positing is general because it is the commonsensical assumption that a world exists with myself located within it. Indeed, 'assumption' is too theoretical a word here because the world simply strikes one as existing. As Husserl puts it, 'The world is always there as an actuality' (*Ideen* I, §30).[21] The positing of the world is necessary and sufficient for the obtaining of the natural attitude. If I posit the world I am in the natural attitude, if I do not posit the world I am not in the natural attitude.

It is this Husserlian thesis that Merleau-Ponty is expressing when he says phenomenology is 'a philosophy for which the world is always "already there"' (PPT, vii).[22] The existence of the world is prior to all philosophising, at least in a chronological sense of 'prior' and for non-phenomenological philosophy in a logical and an epistemological sense too.

Merleau-Ponty also says the world is a 'presence' (PPT, vii) ('présence' PP, 1). This sentence entails Husserl's claim that the world is an 'actuality' ('Wirklichkeit' *Ideen* I, §30) but is not entailed by it. This is because if something is present in the temporal sense of 'present' such that something is present if and only if it exists now, then it follows that if x is present then x is actual. However, Merleau-Ponty's claim is not logically equivalent to Husserl's claim because 'present' has a second sense, not logically entailed by the first. This is the sense in which x is present if and only if x is present to consciousness. At least prima facie (and certainly within the natural attitude) something may exist in the present in the temporal sense of 'present' without thereby being presented to any consciousness. (It would require philosophical argument to show that this claim is false and nothing that is part of the natural attitude needs to be established by philosophical argument in order to be such a part.)

Husserl thinks all knowledge begins in the natural attitude. *A fortiori* all philosophical knowledge and all science begin in the natural attitude. Phenomenology is not unique in adopting a commonsensical starting point for philosophy.[23] However as transcendental philosophy it seeks to explain two possibilities, phenomenology tries to show how all knowledge is grounded in the natural attitude. Yet more radically, phenomenology tries to show how the world of the natural attitude is grounded in conditions that make even common sense possible.

We need to understand now what Merleau-Ponty means by placing the assertions of the natural attitude 'in abeyance' (PPT, vii) ('en suspens' PP, i). ('Arising out of' has no warrant in the French, nor does 'better'). To understand this we need a grasp of Husserl's notion of '*epoché*'.

'*Epoché*' is the Greek word for 'suspension of belief' and it is precisely Husserl's view that transcendental phenomenology requires the suspension of the natural attitude: suspension of belief in the world of common sense. Being clear on this point is crucial to understanding phenomenology. Husserl is manifestly not endorsing a kind of idealism about the external world (even though he sometimes gives his philosophy the Kantian name 'transcendental idealism'). Nor is Husserl endorsing philosophical scepticism about the existence of the external world (even though he sometimes points out some affinities between his own procedures and those of Descartes in the first *Méditation*). Husserl's procedure is exactly this: neither to believe nor disbelieve any belief constitutive of the natural attitude. His adoption of this standpoint is thus well captured by his use of '*epoché*'. Sometimes the suspension of belief and disbelief in the natural attitude is known as the 'phenomenological reduction' or the 'transcendental reduction'. Performing the phenomenological or transcendental reduction is suspending belief in the natural attitude.

Husserl's position may be clarified further by drawing a distinction between not believing something and disbelieving something. If someone disbelieves P then that logically entails that they do not believe P but if someone does not believe P that does not logically entail that they disbelieve P, because that is logically consistent with their being agnostic about P: neither believing P nor disbelieving P.

The suspension of the natural attitude putatively facilitates the phenomenological description of what appears to consciousness just as it does appear. 'En suspens', 'in abeyance', '*epoché*' 'not believing', 'putting in brackets', 'putting in parentheses' and even 'bracketing' are all terms used to denote the refusal to hold the beliefs of the natural attitude. 'Belief' is ambiguous between 'what is believed' and 'the believing of what is believed'. By the *epoché* the believing attitude is witheld from the believed content. We should try now to clarify the logic of belief in both senses when belief is subject to the phenomenological reduction.

Consider some set of sentences {S1 . . . Sn} where these are 'assertions [arising out] of the natural attitude' (PPT, vii) 'les affirmations de l'attitude naturelle' (PP, 1). The members of {S1 . . . Sn} are made true or false by the existence or non-existence of objects and properties that exist in the world of the natural attitude. That world is the world we pre-philosophically and pre-phenomenologically inhabit, so {S1 . . . Sn} are made true or false by the existence or non-existence of certain physical objects, other people, oneself, including the intrinsic and relational properties of those things, including the causal relations they enter into. The truth conditions of {S1 . . . Sn} are thus empirical, commonsensical and pre-philosophical.

By the application of the *epoché* or transcendental reduction, the reality of the world of the natural attitude is placed in ontological abeyance. Crucially, it is no longer assumed that {S1 . . . Sn} have truth conditions, but this is not denied either. {S1 . . . Sn} themselves become objects for phenomenological description, along with the objects that formerly constituted their truth conditions.

The objects of phenomenological description are not numerically distinct from the objects of the world of the natural attitude. There are not two worlds. There is one world towards which two attitudes are adopted. When lived in unreflectively, in a taken for granted way, it is truly designated 'world of the natural attitude' but this same world when subject to phenomenological description is called 'the world of the transcendental reduction' or sometimes 'the world of transcendental subjectivity'.

One of the central aims of the transcendental reduction is the answering of the Kantian questions of how knowledge, experience and the world, are possible. It is argued that the empirical world as it appears to us is an achievement of consciousness, not in any strong idealist sense, but in the sense that its appearing to us just as it does is at least partly to be explained by the kind of consciousness we have of it. This 'transcendental' phenomenology describes fundamental structures of consciousness which 'ground' the world in the sense of explaining why it appears just as it does.

We are now in a position to understand more fully Merleau-Ponty's claim that phenomenology is 'a philosophy for which the world is always "already there" before reflection begins – as an inalienable presence' (PPT, vii).[24] 'World' ('monde') is not only ambiguous between 'what is' and 'what is as we take it to be' but could mean 'existence' in the sense of 'the being of what is or what we take there to be'. On any of these construals phenomenology comes out as presupposing the world. If world means either 'existence' or 'what is' then clearly there can be no phenomenology (nor any other kind of philosophy) unless something is. If there is nothing then *a fortiori* there is no phenomenology. If 'world' means 'what is as we take it to be' (including, paradigmatically, the empirical world) then phenomenology acknowledges the existence of the world of the natural attitude as a presupposition of its own practice. This is a plausible assumption to make because in the procedural order of doing transcendental phenomenology the *epoché* is applied to belief in the world of the natural attitude. This is only feasible if we allow that, in a prior sense, the world of the natural attitude exists.

Much of the effort of doing Husserlian phenomenology is directed at discovering the relationship between the world of the natural attitude and the world of the transcendental reduction. This is why Merleau-Ponty says 'all its efforts are concentrated upon reachieving a direct and primitive contact with the world and endowing that contact with a philosophical status' (PPT, vii).[25] Describing the objects of consciousness just as they are presented to consciousness requires an artistic or aesthetic sensitivity which reveals the world as it is experienced directly, not as we assume it to be for everyday purposes. Ordinary appearances have to be revealed as phenomena.

Clearly, if one of the ambitions of phenomenology is to show how the world of the natural attitude is possible, and if the existence of that world is a presupposition of doing phenomenology, then it follows that the world of the natural attitude and the findings of phenomenology (if true) stand in a relation of reciprocal necessary condition, and, as is entailed by this, a relation of reciprocal sufficient condition. It follows that the findings of phenomenology, if true, are both necessary and sufficient for the world as we take it to be.

3 Being-in-the-world

We need now to make a sharp distinction between two kinds of phenomenologist. Some phenomenologists think a transcendental explanation of the possibility of the natural attitude is possible through the epoché. Others think this impossible. Husserl is overwhelmingly the most important phenomenologist of the first type. Merleau-Ponty, along with Heidegger and Sartre, is of the second type. Crucially, Husserl thinks a complete phenomenological reduction is possible. Merleau-Ponty, Heidegger and Sartre think a complete phenomenological reduction is impossible. For reasons that will become apparent, I label the first kind of phenomenologist 'internalist' and the second kind 'externalist'.

Despite this divergence, the phenomenologies of Husserl, Heidegger and Sartre all logically entail Merleau-Ponty's thesis that 'the world is there before any possible analysis of mine' (PPT, x).[26] Heidegger, Merleau-Ponty and Sartre, however, substitute descriptions of our 'being-in-the-world' ('in-der-Welt-sein', 'être-au-monde') for the putative findings of the phenomenological reduction. While Husserl describes the essence of consciousness the 'existential' phenomenologists describe the existential structures of being-in-the-world.

Merleau-Ponty expresses a thesis common to transcendental and existential phenomenology and so common to Husserl, Heidegger, Sartre and himself when he says of phenomenology:

> It tries to give a direct description of our experience as it is, without taking account of its psychological origin and the causal
> explanations which the scientist, the historian or the sociologist may be able to provide. (PPT, vii)[27]

As we have seen, one consequence of the phenomenological reduction is that no commitment is made to the objective existence and causal properties referred to in the beliefs of the natural attitude. Although the existential phenomenologists think the phenomenological reduction cannot be completed, they inherit the principle that it is no part of phenomenology to establish what causal relations obtain, nor to make any assumption about what exists independently of consciousness. Also, Merleau-Ponty explicitly uses 'description' because despite the goal of providing transcendental explanations, the procedures of phenomenology are essentially descriptive and do not consist in giving any empirical or causal explanation. Nor is phenomenology any kind of conceptual analysis; 'It is a matter of describing, not of explaining or analysing' (PPT, viii).[28]

There are two objections to this characterisation of phenomenology, both of which Merleau-Ponty is aware of. Husserl, in his later writings refers to a 'genetic phenomenology' (PPT, vii) ('"phénoménologie génétique"' (PP, i) and a 'constructive phenomenology' (PPT, vii) ('"phénoménologie constructive"' (PP, i). It could be that the conjunction of the sentences of these projects and those of the earlier 'transcendental' phenomenology entails contradictions ('contradictions' PP, i). Secondly, Heidegger's 'fundamental ontology'[29] in *Sein und Zeit* is so non-psychologistic that to name his procedures there 'the description of experience' is at best misleading and on most plausible interpretations just wrong.

Merleau-Ponty not only views the later Husserl's and Heidegger's departures from transcendental phenomenology as mutually consistent but understands Heidegger as essentially Husserlian:

> the whole of *Sein und Zeit* springs from an indication given by
> Husserl and amounts to no more than an explicit account of the
> 'natürlicher Weltbegriff' or the 'Lebenswelt' which Husserl, towards
> the end of his life, identified as the central theme of phenomenology.
> (PPT, vii).[30]

Merleau-Ponty is suggesting that the replacement of the findings of the transcendental reduction by the existential structures of 'being-in-the-world' is anticipated by the later Husserl's notions of the 'natural concept of the world' ('natürlicher Weltbegriff') and 'lifeworld' ('Lebenswelt'). Even if that is exaggerated, it is clear that all three notions are constitutive of the phenomenology that Merleau-Ponty himself develops in *Phénoménologie de la Perception*.

The most important break Merleau-Ponty makes with Husserl's phenomenology is this:

> The most important lesson which the reduction teaches us is the
> impossibility of a complete reduction. (PPT, xiv).[31]

The decisive objection to the completion of the reduction may be expressed in one sentence: 'we are in the world' (PP, xiv).[32] Merleau-Ponty rejects the Husserlian idea of transcendental subjectivity revealed by the transcendental reduction because we are irreducibly in the world. Merleau-Ponty has two more, logically independent, grounds for rejecting the reduction. So then we have:

1 'We are in the world' (PPT, ix).
2 'Our reflections are carried out in the temporal flux onto which we are trying to seize' (PPT, xiv).
3 'There is no thought which embraces all our thought' (PPT, xiv).[33]

The problem being-in-the-world poses for a complete phenomenological reduction is that the essence of a conscious state cannot be specified without mentioning the object of that conscious state as it really exists in the world (and not just as intended object as Husserl thought). This is externalism and Merleau-Ponty, Sartre and Heidegger are externalists in this sense. The subject's relations with the world are not wholly intrinsic either to the subject or the world so it is not possible to specify what the subject is in abstraction from the world and it is not possible to specify what the world is in abstraction from the subject. On the contrary, a major motivation of the Heideggerian conception, and its hyphening, is capturing the insight that the three ontological components 'being', 'in' and 'the world' although not identical and although denoted by semantically distinct terms, are not ontologically separable. There could be no subject, no world and no relation of 'being-in' in isolation from one another. It is an important theme of Merleau-Ponty's existential phenomenology that what may be separated in thought is not necessarily separable in reality. The most fundamental level at which this holds is denoted by 'being-in-the-world'.

The aspect of being-in-the-world that is logically inconsistent with the completion of the phenomenological reduction is the thesis that the subject's relations to the world are essentially constitutive of the subject: 'we are through and through compounded of relationships with the world' (PPT, xiii).[34] If this is true then it follows that the phenomenological reduction cannot be completed precisely because it entails drawing a clean distinction between subject and world: the field of transcendental subjectivity and the world of the natural attitude. Husserl is an internalist because he thinks the essence of a conscious state may be specified by reference to its intentional object without reference to its real object in the world. However, if consciousness is essentially constituted by relations to the world it is impossible to completely specify the essential properties of consciousness without reference to the world.

Suppose we read Merleau-Ponty's 'le flux temporel' (PP, ix) ('temporal flux' PPT, xiv) to mean a sequence of chronologically ordered thoughts or perceptions {T1 . . . Tn} undergone by a single subject such that {T1 . . . Tn} occur over times {t1 . . . tn} such that there is a one–one mapping between each of {T1 . . . Tn} and each of {t1 . . . tn}. Suppose a 'réflexion' (PP, ix) ('reflection' (PPT, xiv) is an introspective thought by a subject about an occurrent thought of or perception by that subject such that what is thought and what is thought about are simultaneous events in one mind. Suppose further that this thinking is occurring in the context of Husserl's phenomenological reduction. Then we may put Merleau-Ponty's point this way: it is not the case that any reflection is a member of any meta-series of thoughts {T1* . . . Tn*}, numerically distinct from {T1 . . . Tn}, rather any such reflection must itself be a member of {T1 . . . Tn}.

To accept this we have to allow that some of {T1 . . . Tn} may be *about one another*. Merleau-Ponty does not advance any argument for the conclusion that 'any reflection must be a member of {T1 . . . Tn}' is an obstacle to a complete reduction. However, the fact that he thinks that it is an obstacle suggests an argument.

If R is a reflection, and *qua* reflection, is a member of {T1 . . . Tn}, then it follows that either R is chronologically prior to some member of {T1 . . . Tn} or chronologically subsequent to some member of {T1 . . . Tn} or both. The possibility that is ruled out is R being simultaneous with some member of {T1 . . . Tn} (except itself). It follows that *no thought that is about a thought is simultaneous with that thought* (in the same mind). None of my thoughts happens at the same time as the thought it is about. It follows that a thought about another thought in the same mind is either a *memory* of a thought that has happened or an *anticipation* of a thought that has yet to happen. In either case, a thought about a thought is a thought about a thought that does not actually exist.

If we make the (dubious) assumption that reflection can only be an accurate, indubitable or incorrigible thought about another thought if it is simultaneous with that thought, we may accept Merleau-Ponty's point that a thought's being a member of a chronologically ordered sequence is an obstacle to that thought's being certain and veridical. Given that the discovery of the structures of consciousness requires reflection according to Husserl, then Merleau-Ponty has adduced another objection to the project's completion.

Merleau-Ponty's use of 'embrasse' (PP, ix) ('embraces' PPT, xiv) is ambiguous but entails at least that reflections exhibit the intentional feature of being 'about' something. Whether one of my thoughts could be about all of my thoughts (including that one) needs clarifying. When I think any thought using the expression 'all my thoughts' or some synonym in an indicative sentence then I thereby think a thought about all of my thoughts. Clearly, this does not logically entail that I itemise each of my thoughts in my thought, nor, still less that I think a separate thought about each of my thoughts. Both of these are incompletable projects. Each act of reflection would have to be the object of a new act of reflection. Although *any* act of reflection could be the object of a further act of reflection, such a project could never be completed because there would be nothing that it consisted in to have reflected on *all* the acts of reflection. No act of reflection may be 'on' all my thoughts where this means more than thinking a thought about all my thoughts.

It is not clear that Husserl's phenomenological reduction faces such a strong requirement but if it does then Merleau-Ponty has adduced strong grounds for its incompletability.

4 *The critique of science*

Even though phenomenology is not an empirical science and does not provide any causal explanations, Merleau-Ponty says 'It is the search for a philosophy which shall be a "rigorous science"' (PPT, vii).[35] This prima facie logical inconsistency is quickly dispelled however, when we realise that 'science exacte' does not denote any actual or possible natural science but is Merleau-Ponty's translation of Husserl's 'strenge Wissenschaft'. Husserl uses this term to refer to any rigorous body of knowledge which is open to conclusive confirmation. Notably, strict science is to be contrasted with metaphysical speculation. Besides, the ordinary German 'Wissenschaft', French 'science' and English 'science' have it in common to denote not only the natural sciences (physics, chemistry, biology) but any reasonably well organised body of infor-mation, for example in 'Geisteswissenschaften', 'sciences humaines' and 'social sciences' respectively.

Merleau-Ponty is far from saying that phenomenology should adopt the methods of the natural sciences. Merleau-Ponty explicitly repudiates Positivism, the thesis that any problem may, at least in principle, be solved using the methods of the natural sciences.

Phenomenologists provide reasons for being extremely pessimistic about the prospects for an explanation of human thought and action on the model of the natural sciences. If they are right then the scientific and scientifically inspired explanations of human thought and action initiated in the twentieth century are all doomed to failure. Not just psychological behaviourism, neurological determinism, cognitive psy-chology and psychological models derived from artificial intelligence but philosophical legitimations of these such as logical behaviourism, the mind–brain–identity theory in its various permutations, neurophilosophy, eliminativism and Turing machine functionalism are locked within a paradigm which prevents their explaining anything that is distinctively human. Merleau-Ponty's critique of science and positivist philosophy is essentially correct and a valuable contribution to human thought that needs to be endorsed in the twenty-first century.

This is a very large and negative claim and it will take several chapters of this book to substantiate it. However, the essence of the phenomenological objection to scientific explanation may be stated very briefly: *science explains the objective world but can tell us nothing at all about human subjectivity*. Humans are essentially subjective so science can tell us nothing about the essentially human. For example, Merleau-Ponty says,

> I am not the outcome or the meeting point of numerous causal
> agencies which determine my bodily or psychological make-up.
> I cannot conceive of myself as nothing but a bit of the world, a
> mere object of biological, psychological or sociological investigation.
> I cannot shut myself up within the realm of science. (PPT, viii)[36]

This view is common both to Husserlian transcendental phenomenology and to existential phenomenology. Within Husserl's transcendental reduction we have to give up talking about the human (the belief that one is human is part of the natural attitude) but the field of transcendental consciousness that is thereby disclosed is opaque to scientific explanation. It essentially exhibits a subjectivity which the vocabulary of science is inadequate to characterise.

The being that one is is no more amenable to scientific explanation after the existential substitution of being-in-the-world for transcendental subjectivity. It remains true that *I am not presented to myself as one item amongst others that I encounter in the course of my experience of the world*. The objects I encounter are essentially objective but I am essentially subjective and there is no scientific account of subjectivity.

The impossibility of any scientific explanation of the distinctively human is only half of the phenomenological attitude to science. The rest is an explanation of how science is possible. Phenomenology is transcendental philosophy and one of the possibilities phenomenology seeks to explain is science. This is something that concerns Husserl and Merleau-Ponty greatly (if Heidegger less so and Sartre hardly at all).

For Merleau-Ponty the critique of science and the explanation of science are intimately related. Indeed, they are almost the same project because the conditions for the possibility of science cannot be explained scientifically. What makes science possible also gives science its limits.

What makes science possible is the lived experience of the subjective individual who does science and no description of that individual may be reduced to science:

All my knowledge of the world, even my scientific knowledge, is gained from my own particular point of view, or from some experience of the world without which the symbols of science would be meaningless. The whole universe of science is built upon the world as directly experienced ('le monde vécu'). (PPT, viii)[37]

A task of Merleau-Ponty's phenomenology is the reconciliation of the scientific world picture with the world as we experience it. The two pictures do turn out to be mutually consistent but Merleau-Ponty turns the tables on a twentieth-century orthodoxy when he argues that science cannot explain our experience but our experience can explain the possibility of science.

5 Phenomenological reflection

'Phenomenology' may be partly defined through its consistency and inconsistency with Cartesianism and Kant's transcendental philosophy. In each of Cartesianische Meditationen and Die Pariser Vorträge Husserl describes the partial anticipation of phenomenology by Descartes and Kant.

Merleau-Ponty characterises phenomenology as a style or manner of doing philosophy rather than as a set of doctrines. He says, for example, 'phenomenology can be practised and identified as a manner or style [of thinking]' (PP, viii).[38] An aim of phenomenology is to make explicit as many of one's metaphysical and commonsensical assumptions as possible. As we have seen, one crucial intention of Husserl's epoché is to make no realist or objective commitment to answers to the traditional questions of metaphysics; a refusal that is logically equivalent to Kant's eschewal of metaphysical realism. Husserl frequently insists that he is making a fresh start in philosophy; an ambition that is logically equivalent to that of Descartes in the First Meditation. Husserl thinks the transcendental reduction will show that phenomenology is prior to philosophy. Phenomenology will show how philosophy is possible.

Merleau-Ponty provides us with a separate list of anticipators of phenomenology: Hegel, Kierkegaard, Marx, Nietzsche and Freud. Such anticipations do exist, and it is an enormous and piecemeal task for the History of Ideas to detect and prove them. However, Merleau-Ponty. like Husserl, devotes more time to examining the Cartesian and Kantian nature of phenomenology than any of the thinkers listed here.

Merleau-Ponty says that we will not find out what phenomenology is or find out how to do phenomenology, by reading the texts of those who have anticipated the thought of Husserl, Heidegger, Sartre and himself.

Merleau-Ponty says 'We find in texts only what we put into them' (PPT, viii).[39] Against this thesis taken literally is the consequence that it makes learning anything by reading impossible (except learning about oneself): we do learn by reading, therefore the thesis is false. For the thesis, read more subtly, is the ontological fact that a book is a physical object and writing a sequence of black marks on a white background. Reading plausibly consists in *what the reader adds* to these material properties of the book.

Merleau-Ponty suggests instead: 'We shall find in ourselves and nowhere else, the unity and true meaning of phenomenology' (PP, ii).[40] There is a profound sense in which this is right. Doing phenomenology requires perceiving the world in a new way; just as it is presented to consciousness and without taken for granted beliefs about what is perceived. Doing this requires an *epoché* or suspension of belief that facilitates *perception without preconception*. This gives force to Merleau-Ponty's remark that phenomenology discovers afresh our contact with the world.

Because the practice of phenomenology requires an experiential change in the phenomenological practitioner, phenomenology cannot be wholly learned verbally and cannot be wholly learned second-hand or on authority. This is why Merleau-Ponty says, 'It is less a question of counting up quotations than of determining and expressing in concrete form this phenomenology for ourselves' (PPT, viii).[41] A necessary condition for knowing what phenomenology is is engaging in phenomenology as a practice. For this reason, according to Merleau-Ponty, a number of people on reading Husserl and Heidegger for the first time have not so much the impression of learning something new as of recognising within themselves something they tacitly knew all along.

It follows that phenomenology shares this Cartesian epistemological starting point: unless we may know certain first person singular psychological and existential ascriptions to be true then we can know no other propositions to be true. It follows too that phenomenology shares transcendentalism with Kant's critical epistemology. It is facts about consciousness which make possible the world as object of our experience.

However, Merleau-Ponty makes a radical break with Husserl's Cartesian and Kantian presuppositions when he says 'man is in the world' (PPT, ix).[42]

According to Merleau-Ponty Descartes 'detached' the subject from the world. (His term is 'délié' which also has the sense of 'untied' or 'untangled'). Merleau-Ponty replaces Descartes' metaphysical thesis that a person is essentially an immaterial substance which could in principle exist if there were no physical world (and, *a fortiori*, could survive the destruction of his own body) with a new concept of the subject: the subject as essentially embodied and essentially in the world. A disembodied subject could not perceive the world according to Merleau-Ponty. It is because we are ourselves physical that we are able to perceive physical objects. It is only because we are part of the world that we can be aware of it. If this is correct then it is a refutation of Cartesian dualism: if I perceive the world I am not an immaterial substance, I do perceive the world, therefore I am not an immaterial substance.

Merleau-Ponty also thinks Kant's transcendental logic is inconsistent with being-in-the-world. In criticism of Kant's doctrine that the empirical world is constituted by the a priori forms of intuition, space and time, and by the categories, he says the world exists prior to all constitutive synthesis: 'It would be artificial to make it the outcome of a series of syntheses' (PPT, x).[43] The artificiality consists in the fact that sensory contents and the objects putatively synthesised out of them 'have no sort of prior reality' (PPT, x).[44] Kantian synthesis is also a process without a physical subject as Merleau-Ponty understands it, and, as we have seen, for Merleau-Ponty a subject who perceives the physical world is essentially embodied, so disembodied Kantian synthesis is also impossible.

Although Merleau-Ponty explicitly rejects Cartesian mind–body dualism, there is a fundamental tenet of Cartesian epistemology which he endorses. This is the doctrine that certainty about the world as it appears to me depends upon facts about my own subjective existence. In Descartes (in the *Discours* and in the *Méditations*) this is an epistemological doctrine: unless I know that I exist and unless I know that I think then I cannot know anything with certainty. Descartes' foundationalism is an epistemological foundationalism which takes the form: 'unless I can know that P I cannot know that Q'. Merleau-Ponty is also a foundationalist but of a different kind: a phenomenological foundationalist. Phenomenological foundationalism is partly the establishing of quasi-Kantian transcendental grounds where a transcendentally grounds b if and only if if not a then not b, a is not empirical, and b is experience, or knowledge, or the world as we take it to be.

Merleau-Ponty's phenomenological foundationalism, although not epistemological in the way that Descartes' is, is Cartesian on other grounds: the contents of the foundation are to be truly reported by indicative sentences of first person singular form. That Cartesian foundationalism has this grammatical form is paradigmatically evident in Descartes' first person singular existential claim 'I exist' and in his first person singular psychological ascription 'I think'. The Cartesianism in phenomenological foundationalism is evident in Merleau-Ponty's claim that

I am the absolute source, my existence does not stem from my antecedents, from my metaphysical and social environment; instead it moves out towards them and sustains them. (PPT, ix)[45]

I am the 'absolute source' if and only if: I am a ground of everything and nothing is a ground of me. This is a phenomenological rather than an epistemological or metaphysical notion of 'source'. Merleau-Ponty is trying to describe myself and the world as it is given to me. He is manifestly not making the very large metaphysical claim that the whole of existence depends upon his own existence. He means the world as it is presented to his consciousness depends upon his own existence; a claim that may be seen to be true on logical gounds. If the world is presented to my consciousness then that logically entails that I exist.

Merleau-Ponty presents no proof that he is not caused to be, nor caused to be what he is, by his physical and social environment ('entourage physique et social' PP, iii). Phenomenology provides descriptions not explanations. Phenomenology posits no causal explanations, *a fortiori* phenomenology posits no causal explanations of a sociological or physicalist kind.

Merleau-Ponty endorses one thesis common to Descartes and Kant, as he reads them: 'the world is given to the subject because the subject is given to himself' (PPT, x).[46] This is a Cartesian thesis if read epistemologically: knowledge of the external world is possible only if (indubitable) knowledge of one's own existence and psychological states is possible. It is not clearly Kantian because Kant insists that outer experience makes inner experience possible and not *vice versa*. However, Descartes straightforwardly and Kant less so both think that being conscious entails being self-conscious. This is an epistemological doctrine found in different versions in philosophers as diverse as Locke, Descartes, Kant, Hegel, Sartre, and in a revised form, Merleau-Ponty himself. It is one that demands logical clarification because it is part of the foundations of phenomenology.

The possibility of phenomenology depends upon an examination of consciousness by consciousness. Merleau-Ponty wishes to argue for two further facts: that consciousness entails self-consciousness and that self-consciousness makes 'outer' experience possible.

Prima facie, from the fact that some subject, 'S', is conscious it does not logically follow that S is conscious of S, nor, *a fortiori*, conscious of S's consciousness. Further, from the fact that S is conscious of some object, numerically distinct from S, 'x', it does not follow that S is conscious of S. S does not, for example, have to individuate S as a subject of consciousness as a necessary condition for S's being conscious of x. Nor does S have to draw an S/not-S distinction or even an S/x distinction prerequisite to S's consciousness of x. These distinctions (or ones

31

very much like them) do have to *obtain* if S is conscious of x, but S does not have to draw them. They could obtain *anyway*. S may even be conscious of x in these contexts even if S does not know that S exists.

Although Merleau-Ponty is in many ways critical of Descartes and Kant he endorses at least this much of what we could call the 'self-consciousness thesis':

> I could not possibly apprehend anything as existing unless I first
> of all experienced myself as existing in the act of apprehending it.
> (PPT, ix)[47]

Perception presupposes a self-conscious subject of perception (a presupposition which Descartes accepts but which Hume and Sartre, and Kant read correctly, reject).

It is not clear either that I experience myself in the perception of an object by me, nor that this putative fact is a necessary condition for my perceiving anything at all. If some subject, S, apprehends x as existing it is at least true that S comes to know (or at least believe) that x exists and S is thereby aware that x exists. It is clear too that Merleau-Ponty has in mind the case where S perceives x as existing. Now, from 'S perceives x as existing' we cannot validly derive 'S apprehends S as existing'. Also, from the fact that S comes to learn that x exists it does not follow that S apprehends S's own existence. Nor does it follow from the facts that S is aware of x's existence and S perceives x as existing either that S is aware of S's existence or that S perceives S as existing. Each of these claims could of course be true on logically independent grounds, but they do not of themselves support any inference from consciousness to self-consciousness.

It is clear that consciousness is not sufficient for self-consciousness without extra premises and it follows in turn that self-consciousness is not a necessary condition for consciousness.

Phenomenology inherits from Kant and Hegel a set of distinctions between subjectivity and objectivty, some of which are usefully marked by 'subject' ('Subjekt', 'sujet') and 'object' (Objekt', 'objet'). Broadly: S is a subject if and only if S is capable of experience and O is an object if and only if some experience of O is possible, so 'subject' means 'that which experiences' (whatever that is) and 'object' means 'that which is experienced' (whatever that is). Clarifying the subject–object distinction clarifies some differences between Merleau-Ponty and Husserl.

Merleau-Ponty says that the world is not an object. Obviously the world is broadly an object of experience. He means that the totality of what we take there to be is not an item that one could encounter in the course of one's experience. It is not, so to speak, one thing amongst others. It is, rather, a context, or the context, for all the thoughts and actions of the subject:

It is the natural setting of, and field for, all my thoughts and all my explicit perceptions. (PPT, xi)[48]

The world is always already there as the unalienable background ('milieu') in which I operate. It is there prior to all knowledge, not just chronologically but in the transcendental sense that the existence of the world is a necessary condition for knowledge of it.

As we have seen, one reason for Merleau-Ponty's rejection of the *epoché* is that the world survives any putative reduction of it. However, Merleau-Ponty examines two Husserlian theses that he will wish to adapt to his own ends. These are consciousness as meaning-bestowing and the transcendental ego.

Reporting a quasi-Husserlian analysis of the structure of consciousness, Merleau-Ponty says:

My sensation of redness is perceived as the manifestation of a certain redness experienced, this in turn as the manifestation of a red surface, which is the manifestation of a piece of red cardboard, and this finally is the manifestation or outline of a red thing, namely this book. (PPT, xi)[49]

What Merleau-Ponty is deriving from Husserl is the idea of a hierarchy of dependencies between different structures of consciousness. In this visual example:

1 The sensation of red.
2 The red experienced.
3 The red surface.
4 The red material of the surface.
5 The red physical object.

There is only one red. One and the same perceptual content may be subsumed under narrower or wider descriptions. The narrower the description the more psychological and subjective the putative object of that description. The broader the description the more physical and objective the putative object of that description. (Here by 'subjective' I mean: x is subjective if and only if x pertains to the psychology of the subject and by 'objective' I mean: x is objective if and only if x exists independently of the psychology of the subject.)

Merleau-Ponty makes the structure of what appears to consciousness depend closely upon two facts about us as human subjects: our pragmatic interests (or perceived interests) and the fact that we are physical. Neither of these facts is thought to be important by Husserl in *Ideen* I (despite the pragmatic components of the natural attitude) but both are emphasised in *Ideen* II and in the *Krisis*. Crucially, Merleau-Ponty replaces the transcendental ego with the body: not the body of another (as object) but the body as subject; that living human body that I am.

Because of the impossibility of the transcendental reduction there can be no true account of the subject as the transcendental ego. Merleau-Ponty reports Husserl's reduction of the empirical self of the natural attitude:

> In so far as I am a consciousness, that is, in so far as something has meaning for me, I am neither here nor there, neither Peter nor Paul. (PPT, vi)[50]

One putative result of the transcendental reduction is that the self of the natural attitude is suspended. Although I exist after the reduction I am no longer my empirical self because I have ceased to believe in all objective facts about myself. This residual phenomenological self is referred to by Husserl as the 'transcendental ego'. He talks about it as the subjective 'pole' of consciousness. It is what has my experiences and it is what my identity over time consists in; it is what persists as the subject of a series of numerically and qualitatively distinct experiences of mine.

Given that this Husserlian conception requires the withholding of all empirical ascriptions, Merleau-Ponty is clearly right to hold that this putative transcendental subject is not anybody in any empirical sense of 'anybody'. Given that he rejects the phenomenological reduction Merleau-Ponty is clearly also right to reject the transcendental ego. To maintain one but repudiate the other would be inconsistent.

Crucially, Merleau-Ponty thinks that this internalist claim and anything logically equivalent to it is false:

> I and my life remain – in my sense of reality – untouched by whatever way we decide the issue of whether the world is or not. (PL, 9)[51]

My being and my being what I am are partly constituted by my intentional and pragmatic relations to the world. It is not as though I could exist as a kind of conscious residue once the world is suspended. This is not just because *qua* physical body I am part of the physical world but also because my mental states being what they are depend essentially on what they are about and what they are about belongs paradigmatically to the world.

However, Merleau-Ponty still accepts a self–not self or subject–object distinction despite his repudiation of the transcendental ego. In a clear allusion to Husserl's 1929 work *Cartesianische Meditationen*, Merleau-Ponty says, 'as a meditating ego, I can clearly distinguish from myself the world and things' (PPT, xiii)[52] and gives as the reason this; 'I certainly do not exist in the way in which things exist' (PPT, xiii).[53] These two entailments of Husserl's phenomenology of the self are accepted by Merleau-Ponty despite the alleged impossibility of the phenomenological reduction: I and objects in the world are qualitatively distinct because I am not an object and, what is entailed by this, I and the world are numerically distinct. It is worth exploring their plausibility.

Suppose I can distinguish myself from what is not myself if and only if I am able to draw a distinction (in perception or thought or both) between the portion of what is that is truly characterisable using first person singular ascriptions and the remainder which is not so characterisable. Then Merleau-Ponty may be understood as describing the phenomenological differences between these two portions of what is, in virtue of which this grammatical distinction holds.

Large sections of *Phénoménologie de la Perception* are devoted to drawing this distinction, notably, Part One 'The Body' but also the chapter in Part Two: *The World as Perceived* called 'The Thing and the Natural World'. Logically, that there obtains a qualitative difference between the portion of the world that I am and the remainder that I am not is a necessary but not a sufficient condition from my drawing a self–not self distinction. It is logically necessary because in the absence of the distinction it could not be truly drawn, but it is logically insufficient because from the fact that some distinction obtains it does not follow that it is drawn. There is no contradiction in the supposition that some being should not perceive or think the difference between itself and the external world. The existence of the distinction does not entail any consciousness of it.

For both Husserl and Merleau-Ponty the subject does not exist after the manner of a 'thing' but for very different reasons. For Husserl the reduced subject is the transcendental ego and the transcendental subject is not a thing. For Merleau-Ponty the subject in the world is the body-subject and the body-subject does not encounter itself as an 'object'. For Husserl all existential commitment to 'things' is suspended by the *epoché* yet the transcendental ego is not suspended by that reduction. The transcendental ego is not a 'thing': If x can be truly characterised after the *epoché* then x is not a thing, the transcendental ego can be truly characterised after the *epoché*. The transcendental ego is not a thing. Although Merleau-Ponty insists that the subject is physical, and not a transcendental ego, as we shall see in Chapter III below, he nonetheless strongly retains Husserl's thesis that the self is not a physical thing or an object. Although I am physical I am not a physical object. I am a physical subject ('sujet incarné' PP, 515).

III

Existentialism

Existentialism is the movement in nineteenth and twentieth century European philosophy essentially characterised by attempts to solve fundamental problems about human existence. No set of problems or methods is common to all and only existentialists, but typically philosophers otherwise as diverse as Kierkegaard, Nietzsche, Heidegger, Sartre, de Beauvoir, Jaspers and Marcel describe those features of the human condition which matter most to us as individuals and prescribe the exercise of human freedom as the means of authentically facing our situation. Their work is philosophically significant not only because they construe problems of death, anxiety, oneself and other people, sexuality and political and religious commitment as genuine, as not to be dismissed as unscientific, or to be dismissed on linguistic grounds alone. It has also been found to be significant by people thinking outside philosophy. This is perhaps a partial cause and partial consequence of several of the existentialists authoring plays, novels and political tracts and not confining their written output to the philosophical treatise.

Some existentialists, notably Heidegger and Sartre, have denied that they are existentialists but this attempt to distance themselves from one another is rather unsuccessful. Although they do not form a tradition or school in an institutional sense their descriptions and prescriptions about what it is to be, to exist, form a common reaction against concerns with just what it is to be something, to have an essence.

Understanding existentialism is necessary for understanding Merleau-Ponty because his 'existential phenomenology' is a synthesis of existentialism with Husserlian phenomenology. We have seen in the last chapter how Merleau-Ponty replaces the Husserlian concepts of the *epoché*, or phenomenological reduction, and the transcendental ego with the Heideggerian existential category being-in-the-world. We need to examine other existential components of Merleau-Ponty's thought and this requires an examination of Hegel and Sartre. This is not so much because Merleau-Ponty thinks that Hegel was the first existentialist, although that is true, nor is it because Merleau-Ponty wishes to defend Sartre against Catholic and Marxist critics, although that is also true. It is because in seeing what Merleau-Ponty accepts and rejects from Hegel and Sartre we may measure the extent of his own existentialism.

1 *Hegel's existentialism*

Separating out what Merleau-Ponty accepts and repudiates from Hegel, and appreciating the sense in which what is endorsed is existentialist requires a grasp of what is arguably the most radically significant work in French Hegelian studies: Jean Hyppolite's massive and influential *Genèse et Structure de la Phénoménologie de L'Esprit de Hegel* (1946). Hyppolite is the author of the French translation of Hegel's *Phänomenologie des Geistes* and his lectures on Hegel in Paris left a lasting impression upon a generation of French intellectuals. The only French Hegelian scholar whose work may be compared with Hyppolite's for its originality or influence is Alexandre Kojève, whose *Introduction à la Lecture de Hegel* was also read by Sartre and Merleau-Ponty. However it is through the lens of Hyppolite's *Genèse et Structure* that Merleau-Ponty reads Hegel.

In 'L'Existentialisme Chez Hegel' (SNS, 109–21) Merleau-Ponty claims that the philosophies of Marxism, phenomenology and existentialism find their origin in Hegel. No doubt he partly intends this as the historical claim that it was reading Hegel that was a cause of Marx, the existentialists and the phenomenologists writing as they did. What is philosophically significant for existentialism is whether it is an essentially Hegelian movemement. Without providing precise criteria for 'essentially Hegelian' Merleau-Ponty sets about establishing qualitative identities between existentialist thoughts and Hegelian thoughts. For example, he says of Hegel

> It was he who started the attempt to explore the irrational and
> integrate it into an expanded reason which remains the task of our
> century. (SNST, 63)[1]

By 'the irrational' we should not understand the incoherent or contradictory here. Merleau-Ponty means the *non-rational*: the *non-cognitive*, for example the emotional, the lived, the existential. Merleau-Ponty conceives Hegel, rightly, as recommending a kind of thinking which is not constrained by the Kantian distinction between *Verstand* and *Vernunft*. Kant argues in *Kritik der Reinen Vernunft* that human cognitive powers are constrained empirically so that only possible objects of experience are possible objects of knowledge.[2] *Verstand*, or understanding, is the mental faculty which allows, at least in principle, knowledge of those objects. *Vernunft*, or reason, according to Kant becomes a spurious or illegitimate mental faculty in its futile use to acquire putative knowledge of a reality outside our experience. Merleau-Ponty construes Hegel as endorsing a quasi-Kantian *Vernunft* but applying it, not metaphysically, but existentially; as though Kant had not seen that *Vernunft* could be used to reveal the basic structures of human being.

In this passage about Hegel 'Raison' is a clear allusion to *Vernunft* and 'entendement' a clear allusion to *Verstand*:

> He is the inventor of that Reason, broader than the understanding, which can respect the variety and singularity of individual consciousnesses, civilisations, ways of thinking, and historical contingency, but which nevertheless does not give up the attempt to master them in order to guide them back to their own truth. (SNST, 63)[3]

It is not true that Hegel is the inventor of *Vernunft* (Raison). The modern distinction between *Verstand* and *Vernunft* was drawn by Kant. It is Kant for example who calls reason 'dialectical' in the last large section of the *Kritik der Reinen Vernunft* 'Die Transzendentale Dialektik'. However, Merleau-Ponty is right in suggesting that Hegel gives 'dialectic' a sense and dialectic a use that would have appalled Kant.

Merleau-Ponty thinks that Hegel leaves conceptual room for 'historical contingency' (SNST, 63) 'la contingence de l'histoire' (SNS, 110) and this is right. It would certainly be a crude mistake to read Hegel as a historical determinist even though he thinks the thought-world of a community is a set of constraints on or horizons for, thought, perception and action. Hegel's concept of a 'world' ('Welt') is much closer to the existentialist thesis of the exercise of freedom in a situation than to any kind of historically necessitarian context. Crudely speaking, Hegel and the existentialists are compatibilists about freedom and determinism (and this is true even of a prima facie extreme libertarian like Sartre). The 'historical contingency' Merleau-Ponty finds in Hegel is consistent with Sartre's existential 'discovery' that existence, including human existence is contingent. Sartre thinks that everything that is might not have been and everything that is might have been other than it is. Hegel as read by Merleau-Ponty wishes to do full justice to this thought but, like the later Sartre of *Critique de la Raison Dialectique*, he wishes to explore its limitations: the thinkability of its negation.

Despite this, Merleau-Ponty thinks many existentialists are unaware of their intellectual debt to Hegel and points out that some have tried to repudiate Hegel's system. Merleau-Ponty is almost certainly thinking of Kierkegaard and Marx when he says 'Hegel's successors have placed more emphasis on what they reject of his heritage than on what they owe to him' (SNST, 63).[4] Merleau-Ponty thinks putative existentialist refutations of Hegel are pre-empted by Hegel in two ways. They make use of Hegelian language, and so are enacted within an essentially Hegelian framework of background assumptions. Unwittingly they repeat only a part of Hegel's thought without an appreciation of Hegel's appreciation of its limitations. For example, speaking of 'the thankless doctrines which try to forget their Hegelian origin' (SNST, 63)[5] Merleau-Ponty says that it is their Hegelian language that makes their putative opposition to Hegel possible: 'That is where their common language can be found and a decisive confrontation can take place' (SNST, 63).[6] Even though Merleau-Ponty rejects Hegel's 'absolute knowing' ('absolute Wissen') as a metaphysical synthesis of prima facie mutually inconsistent philosophical theses, it remains true for him that Hegel has anticipated the existentialists' 'divergent points of view' (SNST, 63) 'les prises de positions divergentes' (SNS, 110). As he puts it, 'all our antitheses can be found in that single life and work' (SNST, 63).[7] Merleau-Ponty thinks existentialism operates within an essentially Hegelian framework. We need to bear this in mind in studying his philosophy. He may be right. It is an unsolved philosophical and historical problem whether there is *any* kind of philosophy chronologically subsequent to Hegel that has not been anticipated by Hegel.[8] Even more fundamentally, but unnoticed by Merleau-Ponty, is the problem of whether Hegel is essentially a Kantian, and the possible implication of this is that the whole of philosophy since Kant operates within a Kantian paradigm.[9]

Merleau-Ponty accepts that 'Kierkegaard, the first to use "existence" in the modern sense of the word, deliberately set himself up in opposition to Hegel' (SNS, 64).[10] Kierkegaard reacts against Hegel's system historically. It does not follow that Kierkegaard succeeds *philosophically* in being anti-Hegelian or non-Hegelian. (Arguably, Hegel's totalising conception of philosophy implies that being non-Hegelian is being anti-Hegelian.) Although Merleau-Ponty does not allude to it, one not un-obvious reading of Kierkegaard's title *Either/Or* is as a statement of the intrinsic uncompletability of the Hegelian dialectic: as though for any putative speculative synthesis of thesis and antithesis there is only an opposition, as though the Kant of *Die Antinomie der reinen Vernunft* was right.

2 *Being and knowing*

For Merleau-Ponty, Kierkegaard is a Hegelian *malgré-lui*. Despite the justice of some of his remarks about ahistoricity in the later Hegel, Kierkegaard fails to see that Hegel's *absolute Wissen* is existentialist:

> Absolute knowledge, the final stage in the evolution of the spirit as phenomenon wherein consciousness at last becomes equal to its spontaneous life and regains its self-possession, is perhaps not a philosophy but a way of life. (SNST, 64)[11]

Here Merleau-Ponty makes the radical suggestion that the final chapter of *Phänomenologie des Geistes* cannot be only thought but must be *lived*; as though *absolute Wissen* cannot be adequately apprehended intellectually but has to be *enacted* to be understood. What could this mean?

To evaluate the plausibility of this existentialist reading or appropriation of Hegel we need to examine Hegel's statement of it. Hegel says

> The 'I' has neither to cling to itself in the *form* of *self-consciousness* as against the form of substantiality and objectivity, as if it were afraid of the externalisation of itself: the power of Spirit lies rather in remaining the selfsame Spirit in its externalisation and, as that which is both *in itself* and *for itself*, in making its *being-for-self* no less merely a moment than its in-itself; nor is Spirit a *tertium quid* that casts the differences back into the abyss of the Absolute and declares that therein they are all the same; on the contrary, knowing is this seeming inactivity which merely contemplates how what is differentiated spontaneously moves in its own self and returns to its unity.
>
> In this knowing, then, Spirit has concluded the movement in which it has shaped itself, in so far as this shaping was burdened with the difference of consciousness [i.e. of the latter from its object], a difference now overcome. Spirit has won the pure element of its existence, the Notion. (p. 490)[12]

In absolute knowing there is no difference between what is *knowing what it is* and what is *being what it is*: it is what it knows and it knows what it is. All the various dialectical structures of consciousness and self-consciousness are subsumed or *aufgehoben* into the ultimate speculative synthesis of subjectivity and objectivity, epistemology and ontology.

Crucially, if Merleau-Ponty can show that *das absolute Wissen* is existentialist then there is a sense in which he has shown that the whole of Hegel's Phenomenology is existentialist. This is because *das absolute Wissen* is the synthetic whole of Hegel's Phenomenology. (Inferences from wholes to parts do not hold always and everywhere, of course: for example from the fact that x is large it does not follow that every part of x is large.) However, the components of *das absolute Wissen* are only fully what they are in their dialectically ordered mutual dependency in that final speculative synthesis. If *das absolute Wissen* is existential, then the possibility of its dialectical parts being what they are is existential.

Merleau-Ponty suggests that *das absolute Wissen* is not 'a philosophy' (SNST, 64) 'une philosophie' (SNS, 112) but 'a way of life' (SNST, 64) 'une manière de vivre' (SNS, 112). *Das absolute Wissen* is a synthesis or dialectical unity of knowing and being, in particular, of self-knowing and existence. The word Miller translates as 'existence' in the last sentence of the passage quoted from the Phenomenology above is 'Dasein'. 'Dasein' may mean 'existence' in ordinary German, or it can mean 'being there' or 'being somewhere or other' or it can mean 'being determinate', that is, not just being but also being something or other. The latter sense is the most important one in which Hegel uses the term in the *Encyclopaedia Logic* and the *Wissenschaft der Logik*.[13] 'Dasein' is also a technical term in Heidegger's *Sein und Zeit* where it is used to denote the peculiar kind of being that pertains uniquely to human being or being human: a pragmatically situated being-in-the-world that both interrogates being as to its being and functions as the site or clearing ('Lichtung') in which being is disclosed. Heidegger reserves 'existence' ('Existenz') to denote the active, future-directed or 'ecstatic' being that human beings exhibit. So in his fundamental ontology only Dasein has existence, even though other things are.

Merleau-Ponty is not naively assimilating Hegel's use of 'Dasein' to Heidegger's but because of the semantic richness of 'Dasein' it is textually legitimate for Merleau-Ponty to construe Hegel's *das absolute Wissen* as existential.

Most readings of Hegel's Phenomenology are rather over cognitive and underestimate the pragmatic import of his thought. We may read Merleau-Ponty as taking seriously the concept of being in the identification of being and knowing in *das absolute Wissen*. Because being is Dasein being is being someone or being something. On this construal not only is the Hegelian knowing self-consciousness's being what it is identical with what is being what it is; but being is to be understood not just as being tout court but as being something and as something that is done: accomplished. What is has become what it is.

This 'existential' reading of Hegel's *das absolute Wissen* takes seriously that for being in the sense of 'Dasein' there is something that it consists in to be what it is. Dasein is someone.

This realisation of self-consciousness in absolute knowing entails something very much like the existentialist concept of authenticity. It is a *Leitmotif* of existentialist thought that human beings are pervasively inauthentic. This is apparant, for example, in Nietzsche's and Heidegger's concept of ('inauthenticity') and in Sartre's doctrine of mauvaise foi, ('bad faith').[14] If a person is inauthentic or in bad faith then in a sense that person is not really who they are. Their real self is masked from themselves and others by the compromise of role, speech and gesture. In existentialism authenticity or good faith is typically ethically facilitated, for example in Heidegger through the call of conscience or in Sartre through shame. This is true of authenticity in Hegel's Phenomenology because a condition for the progress of *Geist* to *das absolute Wissen* is the transition through the ethical phase or *Gestalt* called 'Der seiner selbst gewisse Geist. Die Moralität' 'Spirit that is certain of itself. Morality' which itself includes the sub-phase or Gestalt-part 'Das Gewissen, die schöne Seele, das Böse und seine Verzeihung' ('Conscience. The "beautiful soul", evil and its forgiveness'). Hegel, Heidegger, and Sartre accept conscience as making possible authenticity.

3 *Being-towards-death*

According to Merleau-Ponty's existentialist definition '[a] man . . . is . . . a being which is not, which denies things, an existence without an essence' (SNST, 66).[15] To say that a person is not is not to say that that person does not exist, but to say that there is nothing that that person is. A person has no fixed, a priori, unchangeable nature. Rather, we make ourselves what we are by our own actions. Each of us defines his or her own essence. People contrast with things in this respect because while in the human case existence is logically prior to essence: being is a necessary condition for being something or someone, in the case of things existence and essence coincide; being and being something are reciprocally dependent. People are also to be distinguished from things by their imagination, especially their negative power to think that things could be other than how they are. This free negativity pertains only to human beings according to Merleau-Ponty.

Merleau-Ponty thinks having these existential features is intimately bound up with death and consciousness of death. There are three dialectical dependencies upon which existentialism relies. There is, according to Merleau-Ponty no life without the consciousness of that life, no life without death and no consciousness of life without consciousness of death. If we separate these dependencies out then they form a hierarchy that may be extracted from Merleau-Ponty's text. The relationship between them, reading downwards, is sufficient condition, and reading upwards, necessary condition.

1 Life
2 Consciousness of Life
3 Consciousness of Death
4 Death

Life presupposes consciousness of life in the sense of 'a life', not in the sense of an only biological phenomenon. Everything one says about one's life is mediated by one's consciousness of it. We have no direct realist access to our lives. We only know our lives through the lens of our reflection on them:

> Of course, all we say about life has to do in reality with
> consciousness of life, since we who talk about it are conscious of it.
> (SNST, 66) [16]

My life and my consciousness of my life are mutually mediating: my life alters my consciousness of it and my consciousness of my life alters my life. This dialectical dependence is so close that it makes no sense to speak of my life and my consciousness of it as existing separately. They are dialectical 'moments' of the single reality that I live.

If this existentialism is true then epistemologists, psychologists and philosophers of mind who seek to examine mental processes but not *qua* the mental processes of a particular living person are studying only abstractions. It is perhaps for this reason that some existentialists have felt more optimistic about gleaning insights into human consciousness from novels and plays than from the philosophy of mind, neurology or, for that matter, Husserlian phenomenology. It is certainly for this reason that phenomenology, in the hands of Merleau-Ponty, becomes existential phenomenology.

Life as I live it presupposes consciousness of life and that consciousness of life presupposses consciousness of death. Merleau-Ponty says

> Consciousness of life, taken radically, is consciousness of death.
> (SNST, 66)[17]

The 'est', 'is', here is the is of dialectical dependence: a and b are dialectically dependent if and only if a depends upon b for its existence and or nature and b depends upon a for its existence and or nature such that a and b either could not be without each other or, at least, could not be what they are without each other. This dialectical sense of 'identical' does not logically entail that a is numerically identical with b (indeed, prima facie it logically precludes it unless these dependencies may obtain between a thing and itself) but, nonetheless the dependencies are very close: so close, in fact, that it is always legitimate to regard a and b as *parts of the same thing* when they are so dialectically related. What a is a part of is what b is a part of.

Merleau-Ponty thinks that 'conscience de la vie' (SNS, 115) 'consciousness of life' (SNST, 66) and 'conscience de la mort' (SNS, 115) 'consciousness of death' (SNST, 66) are dialectically related in this way.

It follows then that consciousness of life depends upon consciousness of death for its existence or nature and consciousness of death depends upon consciousness of life for its existence or nature such that one could not be or at least could not be what it is without the other. The reciprocal dependency is very close and it makes sense to talk of both as aspects or moments of a greater whole: consciousness of life and death.

We can now give some sense to Merleau-Ponty's 'radicalement' (SNS, 115) 'radically' (SNT, 66). Both the French and the English terms come in their etymology from the Latin 'radix' meaning 'root' so Merleau-Ponty is talking about presuppositions. Consciousness of life is the *root* of consciousness of death and consciousness of death is the *root* of consciousness of life. Roots are hidden but could be unearthed. Presuppositions are hidden but may be rendered explicit. In being conscious of one's life one is not thereby overtly conscious of one's death but that kind of consciousness only makes sense, and *a fortiori* only makes sense to onself, if one has a consciousness of one's death.

Why should this be so? Why should consciousness of life presuppose consciousness of death? We may read this at several levels, at least semantic, ontological and psychological (although Merleau-Ponty would in some ways wish to blur the differences between these, or deny sharp differences between them).

Semantically, it is arguable that 'life' and 'death' are mutually dependent concepts. It does not make much sense to claim that everything is alive and deny the intelligibility of 'death', just as it does not make much sense to say that everything is 'good' and deny sense to 'evil' or 'bad' or assert that everything is 'up' and deny sense or reference to 'down'. Unless 'death' has a sense it is hard to see how 'life' has a sense. Unless 'death' has a referent it is hard to see how 'life' has a referent.

Ontologically, it is hard to see how a life could exist unless death exists. Unless some things are, have been, will be or could be dead, or at least, not alive, it is hard to see how other things could be living and how, in particular one's life could be 'a' life: a life with an origin, a duration and an end (whatever that end may be metaphysically).

Psychologically, unless death is thinkable, life is not thinkable. Unless I can represent to myself my death I cannot represent to myself my life. I think of my life as a finite whole: the process which begins with my birth and ends with my death. It is hard to see how I could imagine my life as just that; as my life, without the idea of its being bounded by death.

There is perhaps a more profound reason why Merleau-Ponty thinks life and death mutually dependent. In common with other existentialists he endorses Hegel's thesis that being and nothingness are dialectically related. The title of Sartre's famous 1943 work *L'Etre et le Néant*, *Being and Nothingness*, is an allusion to the fundamental distinction drawn in

Hegel's logic between being, 'Sein' and not being or nothing 'Nichts'. Hegel thinks that *Sein* and *Nichts* are reciprocally dependent, in at least the sense that one is unthinkable without the other. There are semantic and ontological dependencies between *Sein* and *Nichts*, but, like Merleau-Ponty, Hegel thinks it philosophically misleading to draw those distinctions too sharply. The antithesis between *Sein* and *Nichts* may be overcome ('aufgehoben') in a speculative synthesis in *Werden*, 'becoming'. Becoming is the synthesis of being and nothingness. In becoming, at any time, there is beginning to be and ceasing to be (something). That is what becoming is.

According to Merleau-Ponty being depends upon nothingness in the following way:

An absence of being would have to come into the world, a
nothingness from which being would be visible. (SNST, 66)[18]

Without an absence of being, being could not become visible. 'Visible', is a techincal term in Merleau-Ponty's philosophy. The word features in the title of his, unfinished, book *Le Visible et L'Invisible* (which is his best work) and the concept plays a crucial role in his attempt to answer Heidegger's *Seinsfrage*, a theme which I take up in the penultimate chapter of the present work. Here Merleau-Ponty is at least implying that what is could be nothing to us unless we could at least make sense of the idea of what is not being.

It is a theme of Sartre's phenomenological ontology in *L'Etre et le Néant* that the dialectical oppositions between subject and object, *l'être pour-soi* and *l'être en-soi*, freedom and situation, self and other cannot be overcome. There is no Hegelian synthesis that would, as Sartre tendentiously puts it, allow man to be God. Despite this pessimism, and despite Sartre's disclaimers it is a pessimism: a metaphysical pessimism, there is nevertheless a sense in which the tension between being and nothingness is overcome in existentialism. A sense that is anticipated by Hegel's synthesis of *Sein* and *Nichts* in *Werden*.

The existentialist synthesis of being and nothingness is in the living of a life. In self-definition by the performance of one's own actions one effects the transition from being nothing in the sense of having no essence to being something in the sense of having an essence. It follows that according to existentialism a person is in a state of becoming. If we raise the question of whether or how this becoming could end, then two sorts of answer seem possible; both derivable from Hegel. Becoming comes to an end in death, in the sense that it is with death that one not only ceases to be and so ceases to become anything, but also in the Sartrean sense that only in death has a person an essence. It only makes sense at death to say of a person what he is: the totality of his actions.

I am my life. The other answer is that becoming stops when one has authentically become what one is, when one drops the mask of bad faith or inauthenticity and lives according to one's free and sincere choices.

According to Merleau-Ponty there are two fundamental attitudes to death:

> There are two ways of thinking about death: one pathetic and complacent, which butts against our end and seeks nothing in it but the means of exacerbating violence; the other dry and resolute, which integrates death and turns it into a sharper awareness of life. (SNS, 67)[19]

He means at least two and not only two, even if we leave aside attitudes towards what death is and assume just that death is the ending of a person. It is the second of these views that Merleau-Ponty endorses and this is the existentialist attitude anticipated by Hegel.

In the famous section of *Phänomenologie des Geistes* called 'Selbst- ständigkeit und Unselbständigkeit des Selbstbewusstseins; Herrschaft und Knechtschaft', which includes the so called Master and Slave dia- lectic, Hegel advances the controversial thesis that self-consciousness requires an awareness of death, or, more precisely, coming to self- consciousness requires risking one's life.

> For this consciousness has been fearful, not of this or that particular thing or just at odd moments, but its whole being has been seized with dread; for it has experienced the fear of death, the absolute Lord. (p. 117)[20]

Hegel means that full self-consciousness cannot be only intellectual. One must feel oneself to be, in a way that abruptly contrasts with the threat of one's not being, in order to feel that one really exists, to feel 'really alive'. This requirement on self-consciousness is endorsed by existential- ists. It is not only consistent with their view that existing is existing in the face of finitude – being is being-toward-death. It is also an example of Merleau-Ponty's view that consciousness of a life is not purely cog- nitive or abstract. It has to be felt, to be complete. We can see now why Merleau-Ponty endorses the second attitude towards death, the one that 'integrates death and turns it into a sharper awareness of life'.

4 *Merleau-Ponty and Sartre*

The sense in which Merleau-Ponty is an existentialist may be further clarified by examining what he accepts and what he repudiates in the existentialism of Jean-Paul Sartre. In the essay 'La Querelle de L'Existentialisme' (SNS, 123–43) Merleau-Ponty not only defends some central doctrines of *L'Etre et le Néant* against Sartre's Catholic and Marxist critics but also defines his own attitude to Phenomenological Ontology, a Sartrean method which entails existentialism.

Merleau-Ponty thinks the fundamental question addressed in *L'Etre et le Néant* is 'man's relationship to his natural or social surroundings' (SNST, 71) '[le] rapport entre l'homme et son entourage naturel ou social' (SNS, 124)[21] and, arguably, this is also a description under which the concerns of *Phénoménologie de la Perception* could be subsumed. According to Merleau-Ponty a distinction needs to be drawn between two traditional but competing views of this relationship:

> One treats man as the result of the physical, physiological, and sociological influences which shape him from the outside and make him one thing among many. (SNST, 71)[22]

but

> The other consists in recognising an a-cosmic freedom in him, in so far as he is spirit and represents to himself the very causes which supposedly act upon him. (SNST, 71–2)[23]

These two theses are mutually inconsistent, so it follows that at least one of them is false. However, Merleau-Ponty's view is that they are both false. He says 'Neither view is satisfactory' (SNST, 72).[24]

The first view is false because it reduces the subject to an object: reduces the living conscious acting human being to a descriminable item that could be encountered in the course of one's experience of the external world. Merleau-Ponty is not of course denying that we may encounter others, and accepts that other people are presented to us as physical beings. What he denies is that either the totality of what a person is or the essence of what a person's consciousness is is thus presented. In particular, the psychological interiority of a person is not available to this objective perspective and the materialist thesis that a person is a physical object is inconsistent with their consciousness exhibiting intentionality. Even if it should turn out that persons are entirely or essentially physical, it is still a mistake to think of a person as a physical object. A person is a physical subject.

The first view is also false because it is deterministic. As we shall see in the chapter on freedom, below, Merleau-Ponty rejects both conjuncts of the deterministic thesis that every event has a cause and caused events are inevitable and so makes conceptual room for a human freedom which entails that if someone does something there is always a sense in which they could have not done what they did and, perhaps, done something else. The repudiation of necessitarian determinism, and the possibility of always acting otherwise, is consistent with the common existentialist thesis that what is is contingently, and what is is contingently what it is.

The second view is false because it is metaphysical and exaggerated. Although it rightly ascribes mentality and freedom to the human subject it incorrectly identifies that subject with a spiritual item, a soul perhaps, and makes the exercise of its freedom limitless. Merleau-Ponty rejects this picture because it is inconsistent with his thesis that the kind of being that pertains to human beings is 'being-in-the-world' 'être-au-monde'. For Merleau-Ponty it makes no sense to specify mental and physical acts independently of the world in which the agent is embedded. On the second view, however, the spirituality and freedom of the subject are not in the world but 'acosmique' (SNS, 124) 'a-cosmic' (SNST, 72). Merleau-Ponty has no argued refutation of this metaphysical picture. He takes himself to have established the impossibility of any human being not being situated, not being-in-the-world, on independent grounds. If he has proved that then, clearly anything logically inconsistent with it is false.

Merleau-Ponty wishes to retain what is true from both pictures and repudiate what is false. He endorses from the first the thesis that people are physical, but physical subjects not physical objects, and he endorses from the second the view that people are free, but not absolutely or metaphysically free: free within a situation that limits their freedom.

More radically, Merleau-Ponty sees the crucial existentialist departure from previous epistemology and metaphysics in the concepts of being and existence themselves. Following Heidegger's use of 'Existenz' Merleau-Ponty uses 'existence' to refer to the ecstatic and freely spontaneous being that pertains uniquely to human being and asserts that this existence is always 'involved':

> In the modern sense of the word, 'existence' is the movement
> through which man is in the world and involves himself in a
> physical and social situation which then becomes his point of view
> on the world. All involvement is ambiguous because it both affirms
> and restricts a freedom. (SNST, 72)[25]

Merleau-Ponty speaks of existence as a 'movement', not in the sense of physical motion but in the adverbial sense of 'being': being as something that is done, rather than being as something inert or passive. Existence, if not a relation, at least has the inherent property of being relational because paradigmatically it is people that exist and it makes no sense to speak of the existence of people independently of their relations with the world.

Crucially, existentialism is not a kind of epistemology but a philosophy of existence. It does not make cognitive capacities central to its investigations but modes of being; ways of existing. For example, Merleau-Ponty accepts that existentialism inherits the Kantian, Hegelian and Husserlian distinction between subject and object but does not think the primordial relation between them is cognitive: it is existential and active. Indeed, it is human existence that makes cognition possible and it is the neglect of embodiment and action as prerequisites for knowledge that generates traditional epistemological problems:

> The relationship between subject and object is no longer that *relationship of knowing* postulated by classical idealism, wherein the object always seems the construction of the subject, but a *relationship of being* in which, paradoxically, the subject *is* his body, his world, and his situation, by a sort of exchange. (SNST, 72)[26]

By 'classical idealism' Merleau-Ponty means paradigmatically the German idealism of Kant, Fichte, Schelling and Hegel but arguably also Husserlian phenomenology. It is common to these thinkers both to draw a distinction between subject, as that which knows or experiences, and object, as that which is known or experienced, and to argue that the empirical world is, in differing degrees and senses, the cognitive construction of the subject. Despite Merleau-Ponty's use of 'n'est plus' 'is no longer' in this passage, he does not wish to deny the existence of cognitive relations between subject and object nor the subjective constitution of the empirical world. Rather, he wishes to deny that these facts are phenomenologically primitive. It is part of his 'existential' phenomenology that the relations between subject and object are ultimately pragmatic, and it is our ability to pick up, use, or walk around objects which makes possible both their subjective constitution and our knowledge of them.

There are at least two ways of understanding the prima facie paradoxical 'rapport d'être' in which the subject is his world, and situation; one quasi Heideggerian, the other quasi Hegelian. On the Heideggerian construal, 'I am what I am concerned with'. In other words, I am identified with the totality of my pragmatic interests in a situation, including everything that I am confronted with and everything that I try to use as a means to an end, everything with which I am acquainted. On the Heideggarian construal a world or a situation is someone's world or situation. Prima facie, if something is someone's we would not wish to make that conclusive grounds for identifying it with that person.

However, if there is no person without the world that is theirs then, plausibly, their world is essentially what they are.

On the Hegelian construal, 'identical' has to be understood as 'dialectically dependent' such that a and b are dialectically dependent if and only if if not a then not b and if not b then not a. Then we have the thesis that there is no subject without a world and a situation and no world and no situation without a subject. Subject on the one hand and world or situation on the other hand are then 'identical' in the sense that they are parts of a single existential whole, or primordial existential unity. Clearly, on the Hegelian construal 'identical' does not mean 'numerically identical' nor anything synonymous with that.

Merleau-Ponty's thesis that 'le sujet *est* son corps' (SNS, 125) 'the subject *is* his body' (SNST, 72) is logically entailed by the sustained argument of *Phénoménologie de la Perception* that human persons are bodily subjects. Merleau-Ponty thinks subjectivity is physical: not in a materialist reductionist sense which would deny obvious facts about our mental lives in the interests of a brave new pseudo-science, but in a sense which enriches the concept of the body to allow it to think, to perceive.

There is a philosophical problem about whether identity is a relation; about whether a = b should be read as aRb, whether something's being what it is is its being related to itself in some way. Merleau-Ponty assumes in this passage that the answer to this question is 'yes' because the identification of the subject with their body is 'un rapport d'être' 'a relationship of being'. It follows that, for Merleau-Ponty being something is being related to that thing. For example, the subject being their body is a way in which the subject is related to their body. It would seem to follow from this that if something's being something is a way of being related to that thing then it is a way of being related to itself. In general the idea that something should be related to itself is not nonsensical: I can perceive myself, touch myself, be conscious of myself: where this just means that I am both the subject and the object of those actions. I am both perceiver and perceived, toucher and touched, and so on. However, if a subject is their body it is not clear what the two terms of the putative identity relation are. However, if the subject is their body then 'subject' and 'body' admit of only a single referent and this is what the identity of subject and object consists in. Also, if they admit of different senses, or even putatively different senses, then the identification is given sense or semantic content and, controversially, identity could be a relation. For example, if 'subject' means 'that which perceives' and 'body' means 'living human organism' then it makes sense to say 'that which perceives is a living human organism'. The subject is its body by being it.

5 *The synthesis of being and nothingness*

Merleau-Ponty thinks that Sartre's existentialism is not sufficiently Hegelian. The phenomenological ontology of *L'Etre et le Néant* falls short of resolving paradoxes and antitheses concerning the relation of subject and object and 'the book remains too exclusively antithetical' (SNST, 72).[27]

Merleau-Ponty identifies two antitheses which remain unresolved in *L'Etre et le Néant*:

1   the antithesis of my view of myself and another's view of me (SNST, 72)
2   the antithesis of the for itself and the in itself. (SNST, 72)[28]

An antithesis is a pair of semantically and psychologically opposed concepts which putatively refer to one and the same subject matter. An antithesis is paradoxical if and only if either it is at least prima facie inconsistent to give two antithetical concepts the same referent, or if it is psychologically difficult to believe that they could have the same referent, or both. In the two Sartrean cases which Merleau-Ponty considers, then, the view I have of myself and the view others have of me are putatively antithetical and the concepts of the *pour-soi* and the *en-soi* are putatively antithetical.

Clearly, in the case of the consciousness I have of myself and the consciousness others have of me, putatively the same being is the object of both kinds of consciousness. Ultimately, however, there is no philosophical reason why these concepts should be paradoxically antithetical. Not only is there no contradiction in the supposition that a being, including onself, should be the object of qualitatively distinct kinds of consciousness, but also Sartre, notably in *La Transcendence de l'Ego* (1936) maintains that the *way* in which one appears to one's own consciousness is essentially like the way in which one appears to another: as an object not a subject. Presumably Sartre thinks this claim is logically consistent with the phenomenology of the body in *L'Etre et Le Néant* and, prima facie, that I am the object of my consciousness is consistent with certain asymmetries between the physical appearance of self and other.

The distinction between *en-soi* and *pour-soi* is prima facie antithetical because it is a distinction between two kinds of being, and the two categories are mutually exclusive. The antithesis need not be regarded as paradoxical, however, because there is no incoherence in the idea that some portion of being is *pour-soi* and some numerically distinct portion *en-soi*, and this is the position that Sartre holds. *L'être pour-soi* is subjective, conscious and free but *l'être en-soi* is objective, inert and deterministic. It would be prima facie inconsistent to ascribe these properties to all and only the same subject matter, but Sartre maintains that the respect in which what is is *pour-soi* is not the respect in which it is *en-soi* and there is no inconsistency in that.

It follows that Merleau-Ponty is not clearly right to require of Sartre a more Hegelian existentialism, at least to overcome the antitheses of self-consciousness, and subjectivity and objectivity. However, Merleau-Ponty ascribes to Sartre the uncompleted project of effecting a Hegelian synthesis of being and nothingness:

> He is putting off the study of the 'realisation' of nothingness in being – which is action and which makes morality possible – until some other time. (SNST, 72)[29]

There are at least two mutually consistent and quasi-Hegelian interpretations of what the realisation of nothingness in being consists in. Being and nothingness are antithetical concepts and so not just opposites but mutually dependent: semantically, psychologically and, in what they putatively denote, ontologically. If that is right then there is no being without nothingness and no nothingness without being, being is unthinkable unless nothingness is thinkable and nothingness is unthinkable unless being is thinkable and 'nothingness' is meaningless unless 'being' is meaningful and 'being' is meaningless unless 'nothing' is meaningful. We can see here three senses in which nothingness acquires its 'realisation' in being: a is 'realised' in b if and only if either a's being or a's being what a is depends on b's being or b's being what b is or 'a''s meaning depends on 'b''s meaning, or all of these. What this 'realisation' is in the case of being and nothingness is an unsolved philosophical problem because it is not only not clear what it is to be or to not be but is doubtful that either being or not being has an essence. Evaluating the cogency of this realisation therefore depends upon an analysis of being and not being.

The other quasi-Hegelian interpretation of the realisation of nothingness in being emphasises Merleau-Ponty's claim that this 'is action' (SNST, 72) 'est l'action' (SNS, 126). If 'est' here is the 'is' of numerical identity then, whatever interpretation 'realisation' is given it has to be logically consistent with the identification of the realisation of nothingness in being with action.

In the first volume of the *Encyclopädie der Philosophischen Wissenschaften*, in the chapter called 'Die Lehre vom Wesen' which is in the 'Zweite Abteilung der Logik', Hegel exhibits the dialectical relations, as he thinks them, between being (*Sein*), nothingness (*Nichts*) and becoming (*Werden*). Becoming is the speculative synthesis of being and nothingness. There is an insight into what becoming is here: in becoming, at any time, there is beginning to be and ceasing to be. Now, the notion of action that Merleau-Ponty thinks Sartre should deploy in a more dialectically adequate existentialism entails a kind of becoming. By this I mean an indicative sentence including the concept of becoming is true if any indicative sentence in which the existentialist concept of action is embedded is true. If this entailment holds, and if the Hegelian analysis of becoming as the synthesis of being and nothingness is true then Merleau-Ponty is right to suggest that the concept of action overcomes the fundamental dualism of Sartre's phenomenological ontology.

Although Merleau-Ponty's criticism is a clear allusion to the end of *L'Etre et Le Néant* where Sartre raises many questions including that of whether some aspects of being may be lived (but, perhaps, not thematised) and answers:

All these questions, which return us to pure and non-participatory reflection, can only find their answer in the area of morals. We will devote a subsequent work to this.[30]

It is nevertheless true that Sartre makes action, especially freedom of action a prerequisite for the truth of his own existentialism. It would follow then, on Merleau-Ponty's analysis, that Sartre is a dialectician *malgré lui*: that the synthesis of *l'être* and *le néant* is already expressed in *L'Etre et Le Néant*. If this is an implication of Sartre's position on Merleau-Ponty's reading, it is an implication missed not only by Sartre but by Merleau-Ponty.

Merleau-Ponty thinks of Sartre's existentialism as the philosophical synthesis or reconciliation of two prima facie competing tendencies in the Western intellectual tradition. One of these is the Cartesian distinction between mind and matter, the other is the Hegelian thesis that human being and human knowledge are essentially historically situated. These theses are not logically inconsistent: it would not be contradictory to affirm the conjunction of both the non-identity of mind and matter and the historicity of persons *qua* mental and physical beings. However, they are radically different in emphasis. Descartes' soul is unhistorical, unsituated and essentially unchanging. Hegel's *Geist* is essentially dialectical and implicated in the temporality of the world.

Merleau-Ponty draws the distinction between the lessons of Cartesianism and Hegelianism about consciousness this way:

After Descartes, it was impossible to deny that existence as consciousness is radically different from existence as thing and that the relationship of the two is that of emptiness to plentitude. (SNST, 73)[31]

But

> After the 19th century and all it taught us about the historicity of
> spirit, it was impossible to deny that consciousness always exists in
> a situation. (SNST, 73)[32]

It is not mind–body dualism that the existentialist inherits from Descartes.
Merleau-Ponty and Sartre are at pains to repudiate the thesis that mind
and body are numerically distinct substances. Both deny that only consciousness could exist and both deny that only a human body could
exist. However, they endorse the Cartesian thesis that consciousness and
physical objects are radically qualitatively distinct. Notice that this existentialist separation is logically consistent. There is no incoherence in
the supposition that there obtains an important qualitative distinction
between the mental and the physical and yet that neither is a substance,
that is, depends upon nothing except itself for its existence.

It is less clear that the existentialist thesis that the relation between
consciousness and the physical world is that of 'vide au plein' (SNS,
126) 'emptiness to plenitude' (SNST, 73) is anticipated by Descartes.
However, Merleau-Ponty need not be read as affirming that historical
thesis here, but as claiming either that Cartesianism is logically consistent with the distinction between being and nothingness, or that that
is the only appropriate way to describe the phenomenological facts once
Cartesianism is endorsed. Although Merleau-Ponty's existential phenomenology entails that one is one's body, this is consistent with the
thesis that consciousness is a phenomenological nothingness and the
physical world a phenomenological plenitude. That I am my body does
not preclude my apprehending my consciousness as a void and matter
as being.

Merleau-Ponty considers it a merit of existentialism to have synthesised minimal Cartesianism with the Hegelian thesis that consciousness is situated. This Hegelianism may be read on many levels but,
conspicuously, consciousness is consciousness of an object (although,
crucially, subject–object dualism is 'overcome' in *das absolute Wissen*)
and self-consciousness presupposes a confrontation with another consciousness. Many forms of consciousness are distinguished by Hegel,
not only through their internal structure but through their putative
objects and their mutual relations, in existentialist terms, through their
situation.

Merleau-Ponty will consider it a merit of his own existential phenomenology to retain the truth yet overcome the shortcomings of both
Cartesianism and Hegelianism. His thesis that all human being is being-
in-the-world captures the Hegelian insight that all consciousness is situated but is a repudiation of the Cartesianism according to which I am

something metaphysical. His thesis that I am my body lends physical content to the abstractions of Hegel's *Phänomenologie des Geistes* but the way the body is described phenomenologically as 'le corps propre' (PP, 528) leaves room for Cartesian first person singular facts to be true.

IV

The Body

---

1 *The body-subject*

If there is a concept that gives unity to the whole of Merleau-Ponty's work it is that of the body *qua* subject: the idea that I am my body 'Je suis mon corps' (PP, 175). Before examining Merleau-Ponty on the body-subject I provide an intuitive grasp of what he means and state part of its importance for the philosophy of mind.

It is an empirical fact that each of us is acquainted with living human bodies in two kinds of way. First, we each observe through the five senses the bodies of other people; those people who we are not. We could call this 'third person' knowledge of the body (a terminology Merleau-Ponty occasionally has recourse to). Second, however, each of us is acquainted with his or her own body in a more direct way. Knowledge of one's own body by oneself is not only by observation but also by *being* that body. We could call this 'first person singular' knowledge of the body. This distinction between being a person, the one that one is, and observing a person, all the ones that one is not, is essential to grasping the philosophy of mind of many thinkers since Kant, including Hegel, Sartre, Strawson, Nagel and arguably Wittgenstein but certainly Merleau-Ponty.[1]

The obtaining of the distinction is logically consistent with the asymmetry between the empirical truth that part, but not all, of one's knowledge of one's own body is by observation and the fact that none of one's knowledge of someone else's body is derived from one's being that body. It seems to me ultimately a metaphysical and so not a wholly empirical distinction and why it should obtain at all is a profound and unsolved philosophical problem. This is not a problem that Merleau-Ponty addresses, so it follows that his phenomenology rests on at least one unexplained metaphysical assumption. However this is not a very damaging fact as the distinction is so psychologically compelling (once noticed) that it is hard to regard it as vacuous.

Understanding why the idea that I am my body is important for the philosophy of mind requires distinguishing some well known ontologies of the person.[2]

Materialism is the doctrine that a person is a highly complicated physical object and that all the putative mental facts about a person are really physical facts, or at least are logically dependent upon physical facts.

Idealism is the doctrine that a person is a non-physical mind, or consciouness, and that all the physical facts about a person are really mental facts, or at least are logically dependent on mental facts.

Mind–body dualism is the doctrine that a person is essentially a non-physical mind and contingently a non-mental body. On the dualist account a person could, in principle, survive the destruction of their body but could not, even in principle, survive the destruction of their mind.

Merleau-Ponty thinks each of these ontologies is fatally flawed. Materialism reduces the mental and the subjective to the physical and the objective. Idealism reduces the physical and the objective to the mental and the subjective. Neither, it follows, does justice to all the facts: both subjective and objective. Dualism seems to capture both the objective physical facts and the subjective mental facts but leaves wholly unexplained the relation between them.

Merleau-Ponty's originality lies in the idea that subjectivity is physical. None of the three ontologies defined above includes the thesis that I am my body; that I am a subjective object or a physical subject. It is to Merleau-Ponty's detailed phenomenology of the body that we should now turn.

2 *Being my body*

Because phenomenology deals in descriptions not explanations, what Merleau-Ponty offers is a series of differences between the experience of one's own body ('le corps propre' PP, 528) and that of another, or any object in the external world. In the context of his discussion of classical psychology he says:

> my body is distinguishable from the table or the lamp in that I can turn away from the latter whereas my body is constantly perceived. (PPT, 90)[3]

This contrast is not very precisely drawn. It is an empirical fact that I may shift my gaze away from a lamp so that the object no longer falls within my visual field, but it is also an empirical fact that I may do this with my own body. However, Merleau-Ponty says his body is 'constamment perçu' (PP, 106) 'constantly perceived' (PPT, 90) and this does not logically entail 'seen'.

If it is true that my body is constantly perceived by me then this is at best an empirical and contingent truth because it is clearly not a self-contradictory supposition that one is not always perceiving one's body, even if one is one's body. If 'perceived' means 'consciously perceived' then the claim is almost certainly false. For example, it may be doubted whether I am aware of my body the whole time I am asleep, even if when asleep I am aware of some things.

It may be that I am aware of my body without being aware that I am thus aware, or that it is my body that I am aware of, and this would be enough for Merleau-Ponty's claim to go through. However, a test for such awareness would be extremely difficult to devise. It might require the metaphysical possibility of my surviving the destruction of my body and instantly perceiving the loss: a metaphysical possibility Merleau-Ponty emphatically rejects.

A clearer distinction between my body and objects in the external world is this:

It is [. . .] an object which does not leave me. (PPT, 90)[4]

Merleau-Ponty does not consider the converse possibility, that I leave my body, but its negation is entailed by the relevant and intended point: that I do not become separated from my body.

It seems to me a metaphysical possibility that I should become separated from my body; a possibility that cannot be ruled out on phenomenological grounds alone. The notion of a genuine out-of-body experience is not a contradictory one, nor is the supposition that such an experience could continue after the destruction of the body.

We may give Merleau-Ponty's claim a cautious construal; so far it does not appear to my consciousness that I have become separated from my body. Such a claim is not obviously false even if it is logically possible that I have no body, nor ever have had.

It does mark a genuine distinction between my own body and objects in the external world that I am more often perceptually presented with my own body than with any other object. This seems empirically right.

Given that my body does not leave me, Merleau-Ponty raises this question about it: 'But in that case is it still an object?' (PPT, 90).[5] Merleau-Ponty is doubting one of the central tenets of materialism. He does not doubt that we are *physical*, Merleau-Ponty is doubting that we are *objects*.

The phenomenological subject/object distinction is neutral as to whether subjects and objects are mental or physical. When Merleau-Ponty raises the question of whether his body is an object he means 'object' both in the sense of 'intentional object' and 'physical object'. 'Object' in both senses has a single etymological root which 'means that it is standing in front of us' (PPT, 90)[6] but 'physical object' only carries this connotation because physical objects are intentional objects, that is, because they are 'observable' (PPT, 90) 'observable' (PP, 106). Being a possible intentional object is only a necessary condition for being a physical object. From the fact that something is a physical object it follows that it is a possible intentional object. It does not follow from the fact that something is an intentional object that it is a physical object. For this reason Merleau-Ponty tries to distinguish physical objects in particular from intentional objects in general. His example of an intentional object that is not a physical object is 'an idea' (PPT, 90) 'une idée' (PP, 106). Physical objects are distinguished from other intentional objects by this feature:

> An object is an object only in so far as it can be moved away from me, and ultimately disappear from my field of vision. Its presence is such that it entails a possible absence. (PPT, 90)[7]

Merleau-Ponty does not disambiguate 'objet' in its two occurrences in 'an object is an object only . . .' but he means 'the intentional object is a physical object only . . .'.

Prima facie an intentional object other than a physical object could 'disappear from my field of vision': for example the visual illusion of a physical object. In the case of illusory physical objects there may exist an illusionary analogue of moving away from me and there can exist the belief that the illusionary object is absent (even if this belief would have to be false). Despite these facts, Merleau-Ponty's distinction is well founded in that arguably only material particulars are capable of motion and existing either present in or absent from a perceptual field. Not everything physical that may be individuated is straightforwardly a physical object, for example, shadows, gasses and liquids. These too may disappear from my visual field.

Merleau-Ponty claims that my body is not an object in these senses: it does not *stand in front of me* as do objects in the external world. It does not 'ultimately disappear from my field of vision'. (PPT, 90)[8]

If the first of these three claims is taken as logically implying the third then it is true. Although – as Merleau-Ponty will later emphasise – I am visually presented with portions of my body these are not presented in any sense that entails some distance between me and my body. Although there exists some distance between my eyes and the portion of my body I am seeing this is not a distance between me and something else: my body. Although my body does sometimes disappear from my visual field there is a sense of 'ultimately' on which the second claim comes out as true. When my body is not visually presented to me it could always in principle be re-presented. Although this is true it fails as a clear criterion for demarcating my body from external objects. Any physical object may in principle re-appear in my visual field. Merleau-Ponty's claim may be strengthened by adding 'so long as I exist' to it. So long as I exist my body may in principle be visually presented to me where my existence does not guarantee the continued existence and possible reappearance of any external object.

'My body does not ultimately disappear from my field of vision' could mean: so long as I am seeing something then I am seeing (a portion of) my body. If true, this is just empirically true. It amounts to the fact, perhaps, that I see the end of my nose when I see, or perhaps the skin framing my eye sockets at the periphery of my visual field. Again, however, if 'see' means 'consciously see' then the second claim is false. It is not false that I consciously see these things but it is false that I always consciously see them and it may very well be false that I always see them.

The clearest contrast between my body and an external object is that in the case of the latter 'it can be moved away from me' (PPT, 90).[9] My body cannot be moved away from me. Objects can be moved away from me, so my body is not an object.

This argument is certainly valid but it is less clear that it is sound because the second premise is open to metaphysical doubt. It is not incoherent to suppose that my body should move away from me. This is a putative metaphysical possibility which Merleau-Ponty emphatically rejects; my being and my being somewhere depend on my being my body and my being where my body is. Something can only move away from something if both things are physical. Besides, nothing can move away from itself.

However, that my body should move from where I am is not contradictory. Imagine this: the position of the source of my visual field does not change but its content does. My own body appears within my visual field, perhaps walking away from me at first and then stopping to face me. Should the position of the source of my visual field alter it never appears to me that I am looking out of my body.

Imagining this depends on the fact that the source of the visual field does not appear within the visual field. It shows that it is metaphysically possible that my body should move away from me and, if that can happen, then my body can become an 'object': something which in Merleau-Ponty's sense may 'stand in front of' one. Merleau-Ponty wholly neglects the phenomenology of out of body experiences.

Typically and empirically, however, one's body does not move away from one. It follows that Merleau-Ponty has drawn a contrast between one's body and external objects, albeit an empirical and contingent one.

My own body is not an item amongst others that I may encounter during the course of my experience of the external world.

In the case of physical objects, I come across them, I can walk around them, see them from a distance and, if they are not too heavy, pick them up. None of these things is true of my own body.

Merleau-Ponty says my body 'is always presented to me from the same angle' (PPT, 90),[10] but external objects are not. It is an important thesis of Merleau-Ponty's phenomenology of perception that any physical object *qua* object of visual perception is only presented to a subject from a particular angle at a time. Merleau-Ponty endorses Husserl's thesis that an object is presented to a subject through 'profiles' or 'aspects' ('Abschattungen'). For this reason he says,

> It is true that external objects too never turn one of their sides to me without hiding the rest. (PPT, 90)[11]

That in itself does not mark a contrast between my body and external objects. The required contrast partly concerns freedom, and partly the uniqueness of the perspective I have on my own body. In the case of external objects Merleau-Ponty says,

> I can at least choose the side which they are to present to me. (PPT, 90–1)[12]

This freedom is not available in my perception of my own body. The contrast is between degrees of freedom: not between freedom and its absence. By moving my head and the rest of my body I am able to vary the angles from which my body is visually presented to me. The greater freedom I have in the perception of external objects is a consequence of my ability to move around those objects and see more of them, something I seem unable to do with my body. Merleau-Ponty's distinction is just as strong as this impossibility.

Merleau-Ponty thinks the impossibility of an external object presenting an aspect other than the one presented at a time is a different kind of impossibility from the impossibility of my seeing my body from a different angle from the one from which I see it. Each kind of impossibility conceptually depends upon a different kind of necessity. One of these Merleau-Ponty calls 'physical necessity' (PPT, 91) ('nécessité physique' PP, 106), the other he calls 'metaphysical' (PPT, 91) ('métaphysique' PP, 107). He says of external objects:

> They could not appear otherwise then in perspective, but the particular perspective which I acquire at each moment is the outcome of no more than physical necessity. (PPT, 91)[13]

61

Merleau-Ponty does not explain what kind of necessity he intends to express by 'Ils ne sauraient' (translated as 'they could not') except to say that it is not a kind of necessity that imprisons him ('ne m'imprisonne pas' PP, 107) and that it is a kind of necessity he can use ('me servir' PP, 107).

One suggestion is this. If a physical object is perceived visually then it necessarily only presents an aspect or a profile because that is a necessary condition of its being a physical object that is visually presented. If something is visually presented without an aspect or profile being thereby presented then what is presented is not a physical object.

The necessity of, 'They could not appear otherwise than in perspective' (PPT, 91) is; a sufficient condition for a physical object's presenting a profile is that that physical object is perceived visually.

Merleau-Ponty has no further explanation of the notion of necessity he is invoking. If not deductive proof, then something like conceptual evidence may be provided. Lockean primary qualities are necessary conditions for being a physical object in the sense that if something without size, or something without shape, is perceived then what is being perceived is not a physical object. In a parallel way, presenting a phenomenological profile when perceived visually is a necessary condition for being a physical object. It is perhaps hard to make sense of the concept of a physical object seen but not presented to a point of view.

Having provided this much support for Merleau-Ponty, it is not a priori impossible that the whole of (at least the outside) of a physical object should be perceived visually simultaneously. This would have to be by a being with visual sense organs very different from our own: ones which surround the physical object being seen in a visual analogue of a person grasping a ball bearing in their fist and touching all its outer surface at once. As we shall see later, Merleau-Ponty rejects the possibility of visually perceiving the whole of (the outside of) a physical object simultaneously. I would go so far as to accept that it is part of our ordinary concept of a physical object to be visually presented through profiles and not to be seen all at once.

Whatever the necessity of appearing 'in perspective' is, it is not the 'physical necessity' of presenting one perspective rather than another nor the 'metaphysical' necessity that the body only presents one perspective to its owner. Merleau-Ponty does not say what he means by 'physical necessity' and several senses are possible. He says the perspective I 'acquire' (PPT, 91) ('obtiens' PP, 106) 'is the outcome of' (PPT, 91) ('résulte de' PP, 106) physical necessity.

This makes it sound as though a perception, a mental item, is a causal consequence of a property of a physical object in the external world, where the causal relation this entails is a necessary relation. Suppose any causal relation is a necessary relation if and only if the cause, C, is both necessary and sufficient for the effect, E. This means that unless C occurs then E cannot occur but if C does occur then E cannot fail to occur. If we give 'physical necessity' this sense then Merleau-Ponty comes out as committed to this position: unless a physical object presents (a unique) aspect (Abschattung) to a subject that subject does not perceive that aspect. If a physical object does present (a unique) aspect to a subject that subject does perceive that aspect. It is a necessary condition for the perception of a property of a physical object that that property be perceptually presented.

If 'presentation' means anything other than 'perceptual presentation' then the thesis is false.

When Merleau-Ponty says the physical necessity is 'a necessity which I can use' (PP, 91)[14] he gives as an example the visual presentation of a church tower through a window and the possibility of seeing 'the whole church' (PP, 91) 'l'église en entier' (PP, 107) from a different position. The expression 'en entier' has been translated 'the whole' here but it does not mean that. It means 'as a whole'. This is a crucial distinction and one to which Merleau-Ponty is sensitive. From the fact that an object is perceived *as a whole* it does not logically follow that *the whole* of that object is seen, and it is in fact Merleau-Ponty's view that although we may perceive an object as a whole we may not perceive the whole of an object. It is not clear that he is right in this negative claim if the 'cannot' is a logical cannot. It is contingent facts about the powers and positions of our sense organs which produce this impossibility.

Because he holds that it is impossible to perceive the whole of a physical object even in perceiving a physical object as a whole, when he says he may see the church as a whole by changing position, he means enough of the church to assure him it is a church that is perceived.

His phenomenological point is that which aspect of a physical object is presented to a subject is partly dependent upon the physical location of that subject. By voluntarily shifting position the subject has a measure of control over which aspects are seen. This freedom of perception is consistent with particular aspects being 'necessarily' seen from particular points of view in the sense that once I adopt a position I do not have further control over which aspect of the object is presented.

A quite different kind of necessity pertains to my relationships with my body. Two of these relationships exhibit 'metaphysical necessity': 'its permanence near to me' (PPT, 91) ('sa permanence près de moi' PP, 107) and 'its unvarying perspective' PPT, 91) ('sa perspective invariable' PP, 107). Neither is 'a de facto necessity' (PPT, 91) ('une nécessité de fait' PP, 107). The permanence of my body near to me is partly the fact that my body does not leave me, nor I it, but also the fact that when I perceive my body it is never thereby perceived as very far from me.

The 'unvarying perspective' my body presents to me is characterised, for example by the fact that

> My head is presented to my sight only to the extent of my nose end and the boundaries of my eye-sockets. (PPT, 91)[15]

Merleau-Ponty is right to talk of metaphysical necessity here, or, at least of metaphysical facts. The peculiar visual perspective I have on my own body is certainly partly to be explained by the biological contingency of the location of my eye-balls in the front of my head, as it is by other contingencies pertaining to the shape and size of my body.

However, the fact that I see my body only from a certain angle is not wholly explicable by mentioning empirical contingencies. Even if the list of contingent and empirical facts (including all the mental facts) about a certain human body were *per impossibile* complete, the fact that I visually perceive my body only from a certain angle could not validly be derived from such a list. The fact that I am a certain human body is not a further empirical fact about that body. The fact that I perceive my body visually only from a certain angle is to be explained by the fact that I am that body conjoined with all those contingent perceptual facts about that body such as orientation and powers of the eyes.

Merleau-Ponty claims that with respect to his perception of the church, which here stands for any external object, he is not a 'prisoner' (PPT, 91) ('prisonnier' PP, 107). The presentation of any aspect of an external object has only a 'de facto' or 'factual' permanence (PPT, 91) ('permanence de fait' PP, 107). It is a contingent fact that an external object presents a certain aspect to a percipient at a time. This is ultimately contingent because it depends on many contingencies, including the contingencies that there exist physical objects and percipients. The contingency Merleau-Ponty is interested in is the position of the percipient relative to the physical object. He is right in the thought that that contingency is sufficient to make it a contingent fact that any particular aspect of an external object is being perceived. The percipient is not a 'prisoner' in the sense that he or she may shift position and so be presented with fresh aspects of the physical object. The implied contrast is that I am a prisoner in my own body, and so a prisoner in my possible perceptions of my own body. If I am imprisoned in my body this imprisonment is very close; it amounts to identity because I am my body. The metaphor of imprisonment amounts to the fact that *qua* self-perceiver I am not free, to shift position and so perceive my body from different angles, to *tour* my body.

Merleau-Ponty contrasts my body with external objects in another way. He says that although he observes external objects, his own body is not something he observes. This is because it is by means of the body that observation of the external world is possible:

> I observe external objects with my body, I handle them, examine them, walk round them, but my body itself is a thing which I do not observe: in order to be able to do so, I should need the use of a second body which itself would be unobservable. (PPT, 91)[16]

'Observe' does not mean 'perceive' here.

In Merleau-Ponty's sense if something is observed then it is perceived but if something is perceived it does not follow that it is observed. This leaves logical space for the thesis that I perceive my body without observing it.

We need to know now what the difference is between perceiving in general and observing in particular. He says,

> Observation consists in varying the point of view while keeping the object fixed. (PPT, 91)[17]

If that is what observation is then I do not observe my body because I am not able to vary my position *qua* perceiver of it while it remains fixed. That I should do this must, in the end, be a contradictory sup-postion on Merleau-Ponty's terms because I am my body, and it is contradictory to suppose that anything should move while remaining stationary. Although I do not observe my body I do perceive it. Merleau-Ponty describes the phenomenological limits of my visual perception of my body:

> My visual body is certainly an object as far as its parts far removed from my head are concerned, but as we come nearer to the eyes, it becomes divorced from objects, and reserves among them a quasi-space to which they have no access. (PPT, 91–2)[18]

By 'my visual body is certainly an object' Merleau-Ponty allows a respect in which the body–subject is its own object. This captures the insight that, at least so far as the front of my body is concerned, the nearer the head any part of it is, the more it escapes my visual field. In so far as I can see my body it is an object, and *qua* perceiver of it I am a subject. (This escaping admits of degrees because I can move my head and eyeballs.)

The body *qua subject*, however, cannot be perceived as object. This is why Merleau-Ponty says the eyes 'have no access' (PPT, 92) 'n'ont pas

65

accès' (PP, 108) to the quasi-space occupied by my head. This is a quasi-space and not straightforwardly a space because it is a subjective unobservable phenomenological space, where non-quasi-space is public space observable at least via its occupants.

3 Merleau-Ponty and the mind–body problem

The mind–body problem is the problem of stating correctly the relation between the mental and the physical. Putative solutions to the problem oscillate between attempts to prove that the mental is really physical (materialism) or that the physical is really mental (idealism). On both of those theories the relation is putatively numerical identity despite prima facie extreme qualitative differences between what is mental and what is physical. The dualist thesis that both mental and physical items exist and are both numerically and qualitatively distinct succeeds in charac-terising the relation only negatively, in denying that it is identity, and leaves the positive relation obscure even in sometimes claiming it to be causal. The neutral monist thesis that mental and physical are two aspects of some reality which is intrinsically neither mental nor physical typically fails to specify the intrinsic nature of the third kind of entity, or at least, does not avoid using mental or physical predicates in attempt-ing to do so.

Merleau-Ponty's solution to the mind–body problem is phenomeno-logical. Phenomenological solutions to philosophical problems consist in describing the conditions within experience which make the thinking of the problem possible. It is then shown either that the obtaining of these presuppositions is inconsistent with putative solutions to the problem or that the problem itself is a product of reflecting on experience incorrectly. Merleau-Ponty's solution to the mind–body problem may be accurately subsumed under both these descriptions.

Merleau-Ponty argues that being-in-the-world is a primordial existen-tial category with regard to the substantial distinction between mental and physical. A necessary condition for our drawing such a mental–physical distinction is our exhibiting the existential structures of being-in-the-world. The metaphysical mental–physical distinction is not found in immediate experience but is a product of reflection upon experience. Before reflection:

> The unity of man has not yet been broken; the body has not yet
> been stripped of human predicates; it has not yet become a machine;
> and the soul has not yet been defined as existence for-itself.
> (SB, 188).[19]

Crucially, the employment of 'prédicats humains' (SC, 203) 'human predi-cates' (SB, 188) makes the metaphysical employment of mental and physical predicates possible. Being human is prior to being either mental or physical or both. Unless we were human and unless we possessed the category 'human' we would not be able to have the concept of the mental and the concept of the physical as separable. A human predicate is an expression used to denote a property which is essential to being human where such a putative property is not physical but not mental, nor mental but not physical. Paradigmatically such predicates pick out human behaviour but 'behaviour' ('comportement') is not to be understood in any behaviourist or physicalist way. Behaviour is never just mental nor just physical.

When Merleau-Ponty says 'The unity of man has not yet been broken' (CB, 188) he means pre-reflectively the human being has not been divided into mental and physical properties nor mental and physical substances. It is the reflective act of judgement, especially philosophical judgement, which produces the appearance of mind–body dualism.

Merleau-Ponty identifies two kinds of mistake, one materialist and one dualist and idealist. Both mistakes are consequences of one big mistake common to materialists, idealists and dualists alike: the body being 'dépouillé de prédicats humains' (SC, 203) 'stripped of human predicates' (SB, 188). The materialist mistake is to think of the body as a kind of machine ('une machine' SC, 203). The dualist and idealist mistake is to define 'soul' as 'l'existence pour-soi' (SC, 203) 'existence for-itself' (SB, 188). I shall take each in turn.

Materialists, in their attempt to reduce the mental to the physical, either by denying the reality of the mental, or by translating mental predicates into physical predicates, or by identifying mental states with physical states, thereby assume that the human body is just a highly complicated physical object. In fact, according to Merleau-Ponty, as we have seen, the body is not an object. The body is a subject: the subject of its own actions, experiences and acts of thinking.

Idealists and dualists, in their attempt to prove that the mental is not physical, either by denying the existence of the physical or by refusing to identify the mental with the physical, mistakenly think the subject can be mental. In fact, the subject is its body ('le sujet est son corps' SNS, 125): not the inanimate objective mechanical body that I may observe in the external world but the living moving experiencing whole human body that one is: the body, so to speak, I am co-extensive with.

For Merleau-Ponty the body *qua* oneself exhibits the phenomenological–ontological property of being 'pour soi' (SC, 203) 'for-itself' (SB, 188). This terminology, although given widespread use by Sartre in *L'Etre et le Néant* is Hegelian. 'Pour-soi' and 'en-soi' are French translations of Hegel's 'für-sich' and 'an-sich' in *Phänomenologie des Geistes*. The an-sich/für-sich distinction is a distinction between two kinds of being. Something belongs to the realm of being called 'for itself' if and only if it is a subject of thought or experience. Something belongs to the realm of being called 'in itself' if and only if it is the object of thought and experience but not the subject of thought or experience. *Qua* subject it cannot be object. Although Merleau-Ponty's terminology is Hegelian his ontology is not. According to Merleau-Ponty the *pour-soi* cannot be mental or spiritual but Hegel positively insists that the *für-sich* can only be mental or spiritual.

Merleau-Ponty also denies that it is part of pre-reflective common sense that there are psycho-physical causal relations, at least between a mental substance and the body:

> Naive consciousness does not see in the soul the cause of the movements of the body nor does it put the soul in the body as the pilot in his ship. (SB, 188)[20]

Pre-philosophical common sense does not employ the distinction between soul and body nor the idea of causal relations between them. Rather, pre-reflectively, we think of whole human persons performing actions. The idea that a person comprises both a mental substance and a physical substance that might causally interact is not an intuitive one but a product of reflection. Merleau-Ponty says, 'This way of thinking belongs to philosophy; it is not implied in immediate experience' (SC, 188).[21] The distinction between soul and body as putative causes and effects is *thought*, not perceived.

It is not part of pre-reflective common sense to think of one's soul as inside one's body, 'nor does it put the soul in the body as the pilot in his ship' (SB, 188).[22] Pre-philosophically a person experiences him or herself as a whole acting person embedded in the world:

> He lives in a universe of experience, in a milieu which is neutral with regard to the substantial distinctions between the organism, thought and extension; he lives in a direct commerce with beings, things and his own body. The ego as a centre from which his intentions radiate, the body which carries them and the beings and things to which they are addressed are not confused: they are but three sectors of a unique field. (SB, 189)[23]

Merleau-Ponty deploys this existential terminology to depict the structure of our situation before reflection. There are two prima facie paradoxes which need to be dispelled here. It might be (perhaps naively) objected to Merleau-Ponty that commonsensically no-one deploys the vocabulary of existential phenomenology so ordinary experience cannot be as described by that vocabulary. This objection rests upon a fallacious inference. From the fact that some person's pre-reflective experience is not characterised by that person in a certain vocabulary it simply does not follow that it could not be and could not truly be. We should think of Merleau-Ponty as describing not what is not described pre-reflectively but what is experienced.

The other prima facie paradox is more serious, but not insuperable. Merleau-Ponty must reflect upon pre-reflective experience in order to characterise it phenomenologically but reflecting on pre-reflective experience would seem to be an incoherent idea. The experience would cease to be pre-reflective once it is reflected upon.

The phenomenological solution to this paradox is to be as passive as is feasible in the composing of descriptions. The aim is to characterise what is given just as it is given without the imposition of ontological pre-conceptions. If metaphysical ontological commitments are eschewed then, plausibly, the mind–body problem will not arise.

Another response is also possible. It might be that I can remember the pre-reflective nature of my experience and then characterise it phenomenologically. From the fact that I have to think about my pre-phenomenological experience it does not follow that I have to reflect on it while I am having it and from the fact that I do not reflect upon my experience while I am having it it does not follow that I cannot later remember what it is like.

When Merleau-Ponty says the subject inhabits 'a milieu which is neutral' he means ontologically neutral with regard to putative distinctions between mind, body and external world. Although pre-reflectively this threefold distinction does exist, it is not a set of 'distinctions substantielles' (SC, 204) 'substantial distinctions' (SB, 189). What precisely is not given pre-reflectively is a mind that could exist without a body or an external world, a body that could exist without a mind or an external world and an external world that could exist without a mind and a body. 'Mind', 'body' and 'external world' do not denote substances where, if something is a substance, there are no necessary conditions for its existence.

The 'neutral milieu' is the world. 'Milieu' is not translated as 'place' here because the world is not a place. A place has both an interior and an exterior but the world has only an interior. In being-in-the-world the subject is in the world but there is not anything or anywhere the world is in. The world is the totality of what is and it makes no sense to talk of the totality of what is being anywhere.

The distinction between 'the organism', 'thought' and 'extension' although not given as 'substantial' is given pre-reflectively. Crucially, 'they are only three sectors of a unique field' (SB, 189).[24] Something is a *sector* if and only if it is an essential part of being-in-the-world but the world is also essential to it.

Sometimes Merleau-Ponty seems to privilege one of consciousness, the body and the external world over the other two but this privileging is illusory because the existence of each is a necessary condition for the existence of the other two. For example, Merleau-Ponty makes the empirical claim that 'an injury to the eyes is sufficient to eliminate vision' (SB, 189)[25] and concludes from this that 'we must then see through the body' (SB, 189).[26] Merleau-Ponty agrees that consciousness empirically depends upon the well-functioning of the nervous system and sense organs and uses this as a premise for his view that the body uses itself as an instrument to perceive. Taken out of context this thesis is logically consistent with epiphenomenalism but it is clear that the body *qua* body-subject and the external world *qua* object of perception are equally dependent upon consciousness. The privileging of one structure of being-in-the-world over another depends upon emphasising or reading descriptions of some dependencies but not others. Merleau-Ponty's holistic view is that each part of being-in-the-world is a 'indispensible moment of the lived dialectic' (SB, 189).[27]

Any dialectical relation between a and b is at least reciprocal such that a depends upon b and b depends upon a (logically, causally, ontologically, semantically or constitutionally). Although a is not b and b is not a, a's being and a's being a depend both upon a's not being b and b's being and b's being and b's being b depend both on b's not being a and a's being. Where and only where such reciprocal relations obtain, are a and b dialectical 'moments' (SC, 204) 'moments' (SB, 189).

Dialectical philosophy is paradigmatically unifying or synthetic rather than analytical. It exhibits the multiplicity of dependencies between what concepts denote rather than the semantic distinctions between the concepts themselves. Nevertheless, it is possible to think of synthetic and analytical philosophy as themselves dialectically related. One way of reading a subject matter is to look at its components and exhibit their mutual dependencies as parts of a whole (a synthetic procedure). Another is to analyse a whole into its parts by distinguishing between concepts (an analytical procedure). Arguably, if one procedure were in principle impossible so would the other be in principle impossible.

The existential structures of being-in-the-world are dialectical moments so being-in-the-world is itself a dialectically constituted whole: its moments make it what it is. Merleau-Ponty speaks of a 'dialectique vécue' (SC, 204) 'lived dialectic' (SB, 189). He means that being-in-the-world is the set of existential structures it is, partly because of our living participation in it as an essential component. To take one of his examples, 'things' (SB, 189) 'les choses' (SC, 204) are as they are because they present themselves to us perspectivally and because they are the subject matter of an intersubjective discourse. They would not be things *qua* the things we encounter in the world if they were not partly made

70

what they are by our very encounter with them. For example, a physical object being the sort of item that may present a side to us partly depends upon the organisation of our visual and tactile sense organs.

The unity of being-in-the-world makes the mind–body problem thinkable. It is exactly the thinking of certain parts of being-in-the-world as separate that generates the problem of the relations between them. What is existentially inseparable is separated in reflective thought. What is lived as a unity is dispersed in reflection.

Merleau-Ponty thinks an adequate description of being-in-the-world will solve a number of mutually related philosophical problems. For example, the relations between a thing and the perception of thing may be construed as a version of the mind–body problem or as a problem about realism and scepticism about the external world. Merleau-Ponty says:

> The subject does not live in a world of states of consciousness or representations from which he would believe himself able to act on and know external things by a sort of miracle. (SB, 189)[28]

He means that intuitively, or pre-philosophically, we do not draw a distinction between a thing and the perception of it. It is not as though (usually) we are mixed up about the distinction either. Rather we speak of seeing something where there is no doubt that it was a thing that was seen. Common sense postulates no impressions or perceptions as intermediaries. It follows that there is no pre-reflective problem about how there might not be an external world, or how it might not be as we take it to be if we are only directly acquainted with sense impressions. It is philosophical reflection that produces a *doubling* or *duplication* of the world that is absent from primordial experience:

> The world is doubled: there will be the real world as it is outside my body and the world as it is for me, numerically distinct from the first; the external cause of perception and the internal object which it contemplates will have to be separated. (SB, 190)[29]

Pre-reflectively, people are not aware of living in two worlds, one inner and mental, the other external and physical.

One might object to Merleau-Ponty's procedure here as follows: from the fact that pre-reflectively there is no fundamental distinction between mental and physical it does not follow that there is no fundamental distinction between mental and physical and so no problem about the ontological relations between mental and physical. The reason why Merleau-Ponty thinks the content of pre-reflective experience a better guide to what is than philosophical reflection is that it is *existence* rather than just *thought about existence*.

At the end of the *Pariser Vortrāger* Husserl quotes Saint Augustine approvingly: 'Inquire within yourself; the truth inhabits the interior of man.'[30] Merleau-Ponty's existential revision of this phenomenology is:

> Truth does not 'inhabit' only 'the inner man' (sic), or more
> accurately, there is no inner man, man is in the world, and only in
> the world does he know himself. (PPT, xi)[31]

4 *The flesh of the world*

Many of the phenomenological facts which are constitutive of the body being a body-subject are also constitutive of the body not being just one item amongst others in the world. Being it is an obstacle to encountering it, as are facts about action and consciousness. Merleau-Ponty says,

> My body is not only one perceived among others. (VIT, 249)[32]

There are many respects in which this is true for Merleau-Ponty. I could not single out and make a tour of my body as I could a typical physical object that I encounter within my perceptual field. I do not encounter my body as at a distance, as 'over there'. It does not exist at any distance from me (although parts of it exist at some distance from the organs it uses to sense itself). My body is not only one perceived amongst others because my body is not only a perceived. My body is a perceiver. Merleau-Ponty says of one's body:

> It is the mesurant of all, Nullpunkt of all the dimensions of the
> world. (VIT, 249)[33]

To unpack this spatial metaphor, that which measures (a rule for example) *qua* measuring instrument does not measure itself. 'Nullpunkt' is the German for 'zero point' so just as a measuring instrument could give no measurement of itself (except arguably zero) so the body *qua* subject does not appear to itself as an object. *Qua* subject it does not appear to itself as anything at all. Rather as a measuring instrument could in principle be used to measure anything that conformed to its units of measurement so the body is used by the subject it is to perceive the world. That which perceives does not perceive itself in perceiving. The point here is analogous to that made by Wittgenstein in a famous passage of the *Tractatus*. Although Merleau-Ponty insists that our being is in the world and Wittgenstein says in contrast:

5.632
The subject does not belong to the world: rather, it is a limit of the world.[34]

Wittgenstein is saying here that the subject is not an object:

5.633
Where in the world is a metaphysical subject to be found?
   You will say this is exactly like the case of the eye and the visual field. But really you do not see the eye.
   And nothing in the visual field allows you to infer that it is seen by an eye.[35]

Merleau-Ponty and Wittgenstein have in three respects logically equivalent descriptions of subjectivity, even though Wittgenstein takes the example of the eye and Merleau-Ponty is concerned with the whole body *qua* subject. Merleau-Ponty and Wittgenstein agree that the subject *qua* subject is not an object of perception. Merleau-Ponty and Wittgenstein agree that the subject *qua* subject is not a part of the world. On Merleau-Ponty's use of 'monde' ('world') and Wittenstein's use of 'Welt' ('world') something is a possible object of perception if and only if it is a part of the world. Merleau-Ponty and Wittgenstein agree that the subject *qua* subject does not perceive itself (as Wittgenstein puts it, you do not really see the eye). Finally, Merleau-Ponty and Wittgenstein agree not only that the subject *qua* subject makes possible the perception of the world but also that the existence and nature of the subject *qua* subject cannot be logically read off the objective properties of the world. (As Wittgenstein puts it, nothing in the visual field allows one to conclude that it is perceived by an eye.)
   Although Merleau-Ponty is at pains to point out that the body *qua* body-subject is not an object, body-subject and objective world do stand in complex relations of mutual dependence. In particular,

My body is made of the same flesh as the world (it is perceived), and moreoever . . . this flesh of my body is shared by the world, the world reflects it, encroaches upon it and it encroaches upon the world (the felt at the same time the culmination of subjectivity and the culmination of materiality). They are in a relation of transgression or of overlapping. (VIT, 248)[36]

If something is flesh it either perceives or is perceived or both. It follows that the body is paradigmatically flesh because it both perceives and is perceived. Merleau-Ponty says, 'My body is made of the same flesh as the world' because both body and world are perceived. Nothing can be flesh if it neither perceives nor is perceived.

The term 'fait' (VI, 302) 'made' (VIT, 248) is ambiguous: 'fait' (the past participle of 'faire' 'to make' or 'to do') can mean 'made' just in the sense of 'composed', for example 'fait de' means 'composed of'. Or 'fait' can mean 'made' in the sense of 'fabricated' or 'deliberately composed' (by some more or less intelligent agency). Now when Merleau-Ponty says that his flesh ('chair') is 'made' ('fait') he means it only in the sense of 'composed' or 'constituted' and not at all in the sense of 'manufactured' or 'fabricated'. 'Flesh' denotes everything that may be described phenomenologically; everything that is, so to speak, *surface*.

When Merleau-Ponty says 'moreover this flesh of my body is shared by the world'[37] he means that one's body and the world are both perceived.

He also means that the way the world is, and for Merleau-Ponty that can only ever mean the world as it is for us, is due to facts about the body *qua* subject. This is why the the world reflects the body. He says 'the world reflects it'. Wittgenstein says nothing in the visual field could lead one to conclude that it is perceived by an eye but Merleau-Ponty claims the way the world is (for us) is due to the way we are, to our being body-subjects. The world is just what one would expect to be constituted by a body-subject and a body-subject is just what one would expect to be constitutive of such a world. The two positions are in fact mutually consistent. Although a description of the subjective properties of the body cannot be *logically* derived from a description of the objective properties of the world, those objective properties are essentially bestowed by that body-subject.

Body-subject and world are ultimately mutually constituting despite all the emphasis placed just on the subjective constitution of the world in *Phénoménologie de la Perception*. Neither would be what it is without the other. This is what Merleau-Ponty means when he says 'the world . . . encroaches upon it and it encroaches upon the world' (VIT, 248).[38] It follows that Merleau-Ponty's considered view is that body-subject and world are dialectically related: they are mutually constituting.

Although the body-subject is the 'percevant-perçu' (VI, 302) 'perceiving-perceived' (VIT, 248) it is paradigmatically the sensed ('le senti' VI, 302) which is the synthesis of the subjective and the material. We can appreciate this already if we consider that *the sensed* seems to have both experiential and physical properties. For example a pain both hurts and is spatially located in a part of the body. Merleau-Ponty speaks of *the sensed* as 'at the same time the culmination of subjectivity and the culmination of materiality' (VIT, 248).[39] Suppose being F is the 'culmination' of x if and only if being F is essential to being x. In that case being 'the sensed' is essential both to being subjective and to being material. It is possible to give some plausibility to this by insisting that something can only be physical if it is, in principle, an object or content of sensation and by asserting that there can only be subjectivity if there is (or could be) some content that is sensed. On this view it would then be contradictory to maintain that something is physical but is not a possible object of sensation and that something is subjective but is not the possible sensing of some content.

It is possible to interpret 'culmination' (VIT, 248) 'comble' (VI, 302) in a different way here so that both subjectivity and materiality have a single culmination in the sensed. There is a culmination of subjectivity and materiality when the sensed exhibits both subjectivity and materiality.

Within the sensed, subjectivity and materiality can be understood to be 'in a relation of transgression or of overlapping'.[40] In the sensed, it is the physical extension that has the subjective qualitative feel of, say, hurting. Or, to put it another way, the qualitative feel of hurting is physically extended: it has spatial location and even size. It does not make much sense to claim that the sensed is mental but not physical or physical but not mental. It does make sense to speak it as subjective with material aspects or as material with subjective aspects. Merleau-Ponty does not much mind which of these two idioms we choose and in this we see yet another sense in which Merleau-Ponty's phenomenology steers a careful course between idealism and realism.

5 *Who looks into the mirror?*

Some phenomenological facts are constitutive both of being a body and of the body-subject/thing distinction because that there is something it consists in to be a body distinguishes the body *qua* body-subject from things.

> For example it is not one mobile or moving among the mobiles or movings, I am not conscious of its movements as a distance taken by relation to me, it *sich bewegt* whereas the things are moved. (VIT, 249)[41]

A thing in the world may (in principle) be moved by me but I do not move my body by acting on something other than myself or even by acting on myself: I move my body by moving. Merleau-Ponty leaves the third person singular of the reflexive German verb 'sich bewegen' untranslated to capture this idea. This infinitive form means 'to move oneself' so 'il *sich bewegt*' (VI, 302) means 'It moves itself'. My moving my body does not consist in my causing anything to to move (even if, contingently, my moving my body does cause other things to move this is not what my moving my body consists in). It is even wrong to speak of my moving my body consisting in my causing my body to move if this implies the existence of two entities and a causal connection between them: me, my body and my causing my body to move. Because I am it if I move I move it.

Merleau-Ponty's view that I am not aware of the movements of my body as at some distance from me is logically implied by his thesis that I am my body. If I am my whole body then no movement of my body may occur at any distance from myself. I cannot, then be veridically aware of the movements of my body as at some distance from me.

Merleau-Ponty says my knowledge of my own body implies

> a sort of 'reflectedness' (*sich bewegen*), it thereby constitutes itself
> *in itself* – in a parallel way: it touches *itself*, sees *itself*. (VIT, 249)[42]

This is not 'reflection' in any ordinary sense. It is not an epistemological relationship which implies the existence of two relata: something reflecting and something reflected. Rather, I have an implicit or kinaesthetic awareness of the movements of my body. I know that I am moving because I am that which is moving. In seeing I thereby know that I see, not because I reflect on seeing but because in seeing I am what sees. In touching I know that I touch not because I reflect on touching but because in touching I am what touches. (Merleau-Ponty does not mean here that the body is capable of touching itself or that the body is capable of seeing itself although obviously he accepts that).

Why is my being what senses a reason for my knowing that I sense? (I shall take 'senses' in an occurrent and not a dispositional sense because it is the sense Merleau-Ponty intends here.) Clearly, my being what senses is a necessary condition for my knowing that I sense because it would be incoherent to affirm that I know that I sense yet deny that I am what senses. I can only know what is true. But is it sufficient? There is no contradiction in the supposition that one is what senses, in ignorance of that fact. Being what senses provides no *logically* conclusive ground for knowing that one senses.

Suppose being something implies knowing that thing. This thesis has the awkward logical consequence of making it analytic that one knows what one is. This is less than plausible because for many true descriptions of oneself it is not contradictory to assert that one is ignorant of the truth of those descriptions. We need a different notion from 'logically sufficient condition'.

The picture he substitutes is this:

> The touching itself, seeing itself of the body is itself to be
> understood in terms of what we said of the seeing and the visible,

the touching and the touchable. I.e. it is not an act, it is a being at.
(VIT, 249)[43]

The crucial phrase here is 'c'est un être à' 'it is a being at'. 'Being at'
does not mean straightforwardly being spatially located at: as a physical
object might be specifiably located in place at a time. It means at least
'being something': being something which ontologically realises one's
own subjectivity. 'Etre à' may also be read as an appropriation of
Heidegger's 'Sein zu', 'being towards'. We have already seen how in
Phénoménologie de la Perception being a body-subject partly consists in
looking from one's body, being unable to leave one's body and being
co-extensive with one's body. With the notion of 'être à' ('being
towards') Merleau-Ponty is adding to the notion of being something an
intentionality and a teleology. The being that I am, that which realises
me ontologically, is subjectively orientated towards some content. When
there is seeing or touching I am what sees in seeing or touches in touching. I occupy the role of perceiver if and only if I am what the
perceiver is.

This kind of implicit self-knowledge has two consequences, the second
of them prima facie paradoxical. It means both that

To touch oneself, to see oneself, accordingly, is not to apprehend
oneself as an ob-ject, it is to be open to oneself, destined to oneself
(narcissism). (VIT, 249)[44]

and that

Nor therefore is it to reach *oneself*, it is on the contrary to escape
oneself, to be ignorant of *oneself*, the self in question is by
divergence, is *Unverborgenheit of the Verborgen* as such, which
consequently does not cease to be hidden or latent. (VIT, 249)[45]

The first consequence is familiar: I do not single myself out as an object
in the world, in the way that I single out one physical object from
others. By separating 'ob' from 'jet' by the hyphen Merleau-Ponty is
drawing our attention to the fact that in its Latin etymology 'objet' is
derived from the noun 'objectus' which has the sense of 'a casting
before', 'a putting against', 'an opposing' or, perhaps, 'an obstacle'.
However, I precisely do not encounter myself as at some distance from
myself. I am not something that I reach or confront.

The second consequence is paradoxical because in this kind of self-
knowledge there is an 'Unverborgenheit' of the 'Verborgen'. 'Verborgen'
is the ordinary German word for 'hidden' and 'Unverborgenheit' is
'unhiddeness' or 'disclosure' so the 'Unverborgenheit du Verborgen'

(VI, 303) is the 'disclosure of the hidden' or the 'unhiddeness of that which is hidden'.

We need to know what is both hidden and disclosed, and this is 'the self in question' (VIT, 249).[46] It follows that in the implicit kind of self knowledge which consists in 'être à', 'being at' (that is, being realised in a subjective intentional ontology) it is oneself who is both hidden and disclosed.

One misunderstanding needs to be dispelled straight away. Merleau-Ponty is not saying that in this kind of self knowledge at an earlier time one is hidden from oneself and then at a later time one is disclosed to oneself. There would be nothing paradoxical about that. Merleau-Ponty is saying that *at the same time* one is both disclosed to oneself and hidden from oneself, and this is prima facie paradoxical. Despite being disclosed, 'the self in question . . . does not cease to be hidden or latent'.

Nor will it do to construe the disclosed/hidden distinction as an occurrent/dispositional distinction either by saying the self is occurrently hidden but dispositionally disclosed or by saying the self is dispositionally hidden but occurrently disclosed or by saying the self is dispositionally both hidden and disclosed. Even if all these descriptions hold, Merleau-Ponty still wants room for: the self is occurrently both hidden and disclosed.

A clue to the resolution of the paradox is Merleau-Ponty's claim that 'the self in question is by divergence' (VIT, 249) ('le soi en question est d'écart' VI 303). 'Ecart' means 'divergence', 'deviation' or 'aside' so the self has the properties revealed in its implicit self-knowledge so to speak, obliquely (to use an only partly misleading analogy, rather as objects at the periphery of the visual field are seen indirectly). In the kind of self knowledge yielded by being something, by being a subjective intentional and teleological body, the self is not directly presented to itself in the way that, say, a physical object is directly presented in sense perception. In this sense the self 'is diverted from' itself. These phenomenological structures are partly constitutive of being a self. This is why Merleau-Ponty says the self 'est' (VI, 303) 'is' (VIT, 249) by divergence.

Following Hegel, Merleau-Ponty says,

> The self-perception (sentiment of oneself, Hegel would say) or perception of perception does not convert what it apprehends into an object. (VIT, 249)[47]

Merleau-Ponty does not say that in self-perception what is apprehended is not *just an object*: he says it is *not an object* and I take it this implies not any kind of object. It is a *Leitmotif* of phenomenological philosophy since Kant and Hegel that in self-consciousness that which is self conscious is both the subject and the object of its own consciousness: it is

the subject *qua* that which is conscious and it is the object *qua* what that
consciousness is consciousness of. It is also thought that in self-
consciousness, paradigmatically but ultimately not necessarily, something systematically escapes being the object of consciousness: this is
that which is conscious *qua* that which is conscious, or the subject *qua*
subject. Now, in his doctrine of being at ('être à') Merleau-Ponty is
endorsing one half of this quasi-Hegelian picture and repudiating the
other half. What he accepts is the systematic evasiveness of the self *qua*
subject in implicit self-consciousness:

> In fact I do not entirely succeed in touching myself touching, in
> seeing myself seeing, the experience I have of myself perceiving does
> not go beyond a sort of imminence. (VIT, 249)[48]

Merleau-Ponty uses 'pas tout à fait' ('not entirely') to express the
incompleteness of self-consciousness in self-consciousness; *qua* that
which touches I cannot touch myself and *qua* that which sees, I cannot
see myself. This is entailed by the quasi-Hegelian thesis that *qua* subject
I am not an object of consciousness.

What Merleau-Ponty rejects in the quasi-Hegelian picture is the
idea that in implicit self-consciousness the subject is partly an object:
an object for its own consciousness. Of course, in the occurrent
self-consciousness with which we are pre-phenomenologically familiar
Merleau-Ponty does accept that one is both the subject and the object of
one's mental acts. Also, as Merleau-Ponty accepts, Hegel has anticipated the idea that in some kinds of self-consciousness I am not in any
straightforward sense an 'object' of my consciousness. To make sense of
this we need to know more about 'imminence'. Merleau-Ponty says:

> The experience I have of myself perceiving does not go beyond a
> kind of imminence, it terminates in the invisible, simply this invisible
> is its invisible, i.e. the reverse of its specular perception, of the
> concrete vision I have of my body in the mirror. (VIT, 249)[49]

In the mirror I appear as an object. But this is a reversal of the phenomenological facts. As a subject I am what I can *only* see of myself by
using the mirror. I am imminent in that which perceives and in perception because I am that which perceives and the perception.

The idea of the invisible is examined in Chapter XIV below; it has an
essential role in Merleau-Ponty's considered answer to the question of
being. Here he deploys the concept to describe subjectivity. *Qua* the
subject I am, I am invisible.

79

V

Perception

Merleau-Ponty holds that the perceived world is the foundation of all thinking about the world, including philosophical thinking. Unless we were acquainted with the world as it presents itself to us we could hold no beliefs, no theories, no values. The world as we experience it makes possible both common sense and science.

In *Phénoménologie de la Perception* Merleau-Ponty states and argues for this foundationalism but he also addresses a second question: how is the perceived world possible? His sustained answer is that the perceived world is constituted by 'perception' in his broad, pragmatic and non-idealist use of that term. In this chapter I first say something about the relationship between perception and the perceived world according to Merleau-Ponty and then switch attention to the foundationalism. Finally I examine some revisions Merleau-Ponty makes in the phenomenological notion of intentionality.

1 *Perceiving wholes*

Merleau-Ponty says that the theory of the body is already a theory of perception. Like Kant, Merleau-Ponty holds that perception and the perceived world cannot be understood in abstraction from the constitutive contribution of the subject. Merleau-Ponty's subject, however, is a physical subject ('sujet incarné' PP, 515). How the world appears to a subject is partly due to facts about the world but also due to facts about the body-subject. For example, Merleau-Ponty says:

> When I walk round my flat, the various aspects in which it presents itself to me could not possibly appear as views of one and the same thing if I did not know that each of them represents the flat seen from one spot or another. (PPT, 203)[1]

Merleau-Ponty is claiming that any set of aspects ('aspects' PP, 235) or views ('profils' PP, 235) could not be perceived as aspects of one and the same object unless the perceiver of those aspects knows two facts: they are aspects of the same object, and they are aspects presented from numerically and qualitatively distinct spatial positions occupied by the observer.

By 'aspects' and 'views' Merleau-Ponty means a property, or a portion, of an object that may be perceptually presented to a percipient. He does not mean the perception of that property even though 'view' is ambiguous in English between 'what is viewed' and 'the viewing of what is viewed'. The French 'profil' admits only of the first interpretation.

It is not a necessary condition for the perception of a set of aspects as aspects of one and the same object that the perceiver of those aspects knows that they are aspects of that object. A set of aspects may be perceived *as* aspects of one and the same object when in fact they are not that, but aspects of numerically distinct objects.

Suppose, then, Merleau-Ponty means *veridically* perceived as (or 'appear as' veridically). Even if a percipient perceives a set of aspects as aspects of the same object and those aspects are all aspects of that object it would still not be incoherent to affirm those two facts yet deny that the percipient knows that those aspects are all aspects of the same object. A percipient may be ignorant of the fact, or disbelieve the fact that those aspects are aspects of the same object even if that percipient is perceptually presented with those aspects as though they were aspects of the same object, and even though they are aspects of the same object. It is, then, not right that I could not perceive aspects as aspects of an object if I did not know that they represent that object.

There is an unclarity about 'represents' here ('représente' PP, 235). It is not clear what the relationship is between some aspect and some object when that aspect represents that object. Solving that problem depends on specifying the relationship between an object and its perceptible properties. Merleau-Ponty's view is: to say that some properties are properties of the same object is to say that they are properties of each other.

Merleau-Ponty denotes a further relation by 'represents'. Representation in the present context is a three term, not a dyadic relation. So 'represents' can be analysed this way: an aspect *represents* an object only if it is a property of that object and some subject perceives that aspect and thereby ascribes that aspect to that object. Then 'represents' denotes a triadic relation between an aspect, a subject, and an object.

This definition states a necessary but not a sufficient condition for the truth of 'an aspect represents an object'. This is because Merleau-Ponty says 'each of them represents the flat seen from one spot or another' (PPT, 203) 'chacun d'eux représente l'appartement vu d'ici ou vu de là'

PP, 235). It follows that: aspects represent an object if and only if they are properties of that object and some subject perceives those aspects and thereby ascribes those aspects to that object and that object is perceptually presented to that subject when that subject perceives those aspects from some series of numerically distinct places occupied successively by that subject.

Merleau-Ponty's use of 'representing' does not commit him to a representational theory of perception. Following a suggestion of C.D. Broad about Kant interpretation, Merleau-Ponty could have talked about presentation rather than representation to avoid any quasi-Lockean misunderstanding. The object is re-presented because it is presented again; through its various aspects.

If an aspect of an object is presented then that object is presented. To see why, consider the sense in which if a part of an object is perceived it follows logically that that object is perceived. It does not follow that the whole of the object is presented if that object is presented: a conclusion Merleau-Ponty insists is false.

We may now raise the question of whether some aspects may represent an object to a subject only if they represent the object 'seen from one spot or another' (PPT, 203) ('vu d'ici ou vu de là' PP, 235). It is not a necessary condition of some subject truly taking some aspects to be aspects of an object when that subject successively perceives those aspects that they be perceived by that subject from a series of numerically distinct spatial locations occupied by that subject. To see this, consider the case where the object is a physical object and the object rotates, but the subject, while perceiving the object does not change spatial location. It is then possible (on some criteria for individuating aspects, say if an object presents two or more *sides* that object presents more than one aspect) that an object presents numerically distinct aspects to the subject while these are not perceived 'from one spot or another'.

In his thinking about the objects of perception Merleau-Ponty wishes us to appreciate the contribution of the subject. This motivation sometimes leads him to neglect the possibility that knowledge of objects may be generated by keeping constant the spatial location of the percipient but varying the presentation of 'aspects' by the object. Both sorts of things happen in our perception of objects.

Although Merleau-Ponty has not stated a necessary condition for the perception of a set of aspects as aspects of the same object he has succeeded in stating a sufficient condition for this. If a subject perceives some aspects from some series of places and the perception of those aspects causes that subject to truly judge that they are aspects of that object, then it follows that that subject perceives those aspects as aspects of that object. Nothing else is necessary.

Merleau-Ponty maintains another condition is necessary for perceiving some aspects as aspects of the same object. I could not do this

> if I were unaware of my own movements, and of my body as retaining its identity through the stages of those movements. (PPT, 203)[2]

The claim here is that some bodily subject could not perceive some aspects as aspects of some object unless that subject is aware of the movements of his own body, and that subject is aware of his continued identity during the time that he is aware of his bodily movements.

This is not a necessary condition for a subject's truly perceiving some aspects as aspects of the same object. It is part of the widespread philosophical fallacy committed by Descartes, Locke and in a more sophisticated way by Kant, that being conscious entails being self-conscious.

Merleau-Ponty's version of this is: a physical subject must be aware of his or her continued identity through the perception of a set of properties in order to perceive those properties as properties of that object.

All that is in fact necessary is that the subject is in fact numerically identical through the perception of some aspects in order to take them to be aspects of an object. If a subject does perceive some aspects then it logically follows that the same subject perceives those aspects.

It does not logically follow that the subject is spatio-temporally continuous between the beginning and the end of the perceptions of those aspects. There is no contradiction in the idea that the continued existence of the subject is broken but that the subject perceives all of those aspects so long as there are time intervals between the perceptions of some of the aspects.

Merleau-Ponty is right to maintain that the *identity* of the subject between the perceptions of some aspects is a necessary condition for perceiving a series of aspects as aspects of the object. The unbroken continuity of the subject is not necessary.

Further, Merleau-Ponty is not right to hold that a subject's awareness of his identity over the perception of a series of aspects is a necessary condition for his perceiving those aspects as of an object. The subject does not have to be occurrently self-conscious during the whole time of the perceiving, but the subject must not forget, or otherwise be ignorant of perceiving an earlier aspect or he would not be in a position to ascribe both that aspect and later aspects to the same object.

2 *Objectivity and points of view*

If a subject may ascribe a set of properties to one and the same object from different points of view, is it possible for a subject to possess the idea of an object *perceived from no point of view*? If so, how?

Merleau-Ponty says:

> I can of course take a mental bird's eye view of the flat, visualise it or draw a plan of it on paper, but in that case too I could not grasp the units of the object without the mediation of bodily experience, for what I call a plan is only a more comprehensive perspective: it is the flat 'seen from above'. (PPT, 203)[3]

Pre-philosophically we tend to think of a 'bird's eye view' as more objective than a view from or close to the surface of the earth. Merleau-Ponty points out that a view from above is still a view from a point of view: a view from somewhere. It is worth pausing to wonder why, pre-reflectively, we think of the view from above as more objective. In our thinking about God, which is riddled with spatial metaphors, it is the kind of objective view that God is sometimes thought of as enjoying.

I think the causal explanation of the belief is as follows. From above I can typically see *more* of a landscape than when I am on that landscape. I am typically able to perceive what is revealed to the viewpoints of persons on the landscape and more besides. We tend to think, rightly or wrongly, of *more* knowledge as *greater objectivity* in knowledge. We are also typically able to see the points of view of viewers on the landscape where this means 'see the places those viewers view from'. It would be easier to draw a map of the landscape from above – a map with distances not perceptually distorted by the experience of views on the landscape from the landscape. Knowledge from above is also pragmatically important, say in a battle, when from a reconnaissance aircraft one is better able to view the dispositions of the enemy relative to one's own. Arguably, a causal explanation along these lines explains why we ascribe greater objectivity to the view from above.

'Objective' sometimes means 'undistorted by preferences' or 'undistorted by points of view'. Contrasted with the view from the ground, the view from above is often that. This is an empirical (and contingent) distinction that admits of degrees.

Merleau-Ponty is right that the view from above is not a view from nowhere. He could draw a plan of his flat on a piece of paper if he had a view which is 'the flat seen from above' but Merleau-Ponty insists that this is a perspective: a perspective adopted by the bodily subject.

An argument for this is as follows: the view from above is a view from somewhere. A view from somewhere is a view from some *place* and the view of some viewer that occupies that place. Only a physical viewer may occupy a place. The viewer from above is physical.

This argument is valid but it is not clear that it is sound. In particular the claim that only a *physical* viewer may occupy a place may be doubted (because it is not analytic that if x occupies a place then x is physical). It is not incoherent to suppose that the viewer that occupies a place is say, a Lockean spiritual substance which may occupy the same place as a Lockean physical substance and so occupy a place.

Also, if out-of-body experiences may be described in a way that is free from contradiction then such experiences are at least logically possible. Then some quasi-Lockean disembodied subject may perceive from a place but not be perceived at that place.

If it is coherent to suppose that a non-physical subject may occupy a place and have a point of view (say a view from above) then Merleau-Ponty has produced at best an empirical condition but not a logical condition for such a perspective when he claims the subject must be physical.

Merleau-Ponty's claim that 'bodily experience' (PPT, 203) ('L'expérience corporelle' PP, 235) is a prerequisite for a perspectival view (including the view from above) is really two claims. It is the claim that experience is necessary for such a view and is the experience of a bodily subject. Turning to whether experience is necessary for the view, this seems to me analytic. Some subject's having some perception from a point of view entails that subject having at least one experience. Experience is a necessary condition for perception from a point of view, even if that experience need not logically be 'bodily' ('corporelle' PP, 235).

Merleau-Ponty says that from the view from above, 'I am able to draw together in it all habitual perspectives' (PPT, 203).[4] This is not just my suggestion that from above one may view the points of view of those below. Merleau-Ponty claims that this more 'comprehensive perspective' 'is dependent on my knowing that one and the same embodied subject can view successively from various positions' (PPT, 203).[5] In principle, a single bodily subject could successively occupy every point of view. Merleau-Ponty has stated a necessary condition for the existence of any view because if a putative view could not even in principle be adopted by a perceiving subject it is hard to see how it could turn out to be a point of view at all.

Merleau-Ponty next raises the interesting question of whether it is possible to form a conception of an object 'from no point of view' (PPT, 204) ('sans point de vue' PP, 236). His considered view is that we may never perceive an object from no point of view but we may nonetheless think the thought of the object as existing perceived from no point of view. For example:

From the point of view of my body I never see as equal the six sides of the cube, even if it is made of glass, and yet the word 'cube' has a meaning: the cube itself, the cube in reality, beyond its sensible appearances, has its six equal sides. (PPT, 203)[6]

From the point of view of my body the cube may be visually presented like this:

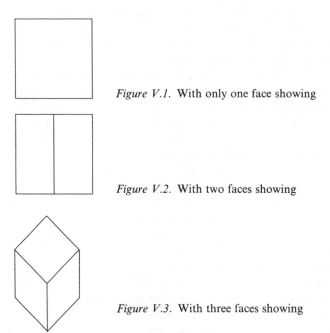

Figure V.1. With only one face showing

Figure V.2. With two faces showing

Figure V.3. With three faces showing

or in a way intermediate between these views. By 'intermediate' here I mean obtained by partly rotating the cube between but not exceeding these positions. If I see the cube and the cube and I are stationary, I see at least one and at most three faces of the cube.

Now, Merleau-Ponty has said that he never sees *as equal* the six sides of the cube The first point to make is that he never sees all six anyway, so that logically entails that he never sees the six as equal.

Suppose he means that *when he is presented* with two or three faces those faces are not seen as 'equal'. This means that the surface areas of the faces and the lengths of the edges appear to him not to be equal.

There is a sense in which Merleau-Ponty is correct and a sense in which he is wrong. He is correct in the sense that the side areas of the surfaces of the drawn cubes are not equal. These are drawings of how cubes are visually presented to a physical subject so, a subject is visually presented with sides of unequal area. We could call these sides 'phenomenological sides'. That is the sense in which Merleau-Ponty is right. This is an empirical and contingent fact about the visual presentation of cubes.

It is not necessarily false that the faces of a cube are visually presented to a subject as equal in area. Indeed, it may sometimes happen that they are visually presented as equal. Consider a partial rotation of Figure V.2: that again, if it is a fact, is an empirical fact.

The sense in which Merleau-Ponty is wrong is this. Even if the surface areas of the faces in the drawings are unequal, and even if cubes are visually presented as with unequal phenomenological faces, the cube will typically thereby *look* to the subject as though it has equal sides.

I mean, being presented phenomenologically with unequal sides may be *just how a cube presents itself to a subject when it presents itself as equal sided*. With unequal phenomenological sides is just how a cube looks when it is truly taken to be equal sided.

Merleau-Ponty says 'the word "cube" has a meaning' (PPT, 203) and 'the cube itself . . . has its equal sides; PPT, 203).[7] If we know the meaning of 'cube' then we have the concept of a cube and if we have the concept of a cube then we know what a cube is. If we know what a cube is we have the idea of a whole cube or a cube perceived from no point of view.

Merleau-Ponty does not say what he means by 'meaning' in this context, but suppose a word has a meaning here if and only if it has either a sense or a reference (or both). Then suppose the sense of 'cube' is 'six sided solid with square faces', and suppose that if the word 'cube' has a reference it refers to a (or the set of, or any) six sided solid with square faces. Then it follows from this definition, and from this specification of a referent that a cube has equal sides because if the sides are square, they cannot be unequal.

Merleau-Ponty tries to answer the question of how it is possible for the word 'cube' to be meaningful if cubes are only ever presented 'perspectively' or from a 'point of view'.

Our concept of a cube is the concept of a whole cube with equal sides. Our visual perception of a cube is a partial perception which presents unequal phenomenological sides. How can the perception give rise to the concept when the content of the concept is in a sense greater than, and in another sense inconsistent with, the content of the perception? How can empiricism about the cube be reconciled with rationalism (or 'intellectualism') about the cube?

Merleau-Ponty's explanation of how the concept of the whole cube may be acquired may be usefully divided into necessary and sufficient conditions for that acquisition.

One such putative necessary condition is this:

> As I move round it, I see the front face, hitherto a square, change its shape, then disappear while the other sides come into view and one by one become square. (PPT, 203)[8]

Again, Merleau-Ponty fails to notice the possibility that the subject does not change spatial location but the object of perception rotates. This would also produce the effect of revealing a succession of sides to the subject. It follows that it is not a necessary condition for perceiving each side of an object in turn that some subject tour that object: i.e. occupy some series of spatial locations circumscribing that object. It could be done in another way.

It might well, however be empiricially necessary for the successive perception of the sides of an object that either the subject circumscribe the object or the object rotate (about some point or other) or both. (If both, the object must not rotate, and the subject move such that, despite both movements, the object continues only to present one side to the subject.)

Merleau-Ponty emphasises that the successive perception of the sides of the cube is only a necessary and not a sufficient condition for the perception of the cube as a whole:

> But the successive stages of this experience are for me merely the opportunity of conceiving the whole cube with its six equal and simultaneous faces. (PPT, 203)[9]

Merleau-Ponty accepts that in visually perceiving only one face (or any one part of the cube) there is a sense in which a cube is seen. This is not sufficient for perceiving that cube as a whole cube. From 'a perceives a part of x' it follows that 'a perceives x', but it does not follow that 'a perceives the whole of x'.

Merleau-Ponty realises this and so says the successive perception of the sides of the cube is only 'the opportunity' for the perception of the cube as a whole.

The sides of the whole cube are identical in area, angle and length of edges. This is just analytic as it semantically unpacks 'cube'. The perception of the sides of the cube is successive but the existence of the sides of the cube is simultaneous. The question is how the concept of six simultaneously existing sides may be acquired through the successive perception of those sides.

Merleau-Ponty says,

> the whole cube with its six equal and simultaneous faces. (PPT, 203)[10]

is

the intelligible structure which provides the explanations of it.
(PPT, 203)[11]

A condition of some subject successively perceiving some aspects of an
object as simultaneous aspects of that object is that that object as a
whole exists as *an intelligible structure*. We grasp the object *qua* whole
and that facilitates the thought of its aspects as simultaneous. But how
do we grasp the object *qua* whole? An intelligible structure may just be
a structure that may be understood in thought.

Merleau-Ponty's argument is in danger of begging the question here.
The account is supposed to explain how the concept of an object as a
whole, or perceived from nowhere, is possible. It will hardly do to
invoke as a premise the thesis that the object is 'an intelligible structure'
if this entails anything like 'already intelligible to the subject' as this
looks disturbingly like the claim that the whole object is something we
have a concept of or understand. That would beg the question.

However, read accurately, Merleau-Ponty is able to evade this circularity. He uses the modal form 'intelligible' and this does not entail
'understood' or 'comprehended' but only 'understandable' or 'comprehensible'. Merleau-Ponty is making the rather analytic point that we
cannot understand an object *qua* whole unless it is intelligible as such.
Crucially, I am able to *walk around* the cube while remembering the
sides I have seen. The unbroken continuity of the perceived sides and
my ability to conduct a 'tour of inspection' (PPT, 203) generate the concept of the whole cube. If I was not a body-subject, Merleau-Ponty
thinks, I could not tour the cube. If I could not tour it, my partial perspective on it would never be adequate to generate the concept of the
whole of it. The whole cube is *an intelligible structure* because it is only
ever thought, not experienced *qua* whole. We know whole physical
objects because we are ourselves physical subjects.

The entire account of the successive perspectival perception of the
object is a putative explanation of how the subject may acquire the concept of the whole object. In the end, the subject has seen the whole of the
outside of the cube and is thereby caused to possess the concept of that.

There are two large deficiences in this account. I am not saying they
could not be made good. The first deficiency, is, as so often in Merleau-
Ponty, that the concept of the visual dominates other perceptual
concepts; Merleau-Ponty's concept of a physical object is for example
paradigmatically the concept of a physical object as seen. In some contexts this is harmless. There is little empirical doubt that humans receive
most of their sensory information through vision. However, in the
present context 'object as a whole' cannot possibly mean just 'object as

a visible whole'. It would help in acquiring the concept of the whole cube to pick it up or kick it over.

The other deficiency is that explaining how an object may, at least in principle, be perceived from every point of view is not at all the same thing as explaining how an object may be thought of as not being perceived from any point of view. The thought of the object as it would be if it were being perceived from all points of view simultaneously is a different thought from the thought of the object as not being perceived at all. Arguably, if Merleau-Ponty's arguments are in the end shown to be sound, he will only have succeeded in showing how we may think of an object perceived from every point of view, not not perceived from any point of view. There is not, for example, any clear inference from possessing the first kind of concept to the second here. Also, it could be that the two concepts are assimilated by Merleau-Ponty.

3 Rationalism and empiricism

A *Leitmotif* of Merleau-Ponty's philosophy is the devising of an existential phenomenology which will overcome the shortcomings of both rationalism and empiricism but exhibit as mutually consistent what is true in each.

This is an admirable philosophical task but, as with Kant and Hegel, Merleau-Ponty allows an obsession with it sometimes to distort his attempts to solve philosophical problems.

In the Chapter 'Le Monde Perçu' Merleau-Ponty has offered an explanation of how we may think of an object from no point of view. This account is partly empiricist because it begins from premises about perceptions and partly rationalist because it ends with a conclusion about thinking. The role of the body-subject is to mediate crucially by practically interacting with the object and making both the perception and the thought of the object possible. The inference from empiricist premises to the rationalist conclusion is achieved using premises about bodily subjectivity.

Although Merleau-Ponty holds that thought and perception are dependent on this new position, he accepts the quasi-Kantian view that thought operates within perception, so in the successive perception of the sides of the cube the subject makes the perceptual judgement that they are the sides of one and the same cube. But any such quasi-Kantian reconciliation of empiricism and rationalism depends on the body-subject's movements through the world.

Although conceptually separable, there are not two really separable cognitive processes here, one sensory, the other intellectual. The intelligibility of the cube *qua* cube structures the succession of perceived sides so that those are perceived as properties of the whole cube.

Merleau-Ponty says

It is a question of tracing in thought that particular form which
encloses a fragment of space between six equal spaces. (PPT, 204)[12]

Whether this is construed as a conceptual component of the perception-
series, or a separate intellectual operation, depends on bodily touring
the cube.

There are further senses in which Merleau-Ponty's phenomenology of
perception is a synthesis of empiricism and rationalism. He thinks there
is a danger of empiricism about perception collapsing into idealism:

the empiricist philosopher considers a subject x in the act of
perceiving and tries to describe what happens: there are sensations
which are the subject's states or manners of being and, in virtue of
this, genuine mental things. (PPT, 207)[13]

Empiricist theories of perception do involve notions such as 'impression', 'sense-datum', 'phenomenon' or 'qualium' to denote some
immediate content of experience. *Qua* empiricist one is not logically
committed to the view that these contents are mental. Of some idealist–
empiricist theories of perception this is true. For Locke and Berkeley
the immediately perceived contents of experience are themselves mental.
For Mill, Hume, Russell and Ayer, however, sense data are intrinsically
neither mental nor physical.[14] Merleau-Ponty's point is that on *any*
empiricist theory of perception there is a liability to fall into idealism.
The sceptic may ask how the empiricist knows that the immediate contents of perception are *not* mental and, if they are all that can be
known, how anything non-mental can be known. Merleau-Ponty has a
reply to this sceptical idealism in the construction of the concept of an
object by the manoeuvres or manipulations of the body-subject.

Empiricist philosophy is an example of the epistemological realism
that Merleau-Ponty calls 'objective thought' (PPT, 207)[15] and 'objective
thought is unaware of the subject of perception' (PPT, 207).[16]

Is empiricism a version of 'objective thought'? Berkeley's empiricism
is a subjective idealism, and Mill, Russell and Ayer hold that physical
objects are logical constructions out of the contents of sense experiences,
where these contents are given just as they are. No classical empiricism
gives a role to the body-subject and on Hume's empiricism there is no
conceptual room for the subject; there being no continued impression
which could give rise to the idea of self. Classical empiricism does, then,
fall under the heading of 'objective thought'.

Merleau-Ponty sees in philosophical rationalism (or 'intellectualism'
(PPT, 207–8) the merit of recognising the subject of perception:

91

Intellectualism certainly represents a step forward in coming to self-consciousness: that place outside the world at which the empiricist philosopher hints, and in which he tacitly takes up his position in order to describe the event of perception, now receives a name, and appears in the descriptions. It is the transcendental ego. (PPT, 207–8)[17]

Empiricism rests on a presupposition that empiricism cannot explain. The subject as condition *for* experience, as transcendental, is not to be encountered *within* experience and so not to be explained in empirical terms. But there is no experience without a subject. Merleau-Ponty has a sound criticism of empiricism. It is, however, open to a Humean to deny that experience presupposes a subject, especially one that is not to be explained as a construct out of (actual or possible) experiences.

Both empiricism and rationalism, underestimate the pragmatic construction of the empirical world. As Merleau-Ponty puts it, 'Intellectualism . . . provides itself with a ready-made world' (PPT, 208).[18] Nothing in rationalism *per se* logically rules out the pragmatic or intellectual construction of the empirical world. It is just that neither philosophy has the conceptual resources to rule it in either. Empiricism and rationalism can explain neither empiricism nor rationalism.

4 *Sexuality and being-in-the-world*

Merleau-Ponty's philosophical motivation in devising a phenomenology of sexuality is to prove his thesis that being-in-the-world is the primordial fact of human existence. He hopes to show that over cognitive conceptions of the human person are damagingly reductionist, and parasitical upon the truth of his own phenomenology for their formulation. For these reasons he says:

Let us try to see how a thing or a being begins to exist for us through desire or love and we shall thereby come to understand better how things and beings can exist in general. (PPT, 154)[19]

According to Merleau-Ponty the existence of sexual desire presupposes some central tenets of his phenomenology. Sexual desire would be impossible without being-in-the-world, the body-subject and the intentional acts of that subject.

The reasons for making these presuppositions are not made clear by Merleau-Ponty, but arguments may be provided for their obtaining. Suppose A desires B sexually, then A stands in an intentional relation to B because it would be incoherent to suppose that A desires B sexually but has no awareness of B. If awareness is an intentional relation, then, so is sexual desire. Desiring is desiring something (whether real or imaginary).[20]

Arguably, too, A may only sexually desire B if A and B are physical and if at least A is a physical subject. This is because the criteria for the individuation of the object of sexual desire are unclear if that object is not physical, or, minimally, spatio-temporal. Also, if the having of genuinely *sexual* desire presupposes the actuality or the possibily of bodily sexual sensations then sexual desire presupposes bodily subjectivity. Only physical subjects may feel sexual desire.

Arguably, sexual desire presupposes being-in-the-world in Merleau-Ponty's sense, or something very much like it, because if A desires B sexually then A and B share a world and there exists at least the conceivability of sexual relations within it.

Merleau-Ponty thinks that once we are persuaded of these presuppositions we will give up any over cognitive conception of sexuality and will endorse this view:

Erotic perception is not a cogitatio which aims at a cogitatum:
through one body it aims at another body, and takes place in the
world, not in a consciousness. (PPT, 157)[21]

The perception of the other as an object of sexual desire is not simply the relation of a knower to a known. The relationship is not only intellectual but involves the whole person or is a 'perception' in Merleau-Ponty's broad sense.

The subject desires the other with his or her own body. Desiring another sexually entails desiring bodily sexual relations with the other. The body-subject is the subject of desire: *qua* my body I desire the other. For this reason sexual desire 'takes place in the world' and 'not in consciousness'. Erotic perception entails sexual desire, so if sexual desire presupposes bodily subjectivity and being-in-the-world then so does erotic perception. A perceives B *erotically* if and only if A perceives B but thereby desires to have sexual relations with B. The desire to have sex with the other is, so to speak, 'read into' the other as object of perception. The perception and the sexual thought are not separate. The perception is a sexual perception:

This objective perception has within it a more intimate perception:
the visible body is subtended by a sexual schema, which is strictly
individual, emphasising the erogenous areas, outlining a sexual
physiognomy. (PPT, 156)[22]

Merleau-Ponty calls this perception an 'emotional totality' (PPT, 156) ('totalité affective' PP, 182). That the body of the other is subsumed under a 'sexual schema' implies that sexual perception is essentially the selective perception of the sexual zones of the other, not only the perception of the other as a whole person. It is a perception that emphasises the bodily sexuality of the other.

The expression 'strictly individual' does not imply that the sexual perception of one object of desire logically or otherwise precludes the perception of another. Rather, sexual perception of an individual is sexual desire for that individual *qua* that individual.

Crucially, because sexual perception exhibits these phenomenological structures 'a body is not perceived merely as any object' (PPT, 156) 'un corps n'est pas seulement perçu comme un objet quelconque' (PP, 182). The other is perceived as a *physical subject*. The perceived body of the other is the exteriority of the other's subjectivity.

Merleau-Ponty claims that erotic perception is not, and is prior to 'understanding' (PPT, 157). It distinguishes understanding from 'erotic comprehension'. 'Understanding', as Merleau-Ponty defines it, denotes the subsumption of some experiential content under an idea. 'Comprehension', in contrast, is not mediated by ideas and is therefore not intellectual'. The thesis that sexual perception is not a kind of understanding, but that understanding, in sexual contexts, presupposes comprehension is intended as a substantiation of his thesis that the engagement of the body-subject in the world is a condition for perception as a kind of consciousness. As he puts it:

> There is an erotic 'comprehension' not of the order of
> understanding, since understanding subsumes an experience, once
> perceived, under some idea, while desire comprehends blindly by
> linking body to body. (PPT, 157)[23]

Merleau-Ponty is not denying that a certain amount of imaginative projection is required to constitute the other as an object of sexual desire. That is part of what is involved in sexual perception not taking its intentional object as just 'any object'. But intellectual reflection upon the object of desire, and one's cognitive relation to that object *qua* sexual, require 'erotic comprehension'. This is why he says 'sexual life is one more form of original intentionality' (PPT, 157) 'une intentionalité originale' (PP, 184). Some intentional relation is an *original* relation if it makes other intentional relations possible. Original intentionality is an 'intentional arc' ('arc intentionel' PP, 184) which makes possible perceptual representations.

Sexuality, then, for Merleau-Ponty is a manner of being-in-the-world. It is a primordial existential relation and only derivatively a cognitive or intellectual one. This thesis gives rise to two questions, the answers to which Merleau-Ponty thinks form a disjunction:

When we generalise the notion of sexuality, making it a manner of being in the physical and inter-human world, do we mean, in the last analysis, that all existence has a sexual significance or that every sexual phenomenon has an existential significance? (PPT, 159)[24]

It seems to me that affirmative answers to both questions are not mutually exclusive. Merleau-Ponty denies outright that all existence has a sexual meaning. His ground is that such a claim would be senseless, the term 'existence' would just be another name for the sexual life. This would be a 'tautology', and, he assumes, tautologies are senseless.

Merleau-Ponty is not right to hold that the claim that all existence has sexual significance is a tautology. It is capable of falsity (which a tautology is not) and, if true, would give new information about existence. Merleau-Ponty fails to see this because he fails to make a distinction between sense and reference. Because (as he rightly holds) 'existence' and 'sexuality' would have a single referent he falsely concludes that 'existence' and 'sexuality' would have the same sense. However, that inference is invalid.

Because the claim that all existence is sexual is not meaningless Merleau-Ponty should have evaluated its truth value more closely. A more cautious claim may in fact be true: any portion of existence may (in principle) be of sexual significance. This is because there is no a priori obstacle to any portion of existence being the object of sexual desire. The meaningfulness of this thought, is however, parasitic upon the 'comprehension' of sexual relations between living beings.

Merleau-Ponty next examines the converse possibility that every sexual phenomenon may have an existential significance. Strangely, he does not attempt to deploy the same kind of 'tautology' argument even though, on his own terms, if 'existence is sexual' is tautologous then so is 'sexuality is existential'. Ironically this is to his advantage as neither sentence is a tautology.

In this context something has 'existential significance' if it is a structure of being-in-the-world. Essentially that is what sexuality is for Merleau-Ponty, so, essentially, sexuality does have existential significance. In a passage marking the extent of his agreement with what he takes to be Freudianism he says:

In so far as a man's sexual history provides a key to his life, it is because in his sexuality is projected his manner of being towards the world, that is, towards time and other men. (PPT, 158)[25]

Although Merleau-Ponty's unconscious sexism in this passage excludes women from his analysis we can read Merleau-Ponty's intended answer as affirmative. All sexuality has existential significance.

The relationship between sexuality and existence (in his sense of the fundamental structures of being-in-the-world) is close and subtle for Merleau-Ponty. He says 'It is at all times present there like an atmosphere' (PPT, 168) 'elle y est constamment présente comme une atmosphère' PP, 196), and 'as an ambiguous atmosphere, sexuality is coextensive with life' (PPT, 169) 'comme atmosphère ambiguë, la sexualité est coextensive à la vie' (PP, 197).

Lived sexuality may be accurately described only in metaphorical and poetic terms, that is why sexuality is an 'atmosphere'. Sexuality *pervades* human relations. It informs speech, perception and bodily movement in a way that is present in them. Sexuality is not an addition to human life but a primordial structure of being-in-the-world that is expressed through human life. As he puts it 'existence permeates sexuality and vice versa' PPT, 169). ('Si l'existence diffuse dans la sexualité, réciproquement la sexualité diffuse dans l'existence' PP, 197).

When he calls sexuality an 'ambiguous atmosphere' he means sexuality is open to numerous interpretations. As we have seen, it is a recurrent *Leitmotif* of Merleau-Ponty's thought that anything can be interpreted. Nothing has only one, perennial meaning. This ambiguity, or amenability to multiple interpretation, is part of what is involved in being human. For this reason he says ambiguity is of the essence of human existence, and everything we live or think has always several 'meanings' (PP, 169) ('sens' PP, 197). He holds this true in two ways. Human beings are essentially interpretative beings and human beings and their mutual relations are essentially open to human interpretation.

Merleau-Ponty thinks that sexuality cannot be wholly explained in scientific terms. He does not deny the obvious biological facts about sexual life, what he denies is that the phenomenology of sex may be captured in any purely scientific description.

The natural sciences treat their subject matter as only 'other'. What escapes analysis is the subjectivity of the subject, the subjectivity of the other, and the lived existential relations between them. For example he says,

> Modesty, desire and love [. . .] are incomprehensible if man is
> treated as a machine governed by natural laws. (PPT, 166)[26]

It is also inadequate to regard a person as 'a bundle of instincts' (PPT, 166) ('faisceau d'instincts' PP, 194).

There is a number of claims here that need separating out. That a person is a machine implies that a person is both physical and objective and has no subjectivity. That a person is governed by natural laws implies that a person is causally determined in his or her own actions.

That a person is, or essentially is, a set of instincts also implies that, but further entails that the determining causes are biological and innate.

Merleau-Ponty argues that sexuality may only be understood when a person is regarded as 'a consciousness and a freedom' (PPT, 166) 'comme conscience et comme liberté' PP, 194). Prima facie these are conditions only for human sexuality: the kind of self-conscious sexuality we in fact have. However, for Merleau-Ponty freedom and self consciousness are necessary for the constitution of the lived world and because sexuality is part of the lived world it follows that it presupposes freedom and consciousness.

The phenomenology of sex – what it is like to experience sexual desire and other sexual relations – cannot be captured in only a scientific description. The sentences of science treat its subject matter only as 'other'. Describing human sexuality adequately requires the use of sentences of the first person singular and first person plural grammatical forms; in particular sentences making first person singular and first person plural psychological ascriptions. Science excludes such sentences so has no room for the fact that sex has a phenomenology.

No first person sentence may be logically derived from any set of third person sentences (no matter how numerous, lengthy, and semantically complex) so Merleau-Ponty is correct in maintaining that there can be no complete natural scientific description of sexuality.

Merleau-Ponty thinks that the reduction of the human person to a scientific object is dehumanising and unethical. What makes us most fully and distinctively human is just what science cannot explain about us.

There is another way in which persons may be treated only as objects. Merleau-Ponty, like Sartre, endorses a neo-Hegelian view of human sexual relations. He speaks of 'a dialectic of the self and the other which is that of master and slave' (PPT, 167) ('une dialectique du moi et d'autrui qui est celle du maître et de l'esclave' PP, 194). In the 'Master and Slave' chapter of Hegel's *Phänomenologie des Geistes* Hegel describes the struggle for mutual recognition between two putative self-consciousnesses in which each seeks the servitude of the other, but each ultimately accepts the self-defeating nature of victory.[27] In applying this antagonistic structure to human sexual relations Merleau-Ponty says:

In so far as I have a body, I may be reduced to the status of an object beneath the gaze of another person, and no longer count as a person for him, or else I may become his master and, in my turn, look at him. (PPT, 167)[28]

This is Hegelianism with the bodily subject. Nothing (in my view) precludes Merleau-Ponty giving the central chapter of Hegel's *Phänomenologie des Geistes* that construal: Hegel's writing there is deliberately abstract so as to be consistent with many contents (or models).

By using 'in so far as' 'en tant que' (PP, 194) Merleau-Ponty is suggesting that embodiment is necessary for the existence of master and slave power relations (and *a fortiori* master and slave sexual relations). Only embodied beings could *meet*. This thought may be right. Master and slave may arguably only be individuated if they are physical, and that master and slave individuate each other is a necessary condition for the power struggle between them. I am thinking of the possibility that only spatio-temporal (or perhaps only spatial) items may be individuated and then only through their spatial properties. If that is right then Hegel's master and slave dialectic conceptually presupposes Merleau-Ponty's notion of the body-subject, or something very much like it.[29]

Merleau-Ponty's view of sexual relations is ultimately optimistic and Hegelian rather than ultimately pessimistic and Sartrean. Like Hegel Merleau-Ponty says

> This mastery is self-defeating, since, precisely when my value is recognised through the other's desire, he is no longer the person by whom I wished to be recognised. (PPT, 167)[30]

If Hegel and Merleau-Ponty are right then we may look forward to a time when sexual relations are no longer power struggles.

5 *The possibility of intentionality*

It is a central tenet of Husserlian phenomenology that intentionality is the essence of consciousness. Intentionality is the putative property of consciousness to be *about* or *of* some object, whether or not that object has what Husserl calls 'existence' ('Existenz'). On Husserl's view, then, the existence of intentionality is necessary and sufficient for the existence of consciousness. In the *Pariser Vorträger* for example he says,

> The essence of consciousness, in which I live as my own self, is (the) so-called intentionality. (PL, 12–13)[31]

In *Logische Untersuchungen* he allows that moods and sensations are mental but denies that they exhibit intentionality. It is thereby left mysterious what their being mental consists in.

In his description of intentionality Husserl distinguishes between the *noēsis*, or act of consciousness, and the *noēma*, or content of consciousness. The *noēma* is what consciousness is directed towards in the restricted sense of what actually appears to consciousness. The *noēsis*, or the noetic act, is the consciousness of the *noēma*. The intentionality of consciousness consists in a noetic act taking a *noēma* as its content.

Understanding Merleau-Ponty on perception requires understanding what he accepts and what he repudiates in at least this minimal picture of Husserl's concept of intentionality.

Merleau-Ponty says about Husserl's notion of intentionality 'it is understandable only through the reduction' (PPT, xvii).[32] It is only through the phenomenological reduction that the various intentional structures of consciousness may be exhibited, including the distinction between *noēsis* and *noēma*. As we saw in Chapter I, Merleau-Ponty thinks the Husserlian *epoché* or phenomenological reduction is impossible or, at least, cannot even in principle be completed. We are left then with the issues of whether Merleau-Ponty may consistently reject the *epoché* yet retain the intentionality of consciousness. This is what he attempts.

Merleau-Ponty replaces the phenomenological reduction of Husserl by the Heideggerian existential category being-in-the-world ('être-au-monde') because describing the subject cannot be conceptually separated from describing the world, in the way that Husserl would wish.

Nevertheless, there is a sense in which many sentences in Husserl's transcendental philosophy may retain their truth values when given a role within Merleau-Ponty's existential phenomenology. They cannot be read as expressing *transcendental* propositions any more, if this entails any claim about transcendental subjectivity or the findings of the reduction. They may however even still be read transcendentally in a minimal Kantian sense that is common to both Merleau-Ponty and Husserl. All three philosophers are trying to describe how experience of the world is possible and for all three a transcendental claim is one that contributes to an explanation of this possibility in what it expresses.

For example, Merleau-Ponty can consistently accept this from Husserl:

All that which exists for me exists by virtue of my cognitive
consciousness; everything is for me the experienced of my
experiencing, the thought of my thinking, the theorized of my
theorizing, the intuited of my intuiting. (PL, 31)[33]

This is not just the quasi-tautological thought that if something is perceptually or intellectually presented to me then it is in some sense the object of my consciousness. It is also the more substantial claim that anything whatsoever with which I am acquainted in any way has this status because it is a possible object of my consciousness: the intentionality of consciousness is a necessary condition for knowledge. According to Husserl:

Everything that is exists for me only as the intentional objectivity of my cogitationes. (PL, 31)[34]

Merleau-Ponty's crucial departure from Husserl is this: we perceive physical objects *only because we are physical subjects.* Husserl's thesis that physical objects are transcendentally constituted by consciousness is at best an abstraction and at worst false. It is because we are body-subjects that we may bodily interact with physical objects: touch them, pick them up, move amongst them. It is this practical and physical interaction with the world that enables us to perceive it as four dimensional.

VI

Space

A *Leitmotif* of Merleau-Ponty's thought is the drawing of a distinction between the abstract and the concrete, or between what is thought to be the case and what is experienced to be the case. Following Kant, he maintains that 'the ultimate court of appeal' (PPT, 244) ('dernière instance' PP, 282) in establishing how things are is experience. This places Merleau-Ponty much more firmly in the empiricist than in the rationalist category of philosophical thought. Despite his professed intention of synthesising rationalism and empiricism he provides something like an empirical account of how rationalism is thinkable. Experience, however, is lived embodied experience, not simply the sense experience and introspection of the British empiricists.[1] Merleau-Ponty's phenomenology of space plays a crucial role in his attempt to 'go beyond' rationalism and empiricism.

1 *The phenomenology of space*

There exist a number of abstract conceptions of space as an 'ideally separable "moment"' (PPT, 243) ('moment idéalement séparable' PP, 281). Each of these is the product of 'an act of reflection' (PPT, 243) ('un acte exprès de réflexion' PP, 281). Each of these conceptions embodies a philosophical mistake according to Merleau-Ponty, even though it is not the case that products of reflection are mistakes just *qua* products of reflection.

Merleau-Ponty says 'there is naturally no question of a relationship of container to content' (PPT, 243)[2] because the container to content relationship pertains only to 'objects' ('des objets' PP, 281). Without argument this criticism is question-begging. Merleau-Ponty needs to show that the container–content metaphor has an empirical genesis in the spatial inclusion relationship between physical objects that restricts its useful application to objects being in space. It could be argued, for

101

example, that if space is not an extra 'thing' over and above all the physical objects then it cannot be a 'container' either, because, plausibly, only a thing can be a container.

Merleau-Ponty also rejects the suggestion that the relationship between space and spatial things is 'a relationship of logical inclusion, like the one existing between the individual and the class' (PPT, 243).[3] The reason he gives for this is 'space is anterior to its alleged parts' (PPT, 243).[4] This claim is partly confused and needs tidying up.

Merleau-Ponty assimilates two ideas: the idea of a spatial thing and the idea of a spatial part. Prima facie a spatial thing is paradigmatically a physical object but a spatial part is paradigmentically a region of space. It might well be that the metaphor of logical inclusion is more apposite in its application to the relation between space and its parts than to the relation between space and spatial things. For example, arguably space could not exist without spatial regions and spatial regions could not exist without space. On the other hand, space could prima facie (even if not metaphysically) exist without spatial things even if spatial things, logically, could not exist without space. Just as in set theory there exists a set without members – the null set – so, analogously, there could in principle exist space without spatial things, the space, so to speak, which the spatial things would occupy were they to exist.

The reason Merleau-Ponty gives for rejecting the set theory metaphor seems rather weak. Even if it is right that space is 'anterior to' (PPT, 243) its alleged parts, it is not clear that the class of x's is not anterior to each x if 'anterior to 'means anything like 'a necessary condition for' here.

Merleau-Ponty also rules out the thought that space is 'a sort of ether in which all things float' (PPT, 43).[5] This metaphor, which is perhaps even cruder than the 'container' metaphor, is to be rejected on similar grounds: it is an empirical thought with an application that lies elsewhere. However, it is not clear that 'float' is used without sense when we think of objects as floating in space. This is a concept that finds an apposite application in situations of minimal gravitational force.

Finally, Merleau-Ponty rejects the possibility of correctly thinking of space in relation to things 'abstractly as a characteristic that they have in common' (PPT, 243).[6] Again, Merleau-Ponty has no argument but one may be supplied. If space were a characteristic, in the sense of an intrinsic property, of physical objects then for each numerically distinct physical object there would then exist a token numerically distinct space. This does not, however, capture our intuitive idea of space. Putatively numerically distinct spaces will turn out to be spatially related and so parts, or regions, of one and the same space. This idea precludes the notion of space as a property of each physical object (even though it is a logical consequence of our intuitive idea of space that each physical object has the property of being spatially located).

It could be objected to this that space as a property of each physical object is a universal: that which they all have in common. Even if common properties are, in this sense, universals it may be doubted that space is a universal in this sense. The uniqueness of space is not a similarity between things.

Merleau-Ponty introduces his own positive view of space through an important distinction; between 'physical space' (PPT, 244) ('l'espace physique' PP, 282) and 'geometrical space' (PPT, 244) ('l'espace géométrique' PP, 282). Sometimes he calls physical space 'spatialised . . . space' (PPT, 244) ('l'espace spatialisé' PP, 282) and geometrical space 'spatialising space' ('l'espace spatialisant' PP, 282). It is his considered view that the experience of physical space makes possible the thought of geometrical space, but first we should examine the properties which he thinks distinguish them.

In the case of physical space:

> My body and things, their concrete relationships expressed in such
> terms as top and bottom, right and left, near and far, may appear to
> me as an irreducibly manifold variety. (PPT, 244)[7]

Here Merleau-Ponty is characterising spatial things and the spatial relationships between them as these are presented to an embodied subject during the ordinary course of experience. It is not so much the unity or uniqueness of space that is perceptually presented as the multiplicity ('multiplicite' PP, 282) of spatial items.

In the case of geometrical space, however, 'I discover a single and indivisible ability to trace out space' (PP, 244).[8] Geometrical space is space as thought, rather than space as directly experienced. Geometry is the abstract mathematics of space. Merleau-Ponty is suggesting that it is in reflection rather than perception that I am presented with space as a single, indivisible whole. Physical space presents 'variously qualified regions' (PPT, 244) ('régions différemment qualifiées' PP, 282) to a subject, suggesting that this presentation is absent from geometrical space.

Merleau-Ponty says geometrical space has 'interchangeable dimensions: homogeneous and isotropic' (PPT, 244)[9] suggesting that these properties are not possessed by physical space.

In the case of geometrical space the following is thinkable:

> A pure change of place which would leave the moving body
> unchanged, and consequently a pure *position* distinct from the
> *situation* of the object in its concrete context. (PPT, 244)[10]

It follows that Merleau-Ponty's conception of geometrical space is essentially Newtonian or absolute. Newtonian space is space that exists in abstraction from spatial things – whether it exists or not is in no way dependent upon the existence of spatial things. In the case of Newtonian space it both makes sense and is true to assert that there are numerically distinct parts or regions of space, the existence of which in no way depends upon those parts or regions being occupied by spatial things.

It is this conception that Merleau-Ponty has in mind when he says geometrical space may contain a 'pure position' (PPT, 244) ('pur position' PP, 282). Pure positions are pure in the sense that their being, and their being the positions that they are, do not depend upon their being occupied, nor upon there being occupants. A situation, on the other hand, is necessarily actually or possibly occupied. Situations are individuated only via actual or possible occupants. Positions are individuated via each other. Physical space contains situations but no positions but geometrical space contains positions but no situations.

It follows that Merleau-Ponty has an essentially Leibnizian or relational view of physical space. He thinks of it as nothing over and above the totality of spatial things and the spatial relations between them. These spatial relations themselves will turn out to be subjectively constituted: made what they are by the perceptual syntheses of the embodied subject.

Merleau-Ponty does not claim this, but his view is logically consistent with each token situation being numerically identical with some token position, so long as we do not accept that there are two spaces one physical and one geometrical. At least, it is coherent to suppose that there exists a one-one mapping between the regions of physical space and the regions of geometrical space. Certainly, the fact that situations are individuated only through actual or possible occupants, and positions are individuated by each other is no a priori or logical obstacle to their being numerically identical. 'Only' in 'only through actual or possible occupants' does not preclude this because we may read 'only' here to mean 'only in the vocabulary of physical space'. Then we can construe Merleau-Ponty as maintaining that there are not two numerically distinct spaces but only one. This space may be experienced directly. Then it is known as 'physical space' and may be characterised using a quasi-Leibnizian relational vocabulary. Or, this space may be thought, abstractly. Then this space is known as 'geometrical space' and is characterised using a quasi-Newtonian absolutist vocabulary. Merleau-Ponty says

> This distinction is blurred in modern conceptions of space, even at the level of scientific knowledge. (PPT, 244)[11]

This is right, I think, in that contemporary Western thought works with a mixture of physical and geometrical concepts of space in Merleau-Ponty's senses.

2 *Subjective and objective space*

Although Merleau-Ponty thinks the experience of physical space makes possible the thought of geometrical space he raises the question of whether the distinction is both genuine and exhaustive:

> Is it true that we are faced with the alternative either of perceiving things in space, or (if we reflect and try to discover the significance of our own experiences) of conceiving space as the indivisible system governing the acts of unification performed by a constitutive mind? (PPT, 244)[12]

To answer these questions Merleau-Ponty examines the role of the subject in the construction of space. Merleau-Ponty takes it as experimentally proven that the way space appears to a subject is at least partly dependent upon facts about that subject. It is not the case that space is simply passively and realistically perceived as it is. It is partly perceptually constructed.

Merleau-Ponty cites the experiments performed by Stratton[13] in which the subject is provided with a pair of spectacles which inverts the retinal images, so that the physical world appears upside down through visual perception. The other sensory modalities are in no way altered. Interestingly, after a day or so of wearing the spectacles the world begins to look the right way up again. The speed of this readjustment depends largely on how active the subject is. The more activities, such as washing his hands, he performs the more tactile and auditory informative overrides and corrects the visual information.

Merleau-Ponty concludes from this experiment that the way physical space is ordinarily perceptually presented to us depends upon our subjective constitution. He says 'We are not among things' (PPT, 246–7)[14] and 'We have as yet only sensory fields' (PPT, 247).[15] The suggestion is that we are not directly presented with spatial relations as they realistically are, but rather with a 'mass of sensations' (PPT, 245) ('masse de sensations' PP, 283) which we subsequently spatially order according to subjective but pragmatic criteria. As Merleau-Ponty puts it:

> One cannot take the world and orientated space as given along with the contents of mere experience or with the body in itself, since experience in fact shows that the same contents can be successively orientated in one direction or another. (PPT, 247)[16]

In making spatial orientation a contribution of the subject Merleau-Ponty claims to be avoiding both empiricism and rationalism about space. For example he criticises

> an empiricist psychology which treats the perception of space as the reception, within ourselves, of a real space. (PPT, 247)[17]

Merleau-Ponty's view does genuinely differ from this kind of empiricism about space. Although on both views space seems to be perceptually 'received', on the empiricist view it genuinely is, on Merleau-Ponty's view it really is not. Merleau-Ponty also says that according to empiricism perceived space is 'a real space' (PPT, 247) ('un espace réel' PP, 286). If 'real' here means anything like 'existing and existing as it appears', then, again, Merleau-Ponty has drawn a genuine distinction between his view of space and the empiricism he characterises, if 'real' logically entails 'mind-independent'. The existence and nature of space are subject-dependent for Merleau-Ponty but not for the empiricism he characterises. (The empiricism Merleau-Ponty describes here has a complex relation to the 'classical' empiricism of Locke, Berkeley and Hume but that cannot be pursued here.)[18]

Merleau-Ponty also distances himself from rationalism or 'intellectualist psychology' when he says that on that view

> the 'upright' and the 'inverted' are relationships dependent upon the fixed points chosen. (PPT, 247)[19]

The 'fixed points' are points within a space that is already orientated, so it only makes sense to talk of some item within a perceived space as 'upright' or 'inverted'. It makes no sense on the rationalist view to speak of perceived space as a whole having a certain orientation. On the rationalist view objects are only upright or inverted in relation to one another, not in relation to a perceiving or constituting subject. Again, Merleau-Ponty has drawn a genuine distinction between his own view and the rationalism he characterises. (This rationalism does not capture very well the position of a 'classical' rationalist like Leibniz, who, like Merleau-Ponty, holds that space is subject-dependent. Merleau-Ponty's constitutive mind is necessarily physical or embodied, however, while Leibniz's is not.)[20]

3 Physical points of view

We should now appraise Merleau-Ponty's thesis that spatial orientation is subject-dependent as argued so far. He says,

> It is easy to show that there can be a direction only for a subject
> who takes it. (PPT, 247)[21]

'Décrit' is here translated as 'takes' but 'describes' is much better. 'Takes'
commits Merleau-Ponty to an extreme subjectivist position on spatial
direction – directions only exist if subjects take them, travel along them.
Clearly it is not Merleau-Ponty's intention to rule out the possibility
of items other than bodily subjects travelling in a direction. A more
cautious, but not the best, construal is this: there can be a direction if
and only if some bodily subject could in principle travel along it. This
fails to make spatial direction subject-dependent in Merleau-Ponty's sense.
It is consistent with the view he rejects: that spatial relations are not
perceptually constituted by the subject.

Suppose we read 'décrit' as 'describes' or 'characterises'. Then we
have: 'There can be a direction only for a subject who describes or
characterises it.' It seems to me right that nothing can be a direction
unless it could be consistently characterised as such but this is a very
weak claim. It amounts to the fact that a necessary condition for the
existence of directions is that the notion of direction be free from contradiction. Construed that way, Merleau-Ponty's thesis is true but barely
informative.

Suppose we read Merleau-Ponty as advocating at least this minimal
subjectivism: 'There can be a direction only in relation to a bodily subject
('sujet incarné' PP, 515).' This reading is entailed by his view that spatial
relations are perceptually constituted and is borne out by his claim that
the subject is necessarily embodied. He says:

> A constituting mind is eminently able to trace out all directions in
> space, but has at any moment no direction, and consequently no
> space, without an actual starting point, an absolute 'here' which
> can gradually confer a significance on all spatial determination.
> (PPT, 247)[12]

This passage contains a *non-sequitur*: from 'x has no direction' it does
not logically follow that 'x is not spatially located' (or has 'no space' as
Merleau-Ponty puts it) because the supposition that x is both motionless and spatially located is not a contradictory one. However, the main
thrust of this passage is that a subject may constitute spatial relations
only if that subject is itself spatially located. If a putative 'constitutive
mind' is disembodied then that mind cannot constitute spatial orientations. Hence there must be a 'here', or subjective space, not only from
which other spatial relations may make sense but in relation to which
they exist.

This claim seems to be extremely doubtful. I see no reason whatsoever to suppose that movement in a direction depends upon movement
in relation to a bodily subject, or embodied observer. Arguably the
following is true: if an object x moves, then x moves nearer to or farther
from a second object y and, further, if x moves in a direction from y
then this is either nearer to or farther from some third object z. Three
objects are required to generate co-ordinates for the plotting of the
movement of one of them.

Once we see this, it can be pointed out that there is no requirement
that one of these objects be an observer. (If this is still thought to be a
requirement then ask which object has to be the bodily observer.)

A mistake which runs through Merleau-Ponty's thinking on space is
the assimilation of two ideas. He correctly sees that many relations that
are thought to be two-term are in fact three-term relations. He then
invalidly infers the false conclusion that the third term – or relatum – is
a perceiving bodily subject. This invalid inference is made, I think,
because Merleau-Ponty has not separated out sufficiently clearly the
mental from the physical dependencies of space on the subject.

This is sufficient to refute the doctrine that directions may exist only
if some bodily observer exists with whom they stand in some spatial
relation. Or, at least, much more argument is needed to exhibit such a
dependence.

One such argument may be constructed on quasi-Merleau-Pontyean
grounds: directions may only exist if *perceptually constituted* by a subject. Subjects are necessarily embodied, therefore, directions may exist
only if embodied subjects exist. This is a valid argument, and one that
yields the conclusion Merleau-Ponty desires. However, it is far from
clear that it is sound. Ascribing a truth-value to the first premise
requires detailed appraisal of the remainder of Merleau-Ponty's writing
on space. The second premise may be true if a kind of materialism is
true but if either idealism or mind–body dualism is true then that
premise is false. Merleau-Ponty himself thinks it is false that there are
or could be non-embodied subjects. In particular he thinks that only a
subject that is itself spatial may have experience of space.

It seems to me not a contradictory supposition that there should be
non-spatial percipients of space, even if we are spatial percipients of
space. If that is right, then it is not necessarily true that there is a 'here'
or a subjective space from which spatial facts are perceived when spatial
facts are perceived even if that is contingently true. It is necessarily true
that if some sense is made of space then there is in some sense a subject
because making sense is making sense to. Nothing follows from that,
however, about the ontology of that subject.

A stronger case may be made for the claim that the *visual* perception
of space presupposes the existence of a perceiving subject who is

embodied. Merleau-Ponty's objection to the idea of a non-embodied mind visually perceiving space is that

> It does not view the spectacle from anywhere. (PPT, 248)[23]

Perceiving visually is perceiving from somewhere. Only an embodied subject can see from somewhere, therefore visual perception is by an embodied subject. Although logically valid this argument is not clearly sound because the second premise may well be false. It is coherent to suppose that visual perceptions may be presented to a subject *as though* that subject occupied a region of physical space without it logically following that that subject does occupy that (or any) space. To see this, consider the analogous fact that images seen 'in the mind's eye' are presented as of three dimensional objects in space. Such images are not, or not straightforwardly, spatially located nor are their intentional contents. If that is coherent then so is the supposition of non-embodied quasi-vision 'from a point of view'.

Prima facie Merleau-Ponty is empirically correct to maintain that each of us is a bodily subject. This is how it appears to most of us most of the time in a psychologically compelling way. To understand the role of the body in the perception of space on Merleau-Ponty's view we have to revert to the distinction made at the beginning of Chapter IV: between being a person and observing one, or between subjective and objective points of view.

The way the world appears to me to be spatially orientated is a function not of the objective location of my body in space but of space as I experience it as occupied by my body. This in turn depends on my pragmatic concerns:

> What counts for the orientation of the spectacle is not my body as it in fact is, as a thing in objective space, but as a system of possible actions, a virtual body with its phenomenal 'place' defined by its task and situation. My body is wherever there is something to be done. (PPT, 249–50)[24]

Merleau-Ponty is right to suppose that from the fact that a bodily subject has a specific objective location in space it does not logically follow that that subject is perceptually presented with objects in one spatial orientation rather than another (if that subject perceives spatially). It follows that the subjective presentation of space is not a logical consequence of objective location in space. However, Merleau-Ponty is wrong to rule out the fact that such objective locations do have a causal role or a 'constitutive' role in dictating spatial presentations.

The fact, for example, that I am standing in front of an object may be one of the causes of my being visually presented with the front of it, and this is fully consistent with the meaning of words like 'front' being partially pragmatically determined.

Merleau-Ponty thinks Stratton's inverting-spectacles experiment shows that under normal conditions the spatial orientation of what is visually presented is subjectively determined. However, that does not follow logically from the results of the experiment. The fact that the re-orientation of the perceived world is an achievement of the subject, an achievement possible partly through bodily action, is consistent with the objective spatial location of the subject having a causal role in presenting spatial orientations under non-experimental conditions.

It is important to realise that, rather like Kantian synthesis, the subjective constitution of spatial orientation that Merleau-Ponty describes is not intended as a chronological process of which the subject is aware. Of course the subject is typically aware of its spatial orientation, and those of the objects with which it is perceptually presented. It is not, however, thereby aware of the constitution of those orientations by itself. Merleau-Ponty says:

> It is of the essence of space to be always 'already constituted', and
> we shall never come to understand it by withdrawing into a
> worldless perception. (PPT, 252)[25]

'A worldless perception' ('une perception sans monde' PP, 291) is a perception of a non-spatial reality. When he says it is 'of the essence of space' ('essentiel à l'espace' PP, 291) to be already constituted he means at least that it is a necessary condition for something, call it 'S', being a space that S be 'already constituted'. It would then be contradictory to suppose that S is a space but not 'already constituted'. He may also mean that if S is 'already constituted' then that is sufficient for 'S is a space'. He had better not mean that however because it is clearly false. It rules out logically the possibility of anything except space being 'already constituted' and on Merleau-Ponty's own terms that is far too restrictive.

Merleau-Ponty is right to hold that consideration of non-spatial realities will help us understand space. The only reservation I would make is that consideration of the absence or non-existence of space may help us to be clearer on what the presence or existence of space is. Because phenomenology – like all post-Kantian movements in philosophy – is metaphysically conservative, Merleau-Ponty wishes us not to raise really fundamental philosophical problems about space. Rather, he wishes us to deal only in phenomenological descriptions:

We must not wonder why being is orientated, why existence is spatial, why, using the expression we used a little while ago, our body is not geared to the world in all its positions, and why its co-existence with the world magnetizes experience and induces a direction in it. The question could be asked only if the facts were fortuitous happenings to a subject and on objects indifferent to space, whereas perceptual experience shows that they are presupposed in our primordial encounter with being, and that being is synonymous with being situated. (PPT, 252)[26]

I have quoted this passage at length because in it we can see some of the limitations of a phenomenological approach to philosophy. In fairness to Merleau-Ponty, he does not say 'we must not wonder' but 'il ne faut pas se demander' (PP, 291) which means 'it is not necessary to ask'. Nevertheless, it is simply not true that metaphysical questions about why space exists and why our perceptual experience is spatial cannot be asked unless subject and object were 'indifferent to space' ('indifférents à l'espace' PP, 291) if this means 'non-spatial'. The ontological fact of our spatial location is no obstacle to an inquiry after metaphysical facts.

It is also doubtful that 'perceptual experience' could show that space is presupposed in our primordial encounter with being. Perceptual experience may reveal to us what is the case but cannot show us what is presupposed by what is the case. This is because if x is a presupposition of y then x is a necessary condition for y, or, to put it another way, the logical relations 'if not x then not y' and 'if y then x' hold between x and y. But no logical relation may be known through perceptual experience, so it cannot be known through perceptual experience that our primordial encounter with being presupposes space. Of course this is consistent with space being primordial with respect to being. Only a certain epistemology of that putative fact is ruled out here.

Consistently with this, Merleau-Ponty may well be right to imply that the first experience that any person has is as of something with spatial properties. This claim, however, is empirical.

Finally, I do not think it is right that:

Being is synonymous with being situated. (PPT, 252)[27]

Even if all human being is Heideggerian 'being-in-the-world' ('in-der-Welt-sein'), as a semantic or lexicographical claim this identification is just false. Suppose something is 'situated' ('situé') if and only if it is either spatial or spatially related to something spatial. Then, from 'x is' or 'x exists' we cannot logically derive 'x is situated'. It is not contradictory to suppose that something non-spatial exists. To think otherwise is to prejudge the issue in favour of phenomenological ontology and against possible non-spatial metaphysics. Heidegger, I think, would have rejected Merleau-Ponty's synonymony claim.

Merleau-Ponty does have an interesting argument for the conclusion that our concept of being is a concept of spatial being (or, our concept of something's being implies the concept of its being spatial). The argument is:

1 Every conceivable being is related either directly or indirectly to the perceived world. (PPT, 253)
2 The perceived world is grasped only in terms of direction. (PPT, 253)

Therefore,

3 We cannot dissociate being from orientated being. (PPT, 253)

Merleau-Ponty also derives a supplementary conclusion from 1, 2 and 3 that is anti-metaphysical:

4 There is no occasion to find a basis for space or to ask what is the level of all levels. (PPT, 253)[28]

Suppose 1 is read as: 'if x is conceivable then x is empirical', 2 as 'if x is empirical then x is spatial' and 3 as 'if x is imaginable then x is imaginable only as spatial'.

The trouble is that the contexts, generated by 'x is conceivable', 'x is empirical' and 'x is imaginable' are referentially opaque, and even if it is true that if x is imaginable then x is empirical and if x is empirical then x is spatial then it still does not logically follow that if x is imaginable then x is only imaginable as spatial. There is no contradiction in the supposition that the imagination of something that is in fact spatial – has spatial properties – does not consist in the imagining of any of its spatial properties. To see this consider the analogous situation where the mind–brain identity theory is true. Then, if someone imagines a mental state then they imagine something that has, in fact, spatial properties. However they do not thereby imagine those properties.

Merleau-Ponty, unfortunately, is unfamiliar with the logical phenomenon of referential opacity. It is clear however that he is trying to present an anti-metaphysical argument familiar in the empiricist epistemologies of, say, Hobbes and Schlick. The idea is that when we think we have succeeded in imagining something non-physical (and so, non-spatial) such as God, a number, a mind, the soul, we have in fact only ever succeeded in imagining something physical (and not non-spatial). Analogously, here, for Merleau-Ponty, 'Nous ne pouvons dissocier l'être

112

de l'être orienté' (PP, 293) 'we cannot dissociate being from orientated being' (PPT, 253).

Merleau-Ponty thinks of the empirical world as essentially spatial. He thinks all concepts are empirical but then erroneously infers that all concepts are spatial. Notice that the invalidity of the argument does not show that Merleau-Ponty's claims are independently false. He might well be right that everything conceivable is empirical, everything empirical is spatial and everything conceivable is only conceivable as spatial. Even if the three claims are not so closely logically related as they appear they may each be true.

The anti-metaphysical conclusion Merleau-Ponty derives from this argument is 4 alone, that there is no room to 'ground' space ('il n'y a pas lieu de "fonder" l'espace' PP, 293).

Now, this conclusion does indeed follow validly from 1, 2 and 3, as premises. Suppose 'x grounds y' if and only if x is a necessary condition for y: either in the sense of y's existence, or in the sense of y's essence or both. Then x grounds y if and only if, if y is, or if y is F, or if y both is and is F, then x is. Suppose now that if y is F then y is spatial. Suppose also we wish to give a value to 'x' so that the sentence 'if y then x' comes out as true (or, 'x grounds y'). Suppose, however, all our concepts are spatial concepts. It logically follows that we lack the conceptual apparatus to give x a value without ascribing to it spatial properties. It follows that Merleau-Ponty is absolutely right in his view that space cannot be 'grounded' if all our concepts are spatial. Clearly, nothing can be the ground of itself in the requisite sense. Although if y then y is always and everywhere true, and although if not y then not y is always and everywhere true, these are only logical truths and so have no ontological import. What Merleau-Ponty has in mind is the quasi-Kantian case where something's possibility is explained by something other than itself. If we can only imagine things as spatial there is no conceptual room ('lieu') to non-spatially 'ground' ('fonder') space. To put it in Kantian terms, space for Merleau-Ponty is an original transcendental ground. To put it in Heideggerian terms, space is primordial.

4 Spaces

The main thrust of Merleau-Ponty's phenomenology of space is essentially Kantian. Space is constituted by the subject, space is a condition for the possibility of spatial objects and for the subject's experience of them. This is familiar from the 'Transcendental Aesthetic'.[29]

Nevertheless, there are two aspects of Merleau-Ponty's phenomenology of space that are non-Kantian, and the second is radically anti-Kantian. They are the theses that *the body* plays an essential role in the constitution of space as it appears to us and the thesis that there exists more than one space. I shall now treat the second of these.

In an important footnote Merleau-Ponty says:

> One might show . . . that aesthetic perception too opens up a new spatiality, that the picture as a work of art is not in the space which it inhabits as a physical thing and as a coloured canvas. That the dance evolves in an aimless and unorientated space. (PPT, 287)[30]

Now, it is an important Kantian thesis that there is only one space. What Kant means is that putatively numerically distinct spaces will turn out to be spatially related and so parts of one and the same space. Putatively discrete 'spaces' are really only places, or parts, or regions, of space. What Merleau-Ponty has done is point to the possibility of spaces that are not spatially related. By 'spatially related' I mean two spaces, S1 and S2, are spatially related if and only if travel is possible between S1 and S2: a physical object could exist in S1 at a time t1 and exist in S2 at a later time t2 and exist at all times between t1 and t2. If, physical travel is the criterion for 'spatially related' then Merleau-Ponty has, in my view, presented examples of spaces that are not spatially related. I cannot walk into the picture, leaving the space of the art gallery for the space of the art-work, even though it is not clear what kind of 'cannot' this is. I can, of course, join a dance and the fact that a dance is not orientated is not sufficient to show that it occupies a space numerically distinct from objective public space.

However, Merleau-Ponty has stronger examples. He says

> The schizophrenic no longer inhabits the common property world, but a private world. (PPT, 287)[31]

and Merleau-Ponty does not restrict this ontological claim to the insane. He says

> There are as many spaces as there are distinct spatial experiences. (PPT, 291)[32]

This is to individuate spaces through spatial experiences; experiences with contents that have spatial properties. This prima facie dubious claim may be supported by the consideration that the content of, say, an olfactory, or auditory experience may not be obviously spatially related to, say, the content of a visual experience even though all may have spatial, or quasi-spatial contents.

Examples of non-spatially related spaces may be multiplied beyond the examples Merleau-Ponty gives. For example, I cannot travel from public space into the space of the image in my minds' eye when, I imagine, for example, Cambridge. I can imagine being in Cambridge, as I can imagine travelling there. Also, if I watch a film at the cinema the space in which the action on the screen takes place is not a space into which I can travel: even though I can perceive it visually. Again, it is not at all clear what kind of impossibility is expressed by 'cannot' here. Anthony Quinton has also provided examples of logically possible spaces which seem to be numerically distinct.[33]

When so much of so called analytical and so called modern continental philosophy is so strongly, if unconsciously, neo-Kantian it is illuminating to read in this part of Merleau-Ponty's phenomenology of space a sharp break with the 'Transcendental Aesthetic'. If we find his numerically distinct spaces implausible then this is probably some measure of our neo-Kantianism.

5 *Schneider's problems*

Merleau-Ponty frequently invokes findings of psychiatry inexplicable by behaviourist or 'objectivist' psychology to displaying the inadequacies of empiricism and rationalism. He then interprets them as substantiations of his own existential phenomenology. The most conspicuous example of this tactic is the extended discussion of the case of Schneider in the chapter 'La Spatialité du Corps Propre' in *Phénoménologie de la Perception*.

Schneider is a wounded first world war veteran whose medical and psychological history has been examined and written up by the German psychologists Gelb and Goldstein.[34] Merleau-Ponty made a close study of their findings.

Those disabilities of Schneider which are thought by Merleau-Ponty most useful for his existential phenomenological purposes are as follows:

Schneider cannot make abstract movements unless his eyes are open. An abstract movement is one, for example, ordered in an artificially contrived experimental situation as opposed to one spontaneously performed in a natural practical situation.

Schneider has little or no kinaesthetic knowledge. For example, he cannot specify the location of his limbs *vis-à-vis* one another nor *vis-à-vis* objects with which they are in contact.

Merleau-Ponty, however, wishes us to bear in mind certain circumstances under which these disabilities can be partly overcome by Schneider.

Schneider is able to perform abstract movements if either he is allowed to open his eyes and watch the limbs he uses to perform them, or, if first he moves his whole body as though he were in a real practical situation, or both.

Schneider also recovers some kinaesthetic knowledge if he rehearses the movements executed by his body as a whole in a practical situation as a preparation. He is then able, for example, to locate some parts of his body and to recognise the size and shape of objects pressed against it.

There are also two respects in which it is relevant to note that Schneider's behaviour is unimpaired: Schneider has greater than normal dexterity and precision in the performance of mundane habitual actions such as blowing his nose or reaching for matches from his pocket.

Schneider works in a factory producing wallets and his production rate is 75 per cent that of the average person employed in this task.

In the case of these habitual movements Schneider can perform them without difficulty as abstract ones when ordered to do so in the experimental situation, even with his eyes closed.

Merleau-Ponty is interested in two distinctions: the distinction between the spatiality of one's own body and 'objective' space, and the distinction between the practical and the abstract. Schneider's disabilities clarify both distinctions. The existence of the distinctions cannot be explained or adequately characterised by objectivist psychology, nor by rationalist and empiricist philosophy.

For example, according to Merleau-Ponty 'traditional' psychology can provide no account of success or failure in the establishment of kinaesthetic knowledge of the kind that Schneider exhibits. Here he is talking about the patient's awareness of the location of parts of his own body:

> Traditional psychology has no concept to cover these varieties of consciousness of place because consciousness of place is always, for such psychology, a positional consciousness, a representation, a Vor-stellung, because as such it gives us the place as a determination of the objective world and because such a representation either is or is not, but, if it is, yields the object to us quite unambiguously and as an end identifiable through all its appearances. (PPT, 104)[35]

Any psychology that ultimately relies on the notion of representation is superficial. My knowledge of my own body does not ultimately consist in mentally presenting it but in being it. Being a bodily agent in the spatial world makes possible any mental representations of which I may be capable.

In what sense is Schneider's case a refutation of rationalism and empiricism? Merleau-Ponty thinks there is no rationalist explanation of the Schneider case and no empiricist explanation of the Schneider case so those two theories are at best derivative and abstract and at worst false. For example, in the laboratory, Schneider is only able to move his arm in a way requested if he visually observes his limb as he moves it. On the other hand, he has no difficulty moving his arm in a physically similar way when making wallets in the factory where he works. There his actions are embedded in a practical situation that habitually elicits them. If empiricism were true we would have to observe our limbs in order to move them. We do not have to do this. Therefore empiricism is false. Similarly, Schneider has no difficulty in blowing his nose or in scratching a point on his leg that has just been bitten by a mosquito but he has immense difficulty in pointing to his nose with a ruler or indicating some point on his leg that is mentioned. He is only able to do these things by *inferring* the location of those parts of his body from facts about his body as a whole. If rationalism were true our knowledge of our own bodies would be by inference. Our knowledge of our own bodies is not by inference. Therefore rationalism is false.

We have self-knowledge as body-subjects not by thinking about our bodies nor by observing them but by *being* them. Our existence as thinkers and observers is made possible by our existence as body-subjects acting in the physical world. The relation between the body-subject's knowledge of itself and its knowledge of space is mutually dependent. We know what kind of movements we are capable of by following a spatio-temporal route through the world and manipulating physical objects. At the same time we understand the world to contain four dimensional objects. Merleau-Ponty even thinks it is abstract and misleading to think of the body-subject as *in* space. That is to think of it on the model of a physical object. He prefers to speak of the body-subject as *of* space. As a body-subject I have my own subjective spatiality. In being-in-the-world body-subject and space are mutually constituting.

The critique of rationalism and empiricism is a critique of *objective thinking*. Thinking of myself as an object is neither necessary nor sufficient for my pre-reflective knowledge of myself as a body-subject. To show this, Merleau-Ponty again draws on the strangeness of certain psychiatric cases to show the inappropriateness of the objective model of self-knowledge. In cases of anosognosia patients do not regard their limbs as their own. They visually observe the flesh and the outline of the limb and do have kinaesthetic awareness of it. They nontheless regard it as something alien (perhaps because it is damaged and they find it psychologically impossible to accept that there is damage to *them*). In a sense such patients have objective knowledge of their bodies. They could be fully appraised of all the relevant physical facts about their limbs. What is crucially missing is the recognition of the subjective fact that their limbs are *part of them*. In the normal case, being one's body provides the essentials of knowledge of one's body.

In other cases, patients have the hallucination of their own face as *seen from the inside*. In the normal case however one's face is never presented to oneself as though one were looking at it. Being one's body is an obstacle to observing it in this quasi-third person way. These subjective facts are not available to objective thought. They are not available to rationalist objective thinking nor to empiricist objective thinking.

VII

Time

1 *The phenomenology of time*

Merleau-Ponty thinks that time is subjective, that is, the existence and nature of time depend upon the existence and nature of a perceiving bodily subject. Before examining his arguments for this conclusion I shall say something about the relations between time and subjectivity according to Merleau-Ponty.

He says,

> all our experiences, in as much as they are ours, arrange themselves in terms of before and after. (PPT, 410)[1]

Now, it is right, indeed a necessary truth that if two experiences occur, call them E1 and E2, then either E1 precedes E2 or E2 precedes E1 or E1 and E2 are wholly simultaneous or E1 and E2 are partly simultaneous.

It is a difficult and unsolved philosophical problem what 'before' and 'after' mean in their temporal sense, but by E1 and E2 being wholly simultaneous I mean that both E1 and E2 occur and that at any time that E1 is occurring E2 is occurring and at any time that E2 is occurring E1 is occurring. This entails that at no time that E1 is occurring is E2 not occurring and at no time that E2 is occurring is E1 not occurring.

By E1 and E2 being partly simultaneous I mean that both E1 and E2 occur and there is a time when both E1 and E2 are occurring but either there is also a time when E1 is occurring but E2 is not occurring or there is also a time when E2 is occurring but E1 is not occurring, or both.

The reason why any pair of experiences exhibits these temporal properties is that all experiences are events and all pairs of events exhibit these properties. Why this should be so, indeed why temporal orderings

119

exist at all, are unsolved philosophical problems but, arguably, an essential part of what we mean by a pair of events being temporal is that they have these properties.

For these reasons Merleau-Ponty is right to claim that each subject's experiences exhibit a before and after ordering. It is also right that their having this ordering is something they have 'in so much as they are ours' (PPT, 410) ('en tant qu'elles sont notres' PP, 469) if this means, in the neo-Kantian idiom, that that is a necessary condition for some set of experiences being my experiences. This is right (unless of course they are simultaneous) because their exhibiting a temporal ordering is a prerequisite for their happening at all and that some experiences happen at all is a necessary condition for their being mine.

I would not want to rule out on logical grounds the empirical peculiarity of the whole set of a being's experiences being simultaneous (and so not successive). It should also be noted that any set of non-simultaneous experiences exhibits the before and after ordering, including any set of token experiences undergone by numerically distinct subjects. Merleau-Ponty does not make the false claim that that a set of experiences exhibits a before and after ordering is a sufficient condition for those being the experiences of only one subject or of one subject, rather than another.

Merleau-Ponty gives a special reason why our experiences are ordered by the before/after relation. It is because,

> temporality, in Kantian language, is the form taken by our inner sense. (PPT, 410)[2]

Kant's thesis that time is the (immediate) form of inner sense (and the mediate form of outer sense) is open to many interpretations, the most plausible being: the temporality of my experience is a necessary condition for my awareness of its content. Merleau-Ponty, however, along with most writers on Kant, reads Kant as an idealist and interprets Kant as holding that time is 'subjective' or pertains only to the inner psychology of the subject.[3]

Whatever the merits or demerits of this reading of Kant Merleau-Ponty is right that it follows from it that experience is ordered by the before/after relation. This is because the exercise of inner sense makes experience temporal and if experience is made temporal it is ordered by the before/after relation. Therefore, if inner sense is exercised then experience is ordered by the before/after relation.

Merleau-Ponty thinks the conclusion that all my experiences are ordered by the before/after relation also follows from another premise. This is [temporality] . . . is the most general characteristic of 'psychic facts'. (PPT, 410)[4]

This inference is clearly valid because if temporality entails the before/after relation and if experiences are psychic facts then if psychic facts exhibit this feature then experiences exhibit this feature.

It is less clear what is meant by saying that temporality is the 'most general characteristic' (PPT, 410) ('le caractère le plus general PP, 469) of "psychic facts" (PPT, 410) ("faits psychiques" PP, 469). It could mean this: consider the elements of a set, S {0, 1, 2, 3, . . . n}. Suppose there is a property, F, of each member of a subset of S. Suppose further that there is a further property, G, possessed by every member of S. It then follows that if any element of S is F then that element is G, but if some element of S is G it does not thereby logically follow that that element is F. When these conditions are met we may say that G is a more general characteristic than F. G is the most general characteristic of the members of S if and only if no property of some members of S is possessed by more members than members that possess G.

Interpreting the members of set S as 'our experiences' (PPT, 410) ('nos expériences' PP, 469) and 'being temporal' as 'being G' and 'having some other characteristic less general than G' as 'being F', then we have:

Any experience of mine is temporal if it has any characteristic less general than temporality, but it does not follow from its temporality alone that any experience of mine has any characteristic less general than temporality. It follows that any experiences of mine exhibit the before/after ordering, on the plausible assumption that any pair of experiences exhibits that ordering if its members are temporal.

Merleau-Ponty excludes two putative temporal properties of the subject. They are:

the subject . . . cannot be a series of psychic events. (PPT, 410)

and

nevertheless cannot be eternal either. (PPT, 410)[5]

The subject is the body-subject ('le sujet est son corps' SNS, 125). The body-subject is neither a series of psychic events nor eternal, therefore, the subject is neither a series of psychic events nor eternal.

It is not clear what kind of 'cannot' ('ne peut') is at work in the first claim. On any construal, if x is a subject then x is not a series of psychic events. This is consistent however with either: 'if x is a subject then x is a series of events' or 'if x is a subject then x is psychic' but not with both. Merleau-Ponty could mean that it is a contingent fact that no subject is identical with any series of psychic events, even though it necessarily follows from the subject's being a body-subject that the subject is not a series of psychic events. Then the necessity pertains to the inference, not to the fact.

Conversely, Merleau-Ponty may mean that if x is a subject it logically follows that x is not a series of psychic events, such that it would be necessarily false to affirm the conjunction of 'x is a subject' and 'x is a series of psychic events': for example because the conjunction is or entails a contradiction once the semantics of each conjunct are made explicit.

On either construal, that any set of experiences undergone by any subject is ordered by a before/after relation is consistent with any such subject not being numerically identical with any such set of experiences. Indeed, a minimal distinction between a subject and his or her experiences is entailed by the thought that such experiences are 'had' or 'undergone' by such a subject. This is to deny that such a subject could be coherently maintained to be nothing over and above the content of their own experience.

Merleau-Ponty says the subject cannot be eternal either. 'Eternal' is equivocal in metaphysical content. It may mean: x is eternal if and only if, x exists and x exists at all times. This means, choose any time you like, x exists at that time. Sometimes, 'eternal' is taken to mean 'non-temporal' such that if x is eternal then x exists but no temporal predicates truly apply to x or, to put it another way, x has no temporal properties. Although x is, there is not any true answer to 'When is x?' Sometimes 'eternal' is used in a third sense such that: x is eternal if and only if x has a beginning but no end. Then x is eternal if and only if x began to be, x is, but x will not not be.

When Merleau-Ponty says the subject is not eternal he does not imply that the subject is not eternal in any of these senses. On Merleau-Ponty's view, if x is a subject, although x exists, x began to exist and x will cease to exist. x exists at a time but there both was time when x was not and will be a time when x will not be. This thesis is logically inconsistent with the thesis that the subject is eternal in any of the senses defined above so, if proven, it proves those theses false.

2 *Temporality*

I turn now to Merleau-Ponty's thesis that time is subjective: made, and made to be what it is, by the constitutive operations of a body-subject. The structure of Merleau-Ponty's argument is rather loose but, roughly, it is this: time is either subjective or objective: these two possibilities are mutually exclusive and collectively exhaustive. The thesis that time is objective is confused and mistaken; therefore, time is subjective.

Merleau-Ponty characterises what he takes to be the objective view of time in this way: 'time passes or flows by' (PPT, 411) and 'we speak of the course of time' (PPT, 411).[6] Centrally, the objective view of time includes this doctrine:

> If time is similar to a river, it flows from the past towards the present and the future. The present is the consequence of the past, and the future of the present. (PPT, 411)[7]

There are two distinct notions which need separating out here. One is the idea that events are ordered by the before/after relation. The other is the idea that events stand in a causal relation. The two notions are not as closely logically related as might appear.

If x and y stand in a before/after relation then either x happens at an earlier time, t1, and y happens only at a later time, t2, or y happens at t1 and x happens at t2. From 'first x then y' we cannot validly infer 'y is a causal consequence of x' and from 'first x then y' we cannot validly infer 'x is a cause of y', but does the chronological ordering follow from the causal ordering?

What causation is is an unsolved philosophical problem but, plausibly, if two events, E1 and E2, are causally related such that E1 is the cause of E2, then it is either both true that if not E1 then not E2 and if E1 then E2 or, it is true that either if not E1 then not E2 or if E1 then E2 but not both. Now, if E1 is the cause of E2 (and, by entailment, E2 is the effect of E1) then it seems the following is true: either E1 chronologically precedes E2 or E1 and E2 are simultaneous or, if there is backwards causation, E2 chronologically precedes E1. If there is forwards or backwards causation then the causally related events are ordered by the before/after relation. If there is simultaneous causation the causally related events are not ordered by the before/after relation.

Merleau-Ponty says the metaphor of time flowing like a river is 'extremely confused' (PPT, 411) ('Très confuse' PP, 470). The reason he gives is this:

> *Looking at the things themselves*, the melting of the snows and what results from this are not successive events, or rather the very notion of an event has no place in the objective world. (PPT, 411)[8]

At least three issues need to be distinguished here. One is the question of the relation between causal relations and the before and after relation. A second is whether there are events in the objective world; events occurring in what exists when what exists is not being perceived or thought to exist. A third is whether either before/after ordering or causal relations are influenced by the objective existence or non-existence of events. Crucially, both before and after ordering and causal relations are logically independent of whether any events are either subjective or objective. To see this, consider some set of empirical events standing both in a before and after relation and a causal relation. First suppose empirical realism is true, so that events perceived or thought to exist (generally) do exist. Now suppose empirical idealism is true, such that those events exist only if they are perceived or thought to exist. Nothing intrinsic to the events, including their mutual temporal and causal relations, is thereby changed. If it is thought to be an objection to this that causal relations may only obtain between physical events it should be noted that empirical idealism *per se* does not logically rule out mental events being physical events (for example brain processes). Admittedly Berkeley's classical empirical idealism is inconsistent with that, but Putnam's 'Brain-in-a-vat' thesis for example, is not. Merleau-Ponty is an empirical idealist about events but thinks the subject is physical.

Merleau-Ponty's claims about time 'flowing' may now be evaluated. He says the melting of the snow and what results from it are not successive. I take it this means, for two events E1 and E2 if E1 causes E2 then E2 does not succeed E1 chronologically. This claim is by and large empirically false; if E1 causes E2 then E2 succeeds E1 chronologically. Of course this is consistent with radical theses about events and causality. For example, there might be no events and no causality, or, as Merleau-Ponty supposes, both events and causation may be subject-dependent.

Merleau-Ponty is nevertheless right to suppose that if E1 and E2 are causally related then it does not logically follow that if E1 causes E2 then E2 succeeds E1 chronologically. As I suggested above, E1 and E2 may be causally related even if E1 and E2 are simultaneous. There by 'simultaneous' I do not mean only 'partly simultaneous', I see no contradiction in the supposition that E1 and E2 are causally related even if wholly simultaneous, even if it is empirically false that there exist such causal relations between such temporally ordered events.

I turn now to Merleau-Ponty's radical thesis that 'the very notion of an event has no place in the objective world' (PPT, 411).[9] One point needs to be cleared up straight away. It is reasonably uncontroversial that the notion of an event is not subject-independent because notions, or ideas, or concepts are plausibly mental occurrences or dispositions in a subject. What Merleau-Ponty means is that there are no subject-independent events, not that there are no subject-independent notions of events (even though that is also true for him).

Suppose I make the claim that two events in the external world, E1 and E2, are chronologically related such that E1 exists at t1 but not at t2 and E2 exists at t2 but not at t1, and suppose further that E1 is the, or a, cause of E2 and E2 is thereby the, or an, effect of E1, then, according to Merleau-Ponty:

> I am tacitly assuming the existence of a witness tied to a certain
> spot in the world, and I am comparing his successive views.
> (PPT, 411)[10]

There is a Kantian insight here which seems correct. If I imagine something, for example a pair of events, such as some snow melting and the resultant flooding, then I imagine these events as they would appear to me were I perceiving them. This is an empirical constraint on the imagination. (It is also the truth contained in the Kantian doctrine that we can only have knowledge of possible objects of experience and not of those things as they are in themselves.) If this empirical constraint on the imagination exists then Merleau-Ponty is right in his view that the imagination of events tacitly presupposes an observer of those events, even if such an observer need only be imaginary. This follows on the assumption, which Merleau-Ponty endorses, that all perceiving is perceiving from a 'point of view' or, from somewhere. This is a logical consequence of his thesis that subjects are embodied; a consequence that he emphasises. 'A certain spot in the world' is the point of view the tacitly assumed observer adopts in the perception of the events we imagine. This observer is where we would be were we to be perceiving those events we imagine.

The claim that in imagining a pair of events both ordered by the before/after relation and causally related, 'I am comparing his (the tacit observer's) successive views' is ambiguous. This is because 'views' ('vues' PP, 470) is ambiguous between 'what is viewed' and 'the viewing of what is viewed'. (In Husserlian phenomenological vocabulary it is ambiguous between denoting an intentional content and denoting an intentional act, or between *noēma* and *noēsis*.)

From the fact that in imagining some events I am tacitly assuming the standpoint of an observer it does not logically follow that those events are subjective or subject-dependent. This is because it is coherent to maintain that what I imagine, and what the tacitly assumed observer perceives, is those events as they realistically are. Some events are imagined or perceived 'as they realistically are' if both the perceiving or imagining of them is veridical and if the perceiving or imagining of them does not cause them to be, nor causes them to be what they are. There is no contradiction in the supposition that some events predate, endure through, and postdate the imagination and/or the perception of them and remain intrinsically unaltered by being the intentional objects of such imagining and/or perceiving. The quasi-Kantian thesis that imagining an object consists in thinking of it as it would be if one were perceiving it is logically consistent with both realism and idealism about perception (as Kant, but not Merleau-Ponty, sees).[11] We do not need to make the additional assumptions that the events imagined idealistically depend upon the tacit observer's perception of them, or on our imagining of them, in order to uphold the quasi-Kantian thesis.

Merleau-Ponty does however have the makings of an argument for such idealism. He says we are really comparing the successive views of the tacit observer when we think we are comparing events in the objective world. Now, if 'views' here means 'the viewing of what is viewed' then Merleau-Ponty's conclusion goes through because the viewing of what is viewed is ideal or subject-dependent because it is a mental event. If, however 'views' means 'what is viewed' then Merleau-Ponty's subjectivism does not follow because what is viewed may be either subject-dependent or subject-independent.

On the first construal Merleau-Ponty is advancing a suggestion analogous to Hume's subjectivism about causation. Hume argues that we mistake our subjective expectation that one impression will be followed by another for an objective and necessary causal relation between the two events those two impressions are impressions of. Merleau-Ponty maintains that we mistake the views of a pair of events by a tacit observer for that pair of events ordered both causally and by the before/after relation. Both Hume and Merleau-Ponty are providing a psychological explanation of how thinking about causally related events is possible. It is part of the theses of both Hume and Merleau-Ponty that from the fact that a particular psychological explanation of our causal thinking is true, it does not logically follow that there are objective causal relations. Merleau-Ponty, and as I interpret him, Hume, also deny that there are such objective causal relations.[12]

Now, from the fact that E1 is imagined to occur at t1 and E2 is imagined to occur at t2, and E1 is imagined to be the or a cause of E2 it does not logically follow that E1 occurs at t1 and E2 at t2, nor does it follow that E1 is the cause of E2 either subject-dependently or subject-independently. It follows that Merleau-Ponty still requires additional argument to show that any event pair that is thought or perceived is subject-dependent.

A premise that Merleau-Ponty advances as a possible constituent of such an argument is this:

The 'events' are [shapes] cut out by a finite observer from the spatio-temporal totality of the objective world. (PPT, 411)[13]

Merleau-Ponty does not in fact say that the events are 'shapes', he only says they are 'cut out' ('découpés') by the observer. This is logically consistent with an event, or an event pair, being selected from a non-ideal totality of events with which the perceiver or thinker could in principle be realistically acquainted. Merleau-Ponty, of course, must reject this suggestion because it contradicts his thesis that there exist no events in the external world. To rule this out, however, he needs to advance another premise. This is:

> If I consider the world itself, there is simply one indivisible and
> changeless being [in it]. (PP, 411)[14]

(The two words 'in it' do not translate anything in the French.) Clearly, Merleau-Ponty's intention is to identify the one indivisible and changeless being with the world.

Now, this rather Parmenidean picture of objective reality may be true and Merleau-Ponty does advance some evidence in its favour. However, prima facie it is logically inconsistent with the claim he made above that the objective world is a 'spatio-temporal totality' (PPT, 411) ('Totalité spatio-temporelle' PP, 470). If x is spatio-temporal then x is temporal and if x is temporal then x changes. Also, if x is changeless then x is not temporal and if x is not temporal, then x is not spatio-temporal.[15] It follows by Leibniz's law that the Parmenidean world is not the spatio-temporal world.

It is best, I think to read 'totalité spatio-temporelle' as a slip, or else give it a much weaker construal, for example, 'the objective world which may be thought of as a spatio-temporal totality by an observer'. This construal is clearly consistent with the Parmenidean thesis Merleau-Ponty wishes to endorse.

The evidence that Merleau-Ponty advances in favour of the Parmenidean thesis is this:

> Change presupposes a certain position which I take up and from
> which I see things in procession before me: there are no events
> without someone to whom they happen and whose finite perspective
> is the basis of their individuality. (PPT, 411)[16]

The kind of presupposition Merleau-Ponty has in mind here cannot possibly be logical entailment because the existence of change does not logically presuppose the perception of that change, nor *a fortiori* the perception of that change from anywhere.

Suppose change is this: x changes if and only if either x lacks a property, F, at t1 and x has that property at t2, or, x has a property, F, at t1 but x lacks that property at t2. In either case it logically follows that x has changed between t1 and t2 and if x has not gained or lost any properties between t1 and t2 then x has not changed between t1 and t2. If x changes between t1 and t2 it follows that an 'event' has happened between t1 and t2 because if anything happens an event happens and if something either gains or loses a property an event happens.

This analysis of change is logically consistent with motion being a kind of change. (Many of Merleau-Ponty's examples of changes are motions.) Suppose motion is this: x is in motion if and only if at t1 x is at some place, P1, and at t2 x is at some other place, P2, but x occupies a juxtaposed series of places between P1 and P2 at every time between t1 and t2.

It follows from this analysis of 'motion' that if x is in motion then x changes, because if x is not at P1 at t2 but is at P2 at t2 but was at P1 at t1 then x has gained and lost a property, and either of those is sufficient for change. If x is in motion then x changes places and if x changes places then x changes.

Now, Merleau-Ponty offers no analysis of 'change' and no analysis of 'motion'. Had he done so then he would have seen, perhaps, that the existence of both is logically independent of the existence of the observing subject. Although from the existence of change the perception of change does not follow logically, it is clear that the existence of an observer follows analytically from the existence of the perception of change. At least, this follows logically with just one additional premise: if there is perception then there is an observer or perceiving subject. This premise is plausible. It is the phenomenological assumption that all perceiving is perceiving by some subject or other; a thesis Merleau-Ponty endorses, and which, perhaps, it does not make much sense to deny.

'Perception' is however ambiguous between 'what is perceived' and 'the perceiving of what is perceived'. Merleau-Ponty needs perception in the first of these two senses to be subject-dependent, in order to prove his Parmenidean thesis. If that kind of perception could be shown to be subject-dependent then Merleau-Ponty's Parmenidean thesis is proven, because; if what is perceived is subject-dependent and if change is perceived then change is subject-dependent. It follows that change is not subject-independent and so not part of the objective world. It follows that the objective world is changeless, or Parmenidean.

Although perception in the sense of 'the perception of what is perceived' is clearly subject-dependent, it is much less clear that perception in the sense of 'what is perceived' is also subject-dependent. The ambiguity here is between perceptual act and perceptual content. Perceptual acts are subject-dependent because they are mental and, plausibly, being mental is sufficent for being subject-dependent. However, being a perceptual content is logically consistent with being either subject-dependent or subject-independent. Although if C is some perceptual content then it logically follows that C is the object of some actual (or perhaps possible) perception it does not follow that C cannot or does not exist unperceived, or that when being perceived C would not exist if not perceived. Of course, *qua* perceptual content C is subject-dependent but C's properties may well not be exhausted by those constituting or constituted by C's subject dependence. There is nothing to suggest that any content is essentially or necessarily subject-dependent except in cases of self-perception. The fact that something is perceived is not logically sufficient for the subject dependence of what is perceived even if events are perceptually 'cut out' (PPT, 411) ('découpés' PP, 470) by a subject.

Merleau-Ponty is right to suggest that the event pairs that preoccupy us in the contemplation of causal relations are typically and paradigmatically event pairs that we have selected for scrutiny according to some tacit or explicit order of priorities governed by our pragmatic interests, or perceived pragmatic interests. This is an empirical claim that is by and large true.

Merleau-Ponty says 'time presupposes a view of time' (PPT, 411)[17] and concludes from this that, 'It is, therefore, not like a river, not a flowing substance' (PPT, 411).[18]

If we raise the question of how much of time is subject-dependent then Merleau-Ponty's answer is, *all of it*. This is a logical consequence of his view that '(the very notion of) event has no place in the objective world' (PPT, 411). Events are subjective, not objective. Time logically depends on events, or things that happen. If x is subjective then what depends on x is also subjective because 'depends on' is a transitive relation. It follows that if events are subjective then the whole of time is subjective if the whole of time depends on events. Although logically valid it is not clear that this argument is sound. This is because the first premise, 'events are subjective', may well be false.

Merleau-Ponty has the makings of an argument for the conclusion that at least part of time is subject-dependent. A premise is extracted from this familiar thought:

It is often said that, with things themselves, the future is not yet, the past is no longer, while the present, strictly speaking, is infinitesimal, so that time collapses. (PPT, 412)[19]

Views like these are discussed by Hobbes, Bergson, McTaggart and, as Merleau-Ponty says, St. Augustine and Leibniz (PPT, 412).[20]

Suppose we endorse the theses about the past and the future but reject the thesis about the present.

Then we have:

1 The past did exist but does not exist.
2 The future will exist but does not exist.

but

3 The present exists now so does exist.

Merleau-Ponty gives no analysis of 'past', 'present', and 'future' so I
suggest these:

1 'Past' means 'before now'.
2 'Future' means 'after now'.
3 'Present' means 'now' or 'when I am'.

'Past' does not mean just 'before' and 'future' does not mean just 'after'
because a pair of events ordered as before and after may occur in the
past or the future. Logically, if 'past' means 'before now' and 'future',
'after now' and 'present', 'when I am' then all of past, present and
future are subject-dependent. I do not mean to imply that there are no
events without subjects – that is Merleau-Ponty's view. But an event's
being a past event, a present event, or a future event is a property that
event has only in temporal relation to a subject. If an event happens
when I am then it is present, if it happens before when I am then it is
past, if it happens after when I am then it is future.

Merleau-Ponty does not see this because he assimilates too closely
together the concepts of before and after and the concepts of past, present and future. He fails to see that although 'before' and 'after' are
needed to define 'past' and 'future', 'past' and 'future' are not needed to
define 'before' and 'after' and a world of objective events could, and
arguably does, exist without thereby being objectively (subject-independently) ordered into past, present and future events. He could use a
famous argument of McTaggart's to conclude that the *temporality* of
before and after depend upon past, present and future.[21]

If the argument I have advanced is sound then Merleau-Ponty's subjectivism about time is too extreme when he says

Time is, therefore, not a real process, not an actual succession that I
am content to record. (PPT, 412)[22]

I hold that change, including beginning and ending, is mainly objectively real, as is duration. The only components of time for which I can

see sound arguments for holding to be subjective are past, present and future.

Merleau-Ponty says, about time, 'It arises from my relation to things' (PPT, 412).[23] As with most varieties of neo-Kantian subjectivism, it is not clear what 'things' ('les choses') we can be related with. The component of truth in Merleau-Ponty's subjectivism about time is that past, present and future do arise from our relations with 'things'. Those things, are however, events and the relations are temporal relations. Merleau-Ponty says,

> past, present and future exist only too unmistakably in the world, they exist in the present. (PPT, 412)[24]

It is an interesting philosophical question how we may have the concepts of past and future if we are only ever acquainted with the present and if past and future are only present. However, past and future cannot possibly be present, so Merleau-Ponty is just wrong here. Of course an event that was future may become present and then past but this is not what Merleau-Ponty has in mind. He is thinking of one event being past, present and future non-consecutively. But it is logically impossible for 'x was', 'x is' and 'x will be' to be true of an event non-consecutively even though they may be true consecutively. Even though it may be true of an event at any time, that it was past, is present and will be future it cannot be true of any event at any time that it is all of past, present and future. This is because past, present and future are not only collectively exhaustive but mutually exclusive temporal categories.

3 The supplement of time

How is a phenomenology of time possible? Merleau-Ponty argues that time may only be described phenomenologically if time constitutes itself, that is, if time makes itself be what it is. A phenomenology of time would be impossible if time could *per impossibile* be understood from a non-temporal point of view, and nothing non-temporal can constitute time:

> The upsurge of time would be incomprehensible as the creation of a supplement of time that would push the whole preceding series back into the past. That passivity is not conceivable. (VIT, 184)[25]

Merleau-Ponty deploys the concept 'supplement' to dispel a compelling but metaphorical view of how any philosophy of time is possible. In thinking of time as a whole one tacitly assumes one's own existence as an atemporal spectator of time as though, so to speak, temporal events were arranged before one or past events behind one.

The supplement of time is the putatively non-temporal subject apprehending time. This is a 'supplement' to time in many senses. It is prima facie something extra added to time: the putative possibility of the non-temporal intelligibility of time from a non-temporal 'position'. The supplement has paradoxical features. It is not just a supplement because if it were possible it would in a sense constitute time. Time would be its 'creation' (VIT, 184) 'création' (VI, 237). To see this, consider that the image of the past as a sequence of events 'behind' one is just an image: a present creation of the subject one is. Clearly, however, if something makes what it supplements what it is then this cannot be just or straightforwardly a supplement.

The supplement has the further paradoxical feature of being prima facie non-temporal yet entailing a kind of temporality. It is seemingly non-temporal because it occupies a site that is outside time: putatively something to which temporal predicates do not truly apply. Yet, the supplement is active in the constitution and the intelligibility of time. The supplement, if it were possible, 'would push' (VIT, 184) 'repousserait' (VI, 237) the time series into the past. It follows that the supplement would be engaged in constitutive activities like those of a Husserlian transcendental ego and those are themselves temporal activities. The idea of non-temporal constitution by the supplement of time is then paradoxical.

Merleau-Ponty takes it that these paradoxes in the concept of supplement cannot be overcome and so the whole model of time as viewed by an atemporal spectator has to be rejected. So too must the idea of a spectator who is both temporal and atemporal.

In this Merleau-Ponty eliminates two metaphysical possibilities which should be preserved. First, sense might be made of the non-temporal intelligibility of time by an observer who understood time, so to speak, all at once. Although what it understands takes time its understanding of time takes no time. Although temporal predicates truly apply to what the observer finds intelligible they do not truly apply either to the observer or its intelligibility. Second, although it is true that nothing can be globally both temporal and non-temporal there is no incoherence in supposing that something should be in some respects temporal and in other respects non-temporal: that some temporal predicates truly apply to it and some do not. (For example, perhaps 'before' and 'after' apply to it but not 'past', 'present' and 'future'. That is not a contradictory supposition.) Here, phenomenological description does not close the metaphysical possibilities it seems to.

Suppose that Merleau-Ponty is right in his view that the paradoxes of the supplement show that any atemporal view of time is incoherent. He is then right to draw the following inferences about any such view: 'The upsurge of time would be incomprehensible' (VIT, 184)[26] and 'That passivity is not conceivable' (VIT, 184).[27] This is not only because the incoherence of any thesis is a sufficient condition for its inconceivablity or (*vel*) incomprehensibility but also because time being fixed in the gaze of the atemporal supplement is inconsistent with one of the essential properties of time: its 'flow' ('surgissement' VI, 237). Merleau-Ponty is suggesting that it is incoherent to hold that time both flows and is passive or static and he is probably right in this. If so he is right about the unintelligibility of the conjunction of these two ideas.

Despite his critique of the supplement there is, ironically, nevertheless a sense in which time needs a supplement according to Merleau-Ponty:

On the other hand every analysis of time that views it from above is insufficient. (VIT, 184)[28]

He means that any thesis according to which the whole of time may be made intelligible by a non-temporal observer or from a non-temporal point of view is inadequate. The necessary supplement of time must be a temporal supplement of time: a 'supplément de temps' not just in the sense of a 'supplement of time' but also in the sense of a 'temporal supplement', a supplement of time to which temporal predicates apply:

Time must constitute itself – be always seen from the point of view of someone who is of it. (VIT, 184)[29]

Merleau-Ponty's strategy, then, is to endorse one part of the constitutive spectator view of the phenomenology of time, but to temporalise it. The constitution of time is a temporal process.

However, Merleau-Ponty still worries that the temporalisation of the subject and the subject's constituting activity may not escape the incoherence of the idea of a supplement of time:

But this seems to be contradictory, and would lead back to one of the two terms of the preceding alternative. (VIT, 184)[30]

The two terms of the preceding alternative are these: either there is a spectator of time who is not temporal, or there is a temporal spectator who is not a spectator of time, but not both. There was no method of reconciling these two theses on the non-temporal supplement of time thesis. Merleau-Ponty needs to find a way of reconciling them on his temporal supplement of time thesis. His solution is this:

> The contradiction is lifted only if the new present is itself a transcendent. (VIT, 184)[31]

4 *The transcendence of time*

We need to know what the new present is and what it is for the new present to be a transcendent.

The new present is the presence of the temporal supplement. This presence may be understood in the double sense of 'presence': the supplement is in the present in the sense of existing at the present time and time is present to – in the presence of – the temporal supplement. This is a 'new' present because it is one established by the temporalisation of the putative observer of time.

This present is not only a transcendent in the familiar phenomenological sense of exceeding any immediate consciousness of it but also in additional senses which Merleau-Ponty itemises. Notably:

> One knows that it is not there, that it was just there. (VIT, 184)[32]

This is the putative observation that if one tries to pay attention to the present time one finds it impossible to be conscious of it *qua* present but only as just having been. It follows from this property of presence that presence is a transcendent in the familiar phenomenological sense because the existence of this property entails that the present *qua* present cannot be wholly immediately intuited. The time when I am is never exactly the present time. Whenever I am, that time is never all and only the present time. This claim is controversial because arguably the present is just when I am (for some conscious subject) and 'present' means 'when I am'. Merleau-Ponty is not relying on the fact that the present is elastic (that the present time could be this century, this microsecond, today etc.) in establishing the thesis that either when I am exceeds the present or the present exceeds when I am. He is relying on the assumption that those events making up the apprehension of time happen at different times from those events making up apprehended time. This is a necessary condition for those prima facie numerically distinct sets of events not being the same events. That would be enough to show that my present was not exactly the same time as an apprehended present (even though there is no a priori reason why two wholly simultaneous sequences of events should not be numerically distinct).

Crucially, the present is not a time interval:

> It is not a segment of time with defined contours that would come
> and set itself in place. (VIT, 184)[33]

By 'defined contours' Merleau-Ponty means a datable or clockable
beginning or end. If so he is right about this because it is metaphysically
impossible to take, say, a stopwatch, set it at the finish of the past, let it
run only for the present, and stop it at the start of the future. (Unless
that is all anyone is ever able to do.)

5 Time constitutes itself

Having putatively shown the impossibility of an atemporal constitution
of time and having advanced the idea of a temporal subject as the right
'supplement' of time, Merleau-Ponty tries to show that this temporal
constitution of time is consistent with the thesis that time constitutes
itself, that, with regard to time, 'Il se constitue' (PP, 244).

To evaluate this purported consistency we need to know what it is for
time to constitute itself. In phenomenology if a constitutes b then a
makes b be what b is, so, if something constitutes itself it makes itself
be what it is. If time constitutes itself time makes itself be what it is.

Merleau-Ponty discusses the self-constitution of time in the context of
a critique of Husserl's phenomenology of internal time consciousness.
In particular Merleau-Ponty is sceptical about the role of receptivity in
Husserl because it seems to presuppose the existence of an ultimately
non-constituting element within the subject that constitutes time.
Merleau-Ponty agrees with Husserl that time constitutes itself but
thinks this truth is inconsistent with Husserl's postulation of receptivity.
Here is the agreement:

> H. is right to say that it is not I who constitute time, that it
> constitutes itself, that it is a *Selbsterscheinung*. (VIT, 190)[34]

But when Merleau-Ponty raises this question,

> What is the 'receptive' element of the absolute consciousness?
> (VIT, 190)[35]

he provides only this answer,

> The term 'receptivity' is improper precisely because it evokes a self
> distinct from the present and who receives it. (VIT, 190)[36]

Merleau-Ponty thinks it is false both that the subject is distinct from the present and that the subject receives the present.

Although Merleau-Ponty thinks it false that the subject exists at all and only at the same time as the present it constitutes, nevertheless there is a sense in which the present of the subject's constitution is partly the same time as the present of the time that is constituted: acts of constitution are partly simultaneous with constituted temporal items. Merleau-Ponty thinks Husserl's use of 'receptivity' commits him to the existence of a subject that is not temporal at all, or at least, not present.

Now, from the fact that some subject is passive or receptive with regard to time it does not follow that that subject is not itself temporal nor, indeed, present. There is no incoherence in the idea of temporal predicates, including the predicate 'is present' truly applying to a subject who passively apprehends or registers the present and in no way constitutes it in a quasi Husserlian or Kantian manner. It follows that Husserl is not logically committed to the position that Merleau-Ponty criticises. (It does not follow, of course, that Husserl is not independently committed to this position.)

Merleau-Ponty has the makings of a refutation of that position in his thesis that the constituting subject is partly simultaneous with the present it constitutes: if something is present then whatever is simultaneous with that thing is also present so if the constituted items are present and if the subject is simultaneous with those items then the subject is present. The trouble with this refutation is that it proves too much. Its conclusion is inconsistent with Merleau-Ponty's own thesis that the present of the subject does not coincide exactly with the present of the constituted present. The price of proving that the constituting subject is temporal is that it is simultaneous with what it constitutes if both are present.

Merleau-Ponty thinks it is false that the subject 'receives' the present and, again, ascribes this view to Husserl. Husserl insists that time is actively constituted by the subject but thinks this is logically consistent with the obtaining of a kind of receptivity. Merleau-Ponty's repudiation of receptivity is not only inconsistent with that view but also with any view on which time is not actively constituted but only 'received'. Two issues arise: whether there is a sense in which the subject is cognitively passive in respect to time and if so, whether this is logically consistent with the thesis that that subject is cognitively active with respect to time.

There is a clear empirical sense in which one is passive with respect to time. One apprehends the order in which events in time happen and notes them as before, after, simultaneous, partly simultaneous, beginning, ending. These orderings are experienced as not dependent upon their being apprehended even though theses in physics and phenomenology show the appearance of independence to be naive. Nevertheless, the ordinary experience of time is a kind of passivity that must be recognised as such. We could call this 'surface' passivity.

This surface passivity, which in the 'Notes de Travail', Merleau-Ponty is logically committed to rejecting, is consistent with the complex constitution of time in *Zür Phänomenologie des inneren Zeitbewusstseins*. We may read Husserl as providing an explanation of the possibility of surface passivity.

The receptivity in Husserl that Merleau-Ponty is seeking to refute is more profound. It is a putative property of absolute consciousness ('la conscience absolue' VI, 244). Despite Husserl's detailed characterisations of the subject's active constitution of time and despite his ascription of temporal properties to those constitutive acts it is true that Husserl thinks there is an ultimate non-temporal ground of time. This is not the transcendental ego because that has the temporal property of enduring as long as the subject endures. It is absolute consciousness. Absolute consciousness includes an awareness of time but is not itself temporal.

This idea is not ultimately incoherent, but the receptivity could not be a sequence of events. Absolute consciousness would have to apprehend temporal items all at once and not consecutively. Absolute consciousness would have to be the kind of atemporal apprehension of time that is sometimes ascribed to God.

Could time constitute itelf? Merleau-Ponty is clearly right that time's self constitution is inconsistent with its constitution by an atemporal subject, whether an atemporal supplement, a Husserlian absolute consciousness or a non-temporal God. This follows because if time is wholly or partly constituted by something non-temporal then time is constituted by something other than itself. (I leave aside the objection that it makes no sense to say that time is temporal and treat the claim as analytic.)

The questions now remain of whether Merleau-Ponty's thesis that time is constituted by the temporal constitutive acts of a temporal subject may be accuratey called 'time constituting itself' and whether the thesis could be true.

The designation seems to me appropriate if we take it to mean that that which makes objective time what it is is itself temporal and not non-temporal. By 'objective time' here I mean those properties of time that are prima facie subject-independent.

The thesis Merleau-Ponty has advanced is internally coherent so there is no a priori or logical obstacle to its essential truth. However, his account only functions as an explanation of objective time. It does not function as an account of the possibility of time as a whole. It is unlikely that time as a whole could be self-constituting: make itself be what it is. If we wish to know how time is possible we have to look outside time.

VIII

Subjectivity

Arguably, Merleau-Ponty's greatest contribution to philosophy is the thesis that subjectivity is physical, even if it was partly anticipated by Husserl and, even if, in the end, it should turn out to be false. However, Merleau-Ponty's account of bodily subjectivty does not exhaust his account of subjectivity and in this chapter I examine his attitude to Cartesian epistemology of the self and his attempts to distance himself from rationalist and empiricist theories of the self.

1 *The cogito*

The 'cogito' is the name sometimes given to the claim made by the seventeenth-century French philosopher and mathematician René Descartes: 'I think therefore I am.'[1] The word 'cogito' is, however, the Latin for 'I think'. It was Descartes' central philosophical project to find some item of knowledge which is so beyond doubt that it could provide the epistemological foundation of our knowledge. His philosophical method was to systematically call into question all the main kinds of knowledge he subscribed to. He doubts the existence of physical objects, the evidence of the senses generally, the truths of mathematics and science and the existence of God. He then happens upon a claim that he cannot truly doubt: the claim that he himself exists as made by him. He was doubting, and doubting is a kind of thinking, so if he thinks then he exists: I think therefore I am. The 'cogito' provides the requisite epistemological foundation and he proceeds to reconstruct our knowledge on its basis.

Merleau-Ponty is concerned to separate out what is true and what is false in the Cartesian cogito. To this end he makes a distinction between three separate interpretations of it:

> The cogito is either this thought which took place three centuries
> ago in the mind of Descartes, or the meaning of the books he
> has left us, or else an eternal truth which emerges from them.
> (PPT, 369)[2]

On the first interpretation, 'I think therefore I am' was a token thought
in the mind of Descartes. Its existence does not predate or postdate
Descartes' thinking it in the seventeenth century, and the thought exists
just so long as Descartes is thinking it.

On the second interpretation, 'I think therefore I am' is the propositional content of at least one sentence in at least one of Descartes'
books. This is to read Merleau-Ponty's 'meaning' (PPT, 369) ('sens' PP,
423) as 'propositional meaning' or 'what is expressed by at least one
indicative sentence'.

On the third interpretation, 'I think therefore I am' is 'an eternal
truth' (PPT, 369) 'une vérité eternelle' PP, 423). A truth, P, is eternal if
and only if P is true, P was true, P will be true and it was never the case
that P was false and it will never be the case that P is false. If P is an
eternal truth then P is true at all times. It seems to me not to follow
from this definition that P is a necessary truth. From the fact that P is
eternally true it does not logically follow that P could not have been
false; only that P is never false. If P is a necessary truth then not only is
P true but P could not have been false. P's being always true is not sufficient for this because P could be always true but contingent.

If that is what Merleau-Ponty means by 'eternal' (and it seems the
only plausible interpretation) then prima facie the claim that the cogito
is an eternal truth is inconsistent with the claim that it 'emerges' (PPT,
369) 'transparaît' (PP, 423) from Descartes' books. This is because
Descartes' books came into existence at datable times in the seventeenth
century in Europe but the cogito has always been true and, in that
sense, has always existed. If 'emerges' means 'began to exist' then this
inconsistency remains. If 'emerges' means anything like 'comes to be
recognised' or 'was expressed in language' then the inconsistency may
be removed. Clearly a truth may exist without being recognised or
expressed in language in the sense that what is the case is logically
independent of being recognised as the case or being reported as the
case.

It is not clear that the truth conditions for 'I think therefore I am' are
eternal but Merleau-Ponty does not notice the inconsistency and so
does not try to resolve it.

Merleau-Ponty's three interpretations of the cogito are not of the
same type. The idea that the cogito was a token thought of Descartes' is
a psychological claim about ontology of the cogito. The idea that it is
the meaning of part of a book is a semantic claim, and the idea that it is

an eternal truth is a claim about truth conditions. None of these, however, tells us what Merleau-Ponty thinks makes the cogito true. It does not tell us either, whether Merleau-Ponty thinks the cogito is necessary or contingent.

'I think therefore I am' is a truth-functional compound sentence containing the atomic sentences 'I think' and 'I am'. Now, it seems to me that 'I think' cannot possibly be a necessary truth and 'I am' cannot be a necessary truth. This is because it is not a necessary truth that anyone is thinking and it is not a necessary truth that anyone exists and there is no reason to suggest that I am any exception to this. There is no contradiction in the supposition that anyone is not thinking and there is no contradiction in the supposition that someone does not exist. If someone thinking is held not to think, or if someone who exists is held not to exist then those two facts are sufficient only to demonstrate the falsity of those two claims, not their incoherence.

It is hard to see how couching a fact in first singular person form could be sufficient to turn a contingent truth into a necessary truth when it is the same fact (proposition) that is expressed in both first and third person form. It is incoherent to maintain that a fact can be both contingent and necessary.

Claims like 'I am' and 'I think' are therefore contingent and not necessary truths. Their appearance of necessity is to be explained, I think, in the following way. 'I exist' is true just so long as it is *produced* and 'I think' is true just so long as it is *produced*. (I use 'produced' here to cover 'thought', 'said' 'written', etc.). It follows that these sentences exist just on condition that they are true. I call this feature of such sentences 'self-confirming' or 'self-verifying'.

Being self-confirming or self-verifying is not the same as being self-evident or necessary. P is self-evident if and only if perceiving the truth of P is a condition for understanding P. P is necessary if and only if not possibly not P. Clearly, however 'P is true if produced' is consistent with both 'P is understood but not perceived to be true' and 'not necessarily P', for example if P is never produced.

Merleau-Ponty has no analysis of the logic of the cogito but he does present something like an analysis of its truth conditions. He says:

> It is I who reconstitute the historical *cogito*, I who read Descartes' text, I who recognize in it an undying truth, so that finally the Cartesian *cogito* acquires its significance only through my own *cogito*.
> (PPT, 371)[3]

The first claim is uncontroversially empirical (so long as we read 'moi' in 'c'est moi qui reconstitute le Cogito Historique' (PP, 425) not to solipsistically preclude other reconstructions by persons other than Merleau-Ponty).

The second two claims are uncontroversial in a parallel way. The problem comes with the claim introduced by 'so that' (PPT, 371): 'Finally the Cartesian *cogito* acquires its significance only through my own *cogito*' (PPT, 371). This claim is a *non sequitur* and is in any case false. It is a *non sequitur* because it does not logically follow from the fact that Merleau-Ponty reads Descartes and reconstitutes the cogito in his own mind that the cogito is only significant through Merleau-Ponty's, or some contemporary person's thinking of it. Not only does this not follow in logic, but, arguably, a presupposition of Merleau-Ponty's reconstituting the cogito of Descartes is that the cogito in fact was significant earlier in Descartes' thinking of it. That historical fact is logically inconsistent with the cogito having significance ('sens' PP, 425) *only* in Merleau-Ponty's thinking of it.

There is, however, a deeper philosophical issue here: who, if anyone, does 'cogito' ('I think') have to be true of for the claim 'I think therefore I am' to be true? Merleau-Ponty, as we have seen, equivocates between Descartes and himself. The answer is, however, *anyone*.

'I think' is true of anyone who thinks it and it is an error to think that Descartes, or Merleau-Ponty, has to think 'I think' in order for 'I think' to be true. Someone has to think it but this need not be one person rather than another. If someone thinks 'I think' then the first person singular pronoun is given a referent. (I assume here that 'I' is a referring expression; the word that each person uses to refer only to himself or herself.) If someone thinks 'I think therefore I am' then both token occurrences of 'I' here have a referent; the same referent. Any referent capable of receiving the requisite first person singular psychological and existential ascription is adequate for the cogito to be true of someone.

A prior philosophical question, which Merleau-Ponty neglects, is, does the cogito have to be true of *anyone* in order to be true? It does not if it is construed as a logical truth equivalent to this conditional: if there exists something that thinks then that thing exists. The trouble is that construal does not capture the indexicality of the first person singular pronoun.

A formulation more adequate to the indexicality of the cogito is: if an 'I' user thinks then that 'I' user exists.[4] Because it is a logical truth, this sentence remains true whether the cogito is thought or not. It follows that the cogito does not have to be thought by Merleau-Ponty, nor by Descartes, nor by anyone else in order to be true. It is then true but not true of anyone.

Merleau-Ponty makes an autobiographical claim about his relation to the cogito. He says:

I should have no thought of it, had I not within myself all that is needed to invent it. (PPT, 371)[5]

Suppose by 'I should have no thought of it', is meant 'I should not have thought it', then this claim is true so long as 'all that is needed to invent it' carries the logical implication that any individual must possess all that is necessary to think the cogito if he thinks it. If x occurs then all the conditions necessary for x's occurrence must be met.

I suggested earlier that 'I think therefore I am' is true just on condition it is produced. If 'I think therefore I am' is produced by Merleau-Ponty that is sufficient for its truth. It follows that Merleau-Ponty is right to imply that the truth-conditions for the cogito are to be found 'within myself' (PPT, 371) 'En moi-même' (PP, 425).

'I think' is true if and only if some 'I' user thinks, and 'I exist' is true if and only if some 'I' user exists. 'I think therefore I am' is true if and only if if there is at least one 'I' user that thinks then there is an 'I' user that exists.

2 *Self-consciousness*

Merleau-Ponty thinks that the certainty, or the indubitability, of 'I think therefore I am' is due to an immediate and incorrigible self-consciousness each person has, not only of their own thought but of their own existence. Merleau-Ponty maintains that all thought is self-conscious thought, and all self-conscious thought is consciousness of one's own existence. It follows from this that all thought is, at least partly, a consciousness of one's own existence. Here is the claim that all thought is self-conscious and a putative justification of it:

All thought of something is at the same time self-consciousness, failing which it could have no object. (PPT, 371)[6]

The idea that thought is thought of something is the phenomenological intentionality doctrine which Merleau-Ponty endorses. Arguably, all thought is thought with content, or thought about, whether or not what any thought is thought about exists. It is difficult to make sense of the idea of thought with no subject matter.

Now, Merleau-Ponty's claim that thought is 'self-consciousness' ('conscience de soi') is ambiguous. It could mean that any thought is or involves the consciousness of a self, or it could mean that any thought is or involves the consciousness of that thought. Merleau-Ponty does not say which he means but the coherence of his text is maximised if he means both.

Taking the claim that all thought entails a consciousness of that thought first, it is not clear that this claim is true. Certainly from 'A is thinking about x' it does not logically follow that 'A is thinking about thinking about x', nor that 'A is thinking about thinking'. There is no contradiction in the supposition that some subject thinks about some (real or imaginary) object but does not thereby think about thinking, nor, *a fortiori* think about thinking about x. This is not a prerequisite for thinking about x 'consciously' if thinking about x 'consciously' means being conscious of x in thinking about x.

It is not necessary either that the whole of A's attention, so to speak, be absorbed by x but, if it is, this shows again that consciousness of thinking is not a condition for thinking.

There are compelling grounds for ruling out the possibility of being conscious of thinking a thought in thinking it. Not every thought could be a self-conscious thought in this sense because that would generate an infinite regress of necessary conditions. Being a self-conscious thought cannot be a prerequisite for being a thought.

If A is thinking about x then, to the extent that A is thinking about thinking about x, A is not thinking about x. If attention is a unitary phenomenon then thinking about x rules out thinking about anything other than x in thinking about x, including thinking about thinking about x.

A possible objection to this line of reasoning is that if A is thinking about thinking about x then A is thinking about x. This entailment does hold but whether what is entailed is true depends upon the point at issue.

Suppose Merleau-Ponty means by 'self-consciousness' (PPT, 371) ('conscience de soi' PP, 426) consciousness of a self, so that if a subject, A, thinks a thought then A is thereby conscious of A. Textual support may be added for this reading when Merleau-Ponty says:

> At the root of all our experiences and all our reflections, we find . . .
> a being which immediately recognises itself, because it is its
> knowledge both of itself and of all things, and which knows its own
> existence, not by observation and as a given fact, nor by inference
> from any idea of itself, but through direct contact with that
> existence. (PPT, 371)[7]

Now, from the fact that A is conscious it does not logically follow that A is conscious of A and from the fact that A is conscious of some object x it does not logically follow that A is conscious of A and from the fact that A is conscious of A's consciousness or conscious of A's consciousness of x it does not logically follow that A is conscious of A. There is no contradiction in the supposition that A is conscious of some thought that is in fact A's without being thereby conscious of itself as the subject of such consciousness.

3 *The subject of consciousness*

Merleau-Ponty is arguably right, however, to maintain that in so far as a subject is conscious of its own mental processes that subject is thereby conscious of itself. This is because the mental processes of a subject, including those mental processes constitutive of that subject's awareness of its own mental states, are partly constitutive of that subject. It follows that if a subject is aware of its own mental processes then it is aware of a part of itself and, in just that sense, aware of itself. It does not follow from this that it is aware of itself *qua* itself; only that it is itself that it is aware of.

This is part of the force of Merleau-Ponty's quasi-Hegelian claim that 'it (the subject) is its knowledge . . . of itself' (PPT, 371). Unlike Hegel, Merleau-Ponty cannot consistently maintain that that is all that a subject is because he holds that the subject of consciousness is physical; and no physical subject of consciousness is exhausted by its consciousness of itself.[8]

Merleau-Ponty here is asserting that a subject is partly constituted by the consciousness it has of itself. I am partly my awareness of myself. This is logically consistent with my being my body, or even, essentially my body, even though it does not follow that in being conscious of myself I am conscious of my body.

Even if from 'A is conscious' it does not follow that 'A is conscious of A' it may be independently true that a subject is a self-conscious subject, in the sense of being conscious of the subject that it is, and in the sense of being aware that it is the subject that it is aware of.

Merleau-Ponty maintains that each of us has a kind of non-perceptual awareness of our own existence. This is partly kinaesthetic, partly a consequence of the consciousness each of us has of his or her own mental states. I have argued that it is implausible to claim that this consequence is logical. Whether there exists a causal connection between the two kinds of self-consciousness seems to me an open but in the last resort empirical question. A necessary condition of such an empirical connection is the existence of both kinds of self-consciousness (because, logically, there are no relations without relata).

Merleau-Ponty says that the kind of consciousness a subject has of its own existence is 'not by observation' (PPT, 371) 'non pas par constatation' (PP, 426), 'nor by inference from any idea of itself' (PPT, 371) 'ou par inférence à partir d'une idée du lui-même' (PP, 426). He is not thereby ruling out these two kinds of self-consciousness, he is merely asserting that the kind of self-consciousness he has in mind is of a different type.

Clearly I may be self-conscious both by observation and by inference. For example, if I visually observe a part of my body then I am thereby conscious of myself because my body is at least a part of what I am. This is a kind of *self-consciousness* if I am conscious of my body and I know that I am (at least partly) my body. A being could in principle be conscious of the body that is its own without thereby being conscious that it is its own body that it is conscious of. We would rightly be reluctant to call this self-consciousness. Being conscious of oneself, the being that one is, is a necessary but not a sufficient condition for being self-conscious. If a being is conscious of itself and knows that it is itself that it is conscious of then that is sufficient for self-consciousness. On these a priori grounds it is coherent to suppose that there may be self-consciousness by observation. *A posteriori* this assumption is also clearly plausible.

I may be conscious of myself by inference from an idea of myself that I may have, so long as being conscious that I am may be construed as a kind of self-consciousness. If I have an idea of myself that is sufficiently accurate to be genuinely an idea of me, then it follows that I think at least one true thought about myself. I could in principle think a thought that is true of the person who in fact I am without thereby being aware that it is myself of whom I am thinking. In such a case although it would in a sense be true that I have an idea of myself this would not genuinely count as a case of self-consciousness: only of consciousness of self.

If I have an idea of myself and know that I am what that idea is of, it follows that I am thereby self-conscious. If I infer from this genuine idea of myself that I exist then I know that I exist by inference from an idea of myself. That there exists self-consciousness by inference from an idea of oneself is coherent. Whether there is such self-consciousness is, broadly, an empirical question.

4 *Immediacy*

I turn now to Merleau-Ponty's claim that I am 'a being which immediately recognises itself' (PPT, 371) and who knows of its own existence 'though direct contact with that existence' (PPT, 371).

Suppose if A 'recognises' A then A knows that A is, A knows that A is A and A may thereby also know further facts about A. This leaves it open what such recognition consists of psychologically, but we know that Merleau-Ponty has explicitly excluded two possibilities. Self-recognition is not self-knowledge by observation and self-recognition is not self-knowledge by inference from an idea of oneself.

Whatever this self-recognition consists in, Merleau-Ponty says it is immediate. 'Immediate' has several philosophical senses and Merleau-Ponty does not stipulate which he is employing.

'Immediate' may mean the opposite of 'mediate' or 'mediated' and so mean 'unmediated'. Then, if A has knowledge of x then what x is to A is not constituted by A's concept of x. On this construal, any quasi-Kantian doctrine on which the objects of knowledge are conceptually constituted makes knowledge mediate, mediated by concepts. Any rejection of this on which the objects of knowledge are known without conceptual intermediaries makes knowledge immediate.

'Immediate' may mean 'punctual' or 'instantaneous'. Then, if A knows x then A's coming to know x is a punctual event, an event without duration. Whether this notion of immediacy is coherent depends on whether the notion of instantaneous happenings is coherent.

A third construal of 'immediate' is: A knows x immediately if and only if A knows x and A does not have to know anything else in order to know x.

So, if Merleau-Ponty is right that there exists immediate self-recognition then either some subject A knows itself without thereby constituting itself conceptually, or A knows itself punctually, or A knows itself without thereby having to know anything other than A, or some combination of these.

The idea that a subject knows itself by 'direct contact' with its own existence is also open to interpretation. This could just mean that A knows that A exists by some method that is neither perception nor inference. Or, it could mean that A knows that A exists by being A. Both readings are borne out by this:

> Self-consciousness is the very being of mind in action. The act
> whereby I am conscious of something must itself be apprehended at
> the very moment at which it is carried out, otherwise it would
> collapse. (PPT, 371–2)[9]

This is partly the claim that all conscious acts are known to their agent but is also the view that in being conscious I am conscious of myself in a way that is neither by observation nor by inference. Suppose I am (partly) a mind in action. Merleau-Ponty is saying that the 'very being' of such a mind is self-consciousness, so what it consists in to be a functioning mind is to be a self-conscious mind. This is entailed by his view that every act of consciousness is a self-conscious act. One candidate for the method of self-knowing that is neither observation nor inference is introspective self-consciousness: being inwardly aware of one's own mental states and, thereby, one's existence.

Merleau-Ponty thinks of introspection as the exercise of a quasi-Kantian inner sense; as a temporal process whereby some subject, A, thinks a thought for the duration t1 . . . t2 and during part or the whole of that time A thinks another thought about that thought or has some cognitive (or doxastic) experience of that thought.

Merleau-Ponty does not deny that persons have thoughts about their own thoughts but he considers it doubtful that that is what every act of self-consciousness consists in.

First, he considers the view that the self-consciousness captured by the cogito is not a temporal process;

the cogito reveals to me a new mode of existence owing nothing to time. (PPT, 372)[10]

This is not simply a reiteration of the claim that the cogito is an 'eternal truth' but a claim about timelessness and self-knowledge.

Second, Merleau-Ponty considers the idea that 'the sole experience of the subject is the one which I gain by coinciding with it' (PPT, 373).[11] I take it that I 'coincide' with a subject if I am numerically identical with that subject.

It now sounds very much as though Merleau-Ponty is entertaining the idea of a kind of self-consciousness which is, or is derived from, *being* a subject, where the existence and even the derivation of this self-consciousness is not temporal.

Clearly, it is a necessary condition of my consciousness of some subject being a case of self-consciousness that I am numerically identical with that subject. If my consciousness of a subject is a case of self-consciousness it logically follows that I am numerically identical with the subject I am conscious of. However, my being numerically identical with some subject is not a sufficient condition for my being self-conscious. This is because my being numerically identical with some subject is logically consistent with that subject not being a self-conscious subject. In claiming that there is a kind of self-consciousness gained from being a person Merleau-Ponty has so far only isolated a necessary condition for self-consciousness and has not stated in what such self-consciousness wholly consists.

We should conjoin this prerequisite for self-consciousness with Merleau-Ponty's claim that 'self-consciousness is the very being of mind in action' (PPT, 371). Then, if I am numerically identical with a self-conscious mind then it logically follows that I am self-conscious. This argument is valid and arguably sound. We can read 'mind' here as 'something that has a capacity to think' and 'self-conscious' as; 'x is self-conscious if an only if x is conscious of x and x knows that it is what it is thereby conscious of'.

147

5 *The trace*

The only obscurity remaining is the putative timelessness of this kind of self-consciousness. Merleau-Ponty considers two possible theses about the relation between the cogito and time. Each includes a different claim about the temporality of the self.

The first possiblity is

1   To reduce experience to a collection of psychological events, of which the I is merely the overall name or the hypothetical cause. (PPT, 372)[12]

and the second possibility is

2   To recognise as anterior to events a field and a system of thoughts which is subject neither to time nor to any other limitation, a mode of existence owing nothing to the event and which is existence as consciousness. (PPT, 372)[13]

The first possibility (1) is clearly empiricist because it is a thesis about the self derived only from experience, and empiricism is the thesis that all knowledge is derived from experience. The second possibility (2) is clearly rationalist because it is a thesis about the self derived by rational reflection upon the presuppositions of thought, and rationalism is the thesis that all knowledge is acquired by rational thought.

Merleau-Ponty self-consciously pursues the Kantian project of criticising both empiricist and rationalist theses about the self. His criticism of the empiricist thesis is:

It is not clear how my existence is more certain than that of
anything, since it is no longer immediate, save at a fleeting instant.
(PPT, 372)[14]

The argument is: on the empiricist thesis my existence is not certain; but my existence is certain, therefore the empiricist thesis is false. This argument is certainly valid and if it is sound it is a refutation of Humean empiricism about the self.[15]

It is open to the empiricist to reply that I am nothing over and above my thoughts, but I am certain that I am thinking at least so long as I am thinking, therefore, I am certain that I exist; because I am that thinking. This would be be to deny the first premise of Merleau-Ponty's argument and so to deny its soundness.

Merleau-Ponty's objection to 2, the rationalist thesis, is, 'my mind is God' (PPT, 372)[16] but then 'the plurality of consciousnesses is

148

impossible' (PPT, 373).[17] His argument is that on the rationalist thesis there is only one mind, but there is a plurality of minds, therefore the rationalist thesis is false.

Again, Merleau-Ponty's argument is valid but is soundness is open to doubt. Spinozistic and Hegelian pantheism does logically entail that there is only one infinite or divine mind, but this is prima facie logically consistent with the existence of a plurality of finite minds. Merleau-Ponty has not proven that the rationalist thesis contradicts a true proposition and is therefore false.

Merleau-Ponty thinks that both the empiricist and the rationalist theories of the self are false. The two theories are mutually inconsistent and so at most one of them can be true and at least one of them is false.

The inconsistency between the two theories of the self concerns time. On the empiricist view I am identical with a totality of thoughts. It follows that the self has whatever temporal properties that totality of thoughts has. Suppose there exists a series of thoughts, T1, T2, . . . Tn over time t1 . . . t2. It is a consequence of the empiricist view that the self may exist intermittently. Suppose there exists a set of thoughts consisting of two subsets T1–T2 which occur from t1 . . . t2 and T3–T5 t3 . . . t6 respectively. Suppose there exists a time, t3, between t2 and t4 when no thought that is a member of either subset (or the set) occurs. Then, if a self is identical with this set of thoughts then this self exists at t1 . . . t2, and at t4 . . . t5 but not at t3. It follows that such a self has an intermittent existence.

On the rationalist view, however, either the self is eternal in the sense that no temporal predicate truly applies to it, or the self is eternal in the sense that the self exists at all times that its thoughts and experiences exist. The atemporal view is inconsistent with empiricism because it is logically impossible that a self should both exist at no time and exist at at least one time.

The second construal of the rationalist view is also inconsistent with the empiricist view if it is construed as the doctrine that the self is not reducible to its thoughts and experiences.

Merleau-Ponty's thesis that the self is a body-subject accepts from empiricism that the self is temporal and accepts from rationalism that the self is not reducible to its thoughts and experiences. It rejects the rationalist thesis that the self is atemporal and rejects the empiricist thesis that it is only its thoughts and experiences. Unless we were body-subjects which acted in the spatio-temporal world the conceptual resources used to formulate empiricism and rationalism would not be available to us. Empiricism and rationalism would be unthinkable.

IX

Freedom

The problem of freedom and determinism in philosophy may be formulated in different ways but one of them is this: If we are free then what we do is the outcome of our choices and we could refrain from doing what we do and do something else. If we are determined then all our actions are caused and, if caused events are inevitable, then we cannot do other than what we do and our freedom is illusionary. Prima facie, freedom and determinism are mutually inconsistent theories, so at most one of them is true and at least one of them is false. The problem of freedom and determinism is stating correctly whether human actions are free or determined.

1 *Freedom and necessity*

Merleau-Ponty says 'It is inconceivable that I should be free in certain of my actions and determined in others' (PPT, 434).[1] Now, this is not obviously right. Whether true or not it seems at least coherent to suppose that some of the actions are performed freely while others are necessitated by causes. This does not seem to be a self-contradictory supposition.

However, there is at least one definition of each of 'freedom' and 'determinism' on which it comes out as contradictory to hold that one and the same action is both free and determined. If an action is performed freely then it was possible not to perform it, and if that action was determined it was not possible not to perform it. It would be incoherent to maintain that one and the same action both could have not been performed and could not have not been performed. On the plausible supposition that logically impossible states of affairs are inconceivable, such an action is inconceivable. There seems no incoherence and so no inconceivability in the idea that some token action could have not been performed but some, numerically distinct, token action could not not have been performed by the same agent.

150

Merleau-Ponty does have the makings of an argument to show that it is at least false that some of a subject's actions are free and some determined.

Merleau-Ponty maintains that freedom is a presupposition of action. He talks for example about 'freedom being anterior to all actions' (PPT, 437).[2] He does not make explicit the reasons for this presupposition but an argument may be brought in its favour. There exists a distinction between two kinds of event: events which are *happenings* and events which are the *doings* of human subjects. One, and perhaps the only, way of marking the distinction between on the one hand what only happens and on the other hand what both happens and is done is to say that all and only what is done is performed freely.

Irrespective of the force of this distinction Merleau-Ponty is right to maintain that it is inconceivable that actions should be determined if freedom is a presupposition of action. This inconceivabily rests on the inconceivabily of the compatibility of freedom and determinism when those two theories are defined as mutually inconsistent.

The view that it is false that I am free in some of my actions, but not all, because I am determined in others relies on establishing that I am free in all my actions.

I am free in all my actions, freedom and determinism are mutually inconsistent theories, therefore, it is not the case that I am determined in any of my actions. As it stands the argument is just valid. It is sound so long as freedom and determinism are incompatible and the first premise can be proven.

However, Merleau-Ponty's formulation is less clear-cut. He says:

1   Once I am free, I am not to be counted among things.
    (PPT, 435)

2   I must then be uninterruptedly free. (PPT, 435)

therefore

3   One cannot be to some extent free. (PPT, 435)[3]

I read this this way:

1   I am free and if I am free I am not a thing (and only things are determined).
2   Therefore any action of mine is free (and there is not a time when I am not free).

therefore,

151

3 I am not free in some of my actions but not others.

Construed this way, with suppressed premises added, Merleau-Ponty has a valid argument. Again, its soundness is only as strong as its premises and the first premise in particular needs argument.

Merleau-Ponty sometimes talks as though the subject is free because the subject is not a thing ('une chose') but he sometimes talks as though the subject is not a thing because the subject is free. For example he says

> In order to be determined . . . by an external factor, it is necessary
> that I should be a thing. (PPT, 434)[4]

The implication is that I am not a thing and so not determined. However, 1 above was 'Once I am free, I am not to be counted among things' (PPT, 435) the implication this time being that I am free and not determined and so not a thing.

There is no incoherence in this, just circularity. It could be that if x is free then x is not a thing and if x is not a thing then x is free. However, in the argumentative order of priorities, Merleau-Ponty either needs to show that the subject is not a thing and derive the freedom of the subject from that, or, he needs to show that the subject is free and derive the conclusion that the subject is not a thing from that.

It is the first course that Merleau-Ponty adopts. He takes it that he has shown by his phenomenology of the body (see Chapters II and III of the present work) that a person is a conscious body-subject, not a mechanical physical object. In Merleau-Ponty's view it is not so much being physical which in Merleau-Ponty's view is incompatible with being causally determined as being a subject and being conscious. Merleau-Ponty regards consciousness as being essentially, or necessarily, free. He says:

> Nothing determines me from outside, not because nothing acts on
> me, but, on the contrary, because I am from the start outside myself
> and open to the world. (PPT, 456)[5]

Here Merleau-Ponty draws an important distinction between causation and determinism. Something 'acts on me' (PPT, 456) ('me sollicite' PP, 520) if and only if something other than me causes some action of mine with a probability of more than zero but less than one, but something 'determines me' (PPT, 456) ('me détermine' PP, 520) if and only if something other than me causes some action of mine but with a probability of one, that is, with necessity.

Merleau-Ponty rightly implies that causation is not logically sufficient for determinism, only logically necessary. Merleau-Ponty characterises our existential situation in two ways. He says 'I am from the start outside myself' and he says he is 'open to the world' (PP, 520). We know that these two characterisations carry the implication that I may be caused but not determined to act.

Merleau-Ponty has no argument for the view that the causes I may be subject to cannot be determining causes. A priori if A causes B then there seems no incoherence in the supposition that if A happens then the probability of B is one. Determinism may be false, but Merleau-Ponty has not proven that the subject is of such a nature that it can be caused but not determined.

When he says he is 'open to the world' he means he is a consciousness that exhibits intentionality. When he says he is 'outside' himself he means he is an agent whose behaviour is teleological, or goal directed.

Some considerations may be adduced for the view that a teleological consciousness may not be wholly determined, even if caused. For example a teleological consciousness alters its own behaviour in the light of perceived and changing goals and so to that degree is self-determining. If A is self-determining then that is potentially logically inconsistent with the complete determination of A by causes outside A. If every action of A is an event necessitated by some cause extraneous to A then that leaves no logical room for A to be, or to be even among, the causes of A's behaviour.

The concept of overdetermination is not incoherent. Suppose E has two causes, C1 and C2, each of which is sufficent for E and each of which occurs. If C1 occurs then E occurs and if C2 occurs then E occurs but if either C1 but not C2 occurs or C2 but not C1 occurs then E nonetheless occurs.

A potential incoherence in the present case arises from the special circumstance of A's being (or being among) the causes of A's action. Suppose C is some external cause of A's action. But suppose further that A is the cause of A's actions. It follows that A may be the cause of some action of A's only if A is the cause of exactly what C causes to happen. It is incoherent to suppose that C and A are both the cause of a single event and thereby cause something qualitatively distinct to happen. Where overdetermination is true then Merleau-Ponty may coherently maintain that there is both external causation and self determination of an action. The inconsistency arises only where the subject determines his or her actions in directions other than effected by external causes. Merleau-Ponty could avoid this by pointing out that the external causes of self-determining actions are not determining.

2 *Self-determination*

We should examine more closely Merleau-Ponty's notion of freedom as self-determination. He says: 'we have indeed always the power to interrupt' (PPT, 438).[6] We have the ability to intervene in the course of our own actions.

Suppose I perform some set of (mental or physical) acts then, on this view, it is within my power to halt these at any point and to initiate (or resume) some other set of actions. It is just this possibility Merleau-Ponty has in mind when he says this power to interrupt 'implies in any case a power to begin' (PPT, 438).[7]

That I have the power to intervene in the course of my own actions must be an empirical and not an a priori fact because it is not something I can know about myself independently of my experience of myself. If all knowledge is either a priori or empirical, but not both, and if we know we intervene in our own actions, then we must know this empirically.

Merleau-Ponty attempts to refute a number of objections to the possibility of human freedom. They are the ideas that my actions determine me, my temperament determines me, the fact that I am subject to weakness of will, and finally, that there are physical constraints on my action.

On the first point, Merleau-Ponty says:

If, as is often said, motives incline me in a certain direction, one of two things happens: either they are strong enough to force me to act, in which case there is no freedom, or else they are not strong enough, and then freedom is complete and as great in the worst torments as in the peace of one's home. (PPT, 435)[8]

It is wrong that one's motives being, or being amongst the causes of one's actions should be considered a constraint on one's freedom. If I act from my own motives, rather than, for example, those of another or from some external cause then that is arguably part of what my being free consists in. There can be little doubt, however, that when Merleau-Ponty says. 'Motives incline me in a sense' he means the agent's own motives.

Merleau-Ponty next presents two possibilities which he takes to be mutually exclusive and collectively exhaustive. The first possibility is motives 'have the force to make me act' and in that case 'there is no freedom', and the second possibility is that 'they do not have it' and in that case 'it [freedom] is complete'.

Suppose some motive is a cause of some action of mine, then Merleau-Ponty is saying if the motive occurs then either it necessitates or does not necessitate the action. If it necessitates the action then I do not have the option not to perform that action. If the motive does not necessitate the action then I have the option either to perform it or not to perform it. Construed that way Merleau-Ponty has said something true. To see that this is right, consider the case where if the motive obtains then it necessitates the action. Then the action cannot not occur given the motive, and it would be contradictory to maintain that the action does not occur, on the grounds that the agent refrains from performing it. However, if the motive does not necessitate the action then there is no contradiction in the supposition that the agent performs the action or refrains from performing the action.

These arguments are sufficient to show that Merleau-Ponty has presented two possibilities that are mutually exclusive. Logically, he is right that if my motives are determining then I am not free, but if my motives are not determining then I may be free. Merleau-Ponty jumps to a conclusion too hastily when he says freedom is complete. Clearly, my motives being non-determining is logically consistent with my actions being determined by causes other than my motives.

We should examine now the question of whether the two possibilities are collectively exhaustive. They are if and only if, if I am not determined then I am free and if I am not free then I am determined (or both, but that has been ruled out). (Two possibilities, P and Q, are collectively exhaustive if and only if if not P then Q and if not Q then P (or both P and Q).)

Suppose some motive is a cause that determines some action of mine (it has 'la force de me faire agir' PP, 497) and so if that motive obtains then the probability of my acting (by that action) is one. Suppose, however, conversely, no motive of mine determines any action of mine, and that my freedom is complete ('elle est entière' PP, 497). It is logically right that if my action occurs with the probability of one then that action does not occur with any probability of less than one. However, if I am free then that action occurs with some probability less than one. This is because if an action is performed freely then it could have not been performed and that is only possible if the probability of its occurrence is less than one. Clearly, in any case, anything that happens either happens with a probability of one or a probability of less than one. This is sufficient to show that Merleau-Ponty is right to maintain that the two possibilities are collectively exhaustive.

When Merleau-Ponty says that if his freedom is complete it is 'as great in the worst torments as in the peace of one's home' he is suggesting that one's freedom may admit of degrees.

The form of the argument here is this: if I am free then my freedom does not admit of degrees. My freedom does admit of degrees, therefore, I am not completely free.

Merleau-Ponty takes it as intuitive that there exist degrees of freedom; that a person under torture is not as free as a person in the peace of their home. That is intuitive. The question is whether the idea of degrees of freedom is coherent.

Suppose the probability of A's doing x is less than one but greater than zero, then it follows that A's doing x is not determined and that (on the present analysis) is a necessary condition for A's doing x freely. It is logically consistent with the probability of A's doing x being less than one that A not do x, and it follows from that that A is free. To model the idea of degrees of freedom we need the idea of an action of A's being partly caused by A and partly caused by causes external to A. This is an idea Merleau-Ponty accepts. Then we have two causal chains issuing in x: one chain external to A and one chain internal to A. If the probability of x's occurrence is greater given both chains than just the chain external to A then A's freedom to do x is greater than if the probability of x given the external chain were not raised by the internal chain.

Merleau-Ponty next considers the possibility that my actions are determined by my temperament and so I am not free. Prima facie it is a mistake to construe this as an objection to freedom. If my temperament is part of what I am, and if my being free partly consists in my being (or being among) the causes of my own actions, and if my temperament causes (some of) my actions, then to that extent I am free, not determined.

Merleau-Ponty's reply to the objection is:

> My temperament exists only for the second order knowledge that
> I gain about myself when I see myself as others see me. In so far as
> I recognise it, confer value upon it, and in that sense, choose it.
> (PPT, 435)[9]

There are several claims here. One is the quasi-Hegelian thesis that part of what I am is a product of a self-reflection that employs concepts gleaned from a third person or 'objective' perspective on the person. One idea is that one's self-conception partly consists in thinking of oneself as others perceive and think of one. Another is: this is *all* that my temperament consists in. Both claims need argument.

It seems empirically right that the self-conception each of us has is partly modelled on the conception we each have of others, partly on the conception others have of us and partly on the conception we have of the conception others have of us. These thoughts have been examined at great length by Hegel and thoughts rather like them have been expressed by Nagel.[10]

Merleau-Ponty's other claim that my temperament 'exists only 'for this knowledge is harder to prove because my having third person or 'objective' epistemological access to my own temperament is logically consistent with two further facts or putative facts: I may have first person singular access to my own temperament (or at least part of it) and, my temperament may cause whatever kind of epistemological access I have to it. The existence of temperament is logically independent of knowledge of it. Merleau-Ponty wishes to rule out these latter two possibilities but he has no argument which does so.

Nor does Merleau-Ponty have an argument for the neo-Sartrean view that I 'choose' my temperament.

I recognise it, confer value upon it, and in that sense choose it. (PPT, 435)[11]

From the fact that I recognise and value my temperament it does not logically follow that I choose it. That is consistent with, and arguably entails its prior existence.

If I choose my temperament then Merleau-Ponty is right to maintain that my temperament may still be among the causes of my actions, but he misses the point that they may be free. If A chooses A's temperament freely then A might not have had that temperament (because A may have chosen otherwise). Given that, A's action may not have had A's actual temperament as its cause. If A freely chooses the cause of A's own actions then that rules out their being externally determined. Then, if A perfoms them, they are performed freely.

Merleau-Ponty next considers weakness of will as a putative objection to freedom. Normally the philosophical problem of weakness of will is thought to be the difficulty of making sense of the fact that we sometimes fail to do what we want to do when we are able to do it and even when we think it is right to do it. Merleau-Ponty has rather a different problem in mind when he uses the expression 'weakness of will' (PPT, 436) ('l'impuissance de la volonté' PP, 498):

And indeed, although I can will myself to adopt a course of conduct and act the part of a warrior or a seducer, it is not within my power to be a warrior or seducer with ease and in a way that 'comes naturally'; really to *be* one, that is. (PPT, 436)[12]

He is considering the case where someone tries to be a particular sort of person by sheer act of will. There is an important insight here. There would seem to be very little that I can do *just* by an effort of will. It is a quasi-Wittgenstein thought that I cannot move my arm off the table just by an act of will: I move my arm by moving my arm.[13] Merleau-

Ponty makes an analogous point here: by willing myself to be a person of a certain kind I do not thereby become that kind of person. As Merleau-Ponty puts it:

> Neither should we seek freedom in the act of the will, which is, in its very meaning, something short of an act. (PPT, 436)[14]

Merleau-Ponty is right not to identify freedom with a kind of inner trying. Freedom is doing with the possibility of not doing and that is consistent with his conception of the body-subject as being-in-the-world.

Merleau-Ponty finally considers the putative physical obstacles to freedom. He maintains that the existence of freedom is a necessary condition for the existence of constraints on freedom. For example he says:

> Even what are called obstacles to freedom are in reality deployed by it. An unclimbable rock face, a large or small, vertical or slanting rock, are things which have no meaning for anyone who is not intending to surmount them, for a subject whose projects do not carve out such determinate forms from the uniform mass of the in itself and cause an orientated world to arise – a significance in things. (PPT, 436)[15]

Although these are Sartrean thoughts that Merleau-Ponty presents, Merleau-Ponty does not avail himself of a very important Sartrean distinction which is of use to him here. Sartre distinguishes my freedom from my power.

For Sartre, my freedom is my capacity to make choices and according to Sartre everybody is always free in that sense. However, Sartre thinks there are many things, includings physical things, that are not within my power. (Many commentators on Sartre miss this distinction and ascribe to him an exaggerated view of freedom.)

Merleau-Ponty agrees with Sartre that the physical world is perceived by the subject as a set of means and obstacles to the fulfilment of that subject's projects. The world is perceived, in the Heideggerian sense, as 'ready to hand'.

In what sense do constraints on freedom presuppose freedom? When he says the constraints are 'deployed' by freedom he means the subject constitutes the objects as constraints and does so freely, that is, with the possibility of not doing so. Merleau-Ponty recognises that from the fact that a physical constraint is constituted by consciousness it does not follow that it is not a physical constraint. These constraints on freedom, the one's that freedom deploys are, however, the only constraints on freedom. He says:

> There is, then, ultimately nothing that can set limits to freedom, except those limits that freedom itself has set in the form of its various initiatives. (PPT, 436)[16]

It follows that the subject is partially self-constraining. The exercise of freedom ironically generates its own constraints. This is true of every action of the subject, not just physical action but also perceptual synthesis. This is why Merleau-Ponty says 'the subject has simply the external world that he gives himself' (PPT, 436).[17]

If, as Merleau-Ponty maintains, the external world is constituted by the projects of the subject then a kind of Kantian constitutive idealism is true, albeit of a highly pragmatic kind. This raises the question of what the world is really like, independently of its constitution through the projects of human subject. Merleau-Ponty's answer is this:

> The world in itself . . . without freedom, would be merely an amorphous and unnamable mass. (PPT, 439)[18]

Freedom is a condition for synthesis and synthesis is a condition for the world being as it appears to a subject so freedom is a condition for the empirical world.

Interestingly, although Merleau-Ponty is a phenomenologist he is committed here, more or less overtly, to the existence of a Kantian thing-in-itself. Husserl and Sartre, following Hegel, claim that phenomenology is possible without the thing-in-itself. This view is certainly mistaken and Merleau-Ponty is more consistent than the other phenomenologists when he sees the need to postulate some reality that is conceptually constituted. If we ask 'What reality?' then that question is as metaphysically awkward for the phenomenologists as for Kant. Of Merleau-Ponty's answer one may ask 'How could this be known?'

3 Compatibilism

Merleau-Ponty's considered view on freedom and determinism is a version of compatibilism. He holds that we are caused, but free, and not determined but constrained:

> What then is freedom? To be born is both to be born of the world and to be born into the world. The world is already constituted, but also never completely constituted; in the first case we are acted upon, in the second we are open to an infinite number of

possibilities. But this analysis is still abstract, for we exist in both ways at once. There is, therefore, never determinism and never absolute choice. (PPT, 453)[19]

In the subject's being-in-the-world there is a reciprocal relationship between subject and world. The world constitutes the subject but the subject constitutes the world. The subject makes the world what it is and the world makes the subject what it is. This is consistent with human freedom because in constituting the world it is open for the subject to act otherwise. Although the world constitutes the subject the world does not necessitate the actions of the subject. Although there is causation, there is no determinism.

Merleau-Ponty says his account is 'still abstract' (PPT, 453) 'encore abstraite' (PP, 517). Two things are abstract if they may be separated in thought but not in reality. Although we may conceive of the world as acting on the subject without thereby conceiving of the subject as acting on the world (and vice versa) we are not thereby conceiving a real possibility. The reciprocal dependence between subject and world is existential. It is instantiated in the existence in the world of a human subject: in being-in-the-world. It is the inextricability of the subject's being from being-in-the-world, and the inseparability in reality of the constitution and the constituting of the subject that has this result:

> It is impossible to determine precisely the 'share contributed by the situation' and the 'share contributed by freedom'. (PPT, 453)[20]

We should not confidently stipulate this a priori. If we can devise sufficiently precise criteria for the individuation of causes and effects the contribution of subject and world may be empirically discerned as separate.

Merleau-Ponty rightly thinks his compatibilism is consistent with his thesis that a person is a body-subject. He says 'I am never a thing and never a bare consciousness' (PPT, 452).[21]

However, caution is needed here. Consciousness with freedom, the physical world with determinism should not be too closely assimilated. The existence of consciousness (or 'pure consciousness' ('conscience nue')) is logically consistent with determinism, and the existence of the physical world (or even only a physical world) is logically consistent with the existence of freedom.

4 The refutation of determinism

Merleau-Ponty's arguments against determinism in *La Structure du Comportement* are deeply embedded in his attempted refutations of behaviourism and materialism in psychology and philosophy. Perhaps because of this, he tends to assimilate these three views when they need to be carefully distinguished.

Determinism is the conjunction of the theses that every event has a cause and caused events are made inevitable by their causes.

Behaviourism in psychology is the thesis that the appropriately scientific subject matter of psychology is behaviour. Behaviour is scientifically explicable because it is publicly observable and environmentally determined.

Behaviourism in philosophy ('analytical behaviourism' or 'logical behaviourism') is the thesis that mentality may be reduced to behaviour: either overt and occurrent bodily and verbal behaviour or dispositions to behave. Here 'reduced' means: as are reducible to bs if and only if any sentence or set of sentences about as may be translated, without loss of meaning, into a sentence of set of sentences about bs.

Materialism is the philosophical thesis that everything that exists is physical.

Merleau-Ponty thinks, rightly, that Behaviourism in psychology logically entails determinism and he thinks, wrongly, that materialism in philosophy logically entails determinism. He also tends to assume that behaviourism in psychology is a kind of materialism which, in a very loose sense, it is. It only deals with physical subject matter. It would be wrong, however, to hold that it entails materialism.

To understand the kind of determinism that Merleau-Ponty seeks to refute we need to understand what he means by 'cause'. He says,

> The cause is the necessary and sufficient condition of the effect considered in its existence and in its nature. (SCT, 161)[22]

This means that C is the cause of an effect E if and only if if not C then not E and if C then E. Merleau-Ponty misses that if C is necessary for E then E is sufficient for C and if C is sufficient for E then E is necessary for C and that if C is necessary and sufficient for E then E is necessary and sufficient for C. This is damaging to his definition of 'cause' because it obliterates the distinction between cause and effect. On some ontology it might be right to obliterate this distinction but on his ontology there is a distinction between cause and effect.

There are several ways of retrieving Merleau-Ponty's position. A distinction could be drawn between on the one hand the conditions necessary for the occurrence of E considered singularly, call them the members of the set 'C': {c1 . . . cn}, and, on the other hand, the conditions necessary for the occurrence of E considered jointly, call them just the set 'C'. Then we may advance the thesis that each member of {c1 . . . cn} is singularly necessary for E but {c1 . . . cn} are jointly sufficient for E. Then we read 'cause' as 'necessary and sufficient condition' as ambiguous between 'each of the conditions considered singularly' and 'all of the conditions considered jointly'. Then 'necessary condition' ascribes a property to each member of {c1 . . . cn} and 'sufficient' ascribes a property to all of {c1 . . . cn}.

Alternatively, Merleau-Ponty could simply drop the claim that the 'cause is a necessary condition' but retain the claim that it is 'sufficient' ('suffisante'). This would have two advantages. It is the putative fact that causes are sufficient conditions for their effects that is necessary for the determinist thesis that caused events are inevitable. So, by adopting this strategy, Merleau-Ponty rules out an essential component of determinism. If he drops the thesis that causes are necessary conditions for their effects then he logically drops everything that is entailed by this, including the consequence that effects are sufficient conditions for their causes. This drops too much because Merleau-Ponty thinks there are causes, but not determining causes.

Merleau-Ponty says that a cause causes both the existence and the nature of an effect. If C is the cause of E then C is both necessary and sufficient for E being and being what E is.

Merleau-Ponty's objections to determinism are of three main kinds: he argues that the essentially situated being of human beings, their being-in-the-world, is inconsistent with determinism. He argues that there are no one–one correlations between single human actions as effects, and occurrences in the external world as causes and, finally, he argues that to regard human actions as the results of determining external causes is to wholly disregard the role of what is internal to the organism in making its actions what they are. These three lines of argument are not always clearly distinguished from one another in Merleau-Ponty's text.

The relations between a body-subject and the world in being-in-the-world which are prima facie causal are not to be understood as mechanical 'mécanique(s)' (SC, 174) but as dialectical 'dialectique(s)' (SC, 174)

> In describing the physical or organic individual and its milieu, we have been led to accept the fact that their relations were not mechanical but dialectical. (SCT, 160)[23]

We need to know now exactly in what the mechanical/dialectical distinction consists.

Some cause, C, and some effect, E, are a mechanical cause and a mechanical effect if and only if both, C determines E but E does not determine C, and every component of C that is causally efficacious on E stands in a one–one mapping with some resulting component of E. Merleau-Ponty means that if C determines E then E does not determine

C in the case of mechanical causation when he says that 'the dependence is uni-directional' (SCT, 160–1) 'la dependence est à sens unique' (SC, 174) and he asserts the one–one mapping between causal parts and resultant parts when he says,

The cause and the effect are decomposable into real elements which have a one-to-one correspondence. (SCT, 160)[24]

Some elements, A and B, are dialectically related if and only if both A determines B and B determines A and if neither A nor B is analysable into discrete causally efficacious components which stand in a mutual one–one correlation. If it makes sense to speak of dialectical relations as causal this is because they are holistic not atomistic, and reciprocal not one-way.

It is also part of the concept of a 'dialectical relation' that dialectical relations are dynamic not static. This means that if A determines B and B determines A such that A and B make each other what they are, then A is not only altered by B but A is altered by B *qua* determinant of B and B is not only altered by A but B is altered by A *qua* determinant of A. It follows that relata that are dialectically related perpetually alter one another *qua* determinants of one another, so long as the dialectical relation obtains. It further follows that it makes sense, derivatively, to speak of A making A what A is via B or B making B what B is via A because if A determines B *qua* determinant of A then A determines A by determining B *qua* determinant of A and if B determines A *qua* determinant of B then B determines B by determining A *qua* determinant of B.

It follows from these definitions that no relation is both mechanical and dialectical because it would be contradictory to affirm either that some relation was both one-way and reciprocal or both constituted by relata that admitted of analysis into causally efficacious components and did not, or both. It follows that if a relation is mechanical it is not dialectical and if a relation is dialectical it is not mechanical. It has been shown, then, that the two kinds of relation are mutually exclusive (but not that they are collectively exhaustive of relation types or even causal relation types).

5 *The dialectic of freedom*

We need to examine next Merleau-Ponty's grounds for repudiating mechanistic explanations of human behaviour and endorsing a kind of dialectic.

In his view there is a sense in which it is false that identifiable parts of the human being respond to external stimuli even though it makes sense to speak of human actions as responses to stimuli. Merleau-Ponty is aware that a person's eyes may be made to dilate by the shining of a light into them, or a person's blood-pressure may be raised by diet or stress but he does not count responses of this type as actions. Action, or behaviour, is something performed by the whole person and not by parts of the person. This is what Merleau-Ponty means when he says 'physical stimuli act upon the organism only by eliciting a global response' (SCT, 161).[25]

Although Merleau-Ponty fully allows that actions performed by the whole person may have external causes and even allows that 'a global response [. . .] will vary qualitatively when the stimuli vary quantitatively' (SCT, 161),[26] nevertheless, such external causes are not deterministic causes. They are what he calls 'occasions' (SCT, 161) 'occasions' (SC, 174).

Merleau-Ponty does not define 'occasion' when he says of such putative external causes 'they play the role of occasions rather than that of cause' (SCT, 161)[27] but a definition may be suggested. As we have seen, a deterministic cause is a sufficient condition for an effect. Whether a given effect happens depends upon whether a deterministic cause of it happens. There is nothing incoherent in the idea that any given effect should have more than one deterministic cause because the concept of overdetermination is free from internal contradiction. Deterministic causes determine whether their effects happen because if a deterministic cause of an event happens then that event happens, but if no deterministic cause of an event happens then that event does not happen. If a deterministic cause happens then something sufficient for an effect has happened. If no deterministic cause has happened then nothing sufficient for an effect has happened.

I suggest that if some event is correctly called the 'occasion' of some effect then it determines not whether that effect will happen but when it will happen. Occasions are triggers or precipitants of events which are the effects of causal chains that lie elsewhere. They just determine the timing of events and it does not much matter whether we decide to apply or withold the name 'causes' from occasions so conceived. (Merleau-Ponty *contrasts* occasions with causes.)

According to Merleau-Ponty it is the human agent who is the cause of his or her own actions and external causes at most determine the timing of those actions. External causes do not determine whether or how an agent will act and in so far as they are causes of actions at all, this depends upon how they are 'taken' by the agent: the meaning the agent attaches to them. For example, Merleau-Ponty says,

> The reaction depends on their vital significance rather than on the material properties of the stimuli. Hence, between the variables upon which the conduct actually depends and this conduct itself

there appears a relation of meaning, an intrinsic relation. (SCT, 161)[28]

It follows that for Merleau-Ponty no token physiological input to the organism is causally sufficient for the occurrence of any token action of that organism *qua* agent. Why should we believe this?

Merleau-Ponty regards deterministic psychology as a scientific failure. It has proven impossible to predict human actions on the basis of a knowledge of external stimuli. Merleau-Ponty presumably thinks that if there were one–one correlations between stimuli types and behaviour types then it would have been possible to predict human behaviour given knowledge of its causes. The fact that such predictions have not been forthcoming suggests that the determinisitic picture is a failure.

Given the failure of deterministic psychology, Merleau-Ponty may be read as providing an explanation of that failure. If something internal to the organism mediates between physiological input and behavioural output then we would not expect to be able to predict human actions given knowledge only of stimuli external to the organism. What is internal to the organism makes a difference to physiological input, behavioural output, and the relations between them.

The way the agent reacts to an external stimulus depends on the 'significance' 'signification' or 'meaning' 'sens' (SCT, 161, SC, 174) the agent bestows on it. What is that?

A stimulus is never presented to an agent *qua* physiological stimulus, but always *qua* part of the human world, or what Merleau-Ponty calls 'L'ordre humain' (SC, 175) 'the human order' (SCT, 162). Following Husserl, Merleau-Ponty says the agent perceives the environment as made up of 'use-objects' (SCT, 162) '"objets d'usage" (Gebrauchob-jekte)' (SC, 175). The world is a human constituted world, not a purely natural world. It follows that human beings are not made what they are by purely natural causes. Self and world are mutually constituting.

X

Language

Merleau-Ponty argues that his phenomenology of language overcomes a number of dualisms in philosophy. As we have seen, he thinks of the body as 'a unity distinct from that of the scientific object' (PPT, 174).[1] The human person is essentially an *expressive* being and the use of language is just one part of this expression. He hopes that this holistic view will enable him to dispense with 'the traditional subject–object dichotomy' (PPT, 174)[2] and provide a phenomenological understanding of how language functions that is not behaviourist, empiricist, or rationalist.

1 *The refutation of linguistic rationalism and empiricism*

One obstacle to understanding Merleau-Ponty's targets is that he assimilates, or treats as one theory, empiricism and behaviourism which are logically distinct philosophical positions.

Empiricism is the theory that all knowledge is acquired through experience (or, sometimes, more narrowly, through sense experience) but philosphical behaviourism is the thesis that minds may be reduced to bodily behaviour and psychological behaviourism is the view that the best explanation of minds is the explanation of behaviour. Empiricism and philosophical behaviourism may even turn out to be logically inconsistent, if empiricism avails itself of a notion of 'experience' that resists behavioural analysis.

The view that Merleau-Ponty roughly characterises as 'empiricist', 'behaviourist', or sometimes 'mechanist' is really a cluster of views about meaning which includes the doctrine, for example, that 'there is no "speaking subject"' (PPT, 174).[3]

Now, the idea that there is no subject of speech is indeed common to behaviourism, some versions of empiricism and various structuralist and post-structuralist positions adopted by Foucault and Derrida.[4] One way of construing behaviourism is as the reduction of the subject to the object, or the translation of sentences of first person grammatical form into sentences of third person grammatical form (without loss of sense or reference). For this reason Merleau-Ponty is right to say that within the behaviourist framework 'speech occurs in a circuit of third person phenomena' (PPT, 175).[5]

If the subject is characterised essentially in first person singular grammatical terms, and if there is nothing essentially characterisable in first person grammatical terms then there is no subject. Then *a fortiori* there is no speaking subject.

Any consistent Humean empiricism must be a philosophy without a subject.[6] According to empiricism, any possible object of knowledge is a possible object of experience. If the subject is not a possible object of experience then the subject cannot be known to exist. It does not follow that there is no subject because empiricism might be false but it does follow that empiricism, like behaviourism, has no logical room for the subject and, *a fortiori*, no room for a speaking subject.

Merleau-Ponty says that on the empiricist view 'There is no speaker, there is a flow of words set in motion independently of any intention to speak' (PPT, 175).[7] From the fact that there is no subject it does not follow that there are no intentions so empiricism is consistent with the thesis that intentions are constitutive of meaning. If intentions may be given a behavioural analysis then behaviourism presents no obstacle to meaning being intending to mean.

Merleau-Ponty is outlining the view that language is itself the vehicle of meaning. Meaning is internal to the rules of language and not a psychological addition to language contributed by a subject. This thesis may be found in Hegel, Nietzsche, Saussure, Wittgenstein, Derrida and other thinkers and, before all these, in Vico and Kant.[8]

Merleau-Ponty next considers the view that:

> The meaning of words is considered to be given with the stimuli or with the states of consciousness which it is simply a matter of naming. (PPT, 175)[9]

Behaviourisms need separating here. Meaning may be identified with the external stimulus or input which causes the organism to speak or meaning could be the disposition to use language or behave linguistically. Distinct from both of these is the empiricist view that the meaning of a word is to be identified with some state of consciousness of the speaker.

Merleau-Ponty suggests that on the behaviourist–empiricist view meaning is *atomistic* and speech is 'an entity of rational origin' (PPT,

175).[10] 'Origin' translates nothing in the French. Merleau-Ponty means linguistic rules inhere in the language itself.

Merleau-Ponty says:

> Since language can disintegrate into fragments, we have to conclude that it is built up by a set of independent contributions. (PPT, 175)[11]

There is a distinction between holism and atomism about meaning and, clearly, disagreement is possible about what the minimal unit of meaning can be; the word (Locke and Saussure), the proposition (Frege, Russell, the early Wittgenstein), the whole of a language or science (Quine).[12] Clearly, too, in the theory of meaning known as Logical Atomism canvassed by Russell and the early Wittgenstein meaning is atomistic because truth is functional; the truth values of compound propositions are logically determined by the truth values of their constituent atomic propositions.[13]

Now, Merleau-Ponty is saying that if language may be analysed into parts then it must be built up out of those parts. To decide whether this is right we need a distinction between analysis and synthesis (an ancient distinction partly revived by Hegel and Sartre). Suppose some non-atomic unit of language, M, may be analysed into {m1 . . . mn} such that M means {m1 . . . mn}, then there is no a priori obstacle to the reverse practice of exhibiting {m1 . . . mn} as jointly constitutive of the meaning of M. This reverse process is synthesis. If language may be analysed into parts it logically follows that language is composed of those parts. No a priori obstacle is thereby shown to the synthesis of language out of those parts.

Both empiricism and behaviourism are consistent with either holism, the view that a language is the minimal unit of meaning and atomism, the view that components of the language are the minimal units of meaning.

Merleau-Ponty defines rationalism (or 'intellectualism') about meaning this way: 'language is but an external accompaniment of thought' (PPT, 177).[14] This view is consistent with the empiricist view that meaning is a mental state of the speaker so for Merleau-Ponty 'intellectualism is hardly any different from empiricism' PPT 177).[15]

What is needed here is a clearer distinction between thought and experience. Then Merleau-Ponty's term 'intellectualism' may be reserved for the view that the meaning of language is the thoughts of the speaker and 'empiricism' may be the view that the meaning of language is the experiences of the speaker. Merleau-Ponty is clearly right to maintain that on all three views, empiricism, behavourism and intellectualism, meaning is external to the language. Experience, stimuli, or thought, respectively, have to be added to language to make language meaningful.

Merleau-Ponty says 'we refute both intellectualism and empiricism by simply saying that the word has a meaning' (PPT, 177).[16] This means that meaning is not bestowed on language but is internal to it.

Merleau-Ponty has boldly stated a position logically inconsistent with the theories he rejects but in the absence of proof this is not yet a refutation.

Before we look for a proof in Merleau-Ponty's text we need to be clearer on the relation between word, thought and meaning in his view.

2 Thought and language

Merleau-Ponty says 'we present our thought to ourselves through internal or external speech' (PPT, 177),[17] but it is clear that for him thought does not exist in abstraction from such presentation, inward or outward.

Writing in an idiom strikingly reminiscent of Kant's doctrine of the transcendental unity of apperception, Merleau-Ponty claims:

A thought limited to existing for itself, independently of the constraints of speech and communication, would no sooner appear than it would sink into the unconsciousness, which means that it would not exist even for itself. (PPT, 177)[18]

Like Kant's putative thought which could not even in principle be an object of self-consciousness, Merleau-Ponty's thought that could not be expressed in speech, either would be nothing to the subject or nothing *tout court*. The ambiguity is in both Kant and Merleau-Ponty.[19]

Merleau-Ponty also affirms in this passage the thesis common to Kant and Wittgenstein that thought is necessarily public in the sense of communicable. Although a cornerstone of the neo-Kantianism of both the so-called 'analytical' and 'continental' philosophical traditions, the doctrine that thought depends upon language and communication seems unlikely to be true. There are empirical grounds for supposing that thought predates language (both in evolution and in the development of the child), and if it is right that thought is chronologically prior to language then it is right that thought is logically independent of language. Also, it is not a self-contradictory supposition that a person be capable of a thought that could not even in principle be communicated. If that is right then the communicability of thought is at best a contingent matter.[20]

Merleau-Ponty also holds that there is no thought that is not expressed either inwardly or outwardly. If 'expressed inwardly' means 'thought' it amounts to the uncontroversial tautology that there is no thought that is not thought. More controversially Merleau-Ponty argues

169

that all thought is expressed in language. The argument is: all thought is expressed, language is the vehicle or medium of expression, therefore, all thought is expressed through language. This is valid if language is the only medium of expression for thought. Merleau-Ponty himself rejects the premise that language is the only vehicle of expression (the body itself, and the work of art are also expressive media). In that case more argument is needed to show that thought depends on language.

Merleau-Ponty says,

> the word, far from being the mere sign of objects and meanings, inhabits things and is the vehicle of meanings. (PPT, 178)[21]

A kind of conceptual idealism is at work here. Merleau-Ponty thinks empirical objects being what they are to us partly depends upon the language we use to characterise them. This is the familiar neo-Kantian structuralist doctrine that the empirical world is presented to us as constituted by our conceptual apparatus.[22] Merleau-Ponty draws an important conclusion from this however: if we recognise things this is because they are partially linguistically constituted, so the recognition of things requires language. We do recognise things, therefore recognition presupposes language. He says 'the most familiar thing appears indeterminate so long as we have not recalled its name' (PPT, 177).[23]

The soundness of this argument would be enough to show that thought presupposes language, but it would not be sufficient to tie thought to language in the close, expressive way that Merleau-Ponty seeks. It is for example logically consistent with thought presupposing language that although if any thinker is a language user not all thinking is language use.

3 *Expression*

Merleau-Ponty says 'we present our thought to ourselves through internal or external speech' (PPT, 177).[24] Again, in a neo-Kantian idiom, he claims 'it is through expression that we make it our own' (PPT, 177).[25] Only if a subject expresses a thought is that thought a thought of that subject.

We lack precise criteria for the ascription of numerically distinct thoughts to numerically distinct subjects partly because we lack precise criteria for the individuation of thoughts. Merleau-Ponty thinks that a thought has to be something to a subject in order to be a thought by that subject. The expression of a thought is at least a necessary condition for that thought's being a self-conscious thought. It is not clear whether he also thinks it sufficient.

He says 'the thinking subject himself is in a kind of ignorance of his thoughts so long as he has not formulated them for himself' (PPT, 177).[26] I think, conversely, if a person expresses his or her thoughts (in such a way as to be conscious of having them or not) then that is a sufficient condition of those thoughts being that person's thoughts. *Pace* Merleau-Ponty, it is not clear that it is necessary. It is not incoherent to suppose that there are unexpressed thoughts. The prior existence of thoughts is arguably a necessary condition for their expression.

Merleau-Ponty, in a strikingly Wittgensteinian turn of phrase, says:

> I begin to understand the meaning of words through their place in
> a context of action, and by taking part in a communal life.
> (PPT, 179)[27]

For Wittgenstein and for Merleau-Ponty meaning is both pragmatic and social. The idea of meaning as a mental process, or as a psychological accompaniment of language, is an illusionary abstraction from the lived reality of the human world.

Merleau-Ponty thinks the pragmatic and social conditions for language learning become clear when I learn a foreign language in the country where it is spoken. Learning the new language takes the form of learning how to speak or write it and Merleau-Ponty thinks thinking in the language depends on this.

To capture the idea that thought is not prior to language Merleau-Ponty introduces the concept of 'thought in speech' (PPT, 179) 'une pensée dans la parole' (PP, 209). 'In' is obscure here. The spatial metaphor hides an unclarity about what the exact relation is between thought and speech if speech is the expression of thought, and cannot exist independently of that expression.

Two notions, mutual dependency and numerical identity, seem inadequate. If x and y are mutually dependent then x is necessary for y and y is necessary for x and, y is sufficient for x and x is sufficient for y. On Merleau-Ponty's account language and thought are necessary and sufficient for each other. He falls short of saying that language and thought are the same. x and y are numerically identical if and only if x is y and y is x. However, if x is the expression of y that would seem to conceptually preclude 'x is y', just because it seems incoherent or barely sensible to talk about something's being its own expression, so the best analysis is mutual dependence without numerical identity.

'To express' can mean 'to represent' but Merleau-Ponty explicitly rules this interpretation out. He says 'thought in the speaking subject, is not a representation' (PPT, 180)[28] and the reason he gives is that thought in its expression 'in' speech 'does not expressly posit objects or relations' (PPT, 180).[29]

171

I take it the relation between thought and speech is not close enough if speech represents thought. What that close relationship is Merleau-Ponty does not say.

4 *The phenomenology of language*

Merleau-Ponty tries to solve problems bequeathed by Husserl's phenomenology of language, in which he identifies three phases: the discovery of the *essence* of language in *Logische Untersuchungen* and the description of a universal grammar putatively presupposed by any language; the claim in *Formale und Transzendentale Logik* that language exhibits an original intentionality not borrowed from thought; and the thesis in *Ursprung der Geometrie* that thought becomes public, intersubjective and ideal through language. Merleau-Ponty wholly rejects the first of these projects and thinks of himself as completing the other two. The ambiguity, contingency, and historical complexity of language make the search for a universal grammar fruitless, but the pragmatic orientations of the body-subject in the world provide a *ground* for the intentionality, intersubjectivity and ideality of language as described by Husserl.

Merleau-Ponty thinks of scientific approaches to language through logic and structural linguistics not as false but as abstract and systematically incompletable. No philosophically adequate account of the relation between the speaking subject and speech or speech and the world will be achieved by bracketing the being-in-the-world of the body-subject and its network of practical concerns. The body is the key to what appears mysterious or aporetic in these two relations. Merleau-Ponty's aim is not to refute scientific linguistics but to explain its thinkablity.

Merleau-Ponty distinguishes two ways in which language may be presented: 'language as object of thought' and 'language as mine' (ST, 86). He says this partly coincides with de Saussure's distinction, in *Cours de la Linguistique Générale*, between synchronic and diachronic linguistics. Merleau-Ponty rarely reports de Saussure's positions accurately but his misrepresentations are often more philosophically perspicuous than de Saussure's original. Synchronic linguistics is the study of the logical and psychological relations which make the terms of a language into a system: the system that that language is. When a speaker of a language has a grasp of that language as a whole, say German, or English, they know it as the kind of object that synchronic linguistics studies (though, obviously, not necessarily under *that* description). Diachronic linguistics is the study of the successive or historical and piecemeal uses of the terms and expressions of a language by its speakers, largely in abstraction from its a priori logical structure. It is not too misleading to think of synchronic linguistics as the study of a language's atemporal form and diachronic linguistics as the study of its temporally fluctuating content. Clearly, the attempt to do linguistics in one of these two senses cannot wholly eschew the other. (Suppose somebody *says something*. We cannot understand what they say by ignoring the logic and grammar of their language or the peculiar contingencies of the uttered content.) In *Signes* Merleau-Ponty argues that synchronic and diachronic linguistics are dialectically interdependent in complex ways. For example, any language contains a *history* of synchronies. Synchrony may be thought of as *enveloping* diachrony or vice versa. Synchrony is a cross-section of diachrony but there is no cross-section without what there is a cross-section of. Language, Merleau-Ponty concludes, is 'logic in contingency' (ST, 88).

To what extent does de Saussure's synchronic/diachronic distinction coincide with Merleau-Ponty's distinction between language as object of thought and language as mine? We could resist the assimilation by emphasising the variety of ways of *thinking* of a language: geographical, historical, syntactic, semantic, psychological, and so on, and by saying that a language even *as mine* is identical with a language that may be studied synchronically (if de Saussure's project is viable). We could substantiate Merleau-Ponty by saying that language as thought, including the language of synchronic linguistics, is *abstract*; it only exists *qua* object of thought and its existence *qua* that depends upon language as directly experienced. *Langue* is abstracted from *parole*. A priori grammar is isolated by a bracketing of the content of speech. On the other hand, Merleau-Ponty's *language as mine* is phenomenologically more fine grained than de Saussure's *parole*. Merleau-Ponty is trying to capture not only the fluctuating linguistic practices of a community but also the first person singular phenomenology of speech as it is presented to the individual speaker: an *experience* of language.

Merleau-Ponty insists that the *experience* of language is not a contingent epistemological appendage to it. The experience of language is ontologically integral to what language is. To understand why he thinks this we need to understand the role of the body-subject in making language possible.

The being-in-the-world of the body-subject is existentially primordial with regard to language in the sense of being ontologically necessary for its emergence. Merleau-Ponty draws a crucial distinction which distances him from over-cognitive phenomenological and structuralist philosophers of language. He says that language does not arise from the 'I think' but from the 'I can' (ST, 88). Any wholly psychologistic account of language, for example one that attempts to show how meanings are 'constituted' by consciousness, is certain to fail because it is unable to explain 'action at a distance' by language (ST, 89). Language may not only be used to refer to spatially or temporally remote or non-existent objects but the expressions of language themselves may be concatenated *ad infinitum* in chains of signifiers. Indeed, uses of language to refer to spatio-temporally present objects would seem to be a case of 'action at a distance'. It is mysterious on any psychologistic account how the *actuality* of consciousness may explain these *possibilites.*

What is the 'I can'? As a body-subject I am surrounded by a spatio-temporal *Umwelt* of natural objects and human artifacts that I use as means to my ends. I can grasp objects and pick them up, or move through gaps between objects without 'thematising' them, without paying detailed attention to the objects, or measuring the distances between them. Primordial to my sophisticated representations of the world is my ability to move through it and manipulate it with gestures that exhibit 'corporeal intentionality' (ST, 89). This is the existential 'I can'.

When I learn a natural language, the expressions of this language map onto the 'landscape' of the existential 'I can'. A child could not learn a first language simply by memorising the syntax and vocabulary of a language. The child has to learn how to speak. This requires learning how to express its intentions and the having of intentions presupposes the 'I can'. Merleau-Ponty thinks there is a kind of meaning that is intermediate between the sophisticated system of signs making up a natural language and the 'I can' misconstrued reductively as only a possible set of bodily movements. This intermediate kind of meaning he calls '*langagière*' (S, 111) ('language like' ST, 88). It 'mediates' between a non-linguistic intention and the linguistic expression of that intention. Merleau-Ponty says disappointingly little about meaning that is 'langagière' but it is clear from its intended role that it pertains to the 'I can'. Rather as Roland Barthes speaks of the *silent language of things* Merleau-Ponty thinks of the world as *announcing itself* to our practical projects.

Of course there are points of vulnerability in this account. It is an unsolved philosophical problem exactly what *possibility* is so it is obscure what exactly intention and the possibility of referring borrow from the 'I can' when they borrow its possibility. Also, the way I have represented Merleau-Ponty on language makes it look as though the 'I can' is not itself linguistically structured. In fact he subscribes to the post-Kantian orthodoxy common to 'analytical' and 'modern continental' philosophers that linguistic preconceptions categorise the way the world appears to a language user. The fact that the existential facts are primordial with regard to the linguistic facts does not preclude their being conditioned by them.

The 'I can' is not only prior to language, it constitutes it. Merleau-Ponty thinks that many problems in the philosophy of language arise through reflecting on language and trying to analyse it. Existentially, language is a lived reality that can only be adequately apprehended in its *use*.

Language undergoes a transformation when it becomes what he calls 'speech in use' (PW, 116):

> We no more *think* of the words we are saying or that are being said to us than of the very hand we are shaking. The hand is not a bundle of flesh and bone, it is the palpable presence of the other person. Language has, therefore, a peculiar signification which is the more evident the more we surrender ourselves to it, and the less equivocal the less we think of it. (PW, 116)

Language can only be understood through being-in-the-world.

5 *Language and philosophy*

Merleau-Ponty thinks the role of language in philosophy is over-estimated by twentieth-century philosophy. This claim is worth examining.

Merleau-Ponty thinks that no problems outside the philosophy of language may be resolved only or essentially by the inspection of language. He rejects the positivist thesis that putative philosophical problems may be analysed as meaningful or meaningless and, if meaningless, discarded as pseudo-problems and, if meaningful, rewritten as scientific problems. He rejects the thesis of linguistic analysts that putative philosophical problems arise through a misunderstanding of the grammar, or uses of ordinary language. He rejects too their thesis that a clarification of ordinary language will dissolve such putative problems.

Less obvious, perhaps, is the fact that Merleau-Ponty's repudiation of 'linguistic' approaches to philosophy is also inconsistent with structuralism and post-structuralism. So called 'modern continental' philosophy has been obsessed with language at least as much as its alleged 'analytical' alternative, and if Merleau-Ponty's arguments for the conclusion that the importance of language in philosophy has been exaggerated are sound, then vulnerable targets include not only Ayer, Wittgenstein and Austin but Lévi-Strauss, Lacan and Derrida.

Merleau-Ponty holds the position that what the world is like cannot be read off the properties of language. The inspection of language tells us nothing about non-linguistic reality. There is plausibility in this, because from any set of sentences, no matter how large and complex, which express propositions about language we cannot logically derive any further sentence or set of sentences about non-linguistic reality. Any such putative derivation is bound to be a *non sequitur* even if some relation weaker than deductive derivation may obtain between claims about language and claims about the universe. The exhibition of such non-deductive relations may even contribute to the solution of philosophical problems. Nevertheless, Merleau-Ponty's prima facie case is a strong one.

6 *Ineffability*

In the section called 'Foi Perceptive et Interrogation' which is part of the essay 'Interrogation et Dialectique' in *Le Visible et L'Invisible*, Merleau-Ponty examines a philosophical problem resisting resolution by the examination of language alone: the problem of *what it is for what is to be*.

In Chapter XIV, I discuss Merleau-Ponty's attempts to answer this question. Here we are only concerned with whether it might admit of a purely linguistic resolution.

The question needs to be distinguished from other, superficially similar, questions. Merleau-Ponty says

> We are not asking ourselves if the world exists; we are asking what it is for it to exist. (VIT, 96)[30]

'World' is a name for the totality of what is (whatever is). Whether there is a world is a different question from the question of what it is for the world to be, given, perhaps, that there is a world. We could reformulate the first question as: *Is what is?* the second as: *What is it for what is to be?*

Neither of these questions is *Why is there something rather than nothing?* For example, answering them will not answer that question. The first is not *What is it to be?* although answering the second adequately will probably answer *What is it to be?* because explaining what it is for what is to be will explain what it is for anything to be if we understand by 'what is' 'whatever is'.

Merleau-Ponty raises the issue of a linguistic solution in this way,

> When we ask what it is for the things and for the world to exist, one might think that it is only a matter of defining a word. (VIT, 96)[31]

The distinction between 'les choses' and 'le monde' is not doing any useful work here. 'Les choses' is naturally translated 'things' (and not 'the things' as the translation has it) so Merleau-Ponty is presenting two alternative formulations of the existential problem What is it for what is to be? 'Les choses' and 'le monde' are just different names for what is, whatever is. Merleau-Ponty does not draw any interesting distinction between *being* and *existing* here. He does not, for example, in a quasi Heideggerian way reserve 'exists' and its cognates for human existence. Suppose someone thought they could solve the problem of what it is for what is to be by inspecting language. How should they proceed?

Merleau-Ponty doubts very much that success could consist in having defined a word. However, it is not obviously false that someone who managed to define 'is' (in its existential sense) or 'exists' would have failed to have solved the problem of the being of the world. Two issues need to be clearly separated here: whether 'exists' could be defined, and, if it could, whether that would solve the philosophical problem. 'Exists' seems to be semantically primitive. It could be that Berkeley is right in *The Principles of Human Knowledge* that it is the most mysterious of concepts and resists verbal definition. However, Heidegger has arguably discovered a real presupposition of being in *Temporalität* (temporality) because, intuitively and minimally, if x is then x lasts. It might be incoherent to assert that something *is* but *is for no time*, has no duration; even though the history of philosophy has been happy with atemporal existents, for example, on some construals, numbers, universals, God.

Suppose, however, 'exists' is not semantically primitive or suppose that Heidegger has initiated a semantic process which may be continued when he wrote *Sein und Zeit*, because *Sein und Zeit* entails that 'x is' entails 'x lasts' and further entailments may be found.

Prima facie, defining 'x' and saying what x is are at least mutually dependent even if not identical procedures. For example, if a person were to be presented with the order or request 'define the word "square" (in its geometrical sense)' and suppose that person were subsequently to be presented with the order or request 'explain what a square is in geometry' it is not clear that in carrying out both requests he would be doing two significantly different things, from the point of view of conveying information or solving a problem. He could reply to both requests 'four-sided, right-angled, equilinear closed plane with parallel sides' or something semantically equivalent. Because of the way in which we can individuate responses there is an obvious sense in which he is doing two qualitatively distinct things: he is both defining a word and saying what something is. However, one token response is enough to perform both tasks and so in that sense he is doing one thing. That is enough to show that defining a word may be enough to solve a nonlinguistic problem.

Merleau-Ponty adduces some putative grounds for this view, putative grounds which he regards as inadequate. He says,

After all, the questions take place in language. (VIT, 96)[32]

and

> One can therefore be tempted to count the philosophical question
> concerning the world among the facts of language, and it would
> seem that the response can be sought only in the meanings of
> words, since it is in words that the question will be answered.
> (VIT, 96)[33]

From the fact that the question of being, if it has an answer, will be
answered in words it does not follow that the answer can be found by
inspecting language. On the contrary, Merleau-Ponty invites us to construe language *ontologically*. Language is something that exists, as part
of the world, as part of life. The question of being may be raised about
anything that exists so language, far from offering us the resources to
solve the problem, merely poses the problem in a new way.

Despite his impatience with linguistic philosophy, Merleau-Ponty
thinks of the world as we live it as ambiguously structured like a
language. Many things can be done in performing a bodily action. One
and the same arm movement could be something seductive or something offensive or both. The objects that we see are like a language
because they ambiguously announce to us what they are. Although
language itself is part of the world it is a meta-world or doubling of the
actual world from which it derives its meanings. It is the ironical and
paradoxical situation of the philosopher of being obliged to put into
words what seems to systematically evade linguistic characterisation.

XI

Other Minds

The problem of other minds is the problem of whether, and if so, what, other people think. Sometimes it is presented in a rather different form. It is assumed we know that and what other persons think and the question then becomes how we know that (given that we do know that).

Problems that are closely logically related are the questions of whether inanimate machines, notably computers, can or could think and the question of the extent to which we may successfully reconstruct – say historically – the mentality and life style of a culture that is not our own. I mention these further problems because they show that something like a version of the problem of other minds is faced by intellectual disciplines outside the mainstream of metaphysics and epistemology – in these cases artificial intelligence and history respectively.

1 Self and other

Merleau-Ponty sees that if the problem of other minds cannot be solved then solipsism is difficult to refute. Solipsism is an extreme version of idealism. Idealism is the doctrine that only minds (and their contents) exist. Solipsism is the doctrine that only my mind (and its contents) exists.

Merleau-Ponty formulates the problem of other minds in a traditional and uncontroversial way:

> This is precisely the question: how can the word 'I' be put into the plural, how can a general idea of the I be formed, how can I speak if an I other than my own, how can I know that there are other I's? (PPT, 348)[1]

Merleau-Ponty tackles the problem by suggesting there are respects in which I am not certain of the nature of my own existence and then

179

proceeds to argue that we may be more certain than we believe of the nature of someone else's existence. There is a sound methodological reason for this procedure.

The problem of other minds is frequently presented through this stark contrast: I am certain beyond any possible doubt that my own mind exists and I am certain beyond any possible doubt what I am thinking when I am thinking. In the case of any other mind, or putative mind, exactly the opposite is true. I can have no certainty that other people have minds and, if they do, I can have no certainty what they think.

Merleau-Ponty's strategy is to undermine the contrast from both sides: one is both more certain of the existence and nature of other people's minds than one may suppose and less certain of the existence and nature of one's own mind than one may suppose.

He points out that past states of one's own mind may be as epistemologically inaccessible to oneself as states of another person's mind. In particular

I can never be sure of reaching a fuller understanding of my past than it had of itself at the time I lived through it. (PPT, 346)[2]

This is so even if Merleau-Ponty tries to imaginatively reconstruct the phenomenology of his childhood in the present, even if 'I take myself back to those years as I actually lived them' (PPT, 346).[3]

Our knowledge of the existence and nature of minds may admit of degrees, so scepticism about minds may therefore also admit of degree. Even where the object of knowledge is one's own mind 'my hold on the past and the future is precarious' (PPT, 346).[4]

The problem of other minds may be given a construal that is more or less empiricist and a construal that is more or less rationalist.

Empirically, the problem is that one has no experience of any mind other than one's own. If there is no knowledge of other minds by experience it follows on empiricism that we have no knowledge of other minds.

The rationalist construal is: from the fact that one has knowledge of (the existence and nature of) one's own mind it does not logically follow that any other mind exists, or that such a putative mind has a particular content. The existence and nature of other minds does not follow logically from the existence and nature of one's own mind. Given that, any putative inference from one's own mind to other minds may at best be inductive. (Notice that as an inductive inference it is very weak. Strong inductive inferences are many–one inferences, but this is a one–many inference.) It follows that there can be no rationalist proof of the existence and nature of other minds.

Merleau-Ponty always tries to avoid the stark alternatives: empiricism or rationalism. It is an important feature of being-in-the-world that it is existentially primordial and so prior to the empiricist/rationalist distinction. Nevertheless, Merleau-Ponty's claim about his past mental states may be given a rationalist or an empiricist construal.

The empiricist construal is this: he has no present experience of his earlier mental states and if only the present content of experience may with certainty be known to exist then it follows that he cannot know with certainty that his past mental state existed.

Construed rationalistically, the claim is: from the existence and nature of his present mental states nothing logically follows about the existence and nature of his past mental states. I see no reason to doubt that there are coherent formulations of epistemological scepticism about one's past mental states, despite Merleau-Ponty's attempts to undermine the rationalist/empiricist distinction.

2 The deferral of self-presence

Interestingly, and more controversially, Merleau-Ponty seeks to demonstrate that one's knowledge of the content of one's present experience is not indubitable. Merleau-Ponty argues that there is no such thing as absolute self-presence:

> The transcendence of the instants of time is both the ground of, and the impediment to, the rationality of my personal history: the ground because it opens a totally new future to me in which I shall be able to reflect upon the element of opacity in my present, a source of danger in so far as I shall never manage to seize the present through which I live with apodeictic certainty, and since the lived is thus never entirely comprehensible, what I understand never quite tallies with my living experience, in short, I am never quite at one with myself. (PPT, 347)[5]

Here Merleau-Ponty deconstructs time, self-presence, and the empiricism–rationalism distinction. By 'deconstructs' here (not a term Merleau-Ponty uses) I mean A deconstructs x if and only if A both shows the possibility of x, and A is a critique of x (for example in the sense of exhibiting the difficulties in distinguishing x from non-x, or in showing the putative definition of 'x' to be incoherent).

It follows that deconstruction is an essentially Kantian enterprise and in this respect Merleau-Ponty, like Derrida after him, does not escape the fundamentally Kantian assumptions of modern philosophy.[6]

For example Merleau-Ponty charactersises 'the transcendence of the instants of time' (PPT, 347) ('La transcendence des moments du temps' (PP, 398–9) in two ways. He says, this is both 'the ground of' (PPT, 347)

('Fonde' PP, 399) and 'the impediment to' (PPT, 347) ('compromet' PP, 399) 'the rationality of my personal history' (PPT, 347) 'La rationalité de mon histoire' (PP, 399). The two components of deconstruction as I have defined it are both present.

If x grounds y then x makes y possible or, if not x then not y and if y then x. If x is an impediment to y then either x exhibits the incoherence of the definition of 'y' or x exhibits the difficulties in drawing a y- non-y distinction or both.

On this analysis, Merleau-Ponty's deconstruction is not incoherent because there is no contradiction in the supposition than one and the same value for 'x' – here the transcendence of the instants of time – both makes y (here self-description) possible and is invoked in a critique of a precise formulation of which y (here such self-description), consists.

There are two senses in which the instants of time are 'transcended'. Merleau-Ponty thinks he has an explanation of how it is possible for there to be instants of time for oneself, and an explanation of why one's understanding of an instant of time may never be complete.

I interpret the content of my own experience and this is facilitated by my conceptually dividing it into discrete temporal units. Merleau-Ponty does not have an argument for this. However, suppose my awareness of my own mental content is an awareness of a set of thoughts or experiences (or both). Then, thought T1 is either wholly simultaneous with thought T2 or T1 wholly predates T2 or T2 wholly predates T1 or T1 and T2 are only partly simultaneous. If T1 and T2 are only partly simultaneous then either T1 partly predates T2 or T2 partly predates T1. In these cases it is entailed that if T1 and T2 stand in some temporal relation then there exist numerically distinct times except in the case where T1 and T2 are wholly simultaneous. Then T1 happens at all and only the time T2 happens and so that does not entail more than one time. In every other case it follows that there exists some number of times greater than one on the plausible assumption that we may individuate times through thoughts that occur at them in this context. This is plausible because it is an application of the more general principle that times are to be individuated through what happens at them. When at least two non-simultaneous events occur that is a sufficient condition for the existence of at least two times. Taking these facts as premises we may logically derive a one–one mapping of non-simultaneous events onto times such that for every thought ordered by the before/after relation {T1 . . . Tn} there exists a time {t1 . . . tn}. Given this, Merleau-Ponty is right to hold that the awareness of one's own mental states presupposes the existence of numerically distinct times, or 'instants of time' (PPT, 347) ('moments du temps' PP, 399). (Notice that the English translation, but not the original French carries the connotation of a durationless time past.)

What does not logically follow is that when I am aware of my own mental states I am aware of the times at which they happen if this means that I am aware that they happen at those times. If I am aware of {T1 . . . Tn}, and I am aware of {t1 . . . tn} in only the minimal and truncated sense then I am aware of temporally ordered events.

Nothing stronger follows about my awareness of time here. It does not even follow that I am aware of those mental events as temporal events if this implies that I think of them as temporal events. This is not implied by my being aware of events that are in fact temporal nor is it implied by the fact, if it is a fact, that my awareness of those temporal events is itself temporal.

If I am aware of my mental events as temporal events then this does presuppose that I minimally judge them to be temporal events. This is, however, quite neutral as to whether they are idealistically constructed as temporal or whether they are passively and realistically judged to be temporal.

Any such understanding of the temporality of one's own mental states can never be complete and can never be quite accurate. Merleau-Ponty deploys the concept 'postponement' (PPT, 346) ('différée' PP, 398) to undermine the idea that I may be fully present to myself in self-understanding:

> My possession of my own time is always postponed until a stage
> when I may fully understand it, yet this stage can never be reached.
> (PPT, 346)[7]

'Différée' is open to several translations, including 'differed', 'deferred' and 'postponed'. On these readings, which are complementary, not mutually exclusive, Merleau-Ponty is saying variously that self-understanding can never quite achieve the complete self-presence that that concept seems to require, that such self-presence is perpetually deferred or postponed.

The postponement or deferral must be perpetual because the moment of full self-understanding 'can never be reached' (PPT, 346). The translation's 'never' has no linguistic equivalent in the French text. However, this is not a philosophically illegitimate insertion as Merleau-Ponty's 'ce moment là ne peut pas arriver' (PP, 398) entails that that moment can never be reached, on the plausible assumption that if some event cannot happen it will not ever happen. In the French Merleau-Ponty is claiming that he will not entirely understand himself ('me') and not his own time 'it' as the translation has it (even though the two impossibilities are mutually dependent).

In what sense is the transcendence of the instants of time an impediment to one's self-understanding? Merleau-Ponty is ruling out the

possibility that one be in a mental state (call it 'MS') which is an awareness of one of one's mental states (one of {T1 . . . Tn}) such that MS
exists all and only during that member of {T1 . . . Tn}, and such that
the nature of that member of {T1 . . . Tn} is wholly grasped in its
apprehension by MS.

Although what he rules out is not contradictory it probably does not
happen. It may be, as Ryle (see note 16) thinks, it is simply not the case
that a subject is in two numerically distinct yet wholly simultaneous
mental states, one of which is the awareness of the other. Merleau-
Ponty certainly sees no phenomenological grounds for postulating a
double mental life – one life of mental states and another which is the
awareness of these.

Ironically and paradoxically it is in the nature of the present never to
be fully present. This is why 'I never manage to seize the present
through which I live' (PPT, 347).[8] ('I could never seize the present that
I live' would be a better translation.) In so far as my present is intrinsic to what I am it follows that my certainty of my own nature is
undermined.

Merleau-Ponty says I cannot grasp my lived present 'with apodeictic
certainty', (PPT, 347) ('Avec une certitude apodictique' PP, 399). I take
it some proposition, P, is apodeictic if and only if P is necessary. Here
the putative value of P is some first person singular psychological
ascription. Merleau-Ponty's claim is then logically equivalent to the
claim that no first person singular psychological ascription is a necessary truth. Whether this is right or not is a complex and piecemeal
matter to decide. It may be, for example, that 'I am thinking' may be
formulated just on condition that it is true but then much rests on just
what is formulated. If, for example, it is a thought that is thus formulated then the inference clearly goes through. Not only is P not necessary on Merleau-Ponty's view if P is a first person singular
psychological ascription, but P is not certain. It follows that one has no
certainty of the existence and nature of one's own mind.

In a striking reversal of a fundamental Cartesian tenet, Merleau-
Ponty says 'I am never quite at one with myself: (PPT 347).[9] This could
be interpreted in many ways but two are these: my consciousness of
myself is never numerically identical with myself as the object of that
consciousness, and, when I am conscious of myself I either ascribe some
property to myself that I lack or I fail to ascribe some property to
myself that I possess (even where self ascriptions are partly accurate, for
example they possess the minimal accuracy to make them still count as
first person singular psychological ascriptions).

On either reading it remains true for Merleau-Ponty that my judgements about my own mental stages lack 'certainty' (PPT, 347) ('certitude' PP, 399). If P is not certain if and only if P is dubitable and if P is

dubitable if and only if it is psychologically possible to disbelieve P, then Merleau-Ponty is committed to the view that it is psychologically possible to disbelieve one's own first person singular psychological ascriptions.

In this sense one side of the problem of other minds is undermined. It is not true that one is certain of the existence and nature of one's own mind but uncertain of the existence and nature of other minds because one is not certain of the existence and nature of one's own mind. This position is as strong as Merleau-Ponty's critique of self-presence.

3 The trace and the presentation of absence

In a parallel way, I am more certain of the existence and nature of other people's minds than the philosophical sceptic would have us believe. Crucial to understanding Merleau-Ponty's strategy here is the concept of the 'trace'.

Merleau-Ponty says:

> When I turn towards perception, and pass from direct-perception to thinking about that perception, I re-enact it, and find at work in my organs of perception a thinking older than myself of which those organs are merely the trace. In the same way I understand the existence of other people. Here again I have only the trace of a consciousness which evades me in its actuality. (PPT, 351–2).[10]

The idea of the 'trace' is designed to show up the shortcomings of a simple and clean distinction between the physical exterior and psychological interior of another person. The trace bridges the gap between interior and exterior, mental and physical.

It is because he rejects this distinction, or does not start by assuming it, that Merleau-Ponty rules out the possibility that one infers the existence and nature of other minds, either from the existence and nature of one's own mind or from facts about the physical exterior of the other. As he puts it

> There is nothing here resembling 'reasoning by analogy'. (PPT, 35)[11]

The trace of the other consciousness is partly what impedes the actuality of the other's consciousness for me and for the other. That is why Merleau-Ponty says

> I have only the trace of a consciousness which evades me in its actuality. (PPT, 352)[12]

It follows that consciousness is not only not fully self-present but also not fully present to the consciousness of another.

The central phenomenological ground for the rejection of the clear mental interior/physical exterior distinction is the postulation of the body-subject. Crucially, 'the body of another, like my own, is not inhabited' (PPT, 349).[13] This is not just a repudiation of Cartesian mind–body dualism (though it is that) it is also the thesis that there is nothing mental that, so to speak, occupies the body. It is not as though finding out that and what other people think could take the form of making discoveries about a mind that is hidden inside a body, or hidden 'behind' the physical exterior of a body. On the contrary, the body is a physical subject, that is, a psycho-physical whole that cannot be reduced to the mechanical object of materialist and behaviourist psychology, yet which does not resist this reduction through being 'occupied' by a Cartesian consciousness.

Merleau-Ponty modestly says, 'What we have said about the body provides the beginning of a solution to this problem' (PPT, 349).[14] I think the problem of other minds is still unsolved but one promising strategy is to reject, as Merleau-Ponty has done, the clean distinction between the obvious physical exterior of the other and the inscrutable mental interior. Because of this it is worth exploring further Merleau-Ponty's remarks on the body. He says:

> At the same time as the body withdraws from the objective world, and forms between the pure subject and the object a third genus of being, the subject loses its purity and its transparency. (PPT, 350)[15]

The pure subject ('le pur sujet' PP, 402) is the putative Cartesian consciousness; that which is always subject but never object, always mental but never physical. This is here contrasted with the Cartesian object ('L'objet' PP, 402) which is only objective so not subjective and only physical and so not mental.

Merleau-Ponty postulates the body-subject as both subjective and objective, both physical and mental. The reason why 'the subject loses its purity' is that the subject is also an object, but not in the reductionist sense of materialism or behaviourism. The subject is not (incoherently) just an object. The body-subject is a psycho-physical whole that is also an object ('objet pour lui' PP, 123fn.).

Similarly, 'the body withdraws from the objective world' in the sense that the body-subject cannot be adequately characterised by any set of third person singular physical ascriptions, no matter how large or complete. This is not because the body-subject is inhibited by an extra being, a Cartesian mind or consciousness. It is because the body is not only an object but also a subject. The body-subject ('sujet incarné' PP, 175) is not (incoherently) just a subject but a psycho-physical whole.

It is sometimes pointed out – I have in mind Mary Warnock for example – that there are interesting parallels between Merleau-Ponty and Gilbert Ryle on what people are.[16] I think this is right. Both are concerned to repudiate mind–body dualism in a way that both does not commit them to reductionist materialism and does justice to the reality of our mental lives. I should say, however, that in the last resort Ryle is a logical behaviourist – he thinks our psychological vocabulary takes on meaning through reference to overt and covert (occurrent and dispositional) bodily behaviour.[17] Merleau-Ponty rejects this and the contrast can be pointed out in this way: logical behaviourism is the reduction of the subjective to the objective but phenomenology is the reduction of the objective to the subjective. Ryle and Merleau-Ponty would doubtless resist this stark contrast but I think it obtains nonetheless.

If logical behaviourism is, essentially, the doctrine that any sentence or set of sentences about minds (or mental states) may be translated without loss of meaning into a sentence or set of sentences about overt or covert bodily behaviour, phenomenology (say, for the purposes of Husserl's transcendental reduction) is the doctrine that any sentence or set of sentences about physical objects (or events) may be translated without loss of meaning into a sentence or set of sentences about intentional states and their contents. It is an interesting philosophical question whether, formulated these ways, logical behaviourism and phenomenology are mutually inconsistant doctrines or, *pace* their practitioners, logically equivalent. This thought is prompted by the question: what is translated in each case? Ryle would resist my formulation because he does not wish to be taken as denying well known facts about our mental lives. Merleau-Ponty would resist it because the body is both subject and object – subject of its own perceptions and object of the perceptions of others (and, to an extent, the object of its own perceptions too).

Merleau-Ponty says the body forms 'a third genus of being' (PPT, 350): a type that is both subject and object and neither only subject nor only object.

Now, it could be objected that this procedure is question-begging *vis-à-vis* the stark formulation of the problem of other minds. On this, although the onus is on Merleau-Ponty to provide independent argument for the existence of the body-subject, I take it this is what he has done in the chapter on the body in *Phénoménologie de la Perception.*

Similarly, however, the onus is on the theorist who advocates the stark formulation of the problem of other minds to provide independent arguments for the conclusion that we have knowledge of our own mind but do not (or may not have) knowledge of other minds. Neither is prima facie more intuitive than the other (even though either may appear intuitively right until the other is suggested). For example it seems that sometimes one does know what other people are thinking and at other times one does not and that, by and large, one knows that other people have minds.

Merleau-Ponty presents a number of supplementary arguments for the existence of other minds. He describes some structural features of being-in-the-world, for example: 'natural time is always there' (PPT, 347),[18] one is surrounded by natural objects, and:

> Not only do I have a physical world, not only do I live in the midst
> of earth, air and water, I have around me roads, plantations,
> villages, streets, churches, implements, a bell, a spoon, a pipe. Each
> of these objects is moulded into the human action which it serves.
> (PPT, 347)[19]

The sceptic about other minds will argue that from the existence of the putative artefacts itemised by Merleau-Ponty it does not logically follow that they are the product of any mind: *a fortiori*, it does not follow that they are the product of other minds. If they are mental products then that is logically consistent with their being produced by one's own mind so the existence of artefacts is consistent with solipsism.

However, Merleau-Ponty rejects the strict distinction between an arte-fact and the mind of its producer. The existence of what one might like to call 'mentality' partly consists in the existence of artefacts, or, better, a human-manipulated world.

Merleau-Ponty's characterisations of mentality as in the world are partly poetic and partly Hegelian. About artefacts he says, 'Each one spreads round it an atmosphere of humanity' (PPT, 347)[20] and the acts of humans on the world are 'deposited like some sediment' (PPT, 348).[21] The Hegelianism of the rejection of a clear mental–physical distinction is evident in his claim that in 'the cultural world' (PPT, 348) ('le monde culturel' PP, 400) there is 'an objective spirit (PPT, 348) ('Un esprit objectif' PP, 400).[22]

The rejection of the presuppositions of the stark formulation of the problem of other minds is entailed by Merleau-Ponty's view that mentality, in this rather Hegelian way, does not exist in abstraction from its expression. Merleau-Ponty is not making any inductive infer-ence from the existence of the artefact to the existence of minds when he says:

> In the cultural object, I feel the close presence of others beneath a
> veil of anonymity. Someone uses the pipe for smoking, the spoon

for eating, the bell for summoning, and it is through the perception of a human act and another person that the perception of a cultural world could be verified. (PPT, 348)[23]

Rather, the grasp of the mentality of the other is very direct. In perceiving artefacts, in perceiving the cultural world, I am perceiving mentality. This idea only appears contradictory if we reject Merleau-Ponty's thesis that the products of human expression are partly constitutive of mentality. Merleau-Ponty holds that human mentality may, so to speak, be read off or seen in human artefacts. Other minds are not something wholly other than their objective expression.

Merleau-Ponty's Hegelian allusion is apposite here. Part of what Hegel means by 'objective spirit' is the observable manifestations of consciousness or spirit, ('Geist'), not only in the visible attitudes and actions of human beings but also in the manipulations of nature through agriculture, industry, painting, sculpture and so on. Hegel, like Merleau-Ponty, rejects mind–body dualism and rejects any theory on which mentality may exist independently of its expression. On both philosophies, mind is essentially expressive. We could call this view of mind 'expressionism' and note that it is an alternative to that assumed by the formulations of the problem of other minds on which other minds are 'hidden', and it nevertheless does not consist in a behaviouristic reduction of mind to observable behaviour, nor a materialist reduction of mental processes to physical processes.

Another strategy Merleau-Ponty adopts is to assume that the body is expressive and claim that this notion is prior to the idea of the body as mere object. This is a version of his theory of bodily subjectivity and is broadly analogous to Strawson's idea of the person as logically primitive (vis-à-vis the mind–body distinction).[24] Merleau-Ponty is discussing the other:

> In order to think of him as a genuine I, I ought to think of myself as a mere object for him, which I am prevented from doing by the knowledge I have of myself. But if another's body is not an object for me, nor mine an object for him, if both are manifestations of behaviour, the positing of the other does not reduce me to the status of an object in his field, nor does my perception of the other reduce him to the status of an object in mine. (PPT, 352)[25]

Merleau-Ponty begins with a concept that he holds is primitive to the self–other distinction: the concept of the body as manifestation of behaviour. We should bear in mind that the relationship between the body and behaviour is very close – it is not as though behaviour could, logically, exist in abstraction from bodily subjectivity. Merleau-Ponty's

189

concept of behaviour is phenomenological and not behaviourist. Behaviour, in this sense, is largely the expression of mentality.

It follows logically from this account that 'another's body is not an object for me' (PPT, 352).[26] This means not *only* a physical object and not *only* an intentional object, because although being expressive of behaviour rules out being an object in either of those senses *tout court*, it is not logically inconsistent with the body of the other being at least a physical object and at least an intentional object. My body is also not only an object for the other.

If we start from the idea of the whole person as an expressive being who has both subjective and objective properties, and if we then maintain that both self and other are people in this sense, then the problem of other minds, arguably, need not arise. If we are considering people as psycho-physical wholes then Merleau-Ponty is right to suggest that we should think of the cases of self and other as ontologically symmetrical. With this background assumption, if one is sceptical about the existence of other minds, one should be as sceptical about the existence of one's own mind. In both cases one is being sceptical about the view that persons have minds.

Whether this strategy may be made to work in a way that is not question-begging against the sceptic about other minds depends largely on the soundness of arguments that may be addressed for the conclusion that the body-subject is a psycho-physical whole, and the conclusion that the concept of the body-subject is prior (logically, epistemologically, or ontologically) to the self–other distinction.

Merleau-Ponty may be usefully read as advocating a kind of identity theory – not a reductionist or a materialist identity theory, but a subjectivity–objectivity identity theory. Although the living conscious human body is the subject of its own perceptions and the object of others' perceptions, there are not two numerically distinct entities: a subject and an object. Indeed, the self that one is is the self that is perceived:

> The self which perceives is in no particularly privileged position
> which rules out a perceived self: both are, not cogitationes shut up
> in their own immanence. (PPT, 353)[27]

The fact that a self perceives does not rule out the possibility that that same self is perceived. This is the kernel of Merleau-Ponty's solution to the problem of other minds. In perceiving another person we are not failing to perceive a Cartesian entity, a hidden mind. We are perceiving another person: perceiving another perceiver.

4 *The refutation of solipsism*

In two senses of 'solipsism' solipsism is inconsistent with the existence of an external world and, *a fortiori*, the existence of other minds.

That *only my mind exists* entails idealism, but idealism, without additional premises, does not entail solipsism. There is no external world on this kind of solipsism both in the sense that there is no extra-mental world and in the sense that there is nothing external to oneself.

Sometimes 'solipsism' is used as the name of the doctrine that *only I exist* and this does not logically entail idealism nor is it entailed by idealism. There is no external world on this second kind of solipsism just so long as an external world is something I am not.

The first kind of solipsism is stronger than the second in that it claims more. On both kinds of solipsism only I exist but on the first kind it is additionally claimed that I am a mind (or at least, that I 'have' a mind and it is just that that exists).

Merleau-Ponty is interested in both kinds of solipsism but we may take all his arguments for my being a body-subject as putative refutations of the view that I am, or essentially am, a mind and concentrate on his refutation in *Le Visible et L'Invisible* of the thesis that only I exist. His strategy has two components. He tries to prove that something outside him exists and he tries to prove that someone outside him exists. Merleau-Ponty would judge 'proof' something of a misnomer here because the refutation is putatively not formal or 'rationalist' but phenomenological. However, wittingly or not, he relies on argument as well as phenomenological description.

In the *Pariser Vorträger* Husserl says

> To the extent that I apprehend myself as a natural human being,
> I presuppose having apprehended a spatial reality; I have conceived
> of myself as being in space, in which I consequently have an outside
> of myself. (PL 32)[28]

The strategy common to Husserl and Merleau-Ponty is to say that our pre-philosophical, natural view of the world presupposes that solipsism is false. Philosophy, including the postulation of solipsism, presupposes our pre-philosophical, natural view of the world. Therefore, philosophy, including the postulation of solipsism, presupposes that solipsism is false. This argument is valid. If it is sound then it follows that solipsism may be formulated just on condition that it is false.

Merleau-Ponty's starting point is this:

> We are interrogating our experience precisely in order to know how
> it opens us to what is not ourselves. (VIT, 159)[29]

and the answering of this question requires the adoption of the pre-philosophical attitude to the world:

> Let us therefore consider ourselves installed among the multitude of things, living beings, symbols, instruments, and men. (VIT, 160)[30]

Crucially, a self–not-self distinction is presupposed by the natural view of the world and this is a distinction that is to be found within experience. It is not an intellectual construct which is retrospectively imposed upon our experience of the world.[31] It is one that clearly obtains when I use an instrument, encounter another person or thing. It is clear that Merleau-Ponty thinks that these claims are self evident, or at least not psychologically dubitable if one pays sufficiently clear and authentic attention to one's experience rather than to philosophical speculation. One can see and feel, for example, where oneself ceases and the rest of the world continues. He describes how the self–external world distinction and the self–other distinction are drawn pre-philosophically:

> Our first truth – which prejudges nothing and cannot be contested – will be that there is presence, that 'something' is there, and that 'someone' is there. (VIT, 160)[32]

Three claims need to be separated here: that there is presence, that something is there and that someone is there. Although Merleau-Ponty groups them under 'our first truth' they do not have the same epistemological status.

'Presence' is notoriously ambiguous between temporal presence and spatial presence. Prima facie it cannot be said that an ontological commitment to either or both forms 'prejudges nothing and cannot be contested'. Merleau-Ponty himself regards the concept of temporal presence as complex and elusive and many philosophers have thought 'presence' incoherent or the present non-existent or both.[33] It is a concept that is excluded from the physical sciences. Spatial presence too cannot be taken for granted if this entails 'being perceptually presented to' because that concept is epistemologically complex and controversial. Hegel's 'Sinnliche Gewissheit' chapter of *Phänomenologie des Geistes* is perhaps the *locus classicus* of a critique of the putative immediacy, incorrigibility and simplicity of spatial and temporal presence.[34]

Although all this is to be said against Merleau-Ponty's thesis that that there is presence is an incorrigible truth that does not rest on assumptions, an argument may be given in its favour. It requires taking seriously his claim that 'we are interrogating our experience'. Then we construe 'there is presence', 'there is "something"' and 'there is someone' as direct reports of what is experienced. Read this way Merleau-

Ponty is using these expressions to refer to the most pervasive features of ordinary pre-philosophical experience which bear on the problem of other minds.

In the everyday course of things, one never doubts that one is presented with physical objects and other people but Merleau-Ponty is not just making the point that doubt is not ordinarily entertained. He is saying that doubt is impossible. When confronted with colleages, students, computers, buildings and pieces of paper it is not a psychological option to doubt that one is in the presence of something and someone.

The kind of indubitability that Merleau-Ponty is advocating, as so often in his work, is neither rationalist nor empiricist. He is manifestly not claiming that it is an a priori or necessary truth that one is confronted with subject-independent people and physical objects. His indubitability thesis is not the thesis that it would be contradictory to deny that one is confronted with other people and physical objects. Nor is Merleau-Ponty saying that there is no room for empirical error in the identification of physical objects and other people. One may mistake one person for another, one physical object for another.

What Merleau-Ponty means is that when in ordinary life one is confronted with a physical object then it is not possible to doubt that it is presented to one as something other than or alien to oneself. It is presented as at some distance from oneself, as the sort of thing one could wander away from, circumambulate, pick up, drop, throw out of the window. External physical objects are presented to one in radically different ways from the way in which I am presented to myself, as we saw in Chapter IV, on the body.

Similarly, when one encounters a colleague it is not a realistic psychological option to doubt that it is another person that one has met. The experience of encountering another human being is qualitatively dissimilar from encountering an inanimate physical object. The other is presented as 'someone', also, as someone friendly or intimidating, or to be respected, despised or feared. Crucially, these are ways in which the other is presented, not later reactions to the other derived from earlier beliefs. They pervade the encounter.

For Merleau-Ponty the sort of philosophical doubt that is possible about the external world and other minds is inauthentic. It is not possible on his view to really or sincerely doubt these things when one picks up an object or meets a fellow human being.

Despite the force of this argument, which is partly similar to Hume's thesis that it is not psychologically possible to doubt the existence of physical objects, there are strong objections to it.[35] Notably, from the fact that it is psychologically impossible to doubt that P it does not follow that not-P and, notoriously, what is psychologically impossible for one person to doubt may be readily dubitable for another.

On the first objection, from the fact that a person finds it psychologically impossible to doubt that others have minds it does not follow that others do have minds. It follows that the conclusion of Merleau-Ponty's argument is consistent with solipsism and solipsism has not been refuted. However, Merleau-Ponty fully admits that there is no deductive or logical proof of the existence of an external world and other minds in particular (nor any inductive proof either). For example on the subject-independence of physical objects he says,

> Even if the thing, upon analysis, always lies beyond proof and
> figures as an extrapolation, still the fact remains that we see pebbles,
> shells. (VIT, 162)[36]

We may understand him this way: we are presented with a choice of whether to endorse philosophical scepticism about the external world or whether to endorse the everyday attitude. Merleau-Ponty has two grounds for choosing the latter over the former. First, the everyday world makes philosophical scepticism possible: it is prior to it logically, ontologically and epistemologically but philosophical scepticism has no such role in making everday realism possible. Second, everyday assumptions are impossible to disbelieve and philosophical scepticism is hard or even impossible to believe. A plausible explanation of why P is impossible to disbelieve, and not-P impossible to believe, is that P is true.

5 *I and other*

Merleau-Ponty invokes yet another strategy to refute scepticism about the external world and about other minds in particular. He argues that there obtain mutual dependencies both between oneself *qua* subject and the external world *qua* object and between oneself *qua* subject and other persons *qua* others. If it may be proven that these dependencies obtain then his putative refutations are sound, because this is a valid argument: I exist. My existence and the existence of the external world, including other minds, stand in a relation of reciprocal necessary condition. Therefore, the external world including other minds exists. It would be incoherent to affirm the premises but deny the conclusion. No solipsist can deny the first premise because every version of solipsism logically entails it: if only I exist then I exist. Nor can any interesting sceptic about the external world deny it because his answer to 'What is the putative external world external to?' is 'myself'. It is crucial to the solipsist to deny that my existence depends upon the existence of others and crucial to the sceptic about the external world to deny that my existence depends upon the existence of the external world.

Merleau-Ponty conjectures,

Perhaps the self and the non-self are like the obverse and the reverse. (VIT, 160)[37]

If this conjecture is right then self and external world are two properties of some underlying reality. Unfortunately Merleau-Ponty has no argument for this conjecture but some may be provided.

Arguably, what we normally take to be the external world could not appear in a perspectival way unless it were genuinely perceptually presented to some perceiving subject. Conversely, no perceiving subject could appear to itself as such unless it were perceptually presented with an external world.

Arguably 'self' makes no sense unless 'non-self' has a sense and if sense is determined by reference then if 'self' has a sense then 'non-self' has a sense and 'self' has a reference then 'non-self' has a reference. The sceptic accepts that 'self' has a reference but denies that 'non-self' has a reference but if this argument is sound then this denial must be false.

The mutual dependency between I and other is this:

The I–other relation is to be conceived (like the intersexual relation, with its indefinite substitutions . . .) as complementary roles one of which cannot be occupied without the other being also: masculinity implies femininity, etc. (VIT, 220–1)[38]

Merleau-Ponty falls short of the insight that I am the inside of the external world.

XII

Things

1 *The essence of a physical object*

In this chapter I examine Merleau-Ponty's concept of a physical object. He is interested in the question of how it is possible for there to be physical objects for us, or, to put it another way, how it is possible for us to be perceptually presented with physical objects. Merleau-Ponty conceives of this question as part of the wider question, 'How can there be objectivity?' (PPT, 300).[1]

He says 'a thing has "characteristics" or "properties" which are stable, even if they do not entirely serve to define it' (PPT, 299).[2] I shall not distinguish between characteristics and properties but stipulate that x has at least one property, F, if and only if at least one proposition is true of x (leaving aside 'x exists'). A property of x is 'stable' if and only if some proposition, P, is true of x over some relatively long time period {t1 . . . t2}; the limiting case of x possessing a 'stable' property, F, being when x possesses F during all and only {t1 . . . t2} and x exists during all and only {t1 . . . t2}. We could call this 'absolute' stability.

Merleau-Ponty talks of the possibility or impossibility of properties 'defining' objects. Merleau-Ponty often confuses use and mention but this can usually be cleared up without damage to his position. Here he needs a distinction between 'predicate' and 'property'. A property as defined above is not a word, but a predicate is a word or sequence of words that may be used to ascribe a property. Because definitions are (analytic) propositions and propositions are expressed by sentences we may say that predicates may be used in definitions. It also confuses use and mention to talk of defining things but here we may avoid the difficulty by adopting the simple expedient of writing defining 'thing' or 'physical object'.

Construed this way, Merleau-Ponty may be understood as claiming something both coherent and true. Some physical object, x, may possess some stable property, F, but from this it does not logically follow that 'F' may be significantly employed in the definition of 'x'. This is right, because from the fact that x is F, and even that x is F whenever x is, it does not logically follow that x is essentially F because from these facts alone it cannot be established that it would be contradictory to assert that x is not F. So, it does not follow either that 'F' should feature in the definition of 'x'. To put it another way, x may be contingently F even if x is F whenever x is.

In 'even if they do not entirely serve to define it' above, 'entirely' translates nothing in the French. Nevertheless, it is worth asking whether the opposite entailment holds. Although from 'x is always F' it does not follow that 'x is essentially F' and so does not follow either that 'F' is part of the definition of 'x', it does not follow from this that from the fact that x is essentially F or 'F' features in the definition of 'x' that F is not an absolutely stable property of x: that x is F whenever x is. Indeed, this reverse entailment does hold because it would be contradictory to affirm both that x is essentially F and that there is at least one time when x is but x is not F. If x is essentially F then it follows that x is F when x is, or, what is logically equivalent; if 'F' features in the definition of 'x' then F is an absolutely stable property of x.

Merleau-Ponty says, 'a thing has in the first place its size and its shape throughout variations of perspective which are merely apparent' (PP, 299).[3] 'D'abord' ('in the first place') can be read in different ways here. One fruitful reading is this: the truth of 'x has size' and 'x has shape' are each a necessary condition for 'x is a physical object'. It is not true that the truth of 'x has shape' and 'x has size' are singularly, or even jointly, sufficient for the truth of 'x is a physical object'. For example, pools of water, gases and shadows may have sizes and shapes yet none of these is a physical object.

What is needed here is a distinction between being physical and being a physical object in particular. The truth of 'x has shape' and 'x has size' are jointly sufficient for 'x is physical' but not for 'x is a physical object'. 'x has size' is not sufficient for 'x is physical' so a fortiori not sufficient for 'x is a physical object' unless 'size is physical' is made analytic. I see little good ground for doing this. Think for example of large or small numbers, or achievements.

'x has shape' is sufficient for 'x is physical' but not for 'x is a physical object' (think of holograms or reflections). Arguably 'x has shape' is not even sufficient for 'x is physical' if we allow that the contents of mental images may have shape. Clearly, however, it would be contradictory to maintain that x is a physical object and yet deny that x has shape or size so that x has some shape and some size is a necessary condition for being a physical object. Equally clearly it would not be contradictory to maintain that x has size and shape but is not a physical object so that x has shape and size is not a sufficient condition for x's being a physical object.

Another construal of 'd'abord' is this. Unless it were true that a physical object has some determinate shape and size it could not be true that 'variations' in the perception of it are possible. This is to make two properties of a physical object foundational, in the sense that being F and being G is a necessary condition for x's possessing further properties. Now, if having shape and size are necessary conditions for being a physical object then Merleau-Ponty is right to claim that having shape and size are necessary conditions for any physical object's being perceived in a perspectival way. This clearly follows because a prerequisite for the perception of a physical object (perspectival or otherwise) is the existence of that physical object and size and shape are in turn prerequisites for that existence of the physical object.

It does not follow from the fact (which Merleau-Ponty accepts) that size and shape are stable (or absolutely stable) properties of a physical object that size and shape are sufficient conditions for perspectival perceptions of that physical object. This is because from the bare fact that x is F, or x is both F and G between $\{t1 \ldots t2\}$, and even if x exists always and only between $\{t1 \ldots t2\}$, it does not follow that being F and G are prerequisites for any kind of perception of x, including perspectival perception.

Another argument may be adduced here for the view that having a determinate shape and size are necessary conditions for being perceived in a perspectival way. Arguably, x could not be perceived as a physical object unless x could, at least in principle, be perceived as having some shape and size. Smelling or tasting a physical object is not enough to perceive the physical object *qua* physical object. Perceiving that shape and size would not count as perceiving x unless it was the shape and size of x that was perceived. A physical object could only present the appearance of various shapes and sizes from numerically and qualitatively distinct viewpoints if there is some determinate shape and size which that object is. This would rest on the assumption that it is only meaningful to talk of an 'apparent' size and shape if it is meaningful to talk of a 'real' size and shape. 'x is a physical object but x has only an apparent size and shape' would then be a putative proposition that makes no sense.

2 *Perspectival perception*

Merleau-Ponty says,

It is conventional to regard as true the size which the object has

when within reach, or the shape which it assumes when it is in a
plane parallel to the frontal elevation, (PPT, 299)[4]

but crucially adds:

These are no truer than any other. (PPT, 299)[5]

Prima facie it appears that Merleau-Ponty has initially retained the
requisite semantic contrast between 'real' or 'true' shape and size in his
claim that it is 'conventional' to make this distinction. (He construes the
distinction as epistemological and not semantic.) However, the distinction is instantly jettisoned when he says that this shape and this size are
no more 'true' than any other.

There is a sense in which this is right. If an object within reach is felt,
or if an object is seen from the front, it is true that the way that the
object appears is partly dependent upon facts about the subject and
not wholly dependent upon facts about the object. Merleau-Ponty
emphasises this when he says that both views are 'evolved with the help
of our body' (PPT, 299).[6] This is not just a reiteration of his thesis that
being a body-subject is a necessary condition for perceiving the physical
world. It also suggests that the way an object feels depends partly on
the size and shape of the subject's hand and perhaps the strength of his
or her grip. The way an object appears visually 'from the front' depends
partly upon facts about the location and orientation of the eyeballs and
partly on the neuro-biology of the optical system. Seeing the object *as it
is* depends upon subjective facts just as much as seeing it only as it
appears.

Clearly, then, perceiving an object from a point of view is logically
consistent with that object thereby appearing as it is. More generally, an
object appearing is consistent with that object appearing as it is. From
'x appears' we cannot validly derive 'x does not appear as it is'.
Merleau-Ponty, however, attaches no more sense to 'as it is' than 'how
it typically appears' or 'how we conventionally believe it to be'. Felt
size and visual appearance from the front are both 'typical' (PPT, 299)
('typique' PP, 345) and,

We can always recognise them, and so they themselves provide us
with a standard for fixing and distinguishing between fleeting
appearances, for constituting objectivity, in short. (PPT, 299)[7]

Merleau-Ponty has no account of why we may 'always' recognise this
size and this shape in the object. I suggest here that realism about physical objects provides an explanation; a realism that Merleau-Ponty
eschews. It could be that the diamond shaped visual presentation of,

say, a book seen from one of its corners is just how an oblong book would look seen from one of its corners. If an object, x, presents an aspect in a way that is 'perspectival' in Merleau-Ponty's sense this is caused by its being the shape it is. Its presenting an aspect is how it looks from a perspective. We might, for example, expect circular disc-shaped objects to look elliptical as we rotate them – an object that is not round will not present the same elliptical aspect as one that is round.

Merleau-Ponty emphasises that a physical object has 'its size and its shape' (PPT, 299), and says this is true despite perspectival presentations of it. This is not just the proposition that a minimal realism about the shape and size of physical objects is held conventionally or pre-phenomenologically. It is also the claim that shape and size, as properties of a physical object, are properties of something. It is Merleau-Ponty's considered view that the properties of a physical object are not properties of a non-empirical substance but, rather like Ayer and the logical positivists, he holds that what makes a set of properties properties of a single physical object is their relation to one another; not any relation to a putative substratum. In particular, the properties of a physical object are properties of one another.

Nevertheless, there is a way of construing Merleau-Ponty's position here as a logical or analytic truth that is neutral *vis-à-vis* competing ontologies of physical objects. Suppose some subject, A, perceives some physical object, x and thereby perceives some properties of x, or, conversely, suppose A perceives some properties of x and thereby perceives x. On either account, a necessary condition of A's perception of x is that the properties perceived by A be properties of x. 'If A perceives the properties of x then those properties belong to x' is analytic and holds whatever the ontological truth about the relations between a physical object and its properties.

Merleau-Ponty addresses a question which he regards as even more fundamental than the issues of whether a physical object has a real shape and size and what the properties of a physical object are properties of. This is: how is it possible for the properties of a physical object to be presented in perception at all? Partly acknowledging the essentially Kantian nature of his phenomenology he says 'Kant is right in saying that perception is, by its nature, polarized towards the object' (PPT, 301)[8] but according to Merleau-Ponty, what cannot be explained by Kant is 'appearance as appearance' (PPT, 301).[9] Merleau-Ponty is right to suggest that both he and Kant endorse a version of the scholastic doctrine of the intentionality of perception. I leave aside whether Kant explains appearance *qua* appearance and turn to the possibility of there being physical objects for us.

THINGS

3 *Physical subjects and physical objects*

Merleau-Ponty is interested in how a physical object may present *any* aspect to a perceiver, apparent or real. He answers this question within the framework of the two central tenets of his phenomenology: the body as subject and being-in-the-world. Baldly expressed, his thesis is that it is possible for us to perceive physical objects because we are physical subjects:

> There are determinate shapes like 'a square' or 'a diamond shape', or any spatial configuration because our body as a point of view upon things, and things as abstract elements of one single world, form a system in which each moment is immediately expressive of every other. (PPT, 301)[10]

It is not clear what force Merleau-Ponty has given to 'because' ('parce que') here. Prima facie, it could be logical, causal or constitutive. It does not logically follow from the fact that there exist perceptions of properties of physical objects that the subject of those perceptions is embodied or that that subject is 'in the world'. This is not just because it might be coherent to maintain that there might be perceptions without a subject but because even if such perceptions were those of a subject it is not contradictory to maintain that that subject is purely mental or spiritual, or at least, has only a contingent relation to some body. It is by no means incoherent to suppose that such a putative subject does not exhibit those features of participating in the world entailed by 'being-in-the-world' but rather is presented perceptually with properties of physical objects by being a spectator of the world. If we try to deny this by making it analytic that perceivers of physical objects are participants in the world then we blur the distinction between participant and spectator in a way that is not useful.

If this argument is sound then it follows that neither being a body-subject nor being-in-the-world is logically necessary for being perceptually presented with the properties of physical objects. However, this is logically consistent with Merleau-Ponty being right in his three central claims here: we are body-subjects, we exhibit 'being-in-the-world' as our primordial existential location, and we are perceptually presented with properties of physical objects. It is also logically consistent with body-subjectivity and being-in-the-world being causally or constitutively necessary for the perceptual presentation of the properties of physical objects.

It is not clear that being a body-subject ('sujet incarné' PP, 515) or being-in-the-world are logically sufficient for being perceptually presented with the properties of physical objects. From the fact that some subject of experience is physical it does not logically follow that the contents or objects of the perceptions of that subject are physical. It could be that they are wholly mental or otherwise non-physical (for example, abstract or mathematical). Similarly, unless it is stipulatively made analytic that being-in-the-world is being in the physical world and being a perceiver of physical objects in that physical world then being-in-the-world is not sufficient for being perceptually presented with properties of physical objects.

Merleau-Ponty says we may perceive a square or a diamond shape because our body is a 'point of view' (PPT, 301). Now, clearly, shape may be detected through two (and only two) sensory modalities: sight and touch, and although a body-subject sees from a point of view it is less clear that it makes much sense to talk about a subject as 'touching from a point of view'. However, Merleau-Ponty may be construed as making a different point here. Arguably, the difference between a square and a diamond cannot be detected only by touch; if a diamond is a rotated square (or vice versa) then they are the same shape in their intrinsic geometry. The trouble with this is that simlar criteria seem to apply in both the visual and the tactile distinction between a diamond and a square: if two corners are presented as top and base it is a diamond. If two sides are presented as as top and base it is a square. If that is right then the diamond–square distinction, as made by us, does not depend very closely upon our bodies being 'points of view'. In the visual case alone the dependence on a point of view is strong because logical. It is hard to make sense of vision that is not from a point of view, and 'If A sees A sees from some point of view' may be analytic.

Perhaps uncontroversially, Merleau-Ponty talks of 'the thing as an intersensory entity' (PPT, 317).[11] On any theory of physical objects that captures our pre-philosophical intuitions it makes sense to speak of touching, seeing, hearing, tasting and smelling one and the same physical object (which is of course not to say, for any one physical object, that it could be detected through all the sensory modalities, even in principle). Merleau-Ponty, presents a phenomenological explanation of how physical objects may be intersensory objects:

> The thing as presented to sight (the moon's pale disc) or to touch (my skull as I can feel it when I touch it) . . . stays the same for us through a series of experiences. (PPT, 317)[12]

If one and the same physical object is perceived through a number of qualitatively distinct experiences then, on Merleau-Ponty's view, something is experienced as *the same* through those experiences. If this is to be accepted then it can only be through an appeal to experience but from the fact that some physical object, x, is the object of some series of experiences, {E1 . . . En}, it does not logically follow that {E1 . . . En}

have some qualitatively similar content common to them all. This inference does not go through except, arguably, where {E1 . . . En} are
experiences through just one sensory modality, but Merleau-Ponty
clearly has in mind the case where {E1 . . . En} are experiences through
qualitatively distinct sensory modalities. But if a subject sees, smells and
tastes, for example, the same physical object it does not follow that
there is thereby some phenomenologically presented content common to
{E1 . . . En}.

Merleau-Ponty says something consistent with this when he rejects
the idea that the constant in the perception of a physical object is
'a *quale* genuinely subsisting' (PPT, 317).[13] The putative common content is not a given quality, like a colour, sound or shape so clearly no
straightforward empirical account is possible of such a content.

Merleau-Ponty rejects a rationalist account of it too when he insists it
is not 'the notion or consciousness of such an objective property' (PP,
317).[14] This is right because the putative content is a perceptual content
and it does not make much sense to talk of perceiving notions or acts of
consciousness. The content is not the thought of the content.

Rather, the objective content is 'what is discovered or taken up by
our gaze or our movement' (PPT, 317).[15] If 'discovered or taken up' is
just what is entailed by 'perceived' here then the analysis is question-
begging. What Merleau-Ponty has in mind, however, is the point that
the physical object is grasped *as a perceptual whole* in each perception
of it. This perceptual whole is qualitatively similar in each perception of
the same object, even across qualitatively distinct sensory modalities.
He says, for example, 'the object . . . presents itself to the gaze or the
touch' (PPT, 317).[16] This implies not just that it is in fact numerically
the same physical object that is perceived through {E1 . . . En} but also
that {E1 . . . En} present that object as numerically the same physical
object through {E1 . . . En}.

Merleau-Ponty concludes,

> If the constants of each sense are thus understood, the question of
> defining the intersensory thing into which they unite as a collection
> of stable attributes or as the notion of this collection, will not
> arise. (PPT, 317)[17]

This in turn is possible because our relations to physical objects are
primarily physical and interactive and the conceivability of our cognitive
relations to physical objects depends on that. It is because we are physical subjects that we may perceive physical objects.

XIII

Art

1 *Is painting a language?*

Merleau-Ponty's considered view is that 'we must refrain finally from treating painting as a language' (PW, 47)[1] but he says nonetheless that 'the parallel is in principle legitimate' (PW, 47).[2] How may these two claims be reconciled?

The ground for the claim that painting should be treated as a language is ambiguous between the claim that painting is a language and painting is like a language. That painting is like a language does not entail that painting is a language but that painting is a language does entail that painting is like a language because it would be incoherent to maintain that something is qualitatively distinct from something with which it is numerically identical.

The translation has 'in principle' (PW, 47) but the original French is 'un principe' (PM, 66) which should be rendered 'a principle' so then we have 'the parallel is a legitimate principle'. However, the translation is here more philosophically perspicuous than the French original. It implies that it is in principle possible for painting to either be or be like a language. In other words, there is no contradiction in either the identification of painting with a language on which it turns out that painting is like a language. By 'like' here we may mean this; a is like b if and only if a and b share more properties than they do with some further object c. This reading may be extracted from the original French if for 'légitime' ('legitimate') we read 'logically legitimate'. Understood this way, Merleau-Ponty has said something meaningful and true.

The following partial ascriptions of common properties to painting and language may be extracted from Merleau-Ponty's text:

1 The same transmutation. (PW, 48)
2 The same migration of meaning scattered in experience. (PW, 48)

204

3   The same expressive function is at work in both cases. (PW, 48)[3]

I shall discuss each in turn.

A transmutation is a change of form or nature so if *a* is a transmutation of *b* then *a* does not cause *b* to cease to be but changes *b* qualitatively by translating *b* into a different medium. Both painting and language operate on their subject matter so that certain intrinsic properties of that subject matter remain unchanged, yet that subject matter is in the one case translated onto canvas and, in the other, into writing or speech. On this analysis, if some painting or language, PL, is a transmutation of some subject matter, x, then x has at least one property, F, and PL comes to be F by being caused to be F by x's being F.

The analysis of 'transmutation' can be used to read 'migration' in extract 2 but extract 2 says more than extract 1. Extract 2 reports the special case where F is a 'sens' (PM, 67) 'meaning' (PW, 48) and 'meaning' cannot only mean 'linguistic meaning'. Suppose, on the analysis of 'transmutation' or 'migration' x is some experience (other than that involved in understanding PL) and F is a meaning, then, as in 1, x is F and x causes PL to be F but F is known empirically and PL has (at least one) meaning in virtue of being caused to be F by x.

On this analysis it has to make sense to talk of meanings as (at least part of) the subject matter of painting or language where this means something other than: the painting or the language is meaningful. Merleau-Ponty allows, indeed elsewhere emphasises, such a use of 'meaning'. For example, he speaks of 'the active meaning-giving operation which may be said to define consciousness' (PPT, xi).[4] Consciousness bestows a 'meaning' on some (partially or wholly intrinsically indeterminate) subject matter 'x' if and only if consciousness (partly or wholly) makes x be what x is. This analysis gives rise to several issues. One I shall not address is the sense that may be given to 'x' if x is wholly indeterminate, especially the question of whether such a putative subject matter could be individuated. Another is the question of what x is when x is made what it is by consciousness. Here I would say that x is only what it is under a possible description. Merleau-Ponty eschews that linguistic idiom so I say x is what x is in virtue of that which would make some description of x true. That is bestowed by consciousness. It is meanings in this sense of 'meanings' that migrate from experience into both painting and language. I suggest as examples: a painting of x and a definition of 'x'. These have something in common: a depiction of x.

Both painting and language 'express'. 'Express' is not clarified by Merleau-Ponty but 'express' has the literal sense of 'emit' or 'exude' or 'symbolise'. The first two senses may be taken as denoting the causal relation between x and PL and those relata, when x causes PL to be F in virtue of being F. The sense in which 'express' can mean 'to represent by symbols' (as, for example, in the notations of mathematical logic) captures a new similarity between painting and language. It is an unsolved philosophical problem what it consists in for one portion of what is to represent another portion of what is (despite the currency of the concept) but the appearance of the word suggests 'to present more than once (at least twice)': to 're-present'. We may take the first presentation just as the presentation of x. If PL 'represents' x, then, PL presents x without being x. Again, it follows that PL aquaints us with what x is without thereby directly acquainting us with x.

It follows from this account too that both language and painting either are or contain 'symbols'. I shall understand by 'symbol' just whatever it is in the ontology of painting or language in virtue of which painting and language represent. It follows that PL's being or containing a symbol is both necessary and sufficient for PL's being or containing a representation.

We are in a position now to see how Merleau-Ponty's two claims may be reconciled. Clearly, from the fact that it is not a contradictory supposition that painting is or is like a language it does not logically follow that that claim is true. It follows that Merleau-Ponty may consistently reject it even if he sees no logical ground for its negation.

Arguably, whether painting is like, or sufficiently like to be a language are in principle undecidable questions. This does not mean it is philosophically uneducative to try to answer them. The problem is that questions of the form, 'Is x (qualitatively) similar to y?' always logically invite the question, 'In what respect?'. Then we need criteria for counting respects and the task becomes infinite. In this particular case the difficulty is compounded because it is not obvious that there exist necessary and sufficient conditions for something's being a language and necessary and sufficient conditions for something's being a painting. Evaluating Merleau-Ponty's comparison requires solving these prior problems in the philosophy of language and aesthetics.

2 Art and science

In *L'Œil et L'Esprit* Merleau-Ponty argues for two main conclusions: art is phenomenologically prior to science and only an embodied being may be an artist. These are themselves putative substantiations of his theses that science presupposes but does not explain the lived world, and a subject of thought and action is a subject with a body.

Merleau-Ponty ascribes certain properties to science which art allegedly lacks. Notably:

1 Science manipulates things and gives up living in them
2 It comes face to face with the real world only at rare intervals
3 [Science's] fundamental bias is to treat everything as though it were an object in general – as though it meant nothing to us and yet was predestined for our own use. (OE, 159)[5]

I shall take each of these in turn.

'Science manipulates things' is either elliptical for 'science makes possible the technology which physically manipulates things' (or some logically equivalent proposition) or entails that the conception of the world by science is itself a kind of manipulation: a kind of intellectual construal. The two interpretations are mutually consistent and nothing logically forces us to choose one over the other.

The idea that science 'gives up living' in things is consistent with Merleau-Ponty's thesis that science essentially proceeds by ignoring the subject. Indeed, a world without the subject is not a world that can be 'lived in': subjectively inhabited *from the inside*. It follows that something like Merleau-Ponty's subjectless view of science is a logical prerequisite for the impossibility of a scientific account of being-in-the-world. The argument is this: if something is an account of being-in-the-world then it must postulate a subject. Science postulates no subject. Science cannot provide an account of being-in-the-world. This argument is not only valid, but sound because it is true that science has no depiction of the subject and a depiction of the subject is a necessary condition for an account of being-in-the-world.

Art, in contrast, neither manipulates things nor gives up living in the world.

3 *Painting and the body*

Art for Merleau-Ponty is, in a sense, the opposite of science. While science is formal and universal, art, especially painting, depicts content and the particular:

art, especially painting, draws upon this fabric of brute meaning which activism [or operationalism] would prefer to ignore. Art and only art does so in full innocence. (OET, 161)[6]

Science, in so far as it treats of individuals, describes them *qua* occupiers of a functional role, not in virtue of their intrinsic perceptible properties. Art shuns this means-to-ends thinking in order to depict the individual as it is given to consciousness. Art, like phenomenology, is concrete and immediate but science is abstract and mediated.

While science can tell no one how to live, literature and philosophy suggest an ethic. When Merleau-Ponty says:

> From the writer and the philosopher . . . we want opinions and advice. We will not allow them to hold the world suspended. (OET, 161)[7]

he is implicitly presenting a critique of Husserl's transcendental phenomenology which 'suspends' the world by the *epoché*. As we have seen, Merleau-Ponty eschews the *epoché* and substitutes for it the structures of his 'existential' phenomenology, notably being-in-the-world. At this point in Merleau-Ponty's text Husserl's phenomenology is subject to the same critique as the natural sciences: it does not tell us how to live.

Although music is the most formal of the arts, science fails where music succeeds in describing the structure of being:

> Music . . . is too far beyond the world and the designatable to depict anything but certain outlines of Being – its ebb and flow, its growth, its upheavals, its turbulence. (OET, 161)[8]

While it makes sense to say that a painting or a sculpture is *of* something this does not make much sense in the case of music. At least in the case of realist paintings it can be seen what the painting is a painting of (whether or not the object of depiction is something that exists). In music this is far more difficult and Merleau-Ponty thinks the reason is that music has a generality which painting lacks. Music depicts the changes in what is as they might be given to a subject, almost irrespective of what is.

Art is paradigmatically painting for Merleau-Ponty and for two reasons. Painting is revelatory of the visibility of what is, the visibility of what is revelatory of what is is, so painting is revelatory of what is is. Second, painting uncovers the role of the body in the constitution of what is.

Painting is revelatory of the nature of being not only because what is is paradigmatically visible and painting depicts the visible *qua* visible, but also because,

> Only the painter is entitled to look at everything without being obliged to appraise what he sees. (OET, 161)[9]

Painting exhibits an objectivity which not only the sciences but even the other arts lack. Here Merleau-Ponty turns the table on a widely held assumption: art is in some broad sense 'subjective' and science is in some broad sense 'objective'. 'Subjective' and 'objective' are useless words in philosophy unless they can be disambiguated but one sense of subjective is: x is subjective if and only if x is wholly or partly constituted by the psychology of the subject and one sense of 'objective' is 'x is objective if and only if x is and x wholly is what it is irrespective of the psychology of any subject'. As we have seen, Merleau-Ponty thinks science is a 'construction' (OET, 160) and this means not only that the theories and the experiments of science are human artefacts but also the world as depicted by science is itself a human artefact. Its coming, so to speak, to be that world, is a contrivance of human intelligence, human ingenuity. It follows logically that science is subjective in the sense defined above. Of course science might not be thus subjective because some of Merleau-Ponty's premises might be false. They are certainly philosophically contentious. However, the derivation is valid.

Now, art cannot be objective in the sense of 'objective' that contrasts with 'subjective' above. This is because it could not with any plausibility be argued that art is not a 'construction'. Works of art are products of the human world just as much as the theories and experiments of science. But that is not what Merleau-Ponty is claiming. He is claiming that the artist is passive and non-evaluative in the face of his subject matter and that subject matter itself belongs to the lived world. So long as he paints well, then, the painter paints the world as we experience it, as we live through it. There is a profound sense in which it follows that the painter paints the world as it is: the world 'as it is' can only mean 'as it is for us'. This is not a kind of subjectivism, prima facie appearances to the contrary notwithstanding, because we have no conception of any world as it is unless this means as it is for us.

Painting is phenomenologically prior to science. Unless the world is as depicted in painting there could be no science. This is because painting is painting of the lived world and the lived world grounds science. Without the lived world there could be no scientists and no scientific subject matter.

Merleau-Ponty calls painting 'this secret science' perhaps because it contains an objectivity that is usually assumed only to pertain to the strict or natural sciences. Perhaps also because it is a fundamental enquiry into the universe, a more profound inquiry than any scientific inquiry.

Merleau-Ponty asks whether there is anything that grounds painting, anything that makes even painting possible:

What, then, is this secret science which he [the painter] has or which he seeks? That dimension which lets Van Gogh say he must go 'further on'? What is this fundamental of painting, perhaps of all culture? (OET, 161)[10]

Merleau-Ponty is establishing a hierarchy of dependencies: science depends on the lived world. The lived world could not be what it is unless it were a visible world. The lived world *qua* visible world could not be what it is unless it could at least in principle be painted. Now he is asking what has to be the case for something to be a possible object of painting, what the necessary conditions for depiction by painting are.

If this hierarchy seems shocking or provocative it is because it is phenomenological rather than commonsensical or positivist. Non-phenomenologically we would assume that unless the world is as described by science then there could be no painters, no canvases, no paint or brushes and no empirical world to depict by painting. But Merleau-Ponty would say that this hierarchy, however psychologically compelling, however much we think it must be right, is an abstraction. It is an abstraction because it is derived from thinking about the world not from experiencing it. In the background again are the old dualisms Merleau-Ponty seeks to overcome: rationalism and empiricism, idealism and realism. Here the commonsensical and positivist hierarchy is rationalist and ideal. The phenomenological hierarchy is empiricist and real. If we think in terms of what we experience, if we so to speak, pause to look and see, it is possible to see the plausibility in Merleau-Ponty's hierarchy. Unless we were acquainted with a world of everyday physical things it is hard to see how we we could make sense of the postulates of science.

Merleau-Ponty finds a clue to what makes painting possible in the physical activity of painting:

> we cannot imagine how a mind could paint. It is by lending his
> body to the world that the artist changes the world into paintings.
> To understand these transubstantiations we must go back to the
> working, actual body – not the body as a chunk of space or a
> bundle of functions but that body which is an intertwining of
> vision and movement. (OET, 162)[11]

It is perhaps too strong to say that we cannot imagine how a mind could paint – he means a mind without a body. I can imagine this. Suppose one never perceived one's body, for example, suppose one's body never entered one's visual field so that one 'saw' objects which would normally be concealed by one's body. Suppose further that one is aware of one's thoughts and some of these thoughts are intentions and willings to paint parts of a picture. Suppose further, by the mere thinking of these thoughts and the exerting of these acts of will a brush suspended in mid air were to leave paint on the canvas in accordance with one's intention and will. This would be imagining a mind painting.

It is important to separate the idea that this happens from the idea that this can be imagined: the implausibility of its happening is not the impossibility of its being imagined. (Although, its being imagined without contradiction removes all logical obstacles to its happening.) If one baulks at the idea of imagining psycho-physical causal connections, think of the relation between one's own intentions and one's own bodily movements. They are as mysterious or as uncontroversial as moving objects in the external world by mere acts of will.

However, a more modest claim does go through: the painter uses his body to paint. It is then a phenomenologically legitimate project to describe the role of the body in making painting possible (empirically possible or phenomenologically possible. By 'phenomenologically possible' here I mean: x makes y phenomenologically possible if and only if y could not have the phenomenology it has unless x has the phenomenology it has. We could allow an additional sense: x makes y phenomenologically possible if and only if x allows y to be a possible object of experience. Before turning to that, however, we should examine Merleau-Ponty's claim that 'le peintre change le monde en peinture' (OE, 16) 'the artist changes the world into paintings' (OET, 162). ('The painter changes the world into painting' would be a more accurate translation.)

One way of taking this is to consider that a painting is itself, in a sense, a part of the world. A painting is a manipulation of matter and changing of the spatio-temporal location of innumerable physical items. Matter is wrought into a new form. In this sense, part of the world is changed into a painting. Wood, paint and canvas are changed into a painting.

Another interpretation is this: painting the world enables us to perceive the world as like a painting. For Merleau-Ponty this, in some respects, means perceiving the world as it is; that is, as we directly experience it to be as opposed to how we *believe* it to be.

Now, paintings are produced by the painter *qua* body-subject, not *qua* physical object. In the body-subject there is a mutual dependence between vision and movement which painting both reveals and depends upon. According to Merleau-Ponty we would not see what we see unless we could move as we do and we could not move as we do unless we could see as we see. This is why he says there is 'an intertwining of vision and movement' (OET 162). Notably, the world appears visually like a world through which I could travel and the world I travel through feels like the world I see. Here is an interdependence between movement and vision:

My mobile body makes a difference in the visible world, being a part of it; that is why I can steer through the visible. (OET, 162)[12]

211

The visible world would not look how it does unless I could take a mobile route through it, but unless it looked to my how it does I could not take any route through it. Here is a dependence of vision on motion:

> Vision is attached to movement. We see only what we look at. And what would vision be without eye movement? (OET, 162)[13]

However, the bare movement of the eyes *qua* physical objects is not sufficient for vision, they have to be the functioning eyes of a conscious body-subject:

> How could the movement of the eyes bring things together if the movement were blind? If it were only a reflex? (OET, 162)[14]

If only a third person singular physiological description of the eye were possible then we could not conclude from this that the eye sees. It is the phenomenon of being part of a body-subject engaged in the world that is further necessary for vision.

The visible world and the world of my movements are in fact one and the same world, describable either in terms of possible routes or in terms of what can be seen. Each of us has both what Merleau-Ponty calls 'the map of the visible' (OET, 162)[15] and 'the map of the "I can"' (OET, 162):[16] not only the idea of what I can see but the idea of the totality of my possible projects. He says 'each of these two maps is complete' (OET, 162)[17] but adds that although there are two 'maps' there are not two worlds. What they depict is so mutually dependent that we can only talk of one world:

> The visible world and the world of my motor projects are each total parts of the same Being. (OET, 162)[18]

Merleau-Ponty thinks that the philosophical implications of this mutual dependence have been underestimated (at least, this is how I read his claim that we do not think sufficiently about 'cet extraordinaire empiètement' (OE, 17) 'this extraordinary overlapping' (OET, 163). Notably, the numerical identity of the world of motor action and the world of vision prevents our correctly conceiving the world as only a picture or a representation. Merleau-Ponty does not spell out the philosophical implications of this but they may be conjectured.

We may use Merleau-Ponty's identification of the world as a set of routes for my travelling with the visible world to combat a pervasive and recurrent tendency in the philosophy of mind and perception. This is the view, or the sceptical possibility, that the world we experience is only a representation, or, if not that, then in some sense just mental: a set of ideas, impressions, sense data, phenomena and so on. The viability of this view derives from neglecting the fact that the world is one I may travel through and privileging the fact that the world is a visible world. We may use Merleau-Ponty's identification of the motor-world with the visible world to place the onus on the idealist or the sceptic to argue for the privileging of vision over movement; of contemplation over action.

Suppose Merleau-Ponty is right that the world could not have its visible properties unless it was a set of routes for my travels and vice versa. If the world is a visual world then that will then turn out to be a sufficient condition for the world being a motor world. The idealist and the sceptic accept that the world is a visual world, but a necessary condition for the world's being visual is that it be a motor world. But then the world is a motor world and that is inconsistent with idealism and scepticism about the world. This is because it makes no sense to say that I travel through a world that is not physical or is a part of me. If the world is not motor then the world is not visible. The world is visible. Therefore, the world is motor.

If this argument is sound then Merleau-Ponty's exhibition of the dependence of the visual on the motor may be used to solve two long standing and conceptually interrelated problems in philosophy: 'is there an external world?' and 'is the external world only mental?' The answers are, respectively, 'yes' and 'no'.

XIV

Being

To understand Merleau-Ponty on being, a distinction needs to be drawn between these two questions: 'What is there?' and 'What is it to be?' The answer to 'What is there?' is a list of items of different ontological types, putatively for example: electrons, numbers, minds, physical objects, sensations and perhaps much else. Crucially, the answer to 'What is it to be?' does not consist in adding some items to this list. It consists in a specification of what exactly it consists in for anything to be, whatever it is. Merleau-Ponty in deciding 'the meaning of being' (VIT, 6)[1] is entirely concerned with the second question: 'Suppose something is. What is thereby true of it?' and not at all concerned with the first question: 'What exists?'

Although the question of what it is to be is recurrent in Western thought – conspicuously it is tackled by Parmenides, Plato, Aristotle, Aquinas, Berkeley, Kant and Hegel for example – it is Heidegger's attempt to answer it in *Sein und Zeit* that provides Merleau-Ponty with his own model of how it should be addressed.[2] In this chapter I examine Merleau-Ponty's quasi-Heideggerian attempts to answer the question of being and then evaluate his explicit endorsements and repudiations of Heidegger's 'fundamental ontology'.

1 *The meaning of being*

Merleau-Ponty says,

> For us the essential is to know precisely what the being of the world means. (VIT, 6)[3]

If the world is what is then the being of the world is what it consists in for what is to be. The meaning or 'sense' ('sens') of the being of the world is the specification of what it is for what is to be.

The question of the meaning of being is primordial, not in the sense that answering it is a prerequisite for answering empirical questions but in both a conceptual sense and an ontological sense. The conceptual sense is this: a grasp of any concept seems to presuppose a grasp of the concept of being. Unless one had a minimal grasp of what it consists in to be it is hard to see how one could have a grasp of anything else, in particular, being something or other. A grasp of a's being would seem to be at least a psychologically necessary condition for a grasp of a's being F. The ontological sense is this: unless there were something that it consists in to be there could not be anything. More accurately, unless there were being or existence, rather than nothing at all, there could not be any particular things nor sorts of things, including *a fortiori* the things and sorts of things there are.

Philosophically, the question of being is extraordinarily difficult to answer, not only because the concept of being is prima facie logically primitive but also because the distinct question 'What is there?' is easily mistakenly assimilated to it. Then the devising of an ontology becomes an obstacle to stating the meaning of being. Merleau-Ponty's expression of his awareness of this problem is both logically equivalent to Heidegger's distinction between entities and the being of entities in *Sein und Zeit* and logically equivalent to his assertion that an inquiry into entities may be mistaken for an inquiry into their being:[4]

> Philosophy elects certain beings – 'sensations', 'representation', 'thought', 'consciousness', or even a deceiving being – in order to separate itself from all being. (VIT, 107)[5]

The first task of any inquirer into being, therefore, is to avoid being diverted; to avoid privileging some particular being or some sort of being instead of inquiring into what it is for any being to be. This danger is emphasised by Heidegger in *Sein und Zeit* when he claims that Aristotle forgot the question of the being of entities for an inquiry into which entities are. Merleau-Ponty's 'tout être' (VI, 144), 'all being' (VIT, 107) here does not denote the totality of what is but the existence of what is; the fact that is expressed about what is when it is claimed that what there is is.

It is hard to see why anyone should mistakenly assimilate the questions of what there is and what it is for what there is to be but Heidegger and Merleau-Ponty are certainly right in their observation that people do make this assimilation. As so often, grasping a problem *qua* philosophical is a necessary condition for doing philosophy.

Just as essential to the inquiry into the meaning of being is the suspension of all preconceptions (and *a fortiori*, all philosophical scientific and commonsensical preconceptions) about the nature of being.

Answering the question of being requires the adoption of the Husserlian phenomenological ideal of doing presuppositionless philosophy. In particular,

> Here we must presuppose nothing – neither the naive idea of being in itself therefore nor the correlative idea of a being of representation, of a being for the consciousness, of a being for man. (VIT, 6)[6]

Presuppositions must be suspended because thinking of ways in which the world is is only ever going to result in thoughts of the form 'a is F','b is G', or constructions out of these. This kind of thinking takes us no nearer to knowing what it is for a or for b to be. Being F does not explain being.

By 'the naive idea of being in itself' Merleau-Ponty means the intuitive pre-philosophical idea of the world being as it is irrespective of one's thought or perception of it, together with the scientific idea of an 'objective' world premised on that. 'A being of representation', 'a being for [the] consciousness' and 'a being for man' all have it in common to denote a putative world which is what it is because it is presented to a subject. It follows that Merleau-Ponty has distinguished here two pervasive ontologies: metaphysical realism and (in differing degrees) metaphysical idealism. The phenomenological (and so putatively non-metaphysical) semantic equivalent of this distinction is that between 'en-soi', 'in itself', 'an-sich' and 'pour-soi', 'for-itself', 'für-sich'. Interestingly, by his use of 'correlative' Merleau-Ponty suggests that these two prima facie mutually inconsistent ways of thinking might really be mutually dependent.

The inquiry into being is not only more fundamental than any metaphysical ontology and any epistemological distinction between realism and anti-realism. It is more fundamental than non-ontological phenomenology. 'Etre', ('being') is ontologically prior to both 'être en-soi' and 'être pour-soi'. None of these distinctions could obtain if there was nothing.

However, from the fact that traditional philosophical taxonomies cannot be used to explain being it does not logically follow that a solution to the problem of being cannot lead to a rethinking of traditional ontology. Merleau-Ponty claims that this is indeed the case when he says of all the subjective–objective distinctions above: 'these . . . are all notions that we have to rethink' (VIT, 6).[7]

In *Phénoménologie de la Perception* perception, in Merleau-Ponty's broad sense, is used to explain the possibility of the world; how it can be that there is a world for us. No analogous procedure is available to answer the question of being. The world, perception and the veridical or non-veridical relations between them all presuppose being:

The perception of the world is formed in the world, the test for truth takes place in Being. (VIT, 253)[8]

Although the perception of the world, in a minimal sense, logically entails the existence of perception and the world it does not explain it. Saying that there is perception, that there is perception of what is and that what is is what it is, does not say what it is for what is to be. Also, unless what is is it is not possible for what is to be what it is: a perceptually constituted world.

If this line of reasoning is sound then the inquiry into being in *Le Visible et L'Invisible* is logically prior to the phenomenology of *Phénoménologie de la Perception*. This means: the truth of the propositions of *Le Visible et L'Invisible* is a necessary condition for the truth of the propositions in *Phénoménologie de la Perception* but the truth of the propositions of *Phénoménologie de la Perception* is not necessary for the truth of the propositions of *Le Visible et L'Invisible*. If that is right, then *Le Visible et L'Invisible* 'grounds' or 'founds' *Phénoménologie de la Perception* transcendentally.

2 *The invisible*

The problem Merleau-Ponty faces is this: if being is not being something then how can being be being anything at all? We may agree with Heidegger and Merleau-Ponty that a's being is not a's being F but then it is hard to see how 'being' can be given any semantic content. Merleau-Ponty's solution to this problem is ingenious.

Consistently with Heidegger's procedure in *Sein und Zeit* Merleau-Ponty says 'The meaning of being is to be disclosed' (VIT, 253).[9] Crucially, and entailed by the suspension of pre-conceptions, the inquirer must remain cognitively passive in the face of being. Being must unveil or uncover or disclose itself. The being of what is becomes apparent only through the suspension of beliefs about the respects in which what is is what it is. This is what Heidegger means when he says the meaning of being is 'disclosed'.[10]

We come now, however, to a crucial bifurcation between the views of Heidegger and Merleau-Ponty. Famously, or notoriously, Heidegger thinks being is disclosed through *Dasein*. Dasein, or human being in the sense of the being that one oneself is, is the 'site' or 'place' in which being is disclosed. For Merleau-Ponty however, being is not paradigmatically disclosed through human being but through the invisible.

Merleau-Ponty speaks of the invisible as 'L'Etre de ce étant' (VI, 198) 'the Being of this being' (VIT, 151):

The invisible of this world, that which inhabits this world, sustains it, and renders it visible its own and interior possibility, the Being of this being. (VIT, 151)[11]

The being that the invisible is the Being of is the world: what is. As we saw in Chapter V above, the world as perceived is phenomenologically parasitic upon the world as unperceived: what is could not appear just as it does unless, essentially, part of it did not appear. This logically entails that the visible phenomenologically depends on the invisible. However, now Merleau-Ponty is further asserting that the invisible is that through which the being of the world is disclosed. Why does he think this?

Clearly, from the fact that x is (necessarily or contingently) invisible it does not logically follow that x is or discloses what being is nor that x itself is. Nor, even if x is and x is invisible, does it logically follow that x's invisibility is what x's being consists in. Being and being invisible are prima facie logically independent and 'being' and 'being invisible' are prima facie semantically independent. This is because we cannot derive 'there is an x' from 'x is F'.

Invisibility discloses being for the following reason. Thinking of x without thinking of x appearing is just thinking of x being. When one thinks of what is as not perceptually present one nevertheless thinks of what is as existing. The disclosure of being requires the abstraction or mental stripping away of empirical properties, but this process is already facilitated in the thinking of the invisible.

The idea of the invisible that is revelatory of being is 'not a de facto invisibility' (VIT, 151).[12] This is not just a reiteration of Merleau-Ponty's view that invisibility is a phenomenologically necessary condition for visibility. It is also the claim that the conceptual connection between invisibility and being is not contingent. The distinction between being and being F conceptually depends upon the distinction between being invisible and being visible. It might seem prima facie as though there is conceptual room for a distinction between being and being something which does not depend upon a notion of what is and what is not available to perception. In fact, the idea of being but not being something depends upon the idea of not being perceptible. Plausibly, if one only possessed the concept of an object as perceived and no concept of an object unperceived one would always only possess the concept of the object having (empirical) properties and no concept of what being is *tout court*.

There are other clues to the nature of being according to Merleau-Ponty, the most important of which are painting and the body. On painting he says,

> To paint, to sketch, is not to produce something from nothing . . .
> the drawing, the touch of the brush and the visible work are but the
> trace of a total movement of speech, which goes into being as a
> whole. (VIT, 211)[13]

Painting is revelatory of being because it is a depiction of the visible which
makes an awareness of the invisible possible. By construing painting as a
kind of language addressed to being Merleau-Ponty is drawing attention
not only to the fact that paintings are not painted *ex nihilo*, but also to
his claim that the visible presupposes the invisible and the invisible presupposes the visible. The visible and the invisible jointly exhaust what is
(we can see this because for any x either x is visible or invisible). Visibility
is revelatory of what is being what it is but invisibility is revelatory of
what is being *tout court*. Although the perceptible is, the perceptible is
not paradigmatically illustrative of what it consists in to be. The perceptible provides symptoms of being: 'Colours, sounds, and things – like
Van Gogh's stars – are the focal points and radiance of being' (ST, 15).[14]
 On the body as a clue to being, Merleau-Ponty says,

> Carnal being, as a being of depths, of several leaves or several faces,
> a being in latency, and a presentation of a certain absence is a
> prototype of Being. (VIT, 136)[15]

and

> our body, the sensible sentient is a very remarkable variant but
> whose constitutive paradox already lies in every visible. (VIT, 136)[16]

The physical world, especially the body-subject ('sujet incarné' PP, 175)
that one is, is a kind of model of being. The constitutive paradox is the
relation between the presence and the absence of a physical being. Not
only one's own body ('corps propre' PP, 528) but any object *qua* object
of perception is presented as partly present and partly absent. The whole
object is constituted by both what is perceptually absent and what is
perceptually present. Now, this is a model of being because in perception
being *qua* being is absent. If an object is perceived it is perceived to be G,
to be F and so on. However, although one can, so to speak, *perceive that
it is*, it is not the being of the thing that one thereby perceives: as an
extra but peculiar property. On the contrary, being is not being something so the perceptually absent properties of the object are a much closer
depiction of being.
 The presentation of being is 'a presentation of a certain absence'
(VIT, 136) ('une présentation d'une certaine absence' VI, 179). It is, for
example, the presentation of the absence of properties but not the

presentation of absolutely nothing. There is a distinction to be drawn between the presentation of an absence and the presentation of nothing. The presentation of an absence is the presentation of what could be fully present through the presentation of its properties. The presentation of nothing is not the presentation of anything.

The body is 'a remarkable varient' (VIT, 136) on physical being largely because it is a subject: for some I 'I am it' is true, but also both because it is the vehicle or instrument of perception and because it admits of the 'pour-soi'/en-soi' distinction. Both the body and any other physical being exhibit the 'constitutive paradox' because they are composed of what is absent and what is present to perception; what is phenomenal and what is objective. The body admits of this distinction as does any physical being. The paradox consists in something's being present as the thing it is partly consisting in its partly being absent.

Merleau-Ponty refuses to categorise the paradox as purely human,

It is indeed a paradox of Being, not a paradox of man, that we are dealing with here. (VIT, 136)[17]

If the paradox is constitutive of any physical object *qua* possible object of perception then it logically follows that the paradox is not only constitutive of the human body-subject. However, Merleau-Ponty accepts that it is the existence of the body-subject that makes possible the presentation of objects of perception (including itself) and that it is that that makes the constitutive paradox possible. These facts are not logically sufficient to make the paradox human ('de l'homme') in the sense of 'only constitutive of human being'. Any possible physical object of perception admits of a phenomenal/objective distinction which essentially makes it what it is *qua* possible object of perception.

What particularly distinguishes the human body-subject from physical objects of perception is the exhibiting of the *pour-soi/en-soi* distinction. This is not exhibited by any physical object of perception because any such object is only *en-soi* and not *pour-soi*. However, any human body-subject is both *pour-soi* and *en-soi*. Here we should note two important phenomenological breaks which Merleau-Ponty makes, one with Hegel and one with Sartre. Both departures are made here:

The in itself–for itself integration takes place not in [the] absolute consciousness, but in [the] Being in promiscuity. (VIT, 253)[18]

This conjunctive claim is logically inconsistent with both Hegel's and Sartre's specifications of the relations between being in itself and being for itself. It is inconsistent with Sartre's because Sartre thinks there is no 'synthesis' between *l'être en-soi* and *l'être pour-soi*. Being is permanently phenomenologically bifurcated in a way that cannot be dialectically 'overcome' nor transcendentally grounded. Merleau-Ponty's thesis is inconsistent with Hegel's for a different reason. Merleau-Ponty accepts Hegel's view that there is a ground or a synthesis of being in itself and being for itself, but he thinks the synthesis is in being *qua* the being of what is and not in 'absolute consciousness' (VIT, 253) 'conscience absolue' (VI, 307).

Merleau-Ponty neglects two points of Hegelian exegesis here. Hegel does not speak of 'absolute consciousness' but 'absolute knowledge' ('Das absolute Wissen') and *das absolute Wissen* is the culminative speculative synthesis of being and consciousness. In absolute knowing there is no irreducible difference between what is being what it is and what is knowing what it is. In this way the 'contradiction' between being and knowing is overcome and the difference between epistemology and ontology eliminated. Merleau-Ponty should have noted this because the Hegelian distinction between 'an-sich' and 'für-sich' is also subsumed under 'das absolute Wissen'. The distinction and what makes it possible is entailed by the correct specification of *das absolute Wissen*. Nevertheless, Merleau-Ponty's synthesis is inconsistent with Hegel's because Hegel would certainly not accept an overcoming of the in itself/for itself distinction just in the being of what is.

It would be a mistake to identify being with just being in itself or just being for itself or even with both. This would be a mistake even if the totality of what is is being for itself and being in itself. Being is not just subjective being. To think that it is is the mistake of idealism. Being is not just objective being. To think that it is is the mistake of realism. Being is not the totality of what is, subjective and objective being, because the totality of what is is not identical with the *being* of the totality of what is.

Being, then, is putatively the solution to this question which was raised in *Phénoménologie de la Perception* and taken up again in *Le Visible et L'Invisible*:

> Between the two 'sides' of our body, the body as sensible and the body as sentient . . . rather than a spread, there is an abyss that separates the In Itself from the For Itself. (VIT, 136–7)[19]

so

> It is a problem . . . to determine how the sensible sentient can also be thought. (VIT, 137)[20]

There is a reciprocal dependency between the *en-soi/pour-soi* distinction and the phenomenal/objective distinction. Unless we could, in principle, draw one we could not draw the other. Unless there were a distinction between subjective being (or subjects) and objective being (or objects) perception would not be possible. Without something that exists that perceives and without something that exists that is perceived the relation called 'perceiving' cannot obtain. Conversely, however, unless there obtained the relation called 'perceiving' and the distinction that pre-supposes between the way the world appears (phenomenally) and the way the world is (objectively) there could not be portions of what is that are subjective perceivers and objective perceiveds. It is *qua* perceiver that a portion of what is is *pour-soi* and it is paradigmatically *qua* per-ceived that a portion of what is is *en-soi*. However, prima facie no perceiver *qua* perceiver is a perceived and no perceived *qua* perceived is a perceiver. No being for itself *qua* being for itself is a being in itself and no being in itself *qua* being in itself is a being for itself.

The problem, then, is how the thought or the concept of that which is both *pour-soi* and *en-soi* is possible; how the 'sentant sensible' (VI, 180) 'sensible sentient' (VIT, 137) as a whole can be thought.

Merleau-Ponty's answer is that being is prior to both the *en-soi*/pour-soi distinction and the phenomenal/objective distinction. There is a clear sense in which this is right. Being is prior to being anything. Unless something is it cannot have any properties. Being is a necessary condition for being F. Whether this dependency is reciprocal, whether being F is a necessary condition for being is an unsolved philosophical problem but Merleau-Ponty is at least right that the subjective/objective distinctions he is discussing cannot obtain unless there is something rather than nothing.

Also, even if there is something and what is is F it does not follow that being F is logically sufficient for being *en-soi*, or being *pour-soi*, or being phenomenal or being objective. It would not be contradictory to assert that something is and has a property but not a property that is or is entailed by the true ascription of any of those predicates. This is a further reason for thinking the concept of being prior to subjective/objective distinctions. That x is and that x is F is a necessary (but not sufficient) condition for the true ascription of any subjective and objec-tive predicates but the true ascription of some subjective or objective predicate is a sufficient (but not a necessary) condition for the truth of both 'x is' and 'x is F'. It logically follows from this that Merleau-Ponty is right to hold that the concept of being is prior to those distinctions.

The concept of being allows the thinking of being F. It follows that the concept of being allows the thinking of the body-subject as both *pour-soi* and *en-soi*. Although *qua être pour-soi* the body is not *être en-soi* and although *qua être en-soi* the body is not *être pour-soi* it is not contradictory to affirm that one and the same body is both *pour-soi* and *en-soi*. We just have to stipulate that the respect in which it is *en-soi* is not the respect in which it is *pour-soi*. If we ask what it is that is both *pour-soi* and *en-soi* then this question has two kinds of answer. The answer which is presupposed by (or logically entails) that it is both *pour-soi* and *en-soi* is that it is a body-subject. If we ask what it is that is both *pour-soi* and *en-soi* and does not presuppose the *pour-soi/en-soi* distinction then the answer is being. It is being that is both *pour-soi* and *en-soi* and this is consistent with the considered view of Merleau-Ponty (and Hegel and Sartre) that the *en-soi/pour-soi* distinction is a distinction between two kinds of being.

It is also logically consistent with Merleau-Ponty's view that the invisible is paradigmatically revelatory of being because that which is both *pour-soi* and *en-soi* and that which makes the *pour-soi/en-soi* distinction possible is invisible. Being is not nothing, and that entails contra Hegel and Sartre, 'the impossibility of a philosophy of Being and Nothingness' (VIT, 196).[21] Being is the presentation of an absence. Being is invisible.

XV

Parousia

Existential Phenomenology and the
Return of Metaphysics

Since the 'Scientific Revolution' of the seventeenth century Western philosophy has increasingly taken as its paradigm of knowledge scientific knowledge. By 'science' I mean any systematic inquiry that uses empirical experiments and mathematical models to obtain predictive knowledge of its subject matter. It is essential to science that the subjective point of view of the inquirer is suspended so that any findings have a neutrality or objectivity that makes them available to any unbiased learner. It is characteristic of scientific prose to be couched in the grammatical third person and to treat any subject matter as entirely physical.[1]

The greatest contribution of existential phenomenology to Western philosophy is to call this paradigm of knowledge into question. Although Merleau-Ponty is not such a thorough thinker about Being as Heidegger and although Merleau-Ponty has neither the literary talent nor the political dexterity of Sartre, it is he rather than they who provides the most insightful suggestions for a critique of science. I say this despite the observations on the dangers of technology in Heidegger's *Die Frage nach der Technik* and despite Sartre's anti-positivist descriptions of freedom and subjectivity in *L'Etre et le Néant*.[2]

Although contemporary positivistic philosophies have much to learn from existential phenomenology about their own heuristic limitations, existential phenomenology has as much to learn about its own metaphysical presuppositions. Western philosophy since Kant has been in the grip of a Kantian anti-metaphysical paradigm. All the salient movements in philosophy since Kant have been essentially Kantian and philosophically this is a much more significant fact about them than the distinction between 'analytical' and 'modern continental' philosophy which is, in the end, vacuous.[3] Philosophy since Kant is a series of metaphysical suicide attempts. Each movement accepts the impossibility of obtaining metaphysical knowledge (but the human inevitability of attempting it). Given that philosophy as metaphysics is impossible, each movement tries to replace it with something else: Marxism with a critique of capitalism, transcendental phenomenology with a description of appearances, logical atomism with the devising of a logically perfect language in which metaphysical questions will not arise, logical positivism with science, linguistic analysis with definitions of words of natural languages, structuralism with the exposure of a priori rule systems, deconstruction with rereadings of philosophical works through their literary styles.[4]

Existential phenomenology, including Merleau-Ponty's existential phenomenology does not escape this Kantian paradigm. However, it leaves metaphysical questions unanswered which have to be answered, one way or the other, if it is to be complete. It follows that existential phenomenology has a hidden metaphysical teleology which is partly subversive but partly fulfilling; subversive because it exhibits a putatively anti-metaphysical philosophy as ultimately metaphysical; fulfilling because it allows that philosophy to be what it really is: a phenomenology of some metaphysical facts. The philosophy of ambiguity turns out to be a philosophy of ambiguity in its truest sense.

We could call this teasing out of the metaphysical presuppositions of existential phenomenology metaphysical deconstruction. It is deconstruction because it is a radical rewriting which while uncovering a suppressed telos, of which Merleau-Ponty was shy or afraid, exhibits some limits of what existential phenomenology professes itself to be. It is metaphysical because it redepicts some appearances as realities. This metaphysical deconstruction is a deconstruction of deconstruction, mediated by Merleau-Ponty's writing, because the post-structuralist deconstruction of Western metaphysics is putatively anti-metaphysical. The deconstruction of existential phenomenology implies some metaphysics. Usually, deconstruction of metaphysics implies some metaphysics.[5]

I have divided what follows into five sections. In 1 *Subjectivity and the limits of science* I use existential phenomenology to show some limits of scientific explanation and criticise some positivist and pseudo-scientific philosophies as false and unethical.

In 2 *Inside the soul* I argue that Merleau-Ponty was wrong to argue for a form of externalism against Husserl and that a kind of internalism is true. I further show that phenomenological descriptions of the interiority of consciousness are in fact descriptions of the inside of the soul. Although Husserl and Merleau-Ponty provide excellent and insightful descriptions of psychological interiority, in a direct and profoundly non-trivial sense, they did not know what they were talking about.

In 3 *Spiritual space,* I argue that Merleau-Ponty was right in thinking that space is essentially subjective but he misses the insight that space is spiritual. What (obscurely) comes under the heading of 'consciousness' should, I suggest, come under the heading of 'spiritual space'.

In 4 *Metaphysical time*, I argue that Merleau-Ponty was partly right in thinking that time is essentially subjective and I further argue that, in a non-tautological and metaphysically informative sense, it is always now. Now is the time it is inside the soul.

In 5 *What is it to Be?*, I suggest an answer to the question of being which thwarted Merleau-Ponty in *Le Visible et L'Invisible*, Heidegger in *Sein und Zeit*, and many other Western philosophers since Parmenides. I end by suggesting that contemporary philosophy needs to pay far more attention to the findings of the world's great religious mystics and suggest some ways forward for a mystical phenomenological theology.

1 *Subjectivity and the limits of science*

Merleau-Ponty has succeeded in identifying some features of human reality which resist, even in principle, scientific explanation. Conspicuous among these are: consciousness, subjectivity and freedom. To these I add qualitative (as opposed to quantitative) facts, and concrete (as opposed to abstract) existence, and individuality.[6]

Merleau-Ponty argues in *La Structure du Comportement* that behavioural psychology is powerless to provide sufficient conditions for the obtaining of states of consciousness. His conclusion is correct on two construals of 'sufficient condition', logical and causal. Logically, from no set of claims about the physiology of the person, no matter how complete, may we derive any claim about the existence of consciousness. There is a logical 'gap' between the physical and the psychological. Causally, no state of the brain can be shown to be sufficient for any mental state. We know that it is empirically false that similar types of brain state are always and everywhere correlated with similar types of mental state but even if this were true it would not be enough to show that the mental is causally determined by the physiological. This is because the obtaining of such close correlations would be consistent with either bare correlations in the absence of causal connections or with the determination of brain states by mental states.

So far as we know, it is an empirical fact that the obtaining of some brain state is a necessary condition for the obtaining of some mental state. We know this because brain damage impairs thinking and perception (in for example, the ways shown by Merleau-Ponty's use of the Schneider case in *Phénoménologie de la Perception*). This dependency can only be contingent and empirical however. We know it is contingent because mental activity may be restored in a restricted number of brain damage cases if alternative neurological prerequisites for that activity may be made functional. Besides, the dependency cannot be logical

226

because there is no contradiction in the supposition that something other than the brain thinks: a computer, God, the soul.

If we accept that the neurological states of a well functioning brain are causally necessary conditions for thoughts then we should accept an important logical consequence of this: the obtaining of thoughts is a causally sufficient condition for the obtaining of the neurological states of a well functioning brain. This settles the metaphysical question of psycho-physical causation in a particular way. Mental states are sufficient for brain states because brain states are necessary conditions for mental states. Mental states determine brain states but brain states do not determine mental states. We should accept this picture of psycho-physical causation because it is a deductive consequence of a highly plausible empirical fact: brain states are prerequisites for mental states.

We may retain Merleau-Ponty's view that it is the person *qua* body-subject that thinks, or that it is the person's brain that thinks, despite the determination of the neurological by the mental. Merleau-Ponty is right in his view that we ordinarily individuate persons through their bodies. It is thus pragmatically appropriate to think of the body thinking or the brain thinking however ultimately metaphysically misleading. If the brain is necessary for thinking it makes some sense to identify the brain with the thinker. Of course the set of necessary conditions for any event (including any mental event) is very large: that a certain person was born, that there is a physical universe, that there is something rather than nothing etc. (In this sense it makes sense to say that the totality of what is thinks.) However, if we desire some not entirely arbitrary criteria for identifying a subset of the necessary conditions for thought with a thinker, a plausible candidate is Merleau-Ponty's body-subject. This is just because we habitually identify thinkers through their bodies.

This is a sketch of an empirical answer to the mind–body problem. It accepts our empirical knowledge of consciousness and the brain as 'constraining' that answer. It leaves the ontological problem of the psycho-physical relation unsolved. That is because 'causally necessary' and 'causally sufficient' are left very abstract in the claims that the neurological is necessary for the mental and the mental is sufficient for the neurological. It is hopeless to say that future developments in neurology will solve this problem. That thought simply betrays an unscientific faith in science. The brain is only a highly complicated physical object. The brain is only billions of atoms in motion. Even if we knew all the neurological facts about the brain the brain would remain only billions of atoms in motion. Ontologically, it is hard to see how billions of atoms in motion could have any relation to consciousness. It is this that makes consciousness inexplicable to science.

In order to solve the ontological problem of the psycho-physical relation it is necessary to give up the concept of consciousness and replace it with the notion of spiritual space. I pursue this below.

The second obstacle to the scientific explanation of human reality that may be extracted from existential phenomenology is *subjectivity*. We have seen that within the Kantian and Hegelian framework of thought in which Merleau-Ponty is located 'subject' is a name for that which experiences and 'object' a name for that which is experienced. Merleau-Ponty thinks the living conscious human body is a subject. Now, in this respect Merleau-Ponty's acceptance of the reality of subjectivity is an improvement on contemporary materialism which tries to reduce subjectivity to objectivity. While materialism tries to 'downgrade' mind or reduce it to matter, Merleau-Ponty tries to 'upgrade matter' or claim that matter can think. His approach has the merit of trying to do justice to all the facts, both mental and physical, not just some of the facts, the physical facts. He never solves the Cartesian problem of how matter can think, given that it is only matter.

The problem for science is why there should be subjectivity at all. Why is the universe not just an objective universe? No amount of scientific experimentation or mathematical modelling is going to solve this problem. Empirical experiments treat their subject matter as observable, but subjectivity pertains to the observing, not the observed. Mathematical modelling depicts the quantitative but subjectivity is qualitative.

In his phenomenology, Merleau-Ponty has insightfully described subjective features of our incarnation: I do not see my own head, I have a peculiarly partial perspective on the part of my body that I do see. I experience the universe in a 'self-centred' way. We cannot logically infer these subjective facts from any purely physiological description of the human body. As Merleau-Ponty points out, science treats the body only as an object and so is powerless to grasp it as a subject.

Nevertheless, because he is doing descriptive phenomenology Merleau-Ponty himself has no explanation of subjectivity. That there is subjectivity is a phenomenological discovery. Why there is subjectivity is a metaphysical mystery.

Science is essentially deterministic. It attempts to identify antecedent causally sufficient conditions for types of effect and tries to discover natural laws from which predictive claims may be logically derived. If something's causally sufficient conditions obtain it cannot fail to obtain. If something happens in accordance with natural law, and the law holds, it cannot fail to happen. It is arguable that science does contain non-deterministic elements. In practice many scientific explanations are only probabilistic. Also, quantum mechanics admits of probabilistic interpretations and it is possible that probabilities that fall short of determinism are not just attributable to our ignorance of the antecedent sufficient conditions for the events we are trying to explain.

Suppose Merleau-Ponty is right in thinking that human beings are irreducibly free. It follows that if someone performs an action freely they could have refrained from performing that action. Something that is the case could have been otherwise. In other words, freedom implies contingency. On the other hand, on a scientific view, any event has antecedent sufficient causal conditions and if those conditions obtain, then that event cannot fail to obtain. It follows that given antecedent conditions no-one could have not performed the actions they perform. If freedom is real, then, it is scientifically inexplicable.

There are good reasons for supposing that Merleau-Ponty is right about human freedom. The possibility of choosing one course of action rather than another is a lived human reality. Determinism is only a theory. I mean, phenomenologically, freedom is experienced to be the case but determinism is largely only thought to be the case.

It is one of the limitations of Merleau-Ponty's existential phenomenology, and for that matter Sartre's, that it attempts no phenomenology of determinism. A description of the experience of determinism shows up the ineliminability of freedom. There is a clear phenomenological difference between situations in which we feel ourselves compelled or constrained and in which we do not. For example, in walking into a strong wind we feel the wind resistance against our body. In being held at gunpoint we feel powerless. On the other hand, in facing some awkward moral dilemma we feel all too free. Now, it is not clear that we could experience ourselves as *thoroughly* determined. Instead of deciding to get up and leave a room, and then doing that, one would have *the sensation of being taken out of the room by one's body*, perhaps to one's surprise or against one's will. Psychologically, one would be reduced to a passive witness to the movement of one's own body. Perhaps even the psychological reactions of oneself as witness presuppose a minimal freedom. If I experienced myself as totally determined this might just mean that we have to give up talking about 'myself' here. The experience of the exercise of freedom would seem to be an essential part of what it is to be me.

The world described by phenomenology is concrete. The world described by science is abstract. Merleau-Ponty turns the tables on science when he argues that scientific theory and practice rest on phenomenological presuppositions: the lived world, phenomenological space and time, and the experience of freedom. Science is powerless to explain its own phenomenological presuppositions and becomes incoherent when it includes claims inconsistent with those presuppositions, for example, in denying freedom or denying the reality of the present time.

The final subjective limitation of science is this: science is quantitative, phenomenology is qualitative. Scientific explanations work well for subject matters it makes sense to quantify over (paradigmatically, sets of physical objects and the relations between them). Phenomenology on the other hand offers descriptions of what experience is like from the standpoint of the subject. It is hard to individuate thoughts, emotions and actions; hard to see where one begins and another ends. It is therefore hard to quantify over phenomenological contents. Merleau-Ponty's critique of 'the sensation' in *Phénoménologie de la Perception* implies that there are no pure 'qualia'. Putative *qualia* are always already interpreted and always already contexually determined. If this piece of neo-Kantianism is right then, if anything, it makes quantification over phenomenological contents even harder.

I conclude that phenomenology and science are antithetical. Phenomenology is subjective. Science is objective. Existential phenomenology is libertarian. Science is determinist. Phenomenology implies the existence of consciousness. Science (as normally understood) implies materialism. Phenomenology is committed to spatial and temporal presence. Science has no conceptual room for 'here' and 'now'. Phenomenology is qualitative. Science is quantitative.

If phenomenology and science are antithetical, then the prospects for some neo-Hegelian synthesis look grim. Its obstacles are the problems of classical metaphysics.

2 *Inside the soul*

Although Merleau-Ponty's phenomenological descriptions of incarnate subjectivity may be usefully deployed to show some limits of scientific explanation, his own objections to Husserl's phenomenological reduction are invalid. On Husserl's 'internalist' view belief in the existence of the external world may be suspended by the phenomenological *epoché* and the essence of consciousness opened to phenomenological inspection. On Merleau-Ponty's 'externalist' view 'the most important lesson which the reduction teaches us is the impossibility of a complete reduction' (PPT, xiv).

Merleau-Ponty has two arguments against the completability of the *epoché*, one from being-in-the-world and one from reflection.

Because our mode of being is irreducibly being-in-the-world our conscious states and actions paradigmatically take objects which are in the world not in ourselves. It is not possible to make sense of thought and action in abstraction from those objects so it is not possible to study them in abstraction from the world.

Now, this line of argument just begs the question against the Husserl of 1913. Husserl not only accepts but insists that conscious states (with the exception of moods and sensations) take intentional objects. However, through the *epoché* these intentional objects are themselves phenomenologically reduced objects. He draws a crucial distinction between the *noēsis* and the *noēma* of a conscious act. The *noēma*, or noēmatic content, of the act is what is presented to the act just as it is presented, shorn of preconceptions about any unpresented features. The *noēsis* is the kind of act that is directed towards that noēmatic content. Merleau-Ponty has not shown that an object of consciousness cannot be phenomenologically reduced to some noetic content, not even by his questioning, via Heidegger, whether Husserl's *noēma* (*qua* reduced presentation) can capture operative engagement in a world of ready-to-hand things.

Phenomenologically we may put the point this way. What is is given to me as if solipsism were true. I mean *directly* given. Appreciating Husserl's phenomenological reduction involves a shift in attitude from the commonsensical view of an enduring world as intermittent object of my conscious states to an enduring consciousness with changing phenomenological contents. Husserl, it seems, has the imaginative capability to make this switch but Merleau-Ponty does not.

If Husserl may coherently describe the structure and content of the 'transcendental field' thus opened up by the *epoché* and avoid drawing on a vocabulary that depends for its meaning on the existence of the external world then his internalism is to that degree plausible. From this standpoint, the existentialist mode of being 'being-in-the-world', far from being primordial with regard to consciousness, would have to be constructed, or transcendentally 'constituted'.

Merleau-Ponty's second objection to the *epoché* is also unsound. He says 'there is no thought which embraces all our thought' (PPT, xiv). Thoughts of the form 'All my thoughts are F' are well formed, and (unless the value allocated to 'F' leads to Liar-like paradoxes) such a thought need not be an exception to itself. Even if the claim were true, it would not constitute a refutation of the possibility of the *epoché*. This is because a Husserlian could treat any conscious state in abstraction from its object in the external world. Once the field of transcendental subjectivity is opened up, so to speak, *globally*, any conscious state arising within it may be described as only appearing within it.

It follows then that Merleau-Ponty's existential phenomenology does not constitute a refutation of Husserl's transcendental phenomenology. It is merely baldly inconsistent with it. I now show that *pace* both Husserl and Merleau-Ponty, the field of transcendental subjectivity has a metaphysical status.

Although because of his rejection of the *epoché* Merleau-Ponty does not use 'transcendental subjectivity' in his own philosophy, he does use 'phenomenal field' in his critique of empirical psychology in the introduction to *Phénoménologie de la Perception*. I maintain that although 'transcendental field', 'phenomenal field' and 'consciousness' differ in sense they do not differ in reference. They may each be used to refer to what is in so far as what is appears consistent with solipsism.

Merleau-Ponty rightly says the phenomenal field is not 'inner'. It is not inner in the sense in which some token mental state is putatively inner: epistemologically private, accessible only to introspection, and perhaps admitting of incorrigible knowledge. The phenomenal field is neither inner nor outer but the body-subject is located at its phenomenological centre.

The phenomenal field is bounded by the 'horizon' of my experiences, rather in the way that the indeterminate periphery of my visual field bounds my visual experiences. Indeed, the visual field is a part of the phenomenal field.

The phenomenal field is not paradigmatically physical (in just the way that the visual field is not paradigmatically physical). Something is paradigmatically physical if and only if it is composed of matter and is spatially located (so, gravitational and electro-magnetic fields are not paradigmatically physical even though physics treats of them). However, the phenomenal field is not both made of matter and spatially located. Therefore the phenomenal field is not paradigmatically physical. The phenomenal field has no discernible beginning or end in time but its contents change over time. The phenomenal field is, however, *spatial* in the sense in which the visual field is spatial. I explore the temporality and spatiality of the phenomenal field in sections 3 and 4 below.

In a quasi-Humean sense, I am my phenomenal field. To see this we have to accept Merleau-Ponty's repudiation of Husserl's transcendental ego but reject his identification of the self or subject with the body-subject. What Husserl thinks of as the transcendental ego or subjective 'pole' or source of my conscious states is in fact a post-reduction residue of the natural attitude belief that I am the 'owner' of my conscious states. If the reduction had been thoroughly carried through it would have been apparent that the transcendental field is neither subjective nor objective and conscious states, so to speak, arise within it. The fact that they arise within *that* transcendental field makes the transcendental ego redundant as putative unifier of consciousness.

Although Merleau-Ponty is right to hold that the body has subjective properties and that I have a peculiarly subjective point of view on my body, he is wrong to hold that I am essentially my body. This is for roughly Cartesian reasons. From no description of a human body, no matter how detailed and complete, does it logically follow that I am that body. If I were essentially my body, this entailment would hold. The entailment does not hold. Therefore I am not my body. Conversely, from the claim 'I exist' it does not logically follow that any human body

232

exists. If I were essentially my body this entailment would hold. It does not hold. Therefore I am not essentially my body.

We could object to the arguments of the last paragraph on quasi-Kripkean grounds. It could be *metaphysically* necessary that I am my body even if logic is powerless to establish this. I would then be essentially my body even if the entailments of the last paragraph did not hold. My being my body would then be a *de re* necessity, and perhaps an *a posteriori* necessity.

What does 'metaphysically necessary' mean here? If it is metaphysically necessary that I am my body then it is true that I am my body in all possible worlds (in which I exist). What does '*a posteriori* necessity' mean here? If it is necessary *a posteriori* that I am my body then this necessity may be established by experience.

I doubt that any experience could establish that I am my body, still less that I am necessarily my body. Even if I exist at all and only the times that my body exists it does not follow that I am identical with my body. I doubt that I am my body in all possible worlds because there is no conclusive refutation of the possibility that I exist in possible worlds in which my body does not exist. Indeed, my having any veridical out-of-body experience or disembodied after-death experience is both an *a posteriori* refutation of the thesis that it is *de re* necessary that I am my body and a refutation of the thesis that I am my body in all possible worlds. 'I am my body' could never be conclusively verified but it could be conclusively falsified.

It is in any case logically possible that I am not my body because disembodied existence may be described in a way that is free from contradiction. I can coherently imagine my surviving the disappearance of my body. To do this imagine the phenomenal field just as it is except without the appearance of one's own body within it. One experiences the contents one would experience if one's body did not exist. If I were essentially my body it would not be possible to coherently imagine this.

Although Merleau-Ponty is right to say that the phenomenal field is not 'inner' it nevertheless exhibits a certain interiority. It is presented as *an inside without an outside*. We could call this 'absolute interiority'.

These features of the phenomenal field are jointly sufficient to establish that the phenomenal field is *the soul*: the soul of traditional theologies and Platonism. The phenomenal field establishes the horizon of my experiences. It is not physical. It is what the unity of my consciousness consists in. It has no empirical beginning. It has no empirical end. It does not depend upon my body. I am phenomenologically given to myself as it in a way that implies no dualism of subject and object. I know it by being it.

I conclude that Husserl and Merleau-Ponty, unknowingly, are describing the inside of the soul.

3 *Spiritual space*

The distinction Merleau-Ponty draws between space as it is experienced and space as it is thought to be in scientific theory is genuine. Although the latter is usefully termed 'geometrical space', Merleau-Ponty's 'physical space' is a misleading term for space as ordinarily experienced. This is because experienced space is not paradigmatically physical. Indeed, no space is paradigmatically physical. Something is paradigmatically physical if and only if it is composed of matter and spatially located but space is neither composed of matter nor physically located, therefore space is not paradigmatically physical.

Merleau-Ponty has a view of space as it is experienced which is partly Leibnizian and partly anti-Kantian. Experienced space is Leibnizian because it is given as nothing over and above the experienced totality of spatial relationships between myself as body-subject and the things I perceive. It is anti-Kantian because it is not presented as a single indivisible whole but as regions.

Now, from a phenomenological point of view Merleau-Ponty is wrong on both these counts. Phenomenological space is presented as Newtonian, not Leibnizian, because it is presented as the spatial field or background for all phenomenological contents with which I am acquainted. (I use the word 'field' here as a deliberate extension of the use of 'field' in 'visual field'.) The spatial field, or phenomenological field, or subjective field is the private space in which all my experiences happen and in which all phenomenological contents are given to me. This space, I suggest, is given as something rather than nothing. It is the phenomenological limit or 'horizon' of what I experience, rather as the visual field provides a limit to what I can see.

Merleau-Ponty says that Newton's metaphor of space as a 'container' for the things in it is inappropriate to space as experienced but there is a way of rethinking the metaphor that makes it apposite. Merleau-Ponty is thinking of the container *from the outside*: rather as a box may function as a container because it has both an outside and an inside. We should imagine the container *from the inside*. I, as embodied subject with a point of view, am inside the container. The container has no outside that could be perceptually presented as an outside from outside it. This is because the container has no outside. The nature of experienced space is to be precisely this: an inside without an outside.

Now, phenomenologically we are not presented with both psychological interiority and subjective space, both the absolute interiority of 'consciousness' and the absolute interiority of space as we experience it. Phenomenologically, we are directly presented with just one absolute interiority so there are no phenomenological grounds for distinguishing the soul as described in the last section from subjective space. The soul and subjective space have all and only each other's properties so it follows that they are one and the same. While on some materialist views consciousness is reduced to something physical, say a process in the brain, on this phenomenological view consciousness is expanded or 'inflated' into subjective space or the soul.

The phenomenological identification of the soul with space as we experience it has important metaphysical consequences. The soul has a certain spatiality. This subjective spatiality was largely unacknowledged by Plato, the Neo-Platonists and Descartes.[7] The spatiality of the soul makes it intuitively more comprehensible how there should obtain causal relations between mental and physical events. Both are spatial so a mental event may act on a physical event by being where it is. Finally, because the body-subject is located at the centre of subjective space, the assumption of the Platonists that the soul is 'in' the body has to be given up. The soul is not located in the body. *The body is located in the soul.*

4 *Metaphysical time*

Merleau-Ponty's radically subjectivist view of time putatively entails that nothing happens in the external world: 'If I consider the world itself, there is simply one indivisible and changeless being [in it]' (PPT, 411). This Parmenidean metaphysics is arguably inconsistent with his repudiation of Husserl's transcendental phenomenology and his own doctrine of being-in-the-world and it does not follow from his own premises.

Merleau-Ponty rightly holds that past, present and future are 'subjective'. Any token of 'now' refers to when it is thought/uttered or otherwise produced (as any token of 'here' refers to where it is produced). The predicate 'past' may be rightly used to ascribe to any event before now the property of being before now. The predicate 'future' may be rightly used to ascribe to any event later than now the property of being later than now. Events are only past, present or future in relation to beings who are veridically conscious of being in time.

However, from the truth that past, present and future are subjective, Merleau-Ponty fallaciously infers that the whole of time is subjective. This is because he wrongly thinks that the relations before, simultaneous with and after depend upon past, present and future. This is wrong because that some event is before, simultaneous with or after some other event of itself says nothing about its temporal relations to me. Only the converse dependency holds: if some event is past, present or future then it does stand in the temporal relation of being before, simultaneous with or after me (or when I am thinking, experiencing, etc). Once we see that the first inference fails, conceptual room is left for events to happen in the external world.

Although Merleau-Ponty is not sufficiently objectivist about before, simultaneous with, and after, he is not subjectivist enough about past, present and future. To see this we need to examine some metaphysical presuppositions of the use of 'now'.

'Now' I suggest has both a metaphysical and an empirical use but the metaphysical use is truer and more fundamental than the empirical use. 'Now' is used empirically in a claim like, 'It is three o'clock now' or a suggestion like, 'Do it now, not later'. Empirically, different tokens of 'now' may refer to different times. In the first of these examples 'now' means something like 'simultaneously with my uttering this' and in the second example it means something like 'as soon as possible after my saying this'. 'Now' picks out particular, if rather vague times in its empirical use.

Metaphysically there is no time that is not now. There is no time but the present. If we ask what time it is, the empirically uninformative but metaphysically true answer is always 'now'.

The metaphysical now is when all my thoughts and experiences happen. It is a subjective time that is phenomenologically analogous to the subjective space described above. Empirically, now and here are *elastic*. Empirically, now and here admit of duration and extension. For example, 'now' may be used to refer to a certain century, an hour or a second or two. 'Here' may be used to refer to a country, a city, planet earth. In their metaphysical uses, however, 'now' does not denote any time interval and 'here' does not denote any measurable extension. Here is where I am wherever I am. Now is when I am whenever I am.

Subjective time and subjective space are mutually dependent aspects of one reality. It is phenomenologically impossible for one to be presented without the other. This fact is captured by the use of the term 'presence'. 'Present' is ambiguous between temporally present and spatially present. What we normally think of as the contents of consciousness could be more appositely thought of as the changing contents of presence in both these senses.

Post-structuralism and scientifically inspired philosophy are unwittingly allies in their attack upon presence. Derrida is wrong to think of Western philosophy as the history of something called 'the metaphysics of presence'. On the contrary, the rise of positivist philosophy since the Renaissance has emphasised an objectivity that represses the metaphysics of presence. (Although, in positivism's extreme form, logical positivism, it relies on a metaphysics of presence that is subversive of the tenseless physics it would legitimate.)

From the fact that all my experiences happen now it follows that the phenomenal field is now. The phenomenal field is the soul so the soul is now. This does not mean that the time of the soul is to be contrasted with times that predate or postdate it. It means that now is the time it is inside the soul.

5 *What is it to Be?*

Despite the insights of *Le Visible et L'Invisible* Merleau-Ponty is ulti-mately no more successful than Heidegger in answering the question of being. The problem is that being does not seem explicable in terms of being something. Being, it seems, is not being F.

Being, I suggest, should be understood in the following way: *Being is that which nothing lacks.* The sentence is deliberately ambiguous between the expression of two metaphysical propositions: *It is not the case that there is anything that is not* and *Nothing is the absence of existence.*

Even though he too failed to answer the question of being, it was Hegel who had the insight that 'being' and 'nothing' are conceptually interdependent. We can no more make sense of one without the other than 'up' without 'down' or 'here' without 'there' or 'elsewhere'.

Is 'exists' used univocally or are there different *ways* of existing (or *modes* of being or *kinds* of being)? Whenever someone thinks they have found a *kind* of existence or *mode* of being they have at most specified a kind of thing that exists. Atoms, minds, numbers, surfaces, political institutions, emotions and pieces of music, although they are radically different kinds of things, if they exist, exist in exactly the same sense: they are rather than are not. Any putative difference between 'modes of being' will turn out, on inspection, to consist in the possession or lack of possession of a property (for example, a spatio-temporal property, a mathematical property, a political property).

Nevertheless, within phenomenology there are metaphysically signifi-cant attempts to distinguish ways of being. Notably, Heidegger uses 'Dasein' and 'Existenz' uniquely to designate the kind of being exhibited by a human being. Dasein is being in the sense of *being someone*. Husserl talks about transcendental subjectivity as having 'absolute being'.[8]

We draw a distinction between *being* and *being perceived to be*. For example, I am, but the physical objects that surround me are perceived to be. The spiritual time–space of the soul is *tout court* but the changing content of the soul is perceived to be. In the fundamental sense of 'being' all these things are rather than are not, so 'being' is still being used unequivocally at root. Nevertheless, as Husserl, Heidegger, Sartre and Merleau-Ponty recognise, there is an ontological distinction between the being of human reality and the being of the external world.

Husserl ended the *Pariser Vorträger* with the quotation from St. Augustine 'Noli foras ire, in te redi, in interiore homine habitat veritas' ('Do not wish to go out; go back into yourself. Truth dwells in the inner man'). I should say, rather, *the inner man dwells in truth.* Nevertheless, Husserl indicates the way forward for a phenomenological theology. To explore the interiority of the soul we should draw inspiration from the writings of the great medieval mystics, something that the reigning positivist and materialist paradigms in Western philosophy are certain to resist. This would be the beginning of the return of metaphysics.

In one of their conversations in the winter of 1944–5 Claude Lévi-Strauss asked Merleau-Ponty about existentialism. Lévi-Strauss reports,

> He told me that it was an attempt to restore metaphysics such as the great philosophers of the past had illustrated it.

Existentialism is still available for this purpose.[9]

Notes

I *Life and works*

1 For Hegel, see *Phänomenologie des Geistes*, ed. G. Lasson and J. Hoff-
meister (Felix Meiner Verlag, Hamburg, 1952) translated by A.V. Miller as
Hegel's Phenomenology of Spirit (Oxford University Press, 1979). For
Kojève on Hegel see Alexandre Kojève *Introduction à la Lecture de Hegel:
Leçons sur la Phénoménologie de l'Esprit professés de 1933 à 1939 à l'Ecole
des Hautes Etudes reunies et publiées par Raymond Queneau* (Gallimard,
Paris, 1947). This volume appeared in the collection 'Bibliothèque des Idées'
in 1968.

For Husserl see *Cartesianische Meditationen: Eine Einleitung in die Phänomenologie* (Felix Meiner Verlag, Hamburg, 1987) translated by Dorion
Cairns as *Cartesian Meditations: An Introduction to Phenomenology* (Martinus Nijhoff, The Hague, 1960).

2 See Jean Hyppolite *Genèse et Structure de la Phénoménologie de Hegel*
(Aubier, Editions Montaigne, Paris, 1946).

3 *L'Arc*, Aix-en-Provence, No. 46 (1971) p. 43.

4 Maurice Merleau-Ponty *La Structure du Comportement* (Presses Universitaires de France, Paris, 1942), translated as *The Structure of Behaviour* by
Alden L. Fisher (Methuen, London, 1965).

5 Peter Strawson *Individuals: An Essay in Descriptive Metaphysics* (Methuen,
London, 1959). For a summary of the relevance of this book to the mind–
body problem see Stephen Priest *Theories of the Mind* (Penguin Books,
London, 1991) Chapter 6, pp. 170–82.

6 (Louvain, 1951).

7 Jean-Paul Sartre *L'Etre et le Néant: Essai d'Ontologie Phénoménologique*
(Gallimard, Paris, 1943) translated by Hazel Barnes as *Being and Nothingness* (Methuen, London, 1958), *La Nausée* (Gallimard, Paris, 1939), *Nausea*
trans. Lloyd Alexander, (London and New York, 1949), *Les Chemins de la
Liberté*: I *L'Age de Raison* (Gallimard, Paris, 1945), II *Le Sursis* (Gallimard,
Paris, 1945), III *La Mort dans L'Ame* (Gallimard, Paris, 1949). Parts of
the unfinished fourth volume were published in *Les Temps Modernes* in
November and December 1949 as *Drôle d'Amitié* and if completed, was to
be called *La Dernière Chance*. English translations: *The Age of Reason* (1961),
The Reprieve (1963), *Iron in the Soul* (1963) (all Penguin, Harmondsworth).

239

Albert Camus *La Peste* (Gallimard, Paris, 1947) translated as *The Plague*, trans. Stuart Gilbert, (Hamish Hamilton, London, 1948), *L'Etranger* (Gallimard, Paris, 1942) translated by Stuart Gilbert as *The Outsider* (Hamish Hamilton, London, 1957).

8 'Les Préjugés Classiques et le Retour aux Phénomènes' (PP, 7).

9 'la pensée objective' (PP, *passim*).

10 Many epistemological and psychological doctrines fall under the names 'empiricism' and 'rationalism'. Here I am identifying those that are Merleau-Ponty's targets. For the varieties of empiricism see Stephen Priest *The British Empiricists* (Penguin Books, London, 1990) esp. pp. 132, 134, 185 and 204. Gilbert Ryle casts doubt on drawing any clear distinction between rationalism and empiricism in his 'Epistemology' in J.O. Urmson (ed.) *The Concise Encyclopaedia of Western Philosophy and Philosophers* (London, 1960). The historical distinction between empiricist and rationalist philosophers is blurred by empiricist elements in rationalist writings and rationalist elements in empiricist writings. Grasping this presupposes a clearer distinction between rationalist and empiricist *philosophy*. Rationalism is the thesis that thought is the best guide to reality. Empiricism is the thesis that experience is the best guide to reality. This distinction is as sharp as that between thought and experience.

By 'what is realistically the case' I mean 'what is the case independently of the existence of the subject'.

11 'Le Corps' (PP, 79).

12 'l'être-au-monde' (PP, *passim*).

13 'Le Monde Perçu' (PP, 233).

14 'L'Etre-Pour-Soi et l'Etre-Au-Monde (PP, 421).

15 See Edmund Husserl *Die Krisis der Europäischen Wissenschaften und die Transzendentale Phänomenologie* Herausgegeben von Walter Biemel (Martinus Nijhoff, The Hague, 1962) translated by David Carr as *The Crisis of the European Sciences and Transcendental Phenomenology* (Northwestern University Press, Evanston, 1970).

16 See Edmund Husserl *Ideen zu einer reinen Phänomenologie und phänomenologischen Philosophie, I Buch: Allgemeine Einfuhrung in die reine Phänomenologie* (Max Niemeyer Verlag, Halle a.d.S., 1913) translated by F. Kersten as *Ideas Pertaining to a Pure Phenomenology and to a Phenomenological Philosophy First Book: General Introduction to a Pure Phenomenology* (Martinus Nijhoff, The Hague, 1983).

17 Jean-Paul Sartre *La Transcendence de l'Ego: Esquisse d'une Description Phénoménologique* (*Recherches Philosophiques*, VI, 1936–7) translated as *The Transcendence of the Ego: An Existentialist Theory of Consciousness* by Forrest Williams and Robert Kirkpatrick (Farrar, Straus and Giroux, New York, 1958). The subtitle of the English translation has no justification in the French and 'existentialist theory' is an oxymoron.

18 *Le Figaro* 3 Mars 1952: 'L'Existentialisme va't-il entrer officiellement au Collège de France?'. *L'Aurore* 4 mars: 'parmi tous les systèmes [. . .] l'existentialisme [. . .] offre [. . .] sur tous les autres, l'énorme avantage de n'avoir aucune morale.' *Combat* 4 mars: 'Avec M. Merleau-Ponty, c'est l'existentialisme athée, le courant le plus original et plus attractif de la philosophie française depuis la Libération qui rentrerait au Collège de France.'

19 *Humanisme et Terreur* (Gallimard, Paris, 1947), *Les Aventures de la Dialectique* (Gallimard, Paris, 1955).

20 *L'Arc*, 46, (1971) p. 80.

21 Martin Heidegger's *Sein und Zeit* first appeared in 'Jahrbuch für Philosophie und Phënomenologische Forschung' Band VIII (1927) with an introduction by Husserl. An accessible edition is produced by Max Niemeyer
Verlag (Tübingen, 1986).

22 Lévi-Strauss' words are: 'Si l'entreprise structuraliste avait éveillé son intérêt
et sa sympathie en dépit de tout ce que nous savions l'en séparer, c'est sans
doute parce que, comme il devait le dire au cours d'un colloque sur le sens
et l'usage du terme "structure" auquel nous participions, il consentait à
trouver en elle "une nouvelle manière de voir l'être"' *L'Arc*, 46, (1971) p. 44.

23 'si [...] au contraire on admet à titre définitif des significations ouvertes,
inachevées, il faut que le sujet ne soit pas pure présence à soi et à l'objet'
(AD, 290).

24 'son activité significante est plutôt la perception d'une différence entre deux
ou plusieurs significations' (AD, 292).

25 Jacques Derrida *La Voix et le Phénomène* (P.U.F., Paris, 1967).

II *Phenomenology*

1 'Qu' est-ce que la phénoménologie?' (PP, I).
2 'La phénoménologie, c'est l'étude des essences' (PP, I).
3 Essentialism is the doctrine that x's being F is a necessary condition of x's
being the sort of thing it is, or x's existing, or both, so any essentialism
includes propositions of the form $\forall x \, (Fx \rightarrow \square \, Gx)$. Essentialisms may be
distinguished through their ontology of essences. Husserl repudiates Plato's
doctrine that essences are forms (*'eidos'*) existing independently of human
minds and the spatio-temporal universe but his essentialism is partly consistent with the neo-Aristotelian claim that there are *de re* modalites, as
endorsed by Kripke. Husserl agrees with Kripke that objects possessing
some of their properties essentially is not linguistically or psychologically
determined. See Plato *Republic* (many editions) and Saul Kripke *Naming
and Necessity* (Blackwell, Oxford, 1980).

4 Although the anti-metaphysical imagination baulks at this, it seems to me
not a self-contradictory supposition that more than one physical object
should occupy the same place at the same time. Suppose two numerically
distinct physical objects, O1 and O2, occupy two numerically distinct
places, P1 and P2 at some time t1. Suppose then that O1 and O2 fuse, but
not through any juxtaposition of parts, at a later time, t2. Although it
makes sense to talk of two physical objects rather than one because O1 and
O2 occupied numerically distinct places at t1, this also gives sense to O1
and O2 'fusing'. Although one is tempted to say O1 and O2 have thereby
become one I see nothing to force this interpretation. Suppose at some time
later than t2, t3, O1 and O2 bifurcate and occupy two numerically distinct
places (say, P1 and P2 again). If physical objects often behaved in this way,
it might become natural to ask: 'How many physical objects are in this
place at this time?' I see no a priori reason why an infinite numer of physical objects should not simultaneously exist at a place. Husserl and Merleau-
Ponty do not see this but nothing in Husserl's procedure of 'eidetic
variation' would seem to rule it out.

Logically, Husserl is right that *redness* may exist in different places at the
same time. If redness is what tokens of phenomenological red have in
common then redness exists in spatially distributed tokens of phenomenological red (where 'redness' does not mean 'tokens of redness').

5 'Wesens-Notwendigkeit' (*Ideen* I, §2).
6 'Wesens-Allgemeinheit' (*Ideen* I, §2).
7 'eidetische Reduktion' (*Ideen* I, §2).
8 The two phases of the eidetic reduction are:

   1 'Zunächst bezeichnete "Wesen" das im selbst-eigenen Sein eines Individuum als sein Was vorfindiche.'
   2 'Jedes solches Was kann aber "in idee gesetzt" werden.'

9 'Urteile von eidetischer Allgemeingultigkeit' (*Ideen* I, §5).
10 'tous les problèmes . . . reviennent à définir des essences' (PP, I).
11 'l'essence de la perception, l'essence de la conscience' (PP, I). Following his teacher, Franz Brentano, Husserl thinks the essence of consciousness is *intentionality*. As early as *Logical Investigations* (1900–1), however, he draws a distinction between intentional and non-intentional mental states. Sensations and moods, for example, do not necessarily exhibit intentionality. Even though sensations may be non-intentional components of intentional acts, in virtue of what exactly wholly non-intentional mental states count as mental is an unresolved problem in Husserl's phenomenology.
12 'Es gehört zur eigenen Artung gewisser Wesenkategorien, daß ihnen zugehörige Wesen in einer schlichten abgeschlossenen Erscheinung nur "einseitig", im Nacheinander "mehrseitig" und doch nie "allseitig" gegeben sein konnen' (*Ideen* I, §3).
13 'imaginative Modifikation'. See *Ideen* I, Sachregister p. 438.
14 Although the early Husserl of *Uber den Begriff der Zahl: Psychologische Analysen* (Halle, 1887) (his *Habilitationsschrift*) and *Philosophie der Arithmetik* (Halle, 1891) endorsed a psychologistic reduction of logical and mathematical relations to psychological relations he had abandoned this view by the time he wrote *Logical Investigations* (1900–1). The extent of Frege's influence in bringing about this change of mind is a matter of scholarly dispute.
15 For Husserl's uses of 'Begrundung' see *Ideen* I pp. 17, 36, 44, 124, 154ff., 293ff.
16 'philosophie . . . qui met en suspens pour les comprendre les affirmations de l'attitude naturelle' (PP, I).
17 'Ich und meine Umwelt' (*Ideen* I, §27).
18 'Ich bin mir einer Welt bewußt, endlos ausgebreitet im Raum, endlos werdend und geworden in der Zeit' (*Ideen* I, §27).
19 'Auch diese Wert-charaktere und praktischen Charaktere gehoren konstitutive zu "vorhanderen" Objekten als solchen' (*Ideen* I, §27).
20 'Generalthesis der näturlichen Einstellung' (*Ideen* I, §30).
21 '"Die" Welt ist als Wirklichkeit immer da' (*Ideen* I, §30).
22 'une philosophie pour laquelle le monde est toujours "déjà là"' (PP, I).
23 In *Pariser Vorträger* and *Cartesianische Meditationen* Husserl explicitly describes affinities between his own procedures and those of Descartes in the first *Meditation*. It is instructive to compare the constituents of Husserl's world of the 'natural attitude' with the targets of Descartes' project of systematic doubt. For the commonsensical starting points of Hobbes, Locke, Berkeley, Hume, Mill, Russell and Ayer see Stephen Priest *The British Empiricists* (Penguin, London, 1990). Despite the self-justifying circularity of his dialectic, Hegel's starting point in his phenomenology is the more or less commonsensical and naive 'sense-certainty'. The examples could be multiplied.

Pace these philosophers, philosophical questioning reveals common sense to be historically changing. Is belief in God part of common sense? Is belief in science part of common sense? Whose God? How much science? When? Who is common sense common to? 'Sense' in the sense of 'sense perception' or sense in the sense of 'meaning' or 'know-how'?

24 'une philosophie pour laquelle le monde est toujours "déjà là" avant la réflexion, comme une présence inalienable' (PP, I).

25 'tout l'effort est de retrouver ce contact näif avec le monde pour lui donner enfin un statut philosophique' (PP, I).

26 'Le monde est là avant toute analyse que je puisse en faire' (PP, IV).

27 'C'est l'essai d'une description directe de notre expérience telle qu'elle est, et sans aucun égard a sa genèse psychologique et aux explications causales que le savant, l'historien ou le sociologue peuvent en fournir' (PP, I).

28 'Il s'agit de décrire, et non pas d'expliquer ni d'analyser' (PP, II).

29 '*Fundamentalontologie*' Martin Heidegger *Sein und Zeit* (Max Niemeyer Verlag, Tübingen, 1986) (Sechsehnte Auflage) p. 13, 'fundamental ontology' Martin Heidegger *Being and Time*, John Macquarrie and Edward Robinson trans. (Blackwell, Oxford, 1973) p. 34. Heidegger claims that ordinary ontology presupposes fundamental ontology because it includes an unexplicated concept of being. Ordinary or traditional ontology is the attempt to establish what there is. Fundamental ontology is the attempt to establish what it is to be. For this reason, Heidegger says,

> Daher muss die *Fundamentalontologie*, aus der alle andern erst entspringen können, in der *existentialen Analytik des Daseins* gesucht werden (*Sein und Zeit*, p. 13).

> Therefore fundamental ontology, from which alone all other ontologies can take rise, must be sought in the existential analytic of Dasein (*Being and Time*, p. 34).

If traditional ontology tries to allocate all the values of 'x' and 'F' which would make the form ∃x (Fx) into a true sentence, fundamental ontology explains the meaning of the existential quantifier. (The fact that Heidegger does not make the distinction under *this* description is philosophically inconsequential.) *Phénoménologie de la Perception* contains no explicit fundamental ontology, even though the structures of the body-subject's being-in-the-world are partly isomorphic with those attributed to *Dasein* in *Sein und Zeit*. The switch to fundamental ontology is made in *Le Visible et L'Invisible*.

Heideggerian exegesis has been revolutionised by Reinhard May's *Ex Oriente Lux: Heideggers Werk unter ostasiatischem Einfluss* (Steiner Verlag, Stuttgart, 1989) translated by Graham Parkes as *Heidegger's Hidden Sources: East Asian Influences on his Work* (Routledge, London and New York, 1996). Much of what we have thought of as Heidegger's originality is essentially Taoist and Zen and the ramifications of this through Heidegger's influence on Merleau-Ponty's corpus have yet to be identified. May's findings are so important that Heideggerian 'Modern Continental Philosophy' should no longer be studied in abstraction from its East Asian ground.

30 'tout *Sein und Zeit* est sorti d'une indication de Husserl et n'est en somme qu'une explication du "näturlichen Weltbegriff" ou du "Lebenswelt" que Husserl, à la fin de sa vie, donnait pour thème premier à la phénoméno-logie' (PP, I).

Merleau-Ponty's inclusion of 'n'est en somme qu[e]' ('is no more than') makes this claim an exaggeration if May is right about the extent of Taoist and Zen influences on Heidegger's thinking.

31 'Le plus grand enseignement de la réduction est l'impossibilité d'une réduction complète (PP, viii).

32 'nous sommes au monde' (PP, ix).

33

1 'Nous sommes au monde' (PP, xiv).

2 'Nos réflexions prennent place dans le flux temporel qu'elles cherchent à capter' (PP, ix).

3 'Il n'y a pas de pensée qui embrasse toute notre pensée' (PP, ix).

34 'nous sommes de part en part rapport au monde' (PP, viii).

35 'C'est l'ambition d'une philosophie qui soit une "science exacte"' (PP, i).

36 'Je ne suis pas le résultat ou l'entrecroisement des multiples causalités qui déterminent mon corps ou mon "psychisme", je ne puis pas me penser comme une partie du monde, comme le simple objet de la biologie, de la psychologie et de la sociologie, ni fermer sur moi l'univers de la science' (PP, ii).

37 'Tout ce que je sais du monde, même par science, je le sais à partir d'une vue mienne ou d'une expérience du monde sans laquelle les symboles de la science ne voudraient rien dire. Tout l'univers de la science est construit sur le monde vécu' (PP, ii).

The translation has 'the world as directly experienced' for 'le monde vécu' but 'the lived world' is a better translation, not only because the adjective 'vécu' is etymologically related to the verb 'vivre' ('to live') but also because 'le monde vécu' is a technical term in Merleau-Ponty's existential phenomenology. It denotes the world as a component of being-in-the world.

38 'La phénoménologie se laisse pratiquer et reconnaître comme manière ou comme style' (PP, ii).

The translator's 'of thinking' is gratuitous and not wholly philosophically perspicuous. Phenomenology is essentially a manner of *describing*. This describing is facilitated by a special style of *experiencing* rather than thinking.

39 'Nous ne trouvons dans les textes que ce que nous y avons mis' (PP, ii).

40 'C'est en nous mêmes que nous trouverons l'unité de la phénoménologie et son vrai sens' (PP, ii).

41 'La question n'est pas tant de compter les citations que de fixer et d'objectiver cette phénoménologie pour nous' (PP, ii).

42 'l'homme est au monde' (PP, v).

43 'Il serait artificiel de le faire dériver d'une série de synthèses' (PP, iv).

44 'ne doivent pas être réalisés avant elle' (PP, iv).

45 'Je suis la source absolue, mon existence ne vient pas de mes antécédents, de mon entourage physique et social, elle va vers eux et les soutient' (PP, iii).

46 'le monde [. . .] est donné au sujet parce que le sujet est donné à lui même' (PP, iv).

47 'Je ne saurais saisir aucune chose comme existante si d'abord je ne m'éprouvais existant dans l'acte de la saisir' (PP, iii).

48 'Il est le milieu naturel et le champ de toutes mes pensées et de toutes mes perceptions explicites' (PP, v).

49 'Ma sensation de rouge est aperçue comme manifestation d'un certain rouge senti, celui comme manifestation d'une surface rouge, celle ci comme mani-

festation d'un carton rouge, et celle ci enfin comme manifestation ou profil d'une chose rouge, de ce livre' (PP, v–vi).

50 'En tant que je suis conscience, c'est a dire en tant que quelque chose a sens pour moi, je ne suis, ni ici, ni là, ni Pierre, ni Paul' (PP, xi).

51 'Ich und mein Leben in meiner Seinsgeltung unberuhrt bleibt, ob nun die Welt ist oder nicht ist oder wie immer daruber entschieden werden mag' (PV, 10).

52 'comme ego méditant je peux bien distinguer de moi le monde et les choses' (PP, vii).

53 'assurement je n'existe pas à la manière des choses' (PP, vii).

III *Existentialism*

1 'Il inaugure la tentative pour explorer l'irrationnel et intégrer à une raison elargie qui reste la tâche de notre siècle' (SNS, 109).

2 See Immanuel Kant *Kritik der Reinen Vernunft*, herausgegeben von Inge-borg Heidemann (Philipp Reclam Jun. Stuttgart, 1980), *Immanuel Kant's Critique of Pure Reason*, translated by Norman Kemp Smith (Macmillan, London, 1992). Nothing in Merleau-Ponty's existentialist phenomenology suggests that he repudiates the Kantian doctrine of metaphysical 'cognitive closure': human beings are so constituted as to be able to pose metaphysical questions but to be unable to answer them. This metaphysical conservatism has been essential to prima facie competing movements in nineteenth and twentieth-century philosophy. Identifying inconsistencies between Merleau-Ponty's thought and Kant's is a large and piecemeal exercise. For example, Merleau-Ponty thinks there is more than one *space* but Kant thinks there is only one.

3 'Il est l'inventeur de cette Raison plus compréhensive que l'entendement, qui, capable de respecter la variété et la singularité des psychismes, des civilisations, des méthodes de pensée, et la contingence de l'histoire, ne rénonce pas cependant à les dominer pour les conduire à leur propre vérité' (SNS, 109–10).

4 'les successeurs de Hegel ont insisté, plutôt que sur ce qu'ils lui devaient, sur ce qu'ils réfusaient de son héritage' (SNS, 110).

Derrida explores the possibility of escaping the anticipation of modern philosophy by Hegel in 'From Restricted to General Economy: A Hegelian-ism Without Reserve' in his *Writing and Difference* (Routledge, London, 1978). A seductive and cynical reason could be given for agreeing that everything since Hegel is Hegelian: *any* proposition is logically entailed by a contradiction. This move is too crude and hasty however, not only because it makes every claim a Hegelian claim but also because by 'contradiction' ('Kontradiktion', 'Widerspruch') Hegel rarely means 'contradiction' in the sense of the conjunction of a proposition and its negation. He uses it to denote semantic, psychological and even ontological dependencies between concepts. If the present concerns with Asian philosophy, mysticism and the metaphysical presuppositions of science continue to grow in the philoso-phies of the twenty-first century then historical distance will allow Hegel, Merleau-Ponty and Derrida to be seen as essentially Kantian thinkers. Derrida does not see that his preoccupation with Hegel is with a paradigm within a paradigm, a problem within a problem.

5 'les doctrines ingrates qui cherchent à l'oublier [leur origine hégelienne]' (SNS, 110).

6 'C'est là qu'un langage commun pourra être trouvé pour elles et qu'une confrontation décisive pourra se faire' (SNS, 110).
7 'dans cette seule vie et dans cette seule œuvre nous trouvons toutes nos oppositions' (SNS, 110).
8 See Derrida, op. cit.
9 I explore this in *The Critical Turn: Modern Philosophy's Kantian Assumptions* (forthcoming).
10 'Kierkegaard, qui a le premier employé le mot d'existence dans son sens moderne, s'est délibérément opposé a Hegel' (SNS, 111).
11 'Le savoir absolu qui termine l'évolution de l'esprit-phénomène, ou la conscience s'égale enfin à sa vie spontanée et reprend possession de soi, ce n'est peut-être pas une philosophie, c'est peut-être une manière de vivre' (SNS, 112).
12 See *Hegel's Phenomenology of Spirit* translated by A.V. Miller (Oxford University Press, Oxford, 1979) p. 490. Hegel's original reads:

> Weder hat Ich sich in der *Form* des *Selbstbewusstseins* gegen die Form der Substantialität und Gegenständlichkeit festzuhalten, als ob es Angst vor seiner Entäusserung hätte; die Kraft des Geistes ist vielmehr, in seiner Entäusserung sich selbst gleich zu bleiben, und als das *An-* und *Fürsich*seiende, das *Fürsichsein* ebensosehr nur als Moment zu setzen, wie das Ansichsein; noch ist es ein Drittes, das die Unterschiede in den Abgrund des Absoluten zurückwirft, und ihre Gleichheit in demselben ausspricht, sondern das Wissen besteht vielmehr in dieser scheinbaren Untätigkeit, welche nur betrachtet, wie das Unterschiedne sich an ihm selbst bewgt, und in seine Einheit zuruckkert.
>
> In dem Wissen hat also der Geist die Bewegung seines Gestaltens beschlossen, insofern dasselbe mit dem unüberwundnen Unterschiede des Bewusstseins behaftet ist. Er hat das reine Element seines Daseins, den Begriff, gewonnen' G.W.F. Hegel *Phänomenologie des Geistes* (Felix Meiner Verlag, Hamburg, 1988) p. 528.

13 See G.W.F. Hegel *Wissenschaft der Logik*, ed. G. Lasson (Felix Meiner Verlag, Hamburg, 1963) (first edition, Nürnburg, 1812–16), *Hegel's Science of Logic*, trans. W.H. Johnston and L.G. Struthers (George Allen & Unwin, London, 1929) and *Encyclopaedie der philosophischen Wissenschaften im Grundrisse*, published as *System der Philosophie in Sämtliche Werke*, ed. H. Glockner (Stuttgart, 1927) vol. VIII, *Hegel's Logic, Being Part One of the Encyclopaedia of the Philosophical Sciences* (1830) trans. W. Wallace, (Oxford University Press, Oxford, 1978).
14 The most detailed explication of inauthenticity is in Heidegger's *Sein und Zeit* (Max Neimeger Verlag, Tübingen, 1986). For Heidegger's use of 'uneigentlich' follow the index references in Robinson and Macquarrie's translation *Being and Time* (Blackwell, Oxford, 1973) which are mapped onto the German text (seventh edition). The German edition has no index.
References to bad faith are pervasive in Sartre's literary output, but the *locus classicus* and most thorough philosophical examination is in *L'Etre et le Néant: Essai d'Ontologie Phénoménologique* (Gallimard, Paris, 1943) Chapitre II *La Mauvaise Foi*, translated by Hazel Barnes as *Being and Nothingness: An Essay on Phenomenological Ontology* (Methuen, London, 1958) Chapter Two 'Bad Faith'.

15 'un homme . . . est . . . un être qui n'est pas, qui nie les choses, une existence sans essence' (SNS, 115).

16 'Bien entendu, ce que nous disons de la vie concerne en réalité la conscience de la vie, puisque nous qui en parlons sommes conscients' (SNS, 115).

17 'La conscience de la vie est radicalement conscience de la mort' (SNS, 115).

18 'Il faut que vienne au monde une absence d'être d'ou l'être sera visible, un néant' (SNS, 115).

19 'Il y a deux méditations de la mort. L'une, pathétique et complaisante, qui bute sur notre fin et ne cherche en elle que le moyen d'exaspérer la violence; l'autre, sèche et resolue, qui assume la mort, en fait une conscience plus aiguë de la vie' (SNS, 116–17).

20 'Dies Bewusstsein hat nämlich nicht um dieses oder jenes, noch fur diesen oder jenen Augenblick Angst gehabt, sondern um sein ganzes Wesen; denn es hat die Furcht des Todes, des absoluten Herrn, empfunden' (G.W.F. Hegel *Phänomenologie des Geistes*, op. cit. p. 134).

21 '[le] rapport entre l'homme et son entourage naturel ou social' (SNS, 124).

22 'L'une consiste à traiter l'homme comme le résultat des influences physiques, physiologiques et sociologiques qui le détermineraient du dehors et feraient de lui une chose entre les choses' (SNS, 124).

23 'L'autre consiste à reconnaître dans l'homme, en tant qu'il est esprit et construit la représentation des causes mêmes qui sont censées agir sur lui, une liberté acosmique' (SNS, 124).

24 'Aucune de ces deux vues n'est satisfaisante' (SNS, 124).

25 'L'existence au sens moderne, c'est le mouvement par lequel l'homme est au monde, s'engage dans une situation physique et sociale qui devient son point de vue sur le monde. Tout engagement rest ambigu, puisqu'il est à la fois l'affirmation et la restriction d'une liberté' (SNS, 125).

26 'Le rapport du sujet et de l'objet n'est plus ce *rapport de connaissance* dont parlait l'idéalisme classique et dans lequel l'objet apparaît toujours comme construit par le sujet, mais un *rapport d'être* selon lequel paradoxalement le sujet *est* son corps, son monde et sa situation, et, en quelque sorte, *s'échange*' (SNS, 125).

27 'le livre reste trop exclusivement antithètique' (SNS, 125).

28

1 'l'antithèse de ma vue sur moi-même et de la vue d'autrui sur moi' (SNS, 125).

2 'l'antithèse du pour-soi et de l'en-soi' (SNS, 125).

29 'Il se réserve d'étudier ailleurs la "réalisation" du néant dans l'être qui est l'action et qui rend possible la morale' (SNS, 126).

30 'Toutes ces questions, qui nous renvoient à la réflexion pure et non complice, ne peuvent trouver leur réponse que sur le terrain moral. Nous y consacrons un prochain ouvrage' (*L'Etre et le Néant*, op. cit. p. 692) (my translation).

31 'Après Descartes, on ne peut nier que l'existence comme conscience se distingue radicalement de l'existence comme chose et que le rapport de l'une de l'autre soit celui du vide au plein' (SNS, 126).

32 'Après le XIXe siècle et tout ce qu'il nous a appris sur l'historicité de l'esprit, on ne peut nier que la conscience soit toujours en situation' (SNS, 126).

IV *The body*

1 Although Hegel, Sartre, Strawson and Wittgenstein, in their different idioms, draw the distinction between being a person and observing one, Sartre and Nagel see that there is an unsolved metaphysical problem about why that being who is oneself should exist at all: why anything should be *me*. See Hegel *Phänomenologie des Geistes* (op. cit.) especially I, IV A: 'Selbständigkeit und Unselbstandigkeit des Selbstbewusstseins; Herrschaft und Knechtschaft', Sartre *L'Etre et le Néant* (op. cit.) especially Troisième Partie: 'Le Pour Autrui', Peter Strawson *Individuals* (op. cit), Chapter 3 'Persons', Ludwig Wittgenstein *The Blue and Brown Books: Preliminary Studies for the 'Philosophical Investigations'* (Blackwell, Oxford, 1972) pp. 61, 63–4, 66–9, 109, Thomas Nagel *The View From Nowhere* (Oxford University Press, Oxford, 1986) p. 54ff.

2 For a critical summary of the principal ontological options in the philosophy of mind see Stephen Priest *Theories of the Mind* (Penguin Books, London, 1991).

3 'Mon corps se distingue de la table ou de la lampe parce qu'il est constamment perçu tandis que je peux me détourner d'elles' (PP, 106).

4 'C'est un objet qui ne me quitte pas' (PP, 106).

5 'Mais des lors est-ce encore un objet?' (PP, 106).

6 'c'est à dire devant nous' (PP, 106).

7 'L'objet n'est objet que s'il peut être éloigné et donc à la limite disparaître de mon champ visuel. Sa présence est une telle sorte qu'elle ne va pas sans une absence possible' (PP, 106).

8 'à la limite disparaître de mon champ visuel' (PP, 106).

In the English translation 'ultimately' does not capture the sense of 'à la limite' which Merleau-Ponty is using to refer to the rather indefinite limit of the visual field.

9 'il peut être éloigné' (PP, 106).

10 'se présente toujours à moi sous le même angle' (PP, 106).

11 'Il est vrai que les objets extérieurs eux aussi ne me montrent jamais un de leurs côtés qu'en me câchant les autres' (PP, 106).

12 'Je peux du moins choisir à mon gré le côté qu'ils me montreront' (PP, 106).

13 'Ils ne sauraient m'apparaître qu'en perspective, mais la perspective particulière que j'obtiens d'eux à chaque moment ne résulte que d'une nécessité physique' (PP, 106).

14 'une nécessité dont je peux me servir' (PP, 106–7).

15 'Ma tête n'est donnée à ma vue que par le bout de mon nez et par le contour de mes orbites' (PP, 107).

16 'J'observe les objets extérieurs avec mon corps, je les manie, je les inspecte, j'en fais le tour, mais quant à mon corps je ne l'observe pas lui-même: il faudrait, pour pouvoir le faire, disposer d'un second corps qui lui-même ne serait pas observable' (PP, 107).

17 'L'observation consiste à faire varier le point de vue en maintenant fixé l'objet' (PP, 107).

18 'Mon corps visuel est bien objet dans les parties éloignées de ma tête, mais à mesure qu'on approche des yeux, il se sépare des objets, il ménage au milieu d'eux un quasi-éspace ou ils n'ont pas accès' (PP, 107–8).

19 'L'unité de l'homme n'a pas encore été rompue, le corps n'a pas été dépouillé de prédicats humains, il n'est pas encore devenu une machine, l'âme n'a pas encore été définie par l'existence pour-soi' (SC, 203).

20 'La conscience naïve ne voit pas en elle [l'âme] la cause des mouvements du corps et pas d'avantage elle ne la met en lui comme le pilote en son navire' (SC, 203).

21 'Cette manière de penser appartient à la philosophie, elle n'est pas impliquée dans l'expérience immédiate' (SC, 203).

22 'elle ne la met en lui comme le pilote en son navire' (SC, 203).

23 'Il vit dans un univers d'expérience, dans un milieu neutre à l'égard des distinctions substantielles entre l'organisme, la pensée et l'étendue, dans un commerce direct avec les êtres, les choses et son propre corps. L'ego comme centre d'ou rayonnent ses intentions, le corps qui les porte, les êtres et les choses auxquels elles s'addressent ne sont pas confondus: mais ce ne sont que trois secteurs d'un champ unique' (SC, 204).

24 'ce ne sont que trois secteurs d'un champ unique' (SC, 204).

25 'une blessure aux yeux suffit à supprimer la vision' (SC, 204).

26 'c'est donc que nous voyons à travers le corps' (SC, 204).

27 'moment indispensable de la dialectique vécue' (SC, 204).

28 'Le sujet ne vit pas dans un monde d'états de conscience ou de représentations d'ou il croirait par une sorte de miracle agir sur les choses extérieures ou les connaître' (SC, 204).

29 'Le monde se redouble: il y aura le monde réel tel qu'il est hors de mon corps, et le monde tel qu'il est pour moi, numériquement distinct du pre-mier; il faudra séparer la cause extérieure de la perception et l'objet intérieur qu'elle contemple' (SC, 205).

30 'Noli foras ire, in te redi, in interiore homine habitat veritas.' The quotation is from St. Augustine's *De Vera Religione* 39, n. 72. Merleau-Ponty and Husserl are antithetical on self-realisation. Merleau-Ponty, like Sartre, sees us as essentially spiritually empty and recommends self-definition through action in the world. Husserl, like Augustine, recommends a turning away from the world to reveal our essentially non-physical level of being. In the final chapter of the present work I outline a possible metaphysical synthesis of self-realisation though inwardness and outwardness.

31 'La vérite n'"habite" pas seulement l'"homme intérieur", ou plutôt il n'y a pas d'homme intérieur, l'homme est au monde, c'est dans le monde qu'il se connaît' (PP, v).

32 'Mon corps n'est pas seulement un perçu parmi les perçus' (VI, 302).

33 'Il est mésurant de tous, Nullpunkt de toutes les dimensions du monde' (VI, 302).

34

5.632

'Das Subjekt gehört nicht zur Welt, sondern es ist ein Grenze der Welt'.

35

5.633

'Wo in der Welt ist ein metaphysisches Subjekt zu merken?

Du sagst, es verhält sich hier ganz, wie mit Auge und Gesichtsfeld. Aber das Auge siehst du wirklich nicht.

Und nichts am Gesichtsfeld lässt darauf schliessen, dass es von einem Auge gesehen wird.'

36 'Mon corps est fait de la même chair que le monde (c'est un perçu), et ... de plus cette chair de mon corps est participée par le monde, il la réflète, il empiète sur elle et elle empiète sur lui (le senti à la fois comblé de subjecti-vité et comblé de matérialité), ils sont dans rapport de transgression ou d'enjambement' (VI, 302).

37 'de plus cette chair de mon corps est participée par le monde' (VI, 302).
38 'il empiète sur elle et elle empiète sur lui' (VI, 302).
39 'à la fois comblé de subjectivité et comblé de matérialité' (VI, 302).
40 'dans rapport de transgression ou d'enjambement' (VI, 302).
41 'P. ex. il n'est pas un mobile ou mouvant parmi tous les mobiles ou mouvants, je n'ai pas conscience de son mouvement comme *éloignement par rapport à moi*, il *sich bewegt* alors que les choses sont mues' (VI, 302). The English translation has 'the things' for 'les choses' but 'things' is more perspicuous here.
42 'une sorte de "réfléchi" (*sich bewegen*), il se constitue *en-soi* par là – Parallèlement: il *se* touche, *se* voit' (VI, 302).
43 'Le *se toucher, se voir* du corps est à comprendre lui-même d'après ce que nous avons dit du voir et du visible, du toucher et du touchable. *I.e.* ce n'est pas un acte, c'est un être à' (VI, 302–3).
44 '*Se* toucher, *se* voir, d'après cela, ce n'est pas se saisir comme ob-jet, c'est être ouvert à soi, destiné à soi (narcissisme)' (VI, 303).
45 'Ce n'est pas davantage, donc, s'atteindre, c'est au contraire s'échapper, s'ignorer, le soi en question est d'écart, est *Unverborgenheit du Verborgen* comme tel, qui donc ne cesse pas d'être câché ou latent' (VI, 303).
46 'le soi en question' (VI, 303).
47 'la perception de soi (sentiment de soi disait Hegel) ou perception de la perception ne convertit pas ce qu'elle saisit en objet' (VI, 303).
48 'en fait je ne réussis pas tout à fait à me toucher touchant, à me voir voyant, l'expérience que j'ai de moi percevant ne va pas au-delà d'une sorte d'*imminence*' (VI, 303).
49 'l'expérience que j'ai de moi percevant ne va pas au-delà d'une sorte d'*imminence*, elle se termine dans l'invisible, simplement cet invisible est *son* invisible, *i.e.* l'envers de *sa* perception speculaire, de la vision concrète que j'ai de mon corps dans le miroir' (VI, 303).

V *Perception*

1 'Quand je me promène dans mon appartement, les différents aspects sous lesquels il s'offre à moi ne sauraient m'apparaître comme les profils d'une même chose si je ne savais pas que chacun d'eux représente l'appartement vu d'ici ou vu de là' (PP, 235).
2 'si je n'avais conscience de mon propre mouvement, et de mon corps comme identique à travers les phases de ce mouvement' (PP, 235).
3 'Je peux evidément survoler en pensée l'appartement, l'imaginer ou en dessiner le plan sur le papier, mais même alors je ne saurais saisir l'unité de l'objet sans la médiation de l'expérience corporelle, car ce que j'appelle un plan n'est qu'une perspective plus ample: c'est l'appartement "vu d'en haut"' (PP, 235).
4 'Je peux résumer en lui toutes les perspectives coutumières' (PP, 235).
5 'C'est à condition de savoir qu'un même sujet incarné peut voir tour à tour de différentes positions' (PP, 235).
6 'Du point de vue de mon corps je ne vois jamais égales les six faces du cube, même s'il est en verre, et pourtant le mot "cube" a un sens, le cube lui-même, le cube en vérité, au-delà de ses apparences sensibles a ses six faces égales' (PP, 235).
7 'Le cube lui même . . . a ses six faces égales' (PP, 235).
8 'A mesure que je tourne autour de lui, je vois la face frontale, qui était un

carré, se déformer, puis disparaître, pendant que les autres côtés apparaissent et devient chacun à leur tour des carrés' (PP, 235).

9 'Mais le déroulement de cette expérience n'est pour moi que l'occasion de penser le cube totale avec ses six faces égales et simultanées' (PP, 235).

10 'Le cube totale avec ses six faces égales et simultanées' (PP, 235).

11 'la structure intelligible qui en rend raison.' (PP, 235).

12 'Il s'agit de dessiner en pensée cette forme particulière qui renferme un fragment d'espace entre six faces égales' (PP, 236).

13 'le philosophe empiriste considère un sujet X en train de percevoir et cherche à décrire ce qui se passe: il y a des sensations qui sont des états ou des manières d'être du sujet et, à ce titre, de véritables choses mentales' (PP, 240).

14 On empiricist theories of perception see Stephen Priest *The British Empiricists* (Penguin, London, 1990).

15 'le pensée objective' (PP, 240).

16 'Le pensée objective ignore le sujet de la perception' (PP, 240).

17 'L'intellectualisme représente bien un progrès dans la prise de conscience: ce lieu hors du monde que le philosophe empiriste sous-entendait et où il se plaçait tacitement pour décrire l'événement de la perception, il reçoit maintenant un nom, il figure dans la description. C'est l'Ego transcendental' (PP, 240–1).

18 'l'intellectualisme . . . se donne le monde tout fait' (PP, 241).

19 'Cherchons à voir comment un objet ou un être se met à exister pour nous par le désir ou par l'amour et nous comprendrons mieux par là comment des objets et des êtres peuvent exister en général' (PP, 180).

20 Roger Scruton explores intentionality as a necessary condition for sexual desire in his *Sexual Desire* (London, 1986). According to Scruton, sexual desire presupposes rationality to a degree that makes it impossible that non-human animals have sexual desires. Scruton's views may be usefully contrasted with Merleau-Ponty's 'non-cognitive' account.

21 'La perception érotique n'est pas une *cogitatio* qui vise un *cogitatum*; à travers un corps elle vise un autre corps, elle se fait dans le monde et non pas dans une conscience' (PP, 183).

22 'cette perception objective est habitée par une perception plus sécrète: le corps visible est sous-tendu par un schéma sexuel, strictement individuel, qui accentue les zones érogènes, dessine une physionomie sexuelle' (PP, 182).

23 'Il y a une "compréhension" érotique qui n'est pas de l'ordre de l'entendement puisque l'entendement comprend en apercevant une expérience sous une idée, tandis que le désir comprend aveuglement en reliant un corps à un corps' (PP, 183).

24 'Quand on généralise la notion de sexualite, et qu'on fait d'elle une manière d'être au monde physique et interhumain, veut-on dire qu'en dernière analyse toute l'existence a une signification sexuelle ou bien que tout phénomène sexuel a une signification existentielle?' (PP, 185).

25 'Si l'histoire sexuelle d'un homme donne la clef à sa vie, c'est parce que dans la sexualité de l'homme se projette sa manière d'être a l'égard du monde, c'est-à-dire à l'égard du temps et à l'égard des autres hommes' (PP, 185).

26 'la pudeur, le désir, l'amour [...] sont incompréhensibles si l'on traîte l'homme comme une machine gouvernée par des lois naturelles' (PP, 194).

27 For a summary of Hegel's Master and Slave dialectic see Stephen Priest *Theories of the Mind* (Penguin, London, 1991) esp. pp. 92–5.

28 'en tant que j'ai un corps, je peut être réduit en objet sous le regard d'autrui et ne plus compter pour lui comme personne, ou bien, au contraire, je peux devenir son maître et le regarder à mon tour' (PP, 194).

29 The quasi-materialist view that the individuation of putatively non-physical items presupposes the possibility of individuating physical particulars may rest on a circularity. We individuate physical particulars though their spatio-temporal locations. It may be that we cannot individuate spatio-temporal locations without reference to physical particulars. If so, the criteria for the individuation of physical particulars are no clearer than the criteria for the individuation of putatively non-physical items.

30 'mais cette maîtrise est une impasse, puisque, au moment où ma valeur est reconnue par le désir d'autrui, autrui n'est plus la personne je souhaitais d'être reconnu' (PP, 194).

31 'Die Grundeigenschaft der Bewußtseins – weisen, in denen ich als Ich lebe, ist die sogenannte Intentionalität' (PV, 13).

32 'elle n'est compréhensible que par la réduction' (PP, xii).

33 'Alles, was für mich ist, ist es dank meinem erkennenden Bewußtsein, es ist für mich Erfahrenes meines Erfahrens, Gedachtes meines Denkens, Theoretisiertes meines Theoretisierens, Eingesehenes meines Einsehens' (PV, 31).

34 'Es ist für mich nur als intentionale Gegenständlichkeit meiner cogitationes' (PV, 31).

VI *Space*

1 For some varieties of empiricism see Stephen Priest *The British Empiricists* (Penguin, London, 1990).

2 'Il ne s'agit pas, bien entendu, d'un rapport de contenant à contenu' (PP, 281).

3 'un rapport d'inclusion logique, comme celui qui existe entre l'individu et la classe' (PP, 281).

4 'l'espace est antérieur à ses prétendues parties' (PP, 281).

5 'une sorte d'éther dans lequel baignent toutes les choses' (PP, 281).

6 'abstraitement comme un caractère qui leur soit commun' (PP, 281).

7 'Mon corps et les choses, leurs relations concrètes selon le haut et le bas, la droit et la gauche, le proche et le lointain peuvent m'apparaître comme une multiplicité irréductible' (PP, 282).

8 'Je découvre une capacité unique et indivisible de décrire l'espace' (PP, 282).

9 'les dimensions sont substituables, j'ai la spatialité homogène et isotrope' (PP, 282).

10 'un pur changement de lieu qui ne modifierait en rien le mobile, et par conséquent une pure *position* distincte de la *situation* de l'objet dans son contexte concret' (PP, 282).

11 'Cette distinction se brouille au niveau du savoir scientifique lui-même, dans les conceptions modernes de l'espace' (PP, 282).

12 'Est-il vrai que nous soyons devant l'alternative, ou bien de percevoir des choses dans l'espace, ou bien (si nous réfléchissons, et si nous voulons savoir ce que signifient nos propres expériences) de penser l'espace comme le système indivisible des actes de liaison qu'accomplit un esprit constituant?' (PP, 282).

13 For the inverted spectacles experiment see Richard Gregory *Eye and Brain* (Wiedenfeld and Nicholson, London, 1969).

14 'Nous ne sommes pas dans les choses' (PP, 285).

15 'Nous n'avons encore que des champs sensoriels' (PP, 285).

16 'On ne peut prendre le monde et l'espace orienté pour donnés avec les contenus de l'expérience sensible ou avec le corps en-soi, puisque l'expérience montre justement que les mêmes contenus peuvent tour à tour être orientés dans un sens ou dans l'autre' (PP, 285).

17 'une psychologie empiriste qui traite la perception de l'espace comme la réception en nous d'un espace réel' (PP, 286).

18 For empiricism about space see Stephen Priest *The British Empiricists* (Penguin, London, 1990) esp. pp. 67, 83, 84, 108–9, 125–7.

19 'le "droit" et la "renverse" sont des relations et dépendent des repères auxquels on se rapporte' (PP, 286).

20 For Leibniz on space see G.H.R. Parkinson (trans. and ed.) *Leibniz: Philosophical Writings* (Everyman, London, 1973) *passim*.

21 'Il est aisé de montrer qu'une direction ne peut être que pour un sujet qui la décrit' (PP, 286).

22 'Un esprit constituant a éminemment le pouvoir de tracer toutes les directions dans l'espace, mais il n'a actuellement aucune direction et, par suite, aucun espace, faut d'un point de départ effectif, d'un ici absolu qui puisse, de proche en proche, donner un sens à toutes les déterminations de l'espace' (PP, 286).

23 'Il ne considère le spectacle de nulle part' (PP, 286).

24 'Ce qui importe pour l'orientation du spectacle, ce n'est pas mon corps tel qu'il est en fait, comme chose dans l'espace objectif, mais mon corps comme système d'actions possibles, un corps virtuel dont le "lieu" phénoménal est défini par sa situation. Mon corps est là où il y a quelquechose à faire' (PP, 288).

25 'Il est essentiel à l'espace d'être toujours "déjà constitué" et nous ne le comprendrons jamais en nous rétirant dans une perception sans monde' (PP, 291).

26 'il ne faut pas se demander pourquoi l'être est orienté, pourquoi, dans notre language de tout à l'heure, notre corps n'est pas en prise sur le monde dans toutes les positions, et pourquoi sa coexistence avec le monde polarise l'expérience et fait surgir une direction. La question ne pourrait être posée que si ces faits étaient des accidents qui adviendraient à un sujet et à un objet indifférents à l'espace. L'expérience perceptive nous montre au contraire qu'ils sont présupposés dans notre rencontre primordiale avec l'être et que l'être et synonyme d'être situé' (PP, 291).

27 'L'être est synonyme d'être situé' (PP, 291).

28

1 'Tout être concevable se rapporte directement ou indirectement au monde perçu' (PP, 293).

2 'Le monde perçu n'est saisi que par l'orientation' (PP, 293).

3 'Nous ne pouvons dissocier l'être de l'être orienté' (PP, 293).

4 'Il n'y a pas de lieu de "fonder" l'espace ou de demander quel est le niveau de tous les niveaux' (PP, 293).

29 Immanuel Kant *Kritik der Reinen Vernunft* (op. cit.) I. Transzendentale Elementarlehre, Erster Teil: Die Transzendentale Ästhetik, *Critique of Pure*

Reason (op. cit.) I. Transcendental Doctrine of Elements, First Part: Transcendental Aesthetic (A19/B34–A49/B73).

30 'On pourrait montrer, par example, que la perception esthétique ouvre à son tour une nouvelle spatialité, que le tableau comme œuvre d'art n'est pas dans l'espace ou il habite comme chose physique et comme toile colorieé; que la danse se déroule dans un espace sans buts et sans directions . . .' (PP, 333).

31 'La schizophrène ne vit plus dans le monde commun, mais dans un monde privé' (PP, 332).

32 'Il y a autant d'espaces que d'expériences spatiales distinctes' (PP, 337).

33 See Anthony Quinton 'Spaces and Times' *Philosophy*, vol 37, 1962, pp. 130–47.

34 Merleau-Ponty refers to Gelb and Goldstein's *Über den Einfluss des vollstandigen Verlustes des optischen Vorstellungsvermogens auf taktile Erkennen. Psychologische Analysen hirnpathologischer Fälle* and to Goldstein's *Uber die Abhändigkeit der Bewegungen von optischen Vorgangen* and *Zeigen und Greifen* (PP, 119–20, PPT 103).

35 'La psychologie classique ne dispose d'aucun concept pour exprimer ces variétés de la conscience de lieu parce que la conscience de lieu est toujours pour elle conscience positionelle, représentation, *Vor-stellung*, qu'à ce titre elle nous donne le lieu comme détermination du monde objectif et qu'une telle représentation est ou n'est pas, mais, si elle est nous livre son objet sans aucune ambiguïté et comme une terme identifiable à travers toutes ses apparitions' (PP, 121).

VII *Time*

1 'toutes nos expériences, en tant qu'elles sont notres, se disposent selon l'avant et l'après' (PP, 469).

2 'la temporalité, en langage kantien, est la forme du sens intime' (PP, 469).

3 See Immanuel Kant *Kritik der Reinen Vernunft* (op. cit), 'Transzendentale Ästhetik' *Critique of Pure Reason* (op. cit.) 'Transcendental Aesthetic'. Although this chapter is arguably the most idealist of the whole work, Merleau-Ponty's reading of it is not beyond dispute. If we do not understand transcendental idealism as idealism then we do not have to ascribe to Kant the view that space and time are literally parts of our psychology. We may take him to be saying that it is necessary and a priori that any object of our inner experience will be temporal and any object of our outer experience will be spatio-temporal. Because temporality is a necessary condition for experience and because spatio-temporality is a necessary condition for outer experience, nothing within experience can refute 'experience is temporal' and nothing within outer experience can refute 'outer experience is spatio-temporal'. Clearly 'it is necessary that' does not mean 'it is contradictory to deny that' here but 'experience is sufficient for'.

4 '[la temporalité] . . . est le caractère le plus général des "faits psychiques"' (PP, 469).

5 'Le sujet . . . ne peut être une série d'événements psychiques' (PP, 469), 'ne peut cependant être éternel' (PP, 469).

6 'le temps passe ou s'écoule' (PP, 470), 'on parle du cours du demps' (PP, 470).

7 'Si le temps est semblable à une rivière, il coule du passé vers le présent et l'avenir. Le présent est la conséquence du passé et l'avenir la conséquence du présent' (PP, 470).

8 '*A considérer les choses elles-mêmes*, la fonte des neiges et ce qui en résulte ne sont pas des événements successifs, ou plutôt la notion même d'événement n'a pas de place dans le monde objectif' (PP, 470).

9 'La notion même d'événement n'a pas de place dans le monde objectif' (PP, 470).

10 'Je sous-entends un témoin assujetti à une certaine place dans le monde et je compare ses vues successives' (PP, 470).

11 It is extremely doubtful that Merleau-Ponty's idealist phenomenology of time in *Phénoménologie de la Perception* may be shown to be consistent with his realism about our being-in-the-world. One solution would be facilitated by dropping the fallacious inference from 'Events may only be conceived by me as they would be if I were experiencing them' to 'Events ontologically depend upon the psychology of the subject'. On many readings of Kant, including Merleau-Ponty's, Kant is an idealist because we can only know *appearances* ('Erscheinungen'). I see no reason to assume that appearances are mental items. They could be things, paradigmatically physical objects, that appear (rather as a motor car but not some sense data could appear around a street corner). From the fact that we can only imagine objects as they would appear to us if we were perceiving them it does not follow that they are (essentially) mental.

12 See Stephen Priest *The British Empiricists* (op. cit.). For a sophisticated articulation of the contrary view, that Hume was a 'realist' about causal relations, see Galen Strawson *The Secret Connection* (Oxford University Press, Oxford, 1989).

13 'Les "Evénements" sont découpés par un observateur fini dans la totalité spatio-temporelle du monde objectif' (PP, 470).

14 'Si je considère ce monde lui-même, il n'y a qu'un seul être indivisible et qui ne change pas' (PP, 470).

This is a Parmenidean thesis if it is logically equivalent to the conjunction of the Eleatic's claims at Fragment 347 'It is [. . .] one', Fragment 348 'Nor is it divisible' and Fragment 350 '[It is] motionless'. See G.S. Kirk and J.E. Raven *The Presocratic Philosophers* (Cambridge University Press, Cambridge, 1977) pp. 275–6. Parmenides' ascription of these properties is to *being* but Merleau-Ponty's is to *being via 'the world itself'* but here this has the sense and reference of 'l'être-en-soi' (being-in-itself) and Parmenides himself implicitly accepts the *appearance* of change in denying its reality. This suggests an identity of referent between Merleau-Ponty's and Parmenides' ascriptions.

15 A world without change would be a world which lacked many pervasive temporal properties of the actual world: *past, present, future*; *containing beginnings and endings*, and arguably, *before, simultaneous with, after*, orderings. Nevertheless I see no contradiction in the idea that a changeless world should have *duration* (unless ageing is changing).

16 'Le changement suppose un certain poste où je me place et d'où je vois défiler les choses; il n'y a pas d'événements sans quelqu'un à qui ils adviennent et dont la perspective finie fonde leur individualite' (PP, 470).

17 'Le temps suppose une vue sur le temps' (PP, 470).

18 'Il n'est donc pas comme un ruisseau, il n'est pas une substance fluente' (PP, 470).

19 'On dit souvent que, dans les choses mêmes, l'avenir n'est pas encore, le passé n'est plus, et le présent, à la rigeur, n'est qu'une limite, de sorte que le temps s'effondre' (PP, 471).

20 See St. Augustine *Confessions* trans. H. Chadwick (Oxford University Press, Oxford, 1991) Book XI, *Hobbes's Leviathan* reprinted from the edition of 1651 with an essay by the late W.G. Pogson Smith (Oxford University Press, Oxford, 1947), Henri Bergson *Matière et Mémoire: Essai sur la Relation du Corps à L'Esprit* (Presses Universitaires de France, Paris, 1965) translated as *Matter and Memory* by N.M. Paul and W. Scott Palmer (George Allen and Unwin, London, 1970). *Leibniz: Philosophical Writings* ed. G.H.R. Parkinson (Everyman, London, 1973), J. McT.E.McTaggart *The Nature of Existence* (Cambridge University Press, Cambridge, 1988) Vol. II, Chapter XXXIII 'Time'.

21 McTaggart argues that the series of events ordered by the before/after (or earlier than/later than) relation (the 'B-series') is temporally ordered only if it includes change. It includes change only if it is also ordered by the past/present/future distinction (and so forms an 'A-series'). The concept of the A-series is incoherent because no event is past, present and future, so there is no A-series, no change, and so the B-series is not a temporal series. See McTaggart (op. cit.) esp. pp. 11–12.

22 'Le temps n'est donc pas un processus réel, une succession effective que je me bornerais à enregistrer' (PP, 471).

23 'Il naît de mon rapport avec les choses' (PP, 471).

24 'Le passé et l'avenir n'existent que trop dans le monde, ils existent au présent' (PP, 471).

25 'Le surgissement du temps serait incompréhensible comme création d'un supplément de temps qui repousserait au passé toute la série précédente. Cette passivité n'est pas concevable' (VI, 237).

26 'Le surgissement du temps serait incompréhensible' (VI, 237).

27 'Cette passivité n'est pas concevable' (VI, 237).

28 'Par contre toute analyse du temps qui le survole est insuffisante' (VI, 237).

29 'Il faut que le temps se constitue, – soit toujours vu du point de vue de quelqu'un qui en est' (VI, 237).

30 'Mais cela paraît contradictoire, et ramenerait à l'un des deux termes de l'alternative précédente' (VI, 238).

31 'La contradiction n'est levée que si le nouveau présent est lui-même un transcendant' (VI, 238).

32 'on sait qu'il n'est pas là, qu'il vient d'être là' (VI, 238).

33 'Il n'est pas un segment de temps à contours définis qui viendrait se mettre en place' (VI, 238).

34 'H. a raison de dire que ce n'est pas moi qui constitue le temps, qu'il ne constitue, qu'il est une *Selbsterscheinung*' (VI, 244).

35 'Qu'est-ce que l'élément "réceptif" de la conscience absolue?' (VI, 244).

36 'le terme de "receptivité" est impropre justement parce qu'il évoque un Soi distinct du présent et qui le *reçoit*' (VI, 244).

VIII *Subjectivity*

1 The famous claim *Cogito ergo sum* does not appear in *A Discourse on Method*, nor in the *Méditations* but in *The Principles of Philosophy* (Part I, para. VII). See, for example, René Descartes *A Discourse on Method etc.* ed. A.D. Lindsay (Everyman, London, 1949) esp. p. 167.

2 'Le cogito est ou bien cette pensée qui s'est formée il y a trois siècles dans l'esprit de Descartes, ou bien le sens des textes qu'il nous a laissés, ou enfin une vérité éternelle qui transparaît à travers eux' (PP, 423).

3 'C'est moi qui reconstitue le *Cogito* historique, c'est moi qui lis le texte de Descartes, c'est moi qui y reconnais une vérité impérissable, et en fin de compte le *Cogito* cartesien n'a de sens que par mon propre *Cogito*' (PP, 425).

4 Deciding the logical form of *cogito ergo sum* depends on deciding the force of *ergo*. Some possibilites are:

1   $\forall x$ (thinks x) $\rightarrow$ $\exists x$ (thinks x)
2   $\Box\{\forall x$ (thinks x) $\rightarrow$ $\exists x$ (thinks x)$\}$

Neither of these captures the indexicality of *cogito* or *sum*.

5 'Je n'en penserais rien si je n'avais en moi-même tout ce qu'il faut pour l'inventer' (PP, 425).

6 'Toute pensée de quelque chose est en même temps conscience de soi? Faute de quoi elle ne pourrait pas avoir d'objet' (PP, 426).

7 'A la racine de toutes nos expériences et de toutes nos réflexions, nous trouvons donc un être qui se reconnaît lui-même immédiatement, parce qu'il est son savoir de soi et de toutes choses, et qui connaît sa propre existence non pas par constatation et comme un fait donné, ou par inférence à partir d'une idée de lui même, mais par un contact direct avec elle' (PP, 426).

8 See Hegel *Phänomenologie des Geistes* (op. cit) VIII 'Das absolute Wissen'. Compare Merleau-Ponty's claim 'il est son savoir de soi' with, for example:

'Indem seine Vollendung darin besteht, das war er ist, seine Substanz, vollkommen zu wissen, so ist dies Wissen sein Insichgehen, in welchem er sein Dasein verlässt und seine Gestalt der Erinnerung ubergibt' p. 530.

'As its fulfilment consists in perfectly *knowing* what *it is*, in knowing its substance, this knowing is its *withdrawl into itself* in which it abandons its outer existence and gives its existential shape over to recollection' (Hegel's *Phenomenology of Spirit* (op. cit.) p. 492).

In absolute knowing what is does not differ from its knowledge of itself because what is is a substantial self-consciousness. Merleau-Ponty denies that self-consciousness is a substance so, on his view, the subject can only partly be (constituted by) its knowledge of itself.

9 'La conscience de soi est l'être même de l'esprit en exercice. Il faut que l'acte par lequel j'ai conscience de quelque chose soit appréhendé lui-même dans l'instant ou il s'accomplit, sans quoi il se briserait' (PP, 426).

10 'le cogito me révèle un nouveau mode d'existence qui ne doit rien au temps' (PP, 426–7).

11 'La seule expérience du sujet est celle qui j'obtiens en coïncidant avec lui' (PP, 427).

12 'réduire l'expérience à une somme d'événements psychologiques dont le Je ne serait que le nom commun ou la cause hypothètique' (VI, 426).

13 'reconnaître en deçà des événements un champ et un système de pensées qui ne soit assujetti au temps ni à aucune limitation, un mode d'existence qui ne doive rien à l'événement et qui soit l'existence comme conscience' (VI, 426).

14 'on ne voit pas comment mon existence pourrait être plus certaine que celle d'aucune chose, puisqu'elle n'est pas plus immédiate, sauf dans un instant insaissable' (VI, 426).

15 See David Hume *A Treatise of Human Nature* ed. L.A. Selby-Bigge (Oxford University Press, Oxford, 1955) I.4.6.

16 'mon esprit est Dieu' (PP, 427).
17 'La pluralité des consciences est impossible' (PP, 428).

IX *Freedom*

1 'Il est inconcevable que je sois libre dans certaines de mes actions et déterminé dans d'autres' (PP, 496).
2 'La liberté est en deçà de toutes les actions' (PP, 499).
3

   1 'Si une seule fois, je suis libre, c'est que je ne compte pas au nombre des choses' (PP, 497).
   2 'Il faut que je le sois sans cesse' (PP, 497).
   3 'On ne saurait être un peu libre' (PP, 497).

4 'Pour que quelque chose du dehors pût me déterminer . . . il faudrait que je fusse une chose' (PP, 496).
5 'Rien ne me détermine du dehors, non que rien ne me sollicite, mais au contraire parce que je suis d'emblée hors de moi et ouvert au monde' (PP, 520).
6 'Nous avons toujours le pouvoir d'interrompre' (PP, 500).
7 'Suppose en tout cas un pouvoir de commencer' (PP, 500).
8 'Si, comme on dit souvent, des motifs m'inclinent dans un sens, c'est de deux choses l'une: ou bien ils ont la force de me faire agir, et alors il n'y a pas de liberté, ou bien ils ne l'ont pas, et alors elle est entière, aussi grande dans les pires tortures que dans la paix de ma maison' (PP, 497).
   The translator renders 'dans un sens' as 'in a certain direction'. 'Certain' has no warrant in the French even though 'sens' can mean 'direction'. Merleau-Ponty probably means there is a sense in which my motives cause my actions so 'sens' is best rendered 'sense' and the idea of direction dropped.
9 'Mon tempérament n'existe que pour la connaissance seconde que je prends de moi-même quand je me vois par les yeux d'autrui, et pour autant que je le reconnais, le valorise et, en ce sens, le choisis' (PP, 497).
10 See Hegel's 'Master and Slave' chapter in his *Phenomenology of Spirit* (op. cit.) and Nagel's *The View From Nowhere* (op. cit.) *passim* but especially chapters III and IV.
11 'Je le reconnais, le valorise et, en ce sens, le choisis' (PP, 497). Sartre thinks we make ourselves what we are.
12 'Et, en effet, si je peux volontairement adopter une conduite et m'improviser guerrier ou séducteur, il ne dépend pas de moi d'être guerrier ou séducteur avec aisance et "naturel", c'est à dire de l'être vraiment' (PP, 498).
13 Wittgenstein *Philosophical Investigations* (Blackwell, Oxford, 1958) §621–2.
14 'Mais aussi ne doit-on pas chercher la liberté dans l'acte volontaire, qui est, selon son sens même, un acte manqué' (PP, 498).
15 'Même ce qu'on appelle les obstacles à la liberté sont en réalité déployés par elle. Un rocher infranchissable, un rocher grand ou petit, vertical ou oblique, cela n'a de sens que pour quelqu'un qui se propose de le franchir, pour un sujet dont les projets découpent ces déterminations dans la masse uniforme de l'en-soi et font surgir un monde orienté, un sens des choses' (PP, 498).
16 'Il n'est donc rien finalement qui puisse limiter la liberté, sinon ce qu'elle a elle-même déterminé comme limité par ses initiatives (PP, 498).
17 'Le sujet n'a que l'extérieur qu'il se donne' (PP, 498).

18 '[Le] monde en-soi . . . sans elle [la liberté] ne serait qu'une masse amorphe et innommable' (PP, 502).

19 'Qu'est que donc la liberté? Naître, c'est à la fois naître du monde et naître au monde. Le monde est déjà constitué, mais aussi jamais complètement constitué. Sous le premier rapport, nous sommes sollicités, sous le second nous sommes ouverts à une infinité de possibles. Mais cette analyse est encore abstraite, car nous existons sous les deux rapports à la fois. Il n'y a donc jamais déterminisme et jamais choix absolu' (PP, 517).

20 'Il est impossible de délimiter la "part de la situation" et la "part de la liberté"' (PP, 517).

21 'Jamais, je ne suis chose et jamais conscience nue' (PP, 517).

22 'la cause est condition necessaire et suffisante de l'effet consideré dans sone existence et dans sa nature' (SC, 174).

23 'En décrivant l'individu physique ou organique et son entourage, nous avons été aménés à admettre que leurs rapports n'étaient pas méchaniques, mais dialectiques' (SC, 174).

24 'La cause et l'effet sont décomposables en éléments réels qui se correspondent chacun à chacun' (SC, 174).

25 'les stimuli physiques n'agissent sur l'organisme qu'en y suscitant une réponse globale' (SC, 174).

26 'une réponse globale [. . .] variera qualitativement quand ils [les stimuli] varient quantitativement' (SC, 174).

27 '[. . .] ils jouent à son egard le rôle d'occasions plutôt que de causes' (SC, 174).
   The translation has 'cause' for 'causes'.

28 'la réaction dépend, plutôt que des propriétés materielles des stimuli, de leur signification vitale. Ainsi entre les variables d'ou dépend effectivement la conduite et cette conduite même, apparaît un rapport de sens, une rélation intrinsique' (SC, 174).

X Language

1 'une unité distincte de celle de l'object scientifique'(PP, 203).
2 'la dichotomie classique du sujet et de l'objet' (PP, 203).
3 'il n'y a pas de "sujet parlant"' (PP, 203).
4 See, notably, Derrida's deconstructions of Husserl's phenomenology of language in *La Voix et le Phénomène* (Presses Universitaires de France, Paris, 1967) translated by David B. Allison as Jacques Derrida *Speech and Phenomena* (Northwestern University Press, Evanston, 1973). Derrida rejects the thesis that the speaking subject has an original control over his or her speech, and rejects the thesis that the meaning of what is said is transparently available to the speaker in self-presence. Rather, the subject is itself a product of the movement of *difference*.
5 'la parole prend place dans un circuit de phénomènes en troisième personne' (PP, 203–4).
6 Hume is more consistently empiricist than Berkeley on the subject. Both agree that no subject appears within experience (at least *qua* subject) but while Hume therefore refuses to postulate a subject *qua* subject, Berkeley postulates a finite spirit whose being is to perceive. Berkeley has no empirically sufficient grounds for this. See Hume *A Treatise of Human Nature* (op. cit.) esp. I.4.6. and Berkeley *The Principles of Human Knowledge* (op. cit.) *passim*.

7 'il n'y a personne qui parle, il y a un flux de mots qui se produisent sans aucune intention de parler qui les gouverne' (PP, 204).

8 See Giambattista Vico *Scienza Nuova* (Cornell, 1948) and Leon Pompa (ed.) *Vico: Selected Writings* (Cambridge University Press, Cambridge, 1982), Kant *Kritik der Reinen Vernunft* (op. cit.), *Critique of Pure Reason* (op. cit.), Hegel *Phänomenologie des Geistes* (op. cit.), *Hegel's Phenomenology of Spirit* (op. cit.), Ferdinand de Saussure *Cours de la Linguistique Générale*, Course in General Linguistics (Collins, London, 1960), Wittgenstein *Philosophical Investigations* (op. cit.), Derrida *La Voix et le Phénomène* (op. cit.), *Speech and Phenomena* (op. cit.).

Although something of an orthodoxy in the philosophy of mind and language over the last two centuries or more, it is obscure what it consists in for thought to be linguistic. Contrast the case where the sentences of a language you do not understand run through your mind with the case where you think tokens of those sentence types after learning the language. Even if mastery of the public rules of the language explains how the transition is possible, or even what the transition consists in, it does not make clear what the transistion is a transition to inside the mind.

9 'Le sens des mots est considéré comme donné avec les stimuli ou avec les états de conscience qu'il s'agit de nommer' (PP, 204).

10 'un être de raison' (PP, 204).

Because 'origin' has no warrant in the French this expression should be translated 'a rational being' or 'something rational'. The idea that the rules of language are not psychologically bestowed on it may then be retained. Colin Smith's translation suggests the opposite of this.

11 'Le langage peut se désagréger par fragments' and it follows from this that 'il se constitue par une série d'apports indépendants' (PP, 204).

12 See John Locke *An Essay Concerning Human Understanding* ed. A.S. Pringle-Pattison (Clarendon Press, Oxford, 1950), Book III, 'Of Words', Saussure *Cours de la Linguistique Générale* (op. cit.) *Course in General Linguistics* (op. cit.), Ludwig Wittgenstein *Tractatus Logico-Philosophicus* trans. David Pears and Brian McGuinness (Routledge and Kegan Paul, London, 1961) Bertrand Russell *An Inquiry into Meaning and Truth* (Penguin, Harmondsworth, 1973), W.V.O. Quine 'Two Dogmas of Empiricism' in his *From a Logical Point of View* (Cambridge, Mass., 1953).

13 See David Pears (ed.) Russell's Logical Atomism (Collins, London, 1972) and Stephen Priest *The British Empiricists* (op. cit.) p. 213ff.

14 'le langage n'est qu'un accompagnement extérieur de la pensée' (PP, 206).

15 'l'intellectualisme diffère à peine de l'empirisme' (PP, 206).

16 'on dépasse donc aussi bien l'intellectualisme que l'empiricisme par cette simple remarque que le mot a un sens' (PP, 206).

Smith translates 'dépasse' as 'refute' here but 'dépasser' means 'to go beyond'. ('Refuter' is 'to refute'.) Merleau-Ponty is not offering a direct refutation of rationalism and empiricism but an explanation of how both are thinkable that will exhibit their merits and shortcomings.

17 'nous nous donnons notre pensée par la parole intérieure ou extérieure' (PP, 207).

18 'Une pensée qui se contenterait d'exister pour-soi, hors des gênes de la parole et de la communication, aussitôt apparue tomberait à l'inconscience, ce qui revient à dire qu'elle n'existerait pas même pour-soi' (PP, 206).

19 See Kant *Kritik der Reinen Vernunft* (op. cit.), *Critique of Pure Reason* (op. cit.). The crucial ambiguity is at B132 where Kant equivocates between

'would be impossible' and 'or at least would be nothing to me' ('unmöglich, oder wenigstens für mich nichts sein').

20 If we distinguish a Lockean view, according to which thought is prior to communication, from a Wittgensteinian view, according to which communication is prior to thought, then Merleau-Ponty is a Wittgensteinian. See Locke *An Essay Concerning Human Understanding* (op. cit.) Part III 'Of Words' and Wittgenstein *Philosophical Investigations* (op. cit.) §244ff.

21 'Le mot, loin d'être le simple signe des objets et des significations, habite les choses et véhicule les communications' (PP, 207).

22 See Kant *Kritik der Reinen Vernunft* (op. cit.), *Critique of Pure Reason* (op. cit.) esp. A64/B89ff.

23 'l'objet le plus familier nous paraît indéterminé tant que nous n'en avons pas retrouvé le nom' (PP, 206).

24 'nous nous donnons notre pensée par la parole intérieure ou extérieure' (PP, 207).

25 'c'est par l'expression qu'elle devient notre' (PP, 207).

26 'le sujet pensant lui-même est dans une sorte d'ignorance de ses pensées tant qu'il ne les a pas forumlées pour-soi' (PP, 206).

27 'Je commence à comprendre le sens des mots par leur place dans une contexte d'action et en participant à la vie commune' (PP, 209).

28 'la pensée, chez le sujet parlant, n'est pas une représentation' (PP, 209).

29 'ne pose pas expressement des objets ou des relations' (PP, 209).

30 'Nous ne nous demandons pas si le monde existe, nous nous demandons ce que c'est, pour lui qu'exister' (VI, 131).

31 'Quand nous nous demandons ce que c'est, pour les choses et le monde, qu'exister, on pourrait croire qu'il ne s'agit que de définir un mot' (VI, 131).

32 'Apres tout, les questions ont lieu dans le langage' (VI, 131).

33 'On peut donc être tenté de mettre au nombre des faits de langage la question philosophique sur le monde et, quant à la réponse, elle ne peut être cherchée, semble-t-il, que dans les significations de mots, puisque c'est en mots qu'il sera répondu à la question' (VI 131).

XI *Other minds*

1 'La question est justement là: comment le mot Je peut-il se mettre au pluriel, comment peut-on former une idée générale du Je, comment puis-je parler d'un autre Je que le mien, comment puis-je savoir qu'il y a d'autres Je' (PP, 400).

2 'Je ne peux jamais être sur de comprendre mon passé mieux qu'il vécu se comprenait lui-même quand je l'ai vécu' (PP, 398).

3 'si je me reporte à ces années, telles que je les ai vécues' (PP, 398).

4 'mes prises sur le passé et sur l'avenir sont glissants' (PP, 399).

5 'La transcedence des moments du temps fonde et compromet à la fois la rationalité de mon histoire: elle la fonde puisqu'elle m'ouvre un avenir absolument neuf ou je pourrai réfléchir sur ce qu'il y a d'opaque dans mon présent, elle la compromet puisque, de cet avenir, je ne pourrai jamais saisir le présent que je vis avec une certitude apodictique, qu'ainsi le vécu n'est jamais tout à fait compréhensible, ce que je comprends ne rejoint jamais exactement ma vie, et qu'enfin je ne fais jamais un avec moi-meme' (PP, 398–9).

6 In this sense, Kant's *Kritik der Reinen Vernunft* (op. cit.) is an essentially deconstructionist project. It simultaneously seeks to explain the possibility

of metaphysics and demarcate the limits of metaphysics through exhibiting its inner inconsistencies.

7 'La possession par moi de mon temps est toujours différée jusqu'au moment ou je me comprendrais entièrement, et ce moment là ne peut pas arriver' (PP, 398).

8 'Je ne pourrai jamais saisir le présent que je vis' (PP, 399).

9 'Je ne fais jamais un avec moi-même' (PP, 399).

10 'Quand je me tourne vers ma perception et que je passe de la perception directe a la pensée de cette perception, je la re-effectue, je retrouve une pensée plus vieille que moi à l'œuvre dans mes organes de perception et dont ils ne sont que la trace. C'est de la même manière que je comprends autrui. Ici encore, je n'ai que la trace d'une conscience qui m'échappe dans son actualité' (PP, 404).

11 'Il n'y a rien là comme un raisonnement par analogie' (PP, 404).

12 'Je n'ai que la trace d'une conscience qui m'échappe dans son actualité' (PP, 404).

13 'Le corps d'autrui, comme mon propre corps, n'est pas habité' (PP, 401).

14 'A ce problème, ce que nous avons dit sur le corps apporte un commencement de solution' (PP, 401).

15 'En même temps que le corps se retire du monde objectif et vient former entre le pur sujet et l'objet un troisième genre d'être, le sujet perd sa pureté et sa transparence' (PP, 402).

16 See Mary Warnock *Existentialism* (Oxford University Press, Oxford, 1970) and Gilbert Ryle *The Concept of Mind* (Hutchinson, London, 1949).

17 See Stephen Priest *Theories of the Mind* (op. cit.) Chapter 2.

18 'Le temps naturel est toujours là' (PP, 398).

19 'Je n'ai pas seulement un monde physique, je ne vis pas seulement au milieu de la terre, de l'air et de l'eau, j'ai autour de moi des routes, des plantations, des villages, des rues, des églises, des utensiles, une sonnette, une cuiller, une pipe. Chacun de ces objets porte en creux la marque de l'action humaine a laquelle il sert' (PP, 399).

20 'Chacun émet une atmosphère d'humanité' (PP, 399–400).

21 'se sédimentent' (PP, 400).

22 On Hegel on the mental–physical distinction see Priest *Theories of the Mind* (op. cit.) Chapter 3.

23 'Dans l'objet culturel, j'éprouve la présence prochaine d'autrui sous une voile d'anonymat. On se sert de la pipe pour fumer, de la cuiller pour manger, de la sonnette pour appeler, et c'est par la perception d'un acte humain et d'un autre homme que celle du monde culturel pourrait se vérifier' (PP, 400).

24 See Peter Strawson *Individuals: An Essay in Descriptive Metaphysics* (Methuen, London, 1959) esp. Chapter 3 'Persons'.

25 'Pour le penser comme un véritable Je, je devrais me penser comme simple objet pour lui, ce qui m'est interdit par le savoir que j'ai de moi même. Mais si le corps d'autrui n'est pas un objet pour moi, ni le mien pour lui, s'ils sont des comportements, la position d'autrui ne me réduit pas a la condition d'objet dans son champ, ma perception d'autrui ne le réduit pas à la condition d'objet dans mon champ' (PP, 405).

26 'le corps d'autrui n'est pas un objet pour moi' (PP, 405).

27 'Le moi que perçoit n'a pas de privilège particulier qui rend impossible un moi perçu. Tous deux sont, non pas cogitationes enfermées dans leur immanence' (PP, 405).

28 'So wie ich mich als naturlicher Mensch apperzipiere, habe ich ja schön im voraus die Raumwelt apperzipiert, mich im Raum gefässt, in dem ich also ein Ausser-mir habe!' (PV, 32).

29 'Nous interrogeons notre expérience, précisement pour savoir comment elle nous offre à ce qui n'est pas nous' (VI, 159).

30 'Considérons-nous donc installés parmi la multitude des choses, des vivants, des symboles, des instruments et des hommes' (VI, 212).

31 Merleau-Ponty's view is inconsistent with Hegel's on this point. See Priest *Theories of the Mind* (op. cit.) p. 81.

32 'Notre première vérité, celle qui ne préjuge rien et ne peut être contestée, sera qu'il y a présence, que "quelque chose" est là et que "quelqu'un" est là' (VI, 213).

33 See McTaggart *The Nature of Existence* (op. cit.) Vol. II, D.H. Mellor *Real Time* (Cambridge University Press, Cambridge, 1981), Derrida *La Voix et le Phénomène* (op. cit.).

34 Hegel *Phänomenologie des Geistes* (op. cit.) p. 69–78.

35 See Hume *A Treatise of Human Nature* (op. cit.) I.4.2.

36 'Et, de même, quand on dit: même si la chose, à l'analyse, est toujours au-delà de la preuve, et apparaît comme une extrapolation, toujours est-il que nous voyons des cailloux, des coquillages' (VI, 215).

37 'Peut-être, le soi et le non-soi sont comme l'envers et l'endroit' (VI, 212).

38 'Le rapport moi-autrui a concevoir (comme le rapport inter-sexuel, avec ses substitutions indéfinies [. . .]) comme rôles complémentaires dont aucun ne peut être tenu sans que l'autre le soit aussi: masculinité implique femininité, etc' (VI, 274).

XII *Things*

1 'comment il y a de l'objectif?' (PP, 346).

2 'même si elle ne peut être définie par là, une chose a des "caractères" ou des "propriétés" stables' (PP, 345).

3 'une chose a d'abord sa grandeur et sa forme propres sous les variations perspectives qui ne sont qu'apparentes' (PP, 345).

4 'Nous convenons de considérer comme vraies la grandeur que nous obtenons à distance de toucher ou la forme que prend l'objet quand il est dans un plan parallèle au plan frontal' (PP, 345).

5 'Elles ne sont pas plus vraies que d'autres' (PP, 345).

6 'définies à l'aide de notre corps' (PP, 345).

7 'Nous avons toujours le moyen de les reconnaître, et elles nous fournissent elles-mêmes un répère par rapport auquel nous pouvons enfin fixer les apparence fuyantes, les distinguer les unes des autres et en un mot construire une objectivité' (PP, 345).

8 'Kant a raison de dire que la perception est, de soi, polarisée vers l'objet' (PP, 347-8).

9 appearance as appearance (PPT, 301).

10 'Il y a des formes déterminées, quelque chose comme "un carré", "un losange", une configuration spatiale effective, parce que notre corps comme point de vue sur les choses et les choses comme éléments abstraits d'un seul monde forment un système ou chaque moment est immédiatement signicatif de tous les autres' (PP, 347).

11 'la chose intersensorielle' (PP, 366).

12 'La chose visuelle (le disque livide de la lune) ou la chose tactile (mon crâne

tel que je le sens en le palpant) [...] pour nous se maintient la même à travers une série d'expériences' (PP, 366).

13 'un quale qui subsiste effectivement' (PP, 366) 'a *quale* genuinely subsisting' (PPT, 317).

14 'la notion ou la conscience d'une telle propriété objective' (PP, 366).

15 'ce qui est retrouvé ou repris par notre regard ou par notre mouvement' (PP, 366).

16 'l'objet . . . s'offre au regard ou à la palpation' (PP, 366).

17 'Si les constantes de chaque sens sont ainsi comprises, il ne pourra pas être question de définir la chose intersensorielle où elles s'unissent par un ensemble d'attributs stables ou par la notion de cet ensemble' (PP, 367).

XIII *Art*

1 'finalement, nous devons renoncer à traîter la peinture comme un langage' (PM, 66).

2 'le parallèle est un principe légitime' (PW, 66).

3

    1 'La même transmutation' (PM, 67).

    2 'La même migration d'un sens épars dans l'expérience' (PM, 67).

    3 'La même opération expressive fonctionne ici et là' (PM, 67).

4 'l'opération active de signification qui définirait la conscience' (PP, vi).

5

    1 'La science manipule les choses et renonce à les habiter' (OE, 9).

    2 'Elle [...] ne se confronte que de loin en loin avec le monde actuel' (OE, 9).

      The translation has 'real world' not 'actual world' for 'monde actuel'. For Merleau-Ponty 'real world' and 'actual world' have the same referent but differ in sense.

    3 'Elle est [...] ce parti pris de traîter tout être comme "objet en générale", c'est à dire à la fois comme s'il ne nous était rien et se trouvait cependant prédestiné à nos artifices' (OE, 9).

6 'l'art et notamment la peinture puisent à cette nappe de sens brut dont l'activisme ne veut rien savoir. Ils sont mêmes seuls à le faire en toute innocence' (OE, 13).

7 'A l'écrivain, au philosophe, on demande conseil ou avis, on n'admet pas qu'ils tiennent le monde en suspens' (OE, 13–14).

8 'La musique [. . .] est trop en deçà du monde et du désignable pour figurer autre chose que des épures de l'Etre, son flux et son reflux, sa croissance, ses éclatements, ses tourbillons' (OE, 14).

9 'Le peintre est seul à avoir droit de regard sur toutes choses sans aucun devoir d'appréciation' (OE, 14).

10 'Quelle est donc ce science secrète qu'il a ou qu'il cherche? Cette dimension selon laquelle Van Gogh veut aller "plus loin"? Ce fondamental de la peinture, et peut-être de toute la culture?' (OE, 15).

11 'on ne voit pas comment un Esprit pourrait peindre. C'est en prêtant son corps au monde que le peintre change le monde en peinture. Pour comprendre ces transubstantiations, il faut recouvrer le corps opérant et actuel, celui qui n'est pas un morceau d'espace, un faiseau de fonctions, qui est un entrelacs de vision et de mouvement' (OE, 16).

12 'Mon corps mobile compte au monde visible, en fait partie, et c'est pourquoi je peux le diriger dans le visible' (OE, 16–17).
13 'la vision est suspendu au mouvement. On ne voit que ce qu'on regarde.
Que serait la vision sans aucun mouvement des yeux?' (OE, 17).
14 'comment leur mouvement ne brouillerait-il pas les choses s'il était lui-même
réflexe ou aveugle?' (OE, 17).
15 'la carte du visible' (OE, 17).
16 'la carte du "je peux"' (OE, 17).
17 'Chacune des deux cartes est complète' (OE, 17).
18 'Le monde visible et celui de mes projets moteurs sont parties totales du
même Etre' (OE, 17).

XIV *Being*

1 'le sens d'être du monde' (VI, 21).
2 See, for example, Parmenides' *Poem* In Kirk and Raven *The Presocratic
Philosophers* (op. cit.), Plato *Sophist* (many editions), Aristotle *Metaphysics*
(many editions), Aquinas *De Ente et Essentia,* for example in *Aquinas:
Selected Philosophical Writings,* trans. T. McDermott (Oxford University
Press, Oxford, 1993) II.6, Berkeley *The Principles of Human Knowledge* (op.
cit.), Kant *Kritik der Reinen Vernunft* (op. cit.), *Critique of Pure Reason*
(op. cit.) esp. A592/B620-A603/B631, Hegel *Wissenschaft der Logik* (op. cit.),
The Science of Logic (op. cit.) especially the treatments of 'Sein', 'Nichts'
and 'Werden'.
3 'Ce qui nous importe c'est précisément de savoir le sens d'être du monde'
(VI, 21).
4 See Heidegger *Sein und Zeit* (op. cit.) p. 2ff.
5 'Pour se retrancher de tout être, la philosophie élit certains êtres – les "sensations", la "représentation", la "pensée", la "conscience", ou même un
être trompeur' (VI, 144).
6 'Nous ne devons là-dessus rien présupposer, ni donc l'idée naïve de l'être
en-soi, ni l'idée correlative, d'un être de représentation, d'un être pour la
conscience, d'un être pour l'homme' (VI, 21).
7 'ce sont toutes ces notions que nous avons à repenser' (VI, 21).
8 'La perception du monde se fait dans le monde, l'epreuve de la vérité se fait
dans l'Etre' (VI, 307).
9 'Le sens de l'Etre [est] à dévoiler' (VI, 307).
10 The Heideggerian term translated as 'to disclose' is 'erschliessen'. See *Sein
und Zeit* (op. cit.) pp. 75, 175, 180, 220, 269, 334ff.
11 'L'invisible de ce monde, celui qui l'habite, le soutien et le rend visible, sa
possibilité intérieure et propre, L'Etre de ce étant' (VI, 198).
12 'pas [. . .] un invisible de fait' (VI, 198).
13 'Peindre, dessiner, ce n'est pas produire quelque chose de rien, que le trace,
la touche du pinceau, et l'œuvre visible ne sont que la trace d'un mouvement total de parler, qui va à l'Etre entier' (VI, 265).
14 'Les couleurs, les sons, les choses comme les étoiles de Van Gogh, sont des
foyers des rayonnments de l'être' (S, 22).
15 'L'être charnel, comme être des profondeurs, à plusieurs feuillets ou à
plusiuurs faces, être de latence, et présentation d'une certaine absence, est un
prototype de l'Etre' (VI, 179).
16 'notre corps, le sentant sensible, est une variante très remarquable, mais
dont le paradoxe constitutif est déjà dans tout visible' (VI, 179).

17 'C'est bien un paradoxe de l'Etre, non d'un paradoxe de l'homme, qu'il s'agit ici' (VI, 180).

18 'L'intégration en-soi–pour-soi se fait non dans conscience absolue, mais dans Etre de promiscuité' (VI, 307).

19 'Entre les deux "côtés" de notre corps, le corps comme sensible et le corps comme sentant . . . il y a plutôt qu'un écart, l'abîme qui sépare l'En-Soi du Pour-Soi' (VI, 180).

20 'C'est une question . . . de savoir comment le sentant sensible peut être aussi pensée' (VI, 180).

XV *Parousia: existential phenomenology and the return of metaphysics*

1 What it is to be physical is obscure. Possibilities are: 'x is physical iff x is spatial', 'x is physical iff x is spatio-temporal', 'x is physical iff x is three (or four) dimensional', 'x is physical iff composed of matter (or energy)', 'x is physical iff x is (in principle) publicly observable' but each of these faces difficulties. I shall argue below that a non-physical being may have a subjective kind of spatio-temporality. It is not clear what 'matter' and 'energy' refer to, and and it is not incoherent to suggest that there might be things that are in principle unobservable, but physical on the other criteria. ('We', for example, might be systematically inequipped to observe them.)

2 See Martin Heidegger 'Die Frage Nach der Technik' in his *Die Technik und Die Kehre* (Tübingen, 1978), *The Question Concerning Technology and Other Essays* trans. W. Lovitt (New York, 1977), Sartre *L'Etre et le Néant* (op. cit.) *passim.*

3 See Stephen Priest *The Critical Turn: Modern Philosophy's Kantian Assumptions* (forthcoming).

4 Deconstruction putatively exhibits the hidden teleology of a text in a way that exposes its hidden inconsistencies. A paradigm case is Derrida's deconstructions of Husserl in *La Voix et le Phénomène* (op. cit.).

5 All the purportedly anti-metaphysical or non-metaphysical movements in modern philosophy since Kant rest on metaphysical assumptions. The brand of neo-Kantianism fashionable in the late twentieth century called 'deconstruction' or sometimes 'postmodernism' is no exception. It is uncritically assumed that there exist 'texts', 'signifiers', 'signifieds', philosophical 'traditions' including something called 'the Western metaphysical tradition'. In its repudiation of 'the metaphysics of presence' Derrida's metaphysics aligns itself squarely on the side of the natural sciences, which also seek to repress the reality of the present.

6 Consciousness, subjectivity, freedom, qualitative facts, existence and individuality are metaphysical features of reality that cannot just be *cleared up* by science. They are so utterly antithetical to the scientific concepts of matter, objectivity, determinism, quantification, abstraction and generality that it is hopeless to suppose that, say, the theory of evolution, neuro-biology or physics will have anything explanatory to say about them. The idea has to be given up that reality is *mostly* objective or *essentially* objective and conscious subjectivity a minor epiphenomenon (or nothing at all). There is no objective explanation of subjectivity and subjectivity, far from being nothing, is the lived reality that we are.

In order for an adequate scientific theory of subjectivity to be devised a scientific revolution would be necessary at least on the scale of those associated with Copernicus, Newton or Einstein. I see little hope of this so long as scientists and positivist philosophers continue to underestimate the reality of subjectivity. Positivist philosophers will no doubt continue to try to bash square pegs into round holes for many years to come.

7 Platonic and Cartesian philosophy has the merit of postulating the soul as what one's own metaphysical reality consists in. Unlike modern materialists, Plato and Descartes see that there is a profound metaphysical mystery that cannot be dispelled by materialism. However, the soul postulated in Platonic and Cartesian philosophy is abstract rather than phenomenological. What is needed is a synthesis of Platonic and Cartesian philosophy on the one hand with existential phenomenology on the other. This would enable an appreciation of one's own existence *qua* soul. (It would require giving up the Cartesian tenet that the soul is not aware of itself, only of its own operations). Identifying the soul with subjective space essentially facilitates this synthesis. My soul is my subjective space.

8 I discuss this in 'Husserl's Concept of Being' in Anthony O'Hear (ed.) *German Philosophy Since Kant*, Royal Institute of Philosophy Supplement: 44 (Cambridge University Press, Cambridge, 1998).

9 At the time of writing there is something of a renaissance in medieval philosophy and Asian philosophy. The medieval scholastics provide us with an exemplary model of how to do philosophy in their combination of metaphysical imagination and logical rigour. As far as phenomenology is concerned, its deployment against positivist and reductivist philosophy may be combined with an awareness of its debt to Asian philosophy. I have in mind here Reinhard May's *Ex oriente lux: Heideggers Werk unter ostasiatischem Einfluss* (Steiner Verlag Wiesbaden, Stuttgart, 1989) translated by Graham Parkes as *Heidegger's Hidden Sources: East Asian Influences on his Work* (Routledge, London and New York, 1996). However, we should not be content with the scholarship of 'comparative philosophy'. Philosophically it does not matter at all that this piece of philosophy is *like* that piece of philosophy. Nor should we allow philosophy to collapse into a history of ideas. Phenomenology, medieval philosophy and the various Asian philosophies are resources of insight and argument for tackling philosophical problems which are in principle beyond the reach of Western science.

Bibliography

Bibliographies

Good, Paul and Camino, Frederico, Bibliographie des Werkes von Maurice Merleau-Ponty, *Philosophisches Jahrbuch*, 77, 434–443, 1970.

Lapointe, François and Lapointe, Clara, *Maurice Merleau-Ponty and his Critics: an International Bibliography* New York and London: Garland, 1976.

Whiteside, Kerry H. The Merleau-Ponty Bibliography: Additions and Corrections, *Journal of the History of Philosophy*, vol. 21, no. 2, 195–201, 1983.

Works by Merleau-Ponty

Texts

La Structure du Comportement, Paris: Presses Universitaires de France, 1942.

Phénoménologie de la Perception, Paris: Gallimard, 1945.

Humanisme et Terreur, Paris: Gallimard, 1947.

Les Aventures de la Dialectique, Paris: Gallimard, 1955.

Eloge de la Philosophie et autres essais, Paris: Gallimard, 1960.

L'Œil et L'Esprit, Paris: Gallimard, 1964.

Maurice Merleau-Ponty à la Sorbonne: Résumé de ses cours établi par les étudiants et approuvé par lui-même *Bulletin de Psychologie*, vol. 18, no. 236, 3–6 (November 1964).

La Prose du Monde, Paris: Gallimard, 1969.

Signes, Paris: Gallimard, 1960.

Le Visible et L'Invisible, Paris: Gallimard, 1964.

Sens et Non-Sens, Paris: Nagel, 1966.

Résumés de Cours: College de France 1952–1960, Paris: Gallimard, 1968.

La Prose du Monde, Paris: Gallimard, 1969.

Translations into English

The Structure of Behaviour, trans. A.L. Fisher, London: Methuen, 1965.

Phenomenology of Perception, trans. Colin Smith, London: Routledge, 1962.

Humanism and Terror, trans. John O'Neill, Boston: Beacon Press, 1969.

Adventures of the Dialectic, trans. Joseph Bien, Evanston: Northwestern University Press, 1973.

In Praise of Philosophy, trans. J. Wild and J.M. Edie, Evanston: Northwestern University Press, 1963.

Consciousness and the Acquisition of Language, trans. Hugh J. Silverman, Evanston: Northwestern University Press, 1973.

The Primacy of Perception, J.M. Edie (ed.), Evanston: Northwestern University Press, 1964.

Signs, trans. Richard C. McClearly, Evanston: Northwestern University Press, 1964.

Sense and Non-Sense, trans. Hubert L. Dreyfus and Patricia Allen Dreyfus, Evanston: Northwestern University Press, 1964.

The Visible and the Invisible, trans. Alphonso Lingis, Evanston: Northwestern University Press, 1968.

Themes from the Lectures at the Collège de France 1952–1960, trans. John O'Neill, Evanston: Northwestern University Press, 1970.

The Prose of the World, trans. John O'Neill, Evanston: Northwestern University Press, 1973.

Chronological Bibliography of the Works of Merleau-Ponty

1935

Christianisme et ressentiment. *La Vie Intellectuelle*, 7e année, nouvelle série, T. XXXVI June 10, 278–306, 1935 (review of Max Scheler's book *L'Homme du ressentiment*, Paris: Gallimard, 1933).

1936

Etre et avoir. *La Vie Intellectuelle*, 8e année, nouvelle série, T. XLV October 10, 98–109, 1936 (review of Gabriel Marcel, *Etre et Avoir*, Paris: Aubier, 1935).

Jean-Paul Sartre *L'Imagination, Journal de Psychologie Normale et Pathologique*, 33e année, no. 9–10, November–December 1936 33: 9–10, 756–761 (review of Sartre's book *L'Imagination*, Paris: Librairie Felix Alcan, 1936).

Gurwitsch, Aron (with the collaboration of Merleau-Ponty) Quelques aspects et quelques développements de la psychologie de la forme. *Journal de Psychologie Normale et Pathologique*, 33, 1936.

1939

'L'Agrégation de Philosophie' Intervention à la Société française de Philosophie, séance du 7 mai, 1938. *Bulletin de la Société française de Philosophie*, vol. 38, no. 4, 130–133, July–August, 1939.

1942

La Structure du Comportement, Paris: Presses Universitaires de France (Bibliothèque de philosophie contemporaine) pp. viii + 395. 2nd edition 1949 prefaced by 'Une Philosophie de l'ambiguïté' by Alphonse de Waelhens, pp. xv + 248.

1943

Les Mouches par Jean-Paul Sartre. *Confluences*, 3: 25, 514–516, September–October 1943 (Review of Sartre's play *Les Mouches*).

1945

Phénoménologie de la Perception, Paris: Gallimard, N.R.F. 1945, 4th ed. 1962, xvi + 526.

La guerre a eu lieu. *Les Temps Modernes*, no. 1, 48–66, October 1945 (reprinted in *Sens et Non-Sens*).

La querelle de l'Existentialisme. *Les Temps Modernes*, no. 2, 344–356, November 1945 (reprinted in *Sens et Non-Sens*).

Le doute de Cézanne. *Fontaine*, VI année T. IX, no. 47, 80–100, December 1945 (reprinted in *Sens et Non-Sens*).

Roman et metaphysique. *Cahiers du Sud*, T. XXII, no. 270, 194–207, March/April 1945 (reprinted in *Sens et Non-Sens* as 'Le Roman et la Métaphysique').

Le Cinéma et la nouvelle psychologie. *Les Temps Modernes*, no. 26, 930–947, November 1947 (reprinted in *Sens et Non-Sens*).

1946

Pour la vérité. *Les Temps Modernes*, no. 4, 577–600, January 1946 (reprinted in *Sens et Non-Sens*).

Foi et bonne foi. *Les Temps Modernes*, no. 5, 769–782, February 1946 (reprinted in *Sens et Non-Sens*).

Autour du marxisme. *Fontaine*, nos 48–49, 309–331, February 1946 (reprinted in *Sens et Non-Sens*).

Le Culte du Héros. *Action, Hebdomadaire de la Libération française*, no. 74, 12–13, 1 February 1946 (reprinted in *Sens et Non-Sens* as 'Le Héros, l'Homme').

L'existentialisme chez Hegel. *Les Temps Modernes*, no. 7, 1311–1319, April 1946 (reprinted in *Sens et Non-Sens*).

[à propos d'une Conférence donné par Jean Hyppolite le 16 février 1945 à l'Institut des Hautes Etudes Gérmaniques.]

Marxisme et philosophie. *Revue Internationale* vol. 1, no. 6, 518–526, June/July 1946 (reprinted in *Sens et Non-Sens*).

Faut-il brûler Kafka? *Action, Hebdomadaire de la Libération française*, no. 97, 14–15, 12 July 1946.

Le Yogi et le Prolétaire. *Les Temps Modernes* no. 13, 2–29, October 1946, no. 14, 253–287, November 1946 (reprinted in *Humanisme et Terreur*).

Crise de la conscience européenne. *La Nef*, 3:24, 66–67, November 1946.

Deux philosophies de l'Europe. *La Nef*, 3:24, 87–89, November 1946.

1947

Le Yogi et le Prolétaire: *Les Temps Modernes* 2:16, 676–711, January 1947 (reprinted in *Humanisme et Terreur*).

L'Esprit européen, Rencontres internationales de Genève 1946, Neuchâtel Les Editions de la Baconnière 1947; interventions by Merleau-Ponty: 74–77, 133, 252–256.

Indochine S.O.S. *Les Temps Modernes* 2:18, 1039–1052, March 1947 (reprinted in *Signes* as 'Sur L'Indochine').

Pour les rencontres internationales. *Les Temps Modernes* 2:19, 1340–1344, April 1947.

Apprendre à lire. *Les Temps Modernes* 2:22, 1–27, July 1947 (partly reprinted in the preface to *Humanisme et Terreur*).

Humanisme et Terreur: Essai sur le Problème Communiste, Paris: Gallimard, pp. xliii + 206, 1947.

Les Cahiers de la Pléiade. *Les Temps Modernes* 3: 1151–1152, December 1947.

Jean-Paul Sartre, un auteur scandaleux. *Figaro Littéraire*, 6 December 1947 (reprinted in *Sens et Non-Sens* as 'Un auteur scandaleux').

Le métaphysique dans l'homme. *Revue de Métaphysique et de Morale* 52: 3–4, 290–307, July–October 1947 (reprinted in *Sens et Non-Sens*).

En un combat douteux. *Les Temps Modernes* no. 27, 961–964, December 1947 (editorial).

Lecture de Montaigne. *Les Temps Modernes* no. 27, 1044–1060, 1947 (reprinted in *Signes*).

Le Primat de la perception et ses conséquences philosophiques. *Bulletin de la Société Française de Philosophie* 41:4, October–December 1947.

1948

Sens et Non-Sens, Paris: Nagel, 1948 (2nd edn, 1966).

Le 'Manifeste communiste' a cent ans. *Le Figaro Littéraire* 6–8, 3 April 1948.

Communisme et anti-communisme. *Le Temps Modernes* no. 34, 175–188, July 1948 (reprinted in *Signes* as 'La Politique paranoïaque').

Complicité objective. *Le Temps Modernes*, no. 34, 1–11, July 1948 (editorial).

Dumas, J.-L. Les Conférences. *La Nef*, 5 no. 45, 151–152, August 1948 (summary by Dumas of 'L'Homme et l'objet', an unpublished lecture by Merleau-Ponty).

1949

Machiavelisme et Humanisme. *Les Temps Modernes* 5:48, 577–593, October 1949 (communication au Congrès 'Umanesimo e scienza politica', September 1949, Rome-Florence) (reprinted in *Signes* as 'Note sur Machiavel').

Lukács et l'autocritique. *Les Temps Modernes* 5:50, 1119–1121, December 1949 (reprinted in *Signes* as 'Marxisme et superstition').

1950

Les jours de notre vie. (with J.-P. Sartre) *Les Temps Modernes* 5:51, 1153–1168, January 1950 (reprinted in *Signes* as 'L'U.R.S.S. et les camps').

Mort d'Emmanuel Mounier. *Les Temps Modernes* 5:54, 1906, June 1950.

Réponse à C.L.R. James. *Les Temps Modernes* 5:56, 2292–2294, June 1950.

L'Adversaire est complice. *Les Temps Modernes* 6:57, 1–11, July 1950 (editorial).

Les Sciences de l'homme et la phénoménologie. Première partie. Les Cours de Sorbonne, Paris, Center de Documentation Universitaire 1950–51. Reédité en 1961.

1951

Les Relations avec autrui chez l'enfant. Les Cours de Sorbonne, Paris, Centre de Documentation Universitaire 1951, p. 60.

Le philosophe et la sociologie. *Cahiers Internationaux de Sociologie* no. X, 50–69, July 1951 (reprinted in *Signes*).

Introduction to Michel Crozier 'Human Engineering'. *Les Temps Modernes* no. 69, 44–48, July 1951.

'Sur la phénoménologie du langage', in H.L. Van Breda (ed.) *Problèmes actuels de la Phénoménologie*, Brussels: Actes du premier Colloque international de phénoménologie, 1951; Paris: Desclée de Brouwer, 89–109, 1952 (reprinted in *Signes*).

1952

'L'homme et l'adversité', in *La Connaissance de l'homme au XXe siècle* Rencontres Internationales de Genève 1951; Neuchâtel: Editions de la Baconniere 1952. Conférence; pp. 51–75. Interventions; pp. 182–183, 215–252, 286–287, 293–294 (reprinted in *Signes*).

'Les Sciences de l'homme et la phénoménologie', Les Cours de Sorbonne, Paris, Centre de Documentation Universitaire, 1952.

Le Langage indirect et les voix du silence (I). *Les Temps Modernes* 7:80, 2113–2144, June 1952 (reprinted in *Signes*).

Le Langage indirect et les voix du silence (II). *Les Temps Modernes* 8:81, 70–94, July 1952.

1953

Eloge de la Philosophie, Paris N.R.F.: Gallimard, 1953 [Leçon Inaugurale au Collège de France, le jeudi 15 janvier 1951].

Le Monde sensible et le Monde de l'expression. *Annuaire du Collège de France*, Paris: Imprimerie Nationale, 1953, 145–150.

Recherches sur l'usage littéraire du langage. *Annuaire du Collège de France*, Paris: Imprimerie Nationale, 1953, 150–155.

1954

Ou sont les nouveaux maîtres? *L'Express*, no. 71, 3, 2 October 1954.

Forum: Le Philosophe est il un fonctionnaire? *L'Express*, no. 72, 3, 9 October 1954.

Le libertin est-il un philosophe? *L'Express*, no. 72, 3, 9 October 1954 (reprinted in *Signes* as 'Sur l'érotisme').

La France va-t-elle se renouveller? *L'Express*, no. 74, 3–4, 23 October 1954.

Les femmes sont-elles des hommes? *L'Express*, no. 76, 4, 7 November 1954.

Les Peuples se fâchent-t-ils? *L'Express*, no. 80, 34, 4 December 1954.

Le goût pour les faits divers est-il malsain? *L'Express*, no. 82, 3–4, 18 December 1954 (reprinted in *Signes* as 'Sur les faits divers').

Le probleme de la parole. *Annuaire du Collège de France*, Paris: Imprimerie Nationale, 175–179, 1954.

Matériaux pour une théorie de l'histoire. *Annuaire du Collège de France*, Paris: Imprimerie Nationale, 180–187, 1954.

1955

D'Abord comprendre les communistes. *L'Express*, no. 85, 8–9, 8 January 1955.

A quoi sert l'Objectivité? *L'Express*, No. 88, 4, 29 January 1955.

Comment répondre à Oppenheimer? *L'Express*, no. 91, 3, 19 February 1955.

Claudel était-il un génie? *L'Express*, no. 93, 3–5, 5 March 1955 (reprinted in *Signes* as 'Sur Claudel').

M. Poujade a-t-il une petite cervelle? *L'Express*, no. 95, 3, 19 March 1955.

Le marxisme est-il-mort à Yalta? *L'Express*, no. 98, 3, 9 April 1955 (reprinted in *Signes* as 'Les papiers de Yalta').

'Sartre est un ultra-bolcheviste' . . . déclare Merleau-Ponty. *Le Figaro Littéraire* 7 May 1955, 1.

Einstein et la crise de la raison. *L'Express*, no. 103, 13, 14 May 1955 (reprinted in *Signes*).

Où va l'anti-communisme? *L'Express*, no. 109, 12, 25 June 1955.

La majorité a-t-elle raison? *L'Express*, no. 111, 7–10, 9 July 1955 (reprinted in *Signes* as 'Sur l'abstention').

L'avenir de la révolution. *L'Express*, no. 118, 7–10, 27 August 1955 (reprinted in *Signes*).

Les Aventures de la Dialectique, Paris N.R.F.: Gallimard, 1955, 320.

L'institution dans l'histoire personelle et publique. *Annuaire du Collège de France*, Paris: Imprimerie Nationale, 1955, 157–160.

Le problème de la passivité: le sommeil, l'inconscient, la mémoire. *Annuaire du Collège de France*, Paris: Imprimerie Nationale, 1955, 161–164.

1956

Textes et commentaires sur la dialectique. *Annuaire du Collège de France*, 1956–7, 175–179, 179–180.

Premier dialogue Est–Ouest à Venise. *L'Express*, no. 278, 21–24, 19 October 1956.

Discordia Concors, Rencontre Est–Ouest à Venise. *Comprendre*, 202–301, 16 September 1956, partly reprinted in 'Entre Merleau-Ponty, Sartre, Silone et les écrivains soviétiques: premier dialogue est–ouest à Venise', *L'Express*, 21–24, 19 October 1956. Interventions by Merleau-Ponty; pp. 210–213, 214, 216, 217, 226, 227–228, 229, 237, 252–253, 265, 266, 267, 268, 271, 275–276, 278, 284, 285, 286, 287, 295, 296, 297.

Réforme ou maladie sénile du communisme? *L'Express*, no. 283, 13–17, 23 November 1956 (reprinted in *Signes* as 'Sur la destalinisation').

Les Philosophes Célèbres, (ed.) Paris: Mazenod, 1956. Section introductions by Meleau-Ponty:

1 'Avant-Propos', 7–11 (reprinted in *Signes* as 'La philosophe et le "dehors"').
2 'L'Orient et sa philosophie', 14–18 (reprinted in *Signes*).
3 'Les fondateurs', 44–45.
4 'Christianisme et philosophie', 104–109 (reprinted in *Signes*).
5 'Le grand rationalisme', 134–137 (reprinted in *Signes*).
6 'La découverte de la subjectivité', 250–251 (reprinted in *Signes*).
7 'La découverte de l'histoire'.
8 'Existence et dialectique' (reprinted in *Signes*).

Sur les Rapports entre la mythologie et le rituel. *Bulletin de la Société Française de la Philosophie*, 50:2, July–September 1956.

1957

Comment on Jacques Lacan 'La psychanalyse et son enseignement', *Bulletin de la Société Française de Philosophie*, 51, 65–104, April–June 1956 (Merleau-Ponty's comment pp. 98–99).

Le Concept de Nature (I). *Annuaire du Collège de France*, Paris: Imprimerie Nationale, 1957–8, 201–217.

1958

La démocratie peut-elle renaître en France? *L'Express*, no. 368, 15–17, 3 July 1958 (reprinted in *Signes* as 'Demain . . .').

Du moindre mal à l'union sacre. *Le Monde*, 5 June 1958 (reprinted in *Signes* as 'Sur le 13 mai 1958').

Le France en Afrique. *L'Express*, no. 375, 21 August 1958 (reprinted in *Signes* as 'Sur Madagascar').

Roger Martin du Gard. *L'Express*, no. 376, 28 August 1958.

Le Concept de Nature (suite) II: l'animalité, le corps humain, passage à la culture. *Annuaire du Collège de France*, Paris: Imprimerie Nationale, 213–219, 1958.

1959

Commentaire sur l'idée de la phénoménologie. *Husserl*, Cahiers de Royaumont (Philosophie III) Paris Editions de Minuit 1959. [Intervention by Merleau-Ponty, pp. 157–159.]

'Le Philosophe et son ombre', in H.L. Van Breda and J. Taminiaux (eds) *Phenomenologica no. 4; Edmund Husserl: 1859–1959*, The Hague: Martinus Nijhoff, 1959 (reprinted in *Signes*).

De Mauss à Levi-Strauss. *La Nouvelle Revue française*, no. 8, 1 October 1959 (reprinted in *Signes*).

Possibilité d'une 3e voie entre le 'néocapitalisme' et la planification dictatoriale de l'URSS. *Cahiers de la République*, no. XXII, November–December 1959.

L'avenir du socialisme. [débat présidé par Merleau-Ponty] *Cahiers de la République*, no. XXLL, 27, 31–32, 35, 42, November–December 1959.

Cours sans titre: Réflexions générales sur le sens de l'ontologie de la Nature et sur la possibilité de la philosophie d'aujourd'hui. *Annuaire du Collège de France*, Paris: Imprimerie Nationale, 1959.

1960

Discours prononcé le 19 mai 1959 lors de la séance d'hommage à l'occasion du centenaire de la naissance de Henri Bergson. *Bulletin de la Société française de Philosophie*, 35–45, January 1960 (reprinted in *Signes* as 'Bergson se faisant').

Signes, Paris N.F.R.: Gallimard, 1960, 438.

Preface to A. Hesnard *L'Œuvre de Freud et son importance dans le monde moderne*, Paris: Payot, 1960, 5–10.

La Volonté dans la philosophie de Malebranche. *Bulletin de la Société Française de Philosophie*, 43:3 July–September 1960 [Intervention by Merleau-Ponty, pp. 133–134].

Husserl aux limites de la phénoménologie. *Annuaire du Collège de France*, Paris: Imprimerie Nationale, 1960, 169–173.

Entretien. *Les Ecrivains en personne* par Madeleine Chapsal, Paris: Juillard, 1960, 145–163.

Nature et Logos: le corps humain. *Annuaire du Collège de France*, Paris: Imprimerie Nationale, 1960, 169–173, 173–176.

La philosophie et la politique sont solidaires. [interview with J.-P. Weber] *Le Monde*, 31 December 1960.

1961

L'Œil et l'esprit. *Art de France* 1:1, 187–308, January 1961, and in *Les Temps Modernes*, no. 17, 184–185, 193–227, 1961–62, and reprinted as the book *L'Œil et l'esprit*, Paris: Gallimard, 1964, 93.

Cinq notes sur Claude Simon. *Médiations, Revue des expressions contemporaines*, 4, 5–9, 1961–62:

1 'Vision', October 1960.
2 'Langage, Claude Simon, Butor', October 1960.
3 'Claude Simon et l'intégration "verticale"', November 1960.
4 'Claude Simon', December 1960.
5 'L'association comme initiation', March 1961.

L'ontologie cartésienne et l'ontologie d'aujourd'hui; Philosophie et non-philosophie d'après Hegel. [textes commentés] *Annuaire du Collège de France*, Paris: Imprimerie Nationale, 1961, 163.

1962

Discussion following 'La Phénoménologie contre The Concept of Mind de Gilbert Ryle', in Jean Wahl (ed.) *La Philosophie analytique*, Paris: Editions de Minuit, 1962 [Intervention by Merleau-Ponty, pp. 93–96].

Un inédit de Merleau-Ponty. *Revue de Métaphysique et de Morale*, 67, no. 4, 401–409, October 1962 [Exposé pour sa candidature au Collège de France 1952].

'Colloque sur le mot structure', in *Sens et usages du term structure dans les sciences humaines et sociales*. S-Graven-Hage: Mouton, 1962, 153–155, 156–157.

1963

Van Breda, H.L., Maurice Merleau-Ponty et les Archives-Husserl à Louvain. *Revue de Métaphysique et de Morale*, 67, 1963, 412, 413, 420, 421–422, 429–430 [Fragments of letters written to Van Breda by Merleau-Ponty].

1964

Le Visible et L'invisible, suivi de notes de travail. Texte établi par Claude Lefort accompagné d'un avertissement et d'une postface, Paris N.R.F.: Gallimard, 1964, 361.

Structure et conflits de la conscience enfantine. *Bulletin de Psychologie*, XVIII, 236, 3–6, November 1964.

Maurice Merleau-Ponty à la Sorbonne. Résumé de ses cours établi par des êtudiants et apprové par lui-même. *Bulletin de Psychologie*, Tome XVIII, 103–336, November 1964. Contains:

1 'Méthode en psychologie de l'enfant' (1951–1952) 109–140.
2 'Les sciences de l'homme et la phénoménologie' (1950–1952) 141–170.
3 'Structure et conflits de la conscience enfantine' (1949–1950) 171–202.
4 'Psychosociologie de l'enfant' (1950–1951) 203–225.
5 'La conscience et l'acquisition du langage' (1949–1950) 226–259.
6 'Les relations avec l'autrui chez l'enfant' (1950–1951) 205–336.

1965

Husserl et la notion de nature. (Notes from 14 and 25 March 1957 transcribed by Xavier Tilliette.) *Revue de Métaphysique et de Morale*, 70, 257–269, 1965.

1966

La Philosophe de l'existence. *Dialogue*, vol. 5, no. 3, 307–322, 1966.

1967

Pages d'Introduction à *La Prose du Monde*. (presented by Claude Lefort) *Revue de Métaphysique et de Morale*, 72, no. 2, 139–153, 1967.

Commenté par Merleau-Ponty. [on Claude Simon] *Le Monde [des Livres]*, no. 6932, 26 April 1967, 5.

1968

Résumé de Cours au Collège de France 1952–1960, Avertissement par Claude Lefort. Paris: Gallimard, 1968, 180.

L'Union de l'âme et du corps chez Malebranche, Biran, et Bergson. Notes prises aux cours de Merleau-Ponty à l'Ecole Normale Supérieure, 1946–7, recueillées et redigées par Jean Deprun, Paris: Librairie Philosophique J. Vrin, 1968, 118.

1969
La Prose du Monde. Texte établi et présenté par Claude Lefort, Paris: Gallimard, 1969, 216.

Secondary sources

Abram, David, Merleau-Ponty and the Voice of the Earth. *Environmental Ethics*, 10, 101–120, Summer 1988.
Arce Carrascoso, Jose Luis, Ontologia Y Conocimiento en M. Merleau-Ponty. *Convivium*, 9, 92–116, 1996.
Aronson, Ronald, Vicissitudes of the Dialectic: from Merleau-Ponty's 'Les Aventures de la Dialectique' to Sartre's Second 'Critique'. *Philosophical Forum*, 18, 358–391, Summer 1987.
Ashbaugh, Anne F., The Fool in the Farce: Merleau-Ponty's 'Philosophy Of'. *Philosophy Today*, 27, 326–341, Winter 1983.
—— The Philosophy of Flesh and the Flesh of Philosophy. *Research in Phenomenology*, 8, 217–223, 1978.
Baertschi, Bernard, Le Problème de la Distinction de l'Ame et du Corps. *Revue de Métaphysique et de Morale*, 87, 344–363, July–September 1982.
Baldwin, Thomas, Phenomenology, Solipsism and Egocentric Thought. *Proceedings of the Aristotelian Society*, Supplement, vol. 62, 27–43, 1988.
Ballard, Edward G. The Philosophy of Merleau-Ponty. *Tulane Studies in Philosophy*, 9, 165–187, 1960.
Bannan, John F., Philosophical Reflection and the Phenomenology of Merleau-Ponty. *Review of Metaphysics*, 8, 418–442, March 1955.
—— The Later Thought of Merleau-Ponty. *Dialogue*, 5, 383–403, 1966.
—— Merleau-Ponty On God. *International Philosophical Quarterly*, 6, 341–365, September 1966.
—— Merleau-Ponty Mismanaged. *Journal of Existentialism*, 7, 459–476, Summer 1967.
—— *The Philosophy of Merleau-Ponty*. New York: Harcourt Brace, 1967.
Barral, Mary Rose, *Merleau-Ponty: the Role of the Body-Subject in Interpersonal Relations*. Pittsburgh: Duquesne University Press, 1965.
—— Merleau-Ponty On the Body. *Southern Journal of Philosophy*, 7, 171–179, Summer 1969.
—— Thomas Aquinas and Merleau-Ponty. *Philosophy Today*, 26, 204–216, Fall 1982.
Barrett, Cyril, Merleau-Ponty and the Phenomenology of Perception. *Philosophy*, 21, 123–139, 1987 Supplement.
Bate, Michele, The Phenomenologist As Art Critic: Merleau-Ponty and Cézanne. *British Journal of Aesthetics*, 14, 344–350, Autumn 1974.
Bayer, Raymond, *Merleau-Ponty's Existentialism*. Buffalo, New York: University of Buffalo, 1951.
Behnke, Elizabeth A., At the Service of the Sonata: Music Lessons With Merleau-Ponty *Somatics*, 4 no. 2, 32–34, 1983 and in *Merleau-Ponty: Critical Essays* Pietersma, Henry (ed.) Washington DC: The University Press of America, 1990.

Bender, Frederic L., *Merleau-Ponty and Method: Toward a Critique of Husserlian Phenomenology and of Reflective Philosophy in General.*

Bergeron, André, La Conscience Engagée Dans le Régime des Significations Selon Merleau-Ponty. *Dialogue*, 5, 373–382, 1966.

Bernasconi, Robert, One-Way Traffic: the Ontology of Decolonization and Its Ethics, in *Ontology and Alterity in Merleau-Ponty*. Evanston: Northwestern University Press, 1991.

Bertram, Maryanne, The Different Paradigms of Merleau-Ponty and Whitehead. *Philosophy Today*, 24, 121–132, Summer 1980.

Bien, Joseph, Man and the Economic: Merleau-Ponty's Interpretation of Historical Materialism. *Southwestern Journal of Philosophy*, 3, 121–127, Spring 1972.

—— Two Approaches To History: Phenomenology and Marxism. *Journal of Thought*, 13, 315–319, November 1978.

—— Existential Phenomenology and Marxism: An Encounter. *Journal of the History of Philosophy*, 13, 1–11, May 1982.

Bigwood, Carol, Renaturalizing the Body (With a Little Help From Merleau-Ponty). *Hypatia*, 54–73, Fall 1991.

Boburg, Felipe, Sujeto y Corporeidad en M Merleau-Ponty. *Revista de Filosofia* (Mexico), 21, 45–51, January–April 1988.

—— La Rehabilitacion de la Percepion. *Revista de Filosofia* (Mexico), 28(83), 117–136, May–August 1995.

—— El Sentido Ontologico de là Fenomenologia de Merleau-Ponty. *Revista de Filosofia* (Mexico), 28(84), 284–313, September–December 1995.

Bohme, Gernot, The Body: the Nature Which We Ourselves Are. *Filozof Istraz*, 15(3), 371–383, 1995.

Borg, John Lucian, Le Marxisme dans le Philosophie Socio-Politique de Merleau-Ponty. *Revue Philosophique de Louvain*, 73, 481–510, August 1975.

Borque, Francisca Hernandez, Hume y Merleau-Ponty, Filosofos de la Experiencia. *An. Seminar. Metaf.*, 11, 63–104, 1976.

—— El Sentido Ontologico de la Fenomenologia del Lenguaje de M Merleau-Ponty. *An. Seminar. Metaf.*, 16, 173–179, 1981.

Boudier, C.E.M., Merleau-Ponty en Buytendijk: Relaas Van Een Relatie. Struyker. *Alg Ned Tijdschr Wijs*, 76, 228–246, October 1984.

Bourgeois, Patrick L. The Epistemic Dimensions of Existential Phenomenology. *Philosophy Today*, 30, 43–47, Spring 1986.

—— The Integration of Merleau-Ponty's Philosophy. *South West Philosophical Review*, 5, 37–50, July 1989.

—— Scientific Time and the Temporal Sense of Human Existence: Merleau-Ponty and Mead. *Research in Phenomenology*, 152–163, 1990.

—— Role Taking, Corporeal Intersubjectivity, and Self: Mead and Merleau-Ponty. *Philosophy Today*, 117–128, Summer 1990.

—— Merleau-Ponty and Heidegger: the Intentionality of Transcendence, the Being of Intentionality. *Journal of the British Society of Phenomenology*, 25(1), 27–33, 1994.

—— Merleau-Ponty, Scientific Method, and Pragmatism. *Journal of Speculative Philosophy*, 10(2), 120–127, 1996.

Bourgeois, Patrick and Rosenthal, Sandra B. Merleau-Ponty, Lewis and Kant: Beyond 'Rationalism Or Empiricism'. *International Studies in Philosophy*, 15, 13–24, Fall 1983.

—— Deconstruction Or Reconstruction of the Living Present: Derrida or Merleau-Ponty and Mead. *International Studies in Philosophy*, 26(4), 1–17, 1994.

Brena, G.L. Critica di Merleau-Ponty alla Concezione del Fondamento nella Filosofia Moderna. *Sapienza*, 26, 440–443, July–December 1973.

Brio Mateos, Asterio Del., Ambiguedad y Reduccion en Merleau-Ponty. *An. Seminar. Metaf.*, 17, 85–104, 1982.

Buchanan, James H., Merleau-Ponty's Political Passage *History of European Ideas*, 16(4–6), 909–914, January 1993.

Burke, Patrick, Listening at the Abyss in *Ontology and Alterity in Merleau-Ponty*. Evanston: Northwestern University Press, 1991.

Busch, Thomas W., Merleau-Ponty and the Problem of Origins. *Philosophy Today*, 2, 124–130, Summer 1967.

—— Ethics and Ontology: Levinas and Merleau-Ponty. *Man and World*, 25(2), 195–202, April 1992.

Camele, Anthony M., Time in Merleau-Ponty and Heidegger. *Philosophy Today*, 19, 256–268, Fall 1975.

Cantista, Maria Jose, Reflexao Sobre a Ontologia de Merleau-Ponty. *Revista Portuguesa de Filosofia*, 27, 289–299, July–September 1971.

—— Fenomenologia e Percepcao em Maurice Merleau-Ponty. *Revista Portuguesa de Filosofia*, 41, 385–404, October–December 1985.

Capalbo, Creusa, L'historicité chez Merleau-Ponty. *Revue Philosophique de Louvain*, 73, 511–535, August 1975.

Capra, Silvio, Il Problema del Linguaggio in Maurice Merleau-Ponty. *Rivista Filosofica Neoscolastica*, 64, 446–470, July–September 1972.

Carey, Seamus, A Development of Heidegger and Merleau-Ponty Towards a Holistic Conception of Health. *Conference*, 5(1), 49–62, Spring 1994.

Carruba, Gerald J., The Phenomenological Foundation of Marxism in the Early Works of Maurice Merleau-Ponty. *Dianoia*, 10, 37–55, Spring 1974.

Carvalho, John M., The Visible and the Invisible in Merleau-Ponty and Foucault. *International Studies in Philosophy*, 25(3), 35–46, 1993.

Casalis, Matthieu, Merleau-Ponty's Philosophical Itinerary: From Phenomenology To Onto-Semiology. *Southern Journal of Philosophy*, 6, 63–69, Winter 1975.

Casey, Edward S., Habitual Body and Memory in Merleau-Ponty. *Man and World*, 17, 279–298, 1984.

—— The Element of Voluminousness: Depth and Place Re-examined, in *Merleau-Ponty Vivant*, Dillon, M.C. (ed.), Albany: Suny Press, 1991.

Castilla Lazaro, Ramon, La Filosofia del Lenguaje de Merleau-Ponty. *Dialogos*, 6, 35–73, April–June 1969.

Cataldi, Sue L., The Conception of Line in Heidegger and Merleau-Ponty. *Philosophy Today*, 32, 327–337, Winter 1988.

—— Emotion, Depth, and Flesh: a Study of Sensitive Space – Reflections on *Merleau-Ponty's Philosophy of Embodiment*. Albany: Suny Press, 1994.

Charlesworth, James H., Reflections on Merleau-Ponty's Phenomenological Description of 'Word'. *Philosophy and Phenomenological Research*, 30, 609–613, June 1970.

Charron, Ghyslain, Du Langage: La Linguistique de Martinet et La Phénoménologie de Merleau-Ponty. *Revue de l'Université d'Ottawa*, 40, 260–283, April–June 1970.

Chiari, Joseph, *Twentieth-Century French Thought: From Bergson To Lévi-Strauss*. New York: Gordian Press, 1975.

Clair, André, Merleau-Ponty Lecteur et Critique de Bergson: Le Statut Bergsonien de L'intuition. *Archives de Philosophie*, 59(2), 203–218, April–June 1996.

Clemente, Isabel, O Nilismo de Merleau-Ponty. *Philosophica* (Portugal), 113–122, 1993.

Coenen, Herman, Types, Corporeality and the Immediacy of Interaction. *Man and World*, 12, 339–359, 1979.

Cohen, Lesley, Descartes and Merleau-Ponty on the 'Cogito', in *Human Nature and Natural Knowledge*, Donagan, A. (ed.), 295–312, Dordrecht: Reidel.

Cohen, Richard, Merleau-Ponty, the Flesh and Foucault. *Philosophy Today*, 28, 329–338, Winter 1984.

Collins, Corbin, Body-Intentionality. *Inquiry*, 31, 495–518, December 1988.

Compton, John J., Sartre, Merleau-Ponty, and Human Freedom. *Journal of Philosophy*, 79, 577–588, October 1982.

—— Some Contributions of Existential Phenomenology to the Philosophy of Natural Science. *American Philosophical Quarterly*, 25, 99–113, April 1988.

—— Merleau-Ponty's Metaphorical Philosophy: Review of 'Merleau-Ponty and Metaphor' by Jerry H. Gill. *Research in Phenomenology*, 23, 221–226, 1993.

Cook, Deborah, Writing Philosophy and Literature: Apology for Narcissism in Merleau-Ponty. *Eidos*, 4, 1–9, June 1985.

Coole, Diana, The Aesthetic Realm and the Lifeworld: Kant and Merleau-Ponty. *History of Political Thought*, 5, 503–526, Winter 1984.

Coolsaet, Willy, Merleau-Ponty als Criticus van het Zuiver Theoretisch Weten. *Alg Ned Tijdschr Wijs*, 72, 85–104, April 1980.

—— De Late Filosofie van Merleau-Ponty. *Alg Ned Tijdschr Wijs*, 74, 99–115, April 1982.

Cooper, Barry, Hegelian Elements in Merleau-Ponty's 'La Structure du Comportement'. *International Philosophical Quarterly*, 15, 411–423, December 1975.

Cooper, David E. *Existentialism*. Oxford: Blackwell, 1990.

Cotten, Jean-Pierre, Les Lectures de Merleau-Ponty: à Propos de la 'Phenomenologie de la Perception'. *Revue de Métaphysique et de Morale*, 77, 307–328, July–September 1972.

Cowley, Fraser, L'expression et la parole d'après Merleau-Ponty. *Dialogue*, 5, 360–372, December 1966.

Coyne, Margaret Urban, Merleau-Ponty on Language. *International Philosophical Quarterly*, 20, 307–326, September 1980.

Crossley, Nick, The Politics of the Gaze: Between Foucault and Merleau-Ponty. *Human Studies*, 16(4), 399–419, October 1983.

—— *The Politics of Subjectivity*. Avebury: Brookfield, 1994.

Crosson, Frederick J., Phenomenology and Realism. *International Philosophical Quarterly*, 6, 455–464, September 1966.

Crowther, Paul, Merleau-Ponty: Perception into Art. *British Journal of Aesthetics*, 22, 138–149, Spring 1982.

—— Experience of Art: Some Problems and Possibilities of Hermeneutical Analysis. *Philosophy and Phenomenological Research*, 43, 347–362, March 1983.

—— Merleau-Ponty: Vision and Painting. *Dialogue and Humanism*, 15, 107–118, Winter–Spring 1988.

Culler, Jonathan, Phenomenology and Structuralism. *Human Context*, 5, 35–41, Spring 1973.

Cumming, Robert Denoon, *Starting Point: An Introduction To the Dialectic of Existence*. Chicago: University of Chicago Press, 1979.

Cunningham, Suzanne, Comments On Russow's 'Merleau-Ponty and the Myth of Bodily Intentionality'. *Nous*, 22, 49–50, March 1988.

Dallmayr, Fred R., Marxism and Truth. *Telos*, 29, 130–159, Fall 1976.

—— *Twilight of Subjectivity*. Amherst: University of Massachussetts Press, 1981.

Daly, James, Merleau-Ponty: a Bridge Between Phenomenology and Structuralism. *Journal of the British Society for Phenomenology*, 2, 53–58, October 1971.

—— Merleau-Ponty's Concept of Phenomenology of Language. *St Louis Quarterly* 4, 325–342, 1966.

Dastur, Françoise, Consciousness and Body in the Phenomenology of Merleau-Ponty in *Phenomenology of Life*, Tymieniecka, Anna-Teresa (ed.), 117–125. Dordrecht: Reidel.

Dauenhauer, Bernard P., Renovating the Problem of Politics. *Review of Metaphysics*, 29, 626–641, June 1976.

—— Teleology of Consciousness: Husserl and Merleau-Ponty in *Analecta Husserliana*, Vol IX, Tymieniecka, Anna-Teresa (ed.), Dordrecht: Reidel, 1979.

—— One Central Link Between Merleau-Ponty's Philosophy of Language and His Political Thought. *Tulane Studies in Philosophy*, 29, 57–80, December 1980.

—— Merleau-Ponty's Political Thought: Nature and Challenge in *Phenomenology in a Pluralistic Context*, McBride, William L. (ed.), Albany: Suny Press, 1983.

—— *The Politics of Hope*. New York: Routledge and Kegan Paul, 1986.

Davis, Duane H., Reversible Subjectivity in *Merleau-Ponty Vivant*, Dillon, M.C. (ed.), Albany: Suny Press, 1991.

—— (Trans.), 'Les Fondateurs' and 'La Découverte de L'histoire': Two Short Pieces Excluded From 'Everywhere and Nowhere', by Maurice Merleau-Ponty. *Man and World*, 25(2), 203–209, April 1992.

De Jong, T.J., 'Le Primat de la Perception', Het Zijnde in 'Phenomenologie de la Perception'. *Alg Ned Tijdschr Wijs*, 71, 81–96, April 1979.

De Lattre, A., L'univers de la perception et ses dimensions chez Maurice Merleau-Ponty. *Revue Philosophique*, 164, 273–292, July–September 1974.

De Rezende, Antonio Muniz, Le Point de Départ dans la Philosophie de Merleau-Ponty. *Revue Philosophique de Louvain*, 73, 451–480, August 1975.

De Sanctis, G.B., L'estetica di due Fenomenologhi: Levinas e Merleau-Ponty. *Riv. Stud. Croce*, 9, 27–43, January–March 1972.

De Waelhens, Alphonse, *Une Philosophie de l'Ambiguîté: l'Existentialisme de Merleau-Ponty,* 2nd edition, Nauwelaerts: Louvain, 1967 (1st edition 1951).

—— Merleau-Ponty Philosophe de la Peinture. *Revue de Metaphysique et de Morale*, 67 no. 4, 431–449, October–December 1962.

—— The Philosophical Position of Merleau-Ponty. *Philosophy Today*, 7, 134–149, Summer 1963.

Dean, Thomas, *Post-Theistic Thinking: the Marxist-Christian Dialogue in Radical Perspective*. Philadelphia: Temple University Press, 1975.

Delco, Alessandro, La Natura di Merleau-Ponty: a Proposito di Alcuni 'Inediti' del Filosofo Francese. *Filosofia*, 46(3), 185–212, September–December 1995.

Delivoyatzis, S., Engagement ou Néantisation? (In Greek). *Philosophia* (Athens), 17–18, 168–181, 198–88.

Deutscher, Max, Some Recollections of Ryle and Remarks on His Notion of Negative Action. *Australasian Journal of Philosophy*, 60, 254–264, September 1982.

Devettere, Raymond J., Merleau-Ponty and the Husserlian Reductions. *Philosophy Today*, 17, 297–308, Winter 1973.

—— The Human Body As Philosophical Paradigm in Whitehead and Merleau-Ponty. *Philosophy Today*, 20, 317–326, Winter 1976.

Diaz Diaz, Gonzalo, Maurice Merleau-Ponty En Las Letras Espanolas: Nota Bibliografica. *An. Seminar. Metaf.*, 17, 129–134, 1982.

Dillon, M.C., Gestalt Theory and Merleau-Ponty's Concept of Intentionality. *Man and World*, 4, 436–459, November 1971.

—— Sartre on the Phenomenal Body and Merleau-Ponty's Critique. *Journal of the British Society for Phenomenology*, 5, 144–158, May 1974.

—— Sartre's Inferno. *Thought*, 52, 134–150, June 1977.

—— 'Eye and Mind': the Intertwining of Vision and Thought. *Man and World*, 13, 155–172, 1980.

—— Merleau-Ponty and the Reversibility Thesis. *Man and World*, 16, 365–388, 1983.

—— Merleau-Ponty and the Transcendence of Immanence: Overcoming the Ontology of Consciousness. *Man and World*, 19, 395–412, 1986.

—— Apriority in Kant and Merleau-Ponty. *Kantstudien*, 78, 403–423, 1987.

—— *Merleau-Ponty's Ontology.* Bloomington: Indiana University Press, 1988.

—— Desire: Language and Body, in *Postmodernism and Continental Philosophy*, Silverman, Hugh (ed.), Albany: Suny Press.

—— Ecart: Reply To Lefort's 'Flesh and Otherness' in *Ontology and Alterity in Merleau-Ponty*. Evanston: Northwestern University Press, 1991.

—— (ed.). *Merleau-Ponty Vivant.* Albany: Suny Press, 1991.

Dolgov, K.M., The Philosophy and Aesthetics of Maurice Merleau-Ponty. *Soviet Studies in Philosophy*, 14, 67–92, Winter 1975–76.

Doud, Robert, Whitehead and Merleau-Ponty. *Process Studies*, 7, 145–160, Fall 1977.

—— Sensibility in Rahner and Merleau-Ponty. *Thomist*, 44, 372–389, July 1980.

—— Wholeness as Phenomenon in Teilhard De Chardin and Merleau-Ponty. *Philosophy Today*, 24, 90–103, Summer 1980.

Dreyfus, H.L. and Todes, S.J., The Three Worlds of Merleau-Ponty. *Philosophy and Phenomenological Research*, 22, 559–565, June 1962.

Dreyfus, H.L., The Current Relevance of Merleau-Ponty's Phenomenology of Embodiment. *Filozofia Istraz*, 15(3), 385–399, 1995.

Dubois, Pierre, Ryle et Merleau-Ponty: Faut-Il Exorciser le Fantôme qui se Cache dans la Machine? *Revue Philosophique de la France et de L'Etranger*, 95, 299–317, July–September 1970.

Duchene, J., La Structure de la Phénoménalisaiton dans la 'Phénoménologie de la Perception' de Merleau-Ponty. *Revue de Métaphysique et de Morale*, 83, 373–398, July–September 1978.

Dufrenne, Mikel, Sartre and Merleau-Ponty, in *Jean-Paul Sartre*, Silverman, Hugh (ed.), Pittsburgh: Duquesne University Press, 1980.

—— Eye and Mind, in *Merleau-Ponty: Perception, Structure, Language*, Sallis, John C. (ed.), Atlantic Highlands: Humanities Press, 1981.

Duhan, Laura, Ambiguity of Time, Self, and Philosophical Explanation in Merleau-Ponty, Husserl, and Hume. *Auslegung*, 13, 126–138, Summer 1987.

Dwyer, Philip, *Sense and Subjectivity: a Study of Wittgenstein and Merleau-Ponty.* Leiden, 1990.

Eckblad, Joyce, Nietzsche and Merleau-Ponty: the Body as Attitude in *Abeunt Studia in Mores: a Festschrift For Helga Doblin.* New York: 1990.

Edie, James M., The Significance of Merleau-Ponty's Philosophy of Language. *Journal of the History of Philosophy*, 13, 385–398, July 1975.

—— The Meaning and Development of Merleau-Ponty's Concept in *Merleau-Ponty: Perception, Structure, Language*, Sallis, John C. (ed.), 39–57. Atlantic Highlands: Humanities Press, 1981.

—— Merleau-Ponty: the Triumph of Dialectics over Structuralism. *Man and World*, 17, 299–312, 1984.

—— *Merleau-Ponty's Philosophy of Language: Structuralism and Dialectics*, Washington, D.C.: University Press of America, 1987.

Elliott, Gregory, Further Adventures of the Dialectic: Merleau-Ponty, Sartre, Althusser. *Philosophy*, 21, 195–214, 1987 Supplement.

Ellis, Ralph, *An Ontology of Consciousness*. Dordrecht: Nijhoff, 1986.

—— Prereflective Consciousness and the Process of Symbolization. *Man and World*, 13, 173–192, 1980.

Embree, Lester, Gurwitsch's Critique of Merleau-Ponty. *Journal of the British Society for Phenomenology*, 12, 151–163, May 1981.

—— Merleau-Ponty's Examination of Gestalt Psychology, in *Merleau-Ponty: Perception, Structure, Language*, Sallis, John C. (ed.), 89–121, Atlantic Highlands: Humanities Press, 1981.

Enns, Diane, 'We Flesh' Re-Membering the Body Beloved. *Philosophy Today*, 39(3–4), 263–279, Fall 1995.

Epstein, Fanny L., The Metaphysics of Mind–Body Identity Theories. *American Philosophical Quarterly*, 10, 111–121, April 1973.

Epstein, Michèle F., The Common Ground of Merleau-Ponty's and Wittgenstein's Philosophy of Man. *Journal of the History of Philosophy*, 13, 221–234, April 1975.

Erickson, Glenn W., *Negative Dialectics and the End of Philosophy*. Wolfeboro Longwood, 1990.

Evans, C. Stephen, Behaviorism as Existentialism: Ryle and Merleau-Ponty on the Mind. *Journal of the British Society for Phenomenology*, 14, 65–78, January 1983.

Fairchild, David, *Prolegomena to a Methodology: Reflections on Merleau-Ponty and Austin*. Washington DC: University Press of America, 1978.

Fandozzi, Phillip R., Art in a Technological Society, in *Research in Philosophy and Technology*, Vol. 2, Durbin, Paul T. (ed.), Greenwich, 1979.

Farber, Marvin, Pervasive Subjectivism. *Philosophy and Phenomenological Research*, 25, 527–533, June 1965.

Fielding, Helen, Grounding Agency in Depth: the Implications of Merleau-Ponty's Thought for the Politics of Feminism. *Human Studies*, 19(2), 175–184, April 1996.

Flay, Joseph C., Merleau-Ponty and Hegel: Radical Essentialism, in *Ontology and Alterity in Merleau-Ponty*. Evanston: Northwestern University Press, 1991.

Floistad, Guttorm (ed.), '*Contemporary Philosophy: a New Survey*', Vol. 4, *Philosophy of Mind*. The Hague: Nijhoff, 1983.

Florival, Ghislaine, Sartre et Merleau-Ponty, in *Philosophy and Culture*, Vol. 4, Cauchy, Venant (ed.), 170–174. Montreal.

Flynn, Bernard C., Textuality and the Flesh: Derrida and Merleau-Ponty. *Journal of the British Society for Phenomenology*, 15, 164–179, May 1984.

—— The Question of an Ontology of the Political: Arendt, Merleau-Ponty, Lefort. *International Studies in Philosophy*, 16, 1–24, Spring 1984.

—— Merleau-Ponty and Nietzsche on the Visible and the Invisible, in *Merleau-*

Ponty: Difference, Materiality, Painting, Foti, Véronique M. (ed.), New Jersey: Humanities Press, 1996.

Flyvbjerg, Bent, Sustaining Non-Rationalized Practices: Body–Mind, Power and Situational Ethics – Interview With Hubert and Stuart Dreyfus. *Praxis International*, 93–113, April 1991.

Fornari, A., Sentido y Praxis (Interpretacion Desde Algunos Textos de Merleau-Ponty). *Stromata*, 34, 103–114, January–June 1978.

Foti, Véronique M., Painting and the Re-orientation of Philosophical Thought in Merleau-Ponty. *Philosophy Today*, 24, 114–120, Summer 1980.

—— Heidegger's and Merleau-Ponty's Turn from Technicity to Art. *Philosophy Today*, 30, 306–316, Winter 1986.

—— Merleau-Ponty on Silence, in *The Horizons of Continental Philosophy*, Silverman, Hugh *et al.* (eds), 272–288. Dordrecht: Kluwer, 1988.

—— The Evidences of Paintings: Merleau-Ponty and Contemporary Abstraction, in *Merleau-Ponty: Difference, Materiality, Painting*, Foti, Véronique M. (ed.), New Jersey: Humanities Press, 1996.

—— (ed.), *Merleau-Ponty: Difference, Materiality, Painting*, New Jersey: Humanities Press, 1996.

Fotinis, Athanasios P., Perception and the External World: a Historical and Critical Account. *Philosophia* (Athens), 4, 433–448, 1974.

Foucault, Michel, The Prose of the World. *Diogenes*, 53, 17–37, Spring 1966.

Frantz, John J., Merleau-Ponty's Notion of 'Flesh': a Look at the Development of a New Philosophical Insight. *Dialogue*, 14, 46–51, January 1972.

Free, George, Language, Speech and Writing: Merleau-Ponty and Derrida on Saussure. *Human Studies*, 293–307, October 1990.

Friedman, Robert M., The Formation of Merleau-Ponty's Philosophy. *Philosophy Today*, 17, 272–278, Winter 1973.

—— Merleau-Ponty's Theory of Intersubjectivity. *Philosophy Today*, 19, 228–242, Fall 1975.

Froman, Wayne, Merleau-Ponty on Beginning: An Interrogation of Acting. *Agora*, 4, 58–77, 1979–80.

—— *Merleau-Ponty: Language and the Act of Speech*. East Brunswick: Associated University Press, 1982.

—— Merleau-Ponty and l'écriture, in *Writing the Politics of Difference*, Albany: Suny Press, 1991.

—— Alterity and the Paradox of Being, in *Ontology and Alterity in Merleau-Ponty*, Evanston: Northwestern University Press, 1991.

—— At the Limits of Phenomenology: Merleau-Ponty and Derrida, in *Merleau-Ponty: Difference, Materiality, Painting*, Foti, Véronique, M. (ed.), New Jersey: Humanities Press, 1996.

Fuentas, Joaquin Lomba, Fenomenologia Existencial en Merleau-Ponty. *Pensamiento*, 27, 309–331, July–September 1971.

Fukada, Susumu, L'Art et Le Sens – Essai sur Vues sur Les Arts de Merleau-Ponty. *Bigaku*, 22, 20–33, December 1971.

Fuller, Andrew R., Synthesizing the Everyday World. *Journal of Mind and Behavior*, 4, 369–388, Summer 1983.

Gagnon, Martin, Etonnement et Interrogation. *Revue Philosophique de Louvain*, 93(3), 370–391, August 1995.

Gaines, Jeffrey J., Maine de Biran and the Body-Subject. *Philosophy Today*, 34(1), 67–79, Spring 1990.

Galan Velez, Francisco V., La Idea de la Fenomenologia de Merleau-Ponty. *Revista de Filosofia* (Mexico), 18, 385–408, September–December 1985.

Gallagher, Shaun, Lived Body and Environment. *Research in Phenomenology*, 16, 139–170, 1986.

—— Hyletic Experience and the Lived Body. *Husserl Studies*, 3, 131–166, 1986.

Gallagher, Shaun and Meltzoff, Andrew N., The Earliest Sense of Self and Others. *Studies in Philosophy and Psychology*, 9(2), 211–233, June 1996.

Gans, Steven, Schematism and Embodiment. *Journal of the British Society for Phenomenology*, 13, 237–245, October 1982.

Garcia, Pablo Sebastian, Simetria y Asimetria en La Nocion de Reversibilidad de Merleau-Ponty. *Revista de Filosofia* (Mexico), 28(84), 271–283, September–December 1995.

—— Merleau-Ponty: Una Critica a la Teoria Realista de la Percepcion. *Revista de Filosofia* (Argentina), 3(1), 43–51, May 1988.

Gardner, Sebastian, Other Minds and Embodiment. *Proceedings of the Aristotelian Society*, 94, 35–52, 1994.

Gay, William C., Merleau-Ponty on Language and Social Science: the Dialectic of Phenomenology and Structuralism. *Man and World*, 12, 322–338, 1979.

—— Ricœur on Metaphor and Ideology. *Darshana International*, 32(1/125), 59–70, January 1992.

Gehl, Paul F., An Answering Silence: Claims for the Unity of Truth Beyond Language. *Philosophy Today*, 30, 224–233, Fall 1986.

Geraets, Theodore, *Vers une nouvelle philosophie transcendentale: La genèse de la philosophie de Maurice Merleau-Ponty jusqu'à la 'Phénoménologie de la Perception'*. The Hague: Martinus Nijhoff, 1971.

—— Le Retour à L'Expérience Perceptive et Le Sens du Primat de la Perception. *Dialogue*, 15, 595–607, December 1976.

—— 'Merleau-Ponty's Conception of Nature', in *Soul and Body in Phenomenology*, Tymieniecka, Anna-Teresa (ed.), 310–312. Dordrecht: Reidel, 1983.

Gerber, Rudolph J., Merleau-Ponty: the Dialectic of Consciousness and World. *Man and World*, 2, 83–107, February 1969.

—— Causality and Atheism. *Proceedings of the Catholic Philosophical Association*, 44, 232–240, 1970.

Gervais, Charles, Y a-t-il Un Deuxième Sartre? *Revue Philosophique de Louvain*, 67, 74–103, February 1969.

Gier, Nicholas F., Intentionality and Prehension. *Process Studies*, 6, 197–213, Fall 1976.

—— *Wittgenstein and Phenomenology: a Comparative Study of the Later Wittgenstein, Husserl, Heidegger, and Merleau-Ponty*. Albany: State University of New York Press, 1981.

—— Wittgenstein, Intentionality and Behaviorism. *Metaphilosophy*, 13, 46–64, January 1982.

Gill, Jerry H., Post-Critical Philosophy of Religion. *International Philosophical Quarterly*, 22, 75–86, March 1982.

—— Objectivity and Social Reality: Peter Berger's Dilemma. *Philosophy Today*, 32, 256–269, Fall 1988.

—— Merleau-Ponty, Metaphor, and Philosophy. *Philosophy Today*, 34(1), 48–66, Spring 1990.

—— *Merleau-Ponty and Metaphor*, Atlantic Highlands: Humanities Press, 1991.

—— *Learning To Learn: Toward a Philosophy of Education*, Atlantic Highlands: Humanities Press, 1993.

Gillan, Garth (ed.), *The Horizons of the Flesh: Critical Perspectives On the Thought of Merleau-Ponty*. Carbondale, S. Illinois University Press, 1973.

—— The Question of Embodiment: Marcel and Merleau-Ponty, in *The Philosophy of Gabriel Marcel*, Schilpp, Paul A. (ed.), La Salle: Open Court, 1984.

Glenn Jr, John D., Merleau-Ponty and the Cogito. *Philosophy Today*, 23, 310–320, Winter 1979.

—— Merleau-Ponty's Existential Dialectic. *Tulane Studies in Philosophy*, 29, 81–94, December 1980.

—— The Behaviorism of a Phenomenologist: the Structure of Behavior and the Concept of Mind. *Philosophical Topics*, 13, 247–256, Spring 1985.

Godway, Eleanor M., Wild Being, the Prepredicative and Expression: How Merleau-Ponty Uses Phenomenology to Develop an Ontology. *Man and World*, 26(4), 389–401, October 1993.

Good, Paul and Camino, Frederico, Bibliographie des Werkes von Maurice Merleau-Ponty. *Philosophisches Jahrbuch*, 77, 434–443, 1970 (P.I.D.G.).

Goyard-Fabre, Simone, Merleau-Ponty et La Politique. *Revue de Métaphysique et de Morale*, 85, 240–262, April–June 1980.

Green, André, Du comportement à la chair: Itineraire de Merleau-Ponty. *Critique*, 211, 1017–1042, December 1964.

Grene, Marjorie, The Aesthetic Dialogue of Sartre and Merleau-Ponty. *Journal of the British Society for Phenomenology*, 1, 59–72, May 1970.

—— Polanyi et La Philosophie Française. *Archives de Philosophie*, 35, 3–5, January–March 1972.

—— Merleau-Ponty and the Renewal of Ontology. *Review of Metaphysics*, 29, 605–625, June 1976.

Guibal, Francis, Significations Culturelles et Sens Ethique: à partir d'Emmanuel Levinas. *Revue Philosophique de Louvain*, 94(1), 134–163, February 1996.

Guibal, Francis and Sanabria, Jose Ruben (Trans.), Significaciones Culturales y Sentido Etico: a partir de Emmanuel Levinas. *Revista de Filosofia* (Mexico), 29(85), 17–61, January–April 1996.

Haar, Michel and Foti, Véronique M. (Trans.), Painting, Perception, Affectivity, in *Merleau-Ponty: Difference, Materiality, Painting*, Foti, Véronique M. (ed.), New Jersey: Humanities Press, 1996.

Hachamovitch, Yfat, Ploughing the Delirium in *Merleau-Ponty: Difference, Materiality, Painting*, Foti, Véronique M. (ed.), New Jersey: Humanities Press, 1996.

Hadreas, Peter, *In Place of the Flawed Diamond: An Investigation of Merleau-Ponty's Philosophy*. New York, 1986.

Haight, David, The Source of Linguistic Meaning. *Philosophy and Phenomenological Research*, 37, 239–247, December 1976.

Hall, Harrison, The Continuity of Merleau-Ponty's Philosophy of Perception. *Man and World*, 10, 435–447, 1977.

—— The A Priori and the Empirical in Merleau-Ponty's 'Phenomenology of Perception'. *Philosophy Today*, 23, 304–309, Winter 1979.

—— Painting and Perceiving. *Journal of Aesthetics and Art Criticism*, 39, 291–295, Spring 1981.

—— Merleau-Ponty's Philosophy of Mind, in *Contemporary Philosophy: a New Survey*, Floistad, Guttorm (ed.), 343–361. The Hague: Nijhoff, 1983.

Hall Ronald L., Freedom: Merleau-Ponty's Critique of Sartre. *Philosophical Research*, 6, No. 1391, 1980.

—— The Origin of Alienation: Some Kierkegaardian Reflections on Merleau-Ponty's Phenomenology of the Body. *International Journal for Philosophy of Religion*, 12, 111–122, 1981.

285

Hamrick, William S., Whitehead and Merleau-Ponty: Some Moral Implications. *Process Studies*, 4, 235–251, Winter 1974.
—— Fascination, Fear and Pornography: a Phenomenological Typology. *Man and World*, 7, 52–66, February 1974.
—— Ingarden and Artistic Creativity. *Dialogue and Humanism*, 2, 39–49, Autumn 1975.
—— Towards a Phenomenology of Legal Rules. *Journal of the British Society for Phenomenology*, 10, 9–22, January 1979.
—— Language and Abnormal Behavior: Merleau-Ponty, Hart, and Laing. *Review of Existential Psychology and Psychiatry*, 18, 181–203, 1982–83.
—— Merleau-Ponty 1 Jean-Paul Sartre: Translator's Introduction. *Journal of the British Society for Phenomenology*, 15, 123–127, May 1984.
—— Merleau-Ponty's View of Creativity and Its Philosophical Consequences. *International Philosophical Quarterly*, 34(4), 401–412, December 1994.
Hass, Lawrence, The Antinomy of Perception: Merleau-Ponty and Causal Representation Theory. *Man and World*, 13–25, January 1991.
—— Merleau-Ponty and Cartesian Skepticism: Exorcising the Demon. *Man and World*, 26(2), 131–145, April 1993.
Heelan, Patrick A., Natural Science and Being-In-The-World. *Man and World*, 16, 207–220, 1983.
Heidsiek, François, *L'Ontologie de Merleau-Ponty*. Paris: Presses Universitaires de France, 1971.
Heinzig, Dennis, M Merleau-Ponty and Ludwig Wittgenstein: a Synthesis. *Auslegung*, 14, 19–36, Winter 1987.
Herzog, Maximilian, Entwicklungsdenken bei Piaget und Merleau-Ponty. *Philosophische Rundschau*, 41(4), 321–327, December 1994.
Hoeller, Keith, Phenomenology, Psychology, and Science, II. *Review of Existential Psychology and Psychiatry*, 18, 143–154, 1982–83.
—— (ed.), *Merleau-Ponty and Psychology*. Atlantic Highlands: Humanities Press, 1993.
Hohler, Thomas P., The Limits of Language and the Threshold of Speech. *Philosophy Today*, 26, 287–300, Winter 1982.
Holland, Nancy H., Merleau-Ponty on Presence: a Derridean Reading. *Research in Phenomenology*, 16, 111–120, 1986.
Hottois, Gilbert (ed.), *Philosophies et Sciences*. Bruxelles: Brussells University, 1986.
Howard, Dick, Introduction To Lefort. *Telos*, 2–30, Winter 1974–75.
—— *The Marxian Legacy*, Minneapolis: University Minnesota Press, 1988.
Howarth, J., The Crisis of Ecology: a Phenomenological Perspective. *Journal of Environmental Values*, 4(1), 17–30, February 1995.
Hudac, Michael C., Merleau-Ponty On the Cartesian 'Dubito': a Critical Analysis. *History of Philosophy Quarterly*, 207–219, April 1991.
Hurst, William J., Merleau-Ponty's Concept of the Self. *International Philosophical Quarterly*, 22, 227–240, December 1982.
—— Merleau-Ponty's Ontological Quest. *International Philosophical Quarterly*, 34(3), 335–347, Summer 1994.
Ihde, Don, *Instrumental Realism: the Interface Between Philosophy of Science and Philosophy of Technology*. Bloomington: Indiana University Press, 1991.
Ivaldo, M., L'Impegno Ontologico in un Recente Studio a Carattere Storico-Teoretico. *Sapienza*, 30, 455–464, October–December 1977.
Jacobson, Paul, The Return of Alcibiades: An Approach to the Meaning of

Human Sexuality Through the Works of Freud and Merleau-Ponty. *Philosophy Today*, 22, 89–98, Spring 1978.

—— Language, Thought, and Truth in the Works of Merleau-Ponty: 1948–1949. *Research in Phenomenology*, 9, 144–167, 1979.

Janicaud, Dominique, La Technique et le Langage. *Man and World*, 16, 349–364, 1983.

Janssen, Paul, Reflexion Und Weltbezug: eine Analysis von Merleau Pontys Verstandnis Des Cogito. *Philosophische Forschung*, 31, 252–264, April–June 1977.

—— Phänomenologie als Geschichtsphilosophie in Praktischer Absicht: Den Philosophischen Intentionen Ludwig Landgrebes zur Erinnerung. *Husserl Studies*, 10(2), 97–110, 1993–94.

Johnson, Galen A., Merleau-Ponty's Early Aesthetics of Historical Being: the Case of Cézanne. *Research in Phenomenology*, 17, 211–225, 1987.

—— Husserl and Merleau-Ponty: History, Language and Truth, in *Merleau-Ponty: Critical Essays*, Pietersma, Henry (ed.), Washington DC: University Press of America, 1990.

—— Generosity and Forgetting in the History of Being: Merleau-Ponty and Nietzsche in *Questioning Foundations*, Silverman, Hugh (ed.), New York: Routledge, 1993.

—— Desire and Invisibility in the Ontology of *Eye and Mind*: Some Remarks on Merleau-Ponty's Spirituality in *Merleau-Ponty in Contemporary Perspective*, Burke P. and Van der Veken J. (eds), Kluwer, 1993.

—— Painting, Nostalgia and Metaphysics. *Bulletin de la Société Americaine de Philosophie de Langue Française*, 5 no. 1, 55–70, Spring 1993.

—— The Colors of Fire: Depth and Desire in Merleau-Ponty's 'Eye and Mind'. *Journal of the British Society for Phenomenology*, 25(1), 53–63, January 1994.

—— (ed.), *The Merleau-Ponty Aesthetics Reader: Philosophy and Painting*, Evanston: Northwestern University Press, 1994.

—— Thinking in Color: Merleau-Ponty and Paul Klee, in *Merleau-Ponty: Difference, Materiality, Painting*, Foti, Véronique M. (ed.), New Jersey: Humanities Press, 1996.

Johnson, Galen A. and Smith, Michael B. (eds), *Ontology and Alterity in Merleau-Ponty*, Evanston: Northwestern University Press, 1991.

Jolivet, Regis, The Problem of God in the Philosophy of Merleau-Ponty. *Philosophy Today*, 7, 150–164, Summer 1963.

Joos, Ernest, Remarks On Bertoldi's 'Time in the Phenomenology of Perception'. *Dialogue*, 15, 113–117, March 1976.

—— *Intentionality – Source of Intelligibility: the Genesis of Intentionality*, New York: 1989.

Jung, Hwa Yol, The Concept of the Dialectic in Hegel, Marx and Merleau-Ponty. *Journal of the British Society for Phenomenology*, 8, 56–58, January 1977.

Kaelin, Eugene F., *An Existentialist Aesthetic: the Theories of Sartre and Merleau-Ponty*, Madison: University of Wisconsin Press, 1962.

—— *Art and Existence: a Phenomenological Aesthetics*, Lewisburg Pa.: Bucknell University Press, 1970.

—— Merleau-Ponty, Fundamental Ontologist. *Man and World*, 3, 102–115, February 1970.

—— 'On "Meaning" in Sartre's Aesthetic Theory', in *Jean-Paul Sartre*, Silverman, Hugh (ed.), Pittsburgh: Duquesne University Press, 1980.

Katayama, Hisanki, La Pensée Esthétique de M. Dufrenne (in Japanese). *Bigaku*, 30, 49, December 1979.

Kaufmann, Pierre, De la vision picturale au désir de peindre. *Critique*, 211, 1047–1064, December 1964.

Kearney, Richard, Modern Movements in European Philosophy: Some Introductory Remarks. *Eidos*, 4, 51–61, June 1985.

—— *Modern Movements in European Philosophy*. Manchester: Manchester University Press, 1986.

— *Poetics of Imagining: From Husserl To Lyotard*. New York: Routledge, 1991.

Kerby, Anthony Paul, *Narrative and the Self*, Bloomington: Indiana University Press, 1991.

Kerszberg, Pierre, Husserl et Merleau-Ponty: La Prose Bourdonnante du Monde. *Archives de Philosophie*, 59(2), 179–201, April–June 1996.

—— 'Misunderstanding the Other' in *Merleau-Ponty: Difference, Materiality, Painting*, Foti, Véronique M. (ed.), New Jersey: Humanities Press, 1996.

Kessler, Gary E., Pragmatic Bodies Versus Transcendental Egos. *Transactions of the Peirce Society*, 14, 101–119, Spring 1978.

Kimmerle, Heinz, Das Multiversum der Kulturen: Einstellungen der Zeitgenossischen Europaisch-Westlichen Philosophie zu den Philosophien Anderer Kulturen. *Perspektiven der Philosophie*, 21, 269–292, 1995.

—— *Das Multiversum Der Kulturen*. Amsterdam, 1996.

Klein, Robert, Peinture moderne et phénoménologie: a propos de *L'œil et l'esprit*. *Critique*, 191, 336ff., April 1963.

Knabenschuh De Porta, Sabine, Expresion Artistica y Lenguaje Verbal en Merleau-Ponty. *Revista de Filosofia* (Venezuela), 18, 109–128, 1993.

Kockelmans, Joseph J., Merleau-Ponty On Sexuality. *Journal Existentialism*, 6, 9–30, Fall 1965.

—— (ed.), *Phenomenology; the Philosophy of Edmund Husserl and Its Interpretation*, Garden City, New York: Anchor Books, 1967.

—— The Function of Psychology in Merleau-Ponty's Early Works. *Review of Existential Psychology and Psychiatry*, 18, 119–142, 1982–83.

Kohout, J., Time, Perception, Structure (In Czech). *Filozofia*, 39(2), 239–258, 1991.

Kortooms, A. and Boudier, C. Struyker, Een Bijdrage tot de Geschiedenis van de Husserl-Receptie in Belgie En Nederland, Eerste Deel. *Alg Ned Tijdschr Wijs*, 81, 1–20, January 1989.

—— Een Bijdrage tot de Geschiedenis van de Husserl-Receptie in Belgie en Nederland, Tweede Deel. *Alg Ned Tijdschr Wijs*, 81, 79–101, April 1989.

Kovacs, George, The Personalistic Understanding of the Body and Sexuality in Merleau-Ponty. *Review of Existential Psychology and Psychiatry*, 18, 207–217, 1982–83.

Kovaly, Pavel, Maurice Merleau-Ponty and the Problem of Self-Accusations. *Studies in Soviet Thought*, 17, 225–241, October 1977.

Kozel, Susan, The Diabolical Strategy of Mimesis: Luce Irigaray's Reading of Maurice Merleau-Ponty. *Hypatia*, 11(3), 114–129, Summer 1996.

Krell, David Farrell, M Merleau-Ponty on 'Eros' and 'Logos'. *Man and World*, 7, 37–51, February 1974.

—— Phenomenology of Memory From Husserl To Merleau-Ponty. *Philosophy and Phenomenological Research*, 42, 492–505, June 1982.

—— Foreign Bodies in Strange Places: a Note on Maurice Merleau-Ponty, Georges Bataille, and Architecture. *Philosophy Today*, 43–50, Spring 1991.

Kruks, Sonia, Merleau-Ponty, Hegel and the Dialectic. *Journal of the British Society for Phenomenology*, 7, 96–110, May 1976.

—— Merleau-Ponty: a Phenomenological Critique of Liberalism. *Philosophy and Phenomenological Research*, 37, 394–407, March 1977.

—— *The Political Philosophy of Merleau-Ponty*, Atlantic Highlands: Humanities Press/Sussex: Harvester Press, 1981.

—— Marcel and Merleau-Ponty: Incarnation, Situation and the Problem of History. *Human Studies*, 10, 225–245, 1987.

—— Simone de Beauvoir: Teaching Sartre about Freedom, in *Sartre Alive*, Aronson, Ronald (ed.), Detroit: Wayne St University Press, 1991 and in *Feminist Interpretations of Simone de Beauvoir*, Simons, Margaret A. (ed.), University Park: Penn St University Press, 1995.

Kuang-Ming Wu, Trying Without Trying: Toward a Taoist Phenomenology of Truth. *Journal of Chinese Philosophy*, 8, 143–167, June 1981.

—— *Chuang Tzu: World Philosopher At Play*, New York: Crossroad, 1982.

Kujundzic, Nebojsa and Buschert, William, Instruments and the Body: Sartre and Merleau-Ponty. *Research in Phenomenology*, 24, 206–215, 1994.

Kwant, R.C., De Mens als Oorsprong. *Tijdschr Filosof*, 31, 441–470, September 1969.

—— Merleau-Ponty's Nieuwe Filosofie van de Perceptie, de Natuur en de Logos. *Tijdschr Filosof*, 51(4), 669–695, December 1989.

—— Merleau-Ponty En Wittgenstein Ii. *Tijdschr Filosof*, 32, 3–29, March 1970.

—— Eindigen met een Nieuw Begin: Zien en Denken in De Laatste Geschriften van M. Merleau-Ponty. *Tijdschr Filosof*, 58(4), 716–734, December 1996.

—— *From Phenomenology To Metaphysics: An Inquiry Into the Last Period of Merleau-Ponty's Philosophical Life*, Pittsburgh: Duquesne University Press, 1966.

—— *The Phenomenological Philosophy of Merleau-Ponty*, Pittsburgh: Duquesne University Press, 1963.

Lagueux, Maurice, Merleau-Ponty et la linguistique de Saussure. *Dialogue*, 4, no. 3, 351–364, December 1965.

—— Y a-t-il Une Philosophie de l'histoire Chez Merleau-Ponty. *Dialogue*, 5, 404–417, 1966.

Langan, Thomas, *Merleau-Ponty's Critique of Reason*, New Haven: Yale University Press, 1966.

Langer, Monika, Sartre and Merleau-Ponty: a Reappraisal, in *The Philosophy of Jean-Paul Sartre*, Schilpp, Paul A. (ed.), 300–325. La Salle: Open Court, 1981.

—— Merleau-Ponty and Deep Ecology, in *Ontology and Alterity in Merleau-Ponty*, Johnson and Smith (eds), Evanston: Northwestern University Press, 1991.

Lanigan, Richard L., Rhetorical Criticism: An Interpretation of Maurice Merleau-Ponty. *Philosophy and Rhetoric*, 2, 61–71, Spring 1969.

—— Maurice Merleau-Ponty Bibliography. *Man and World*, 3, 289–319, September–November 1970.

—— Merleau-Ponty's Phenomenology of Communication. *Philosophy Today*, 14, 79–88, Summer 1970.

—— *Speaking and Semiology: Maurice Merleau-Ponty's Phenomenological Theory of Existential Communication*, The Hague: Mouton, 1972.

—— *Phenomenology of Communication: Merleau-Ponty's Thematics in Communicology and Semiology*, Pittsburgh: Duquesne University Press, 1988.

—— Communication Science and Merleau-Ponty, in *The Horizons of Continental Philosophy*, Silverman, Hugh *et al.* (eds), Dordrecht: Kluwer, 1988.

—— *The Human Science of Communicology: a Phenomenology of Discourse in Foucault and Merleau-Ponty*, Pittsburgh: Duquesne University Press, 1992.

—— The Algebra of History, in *The Critical Turn*, Angus, Ian (ed.), Carbondale: South Illinois University Press, 1993.

—— A Good Rhetoric is Possible, in *The Philosophy of Paul Ricœur*, Hahn, Lewis Edwin (ed.), Peru: Open Court, 1994.

Lapointe, François H., The Phenomenological Psychology of Sartre and Merleau-Ponty: a Bibliographical Essay. *Dialogos*, 8, 161–182, November 1972.

—— The Significance of Time in Merleau-Ponty's Phenomenology of the Body and the World. *Modern Schoolman*, 49, 356–366, May 1972.

—— Selected Bibliography on Art and Aesthetics in Merleau-Ponty. *Philosophy Today*, 17, 292–296, Winter 1973.

—— The Body–Soul Problem in Merleau-Ponty's 'The Structure of Behavior'. *Modern Schoolman*, 50, 281–291, March 1973.

—— The Evolution of Merleau-Ponty's Concept of the Body. *Dialogos*, 139–151, April 1974.

Lauer, Quentin, *Triumph of Subjectivity: Introduction To Transcendental Phenomenology*, New York: Fordham University Press, 1958.

Leder, Drew, Merleau-Ponty and the Critique of Kant. *Graduate Faculty Philosophy Journal*, 9, 61–75, Fall 1983.

—— Medicine and Paradigms of Embodiment. *Journal of Medicine and Philosophy*, 9, 29–44, February 1984.

—— Flesh and Blood: a Proposed Supplement To Merleau-Ponty. *Human Studies*, 13(3), 209–219, July 1990.

—— A Tale of Two Bodies: the Cartesian Corpse and the Lived Body, in *The Body in Medical Thought and Practice*, Leder, Drew (ed.), Dordrecht: Kluwer, 1992.

Ledermann, E.K., Conscience and Bodily Awareness: Disagreements With Merleau-Ponty. *Journal of the British Society for Phenomenology*, 13, 286–295, October 1982.

Lefeuvre, Michel, Musique et peinture ou Lévi-Strauss et Merleau-Ponty. *Etudes*, 140, 727–785, May 1974.

Lefort, Claude, L'idée d'être brut et d'esprit sauvage. *Les Temps Modernes*, 17, nos 184–5, 255–286, October 1961.

—— *Introduction to La Prose du Monde de M. Merleau-Ponty*, Paris: Gallimard, 1969.

—— Presenting Merleau-Ponty. *Telos*, 29, 39–42, Fall 1976.

—— *Sur une colonne absente: Ecrits autour de Merleau-Ponty*. Paris: Gallimard, 1978.

—— Flesh and Otherness, in *Ontology and Alterity in Merleau-Ponty*, Johnson and Smith (eds), Evanston: Northwestern University Press, 1991.

Lessing, A., Spinoza and Merleau-Ponty on Human Existence. *Proceedings of the New Mexico and West Texas Philosophy Society*, 20–24, April 1972.

Lévi-Strauss, Claude, De quelques rencontres L'Arc (Aix-en-Provence). 46, 43–7, 1971.

—— On Merleau-Ponty, Christine Gross (Trans). *Graduate Faculty Philosophy Journal*, 7, 179–188, Winter 1978.

Levin, David Michael, The Spacing of Comedy and Tragedy: a Phenomenological Study of Perception. *Journal of the British Society for Phenomenology*, 11, 16–36, January 1980.

—— Eros and Psyche: a Reading of Merleau-Ponty. *Review of Existential Psychology and Psychiatry*, 18, 219–239, 1982–83.

—— Sanity and Myth in Affective Space: a Discussion of Merleau-Ponty. *Philosophical Forum*, 14, 157–189, Winter 1982–83.

—— Hermeneutics as Gesture: a Reflection on Heidegger's 'Logos (Herakleitos B50)' Study. *Tulane Studies in Philosophy*, 32, 69–77, 1984.

—— The Body Politic: Political Economy and the Human Body. *Human Studies*, 8, 235–278, 1985.

—— Mudra As Thinking, in *Heidegger and Asian Thought*, Parkes, Graham (ed.), Honolulu: University of Hawaii Press, 1987.

—— *The Opening of Vision: Nihilism and the Postmodern Situation*, New York: Routledge, 1988.

—— The Body Politic: the Embodiment of Praxis in Foucault and Habermas. *Praxis International*, 9, 112–132, April–July 1989.

—— *Visions of Narcissism in Merleau-Ponty Vivant*, Dillon, M.C. (ed.), Albany: Suny Press, 1991.

—— Justice in the Flesh, in *Ontology and Alterity in Merleau-Ponty*, Evanston: Northwestern University Press, 1991.

—— Making Sense: the Work of Eugene Gendlin. *Human Studies*, 17(3), 343–353, July 1994.

Levine, Stephen K., Merleau-Ponty's Philosophy of Art. *Man and World*, 2, 438–452, August 1969.

Levinson, Daniel, Logic in Contingency: the Origin of Truth in Merleau-Ponty with Constant Reference to Nietzsche. *Graduate Faculty Philosophy Journal*, 5, 132–141, Fall 1975.

Lewis, Philip E., Merleau-Ponty and the Phenomenology of Language, *Yale French Studies*, 36–37, 19–40, 1964–5.

Lingis, Alphonso, Intentionality and Corporeity. *Analecta Husserliana*, 1, 75–90, 1971.

—— The Difficulties of a Phenomenological Investigation of Language. *Modern Schoolman*, 57, 56–64, November 1979.

—— Sensations. *Philosophy and Phenomenological Research*, 42, 160–170, December 1981.

—— Imperatives, in *Merleau-Ponty Vivant*, Dillon, M.C. (ed.), Albany: Suny Press, 1991.

—— Intentionality and the Imperative. *International Philosophical Quarterly*, 34(3), 289–300, September 1994.

—— The Body Postured and Dissolute, in *Merleau-Ponty: Difference, Materiality, Painting*, Foti, Veronique, M. (ed.), New Jersey: Humanities Press, 1996.

Llavona, Rafael, Merleau-Ponty a los Diez Anos de su Muerte: Ensayo Bibliografico. *Pensamiento*, 27, 255–307, July–September 1971.

Lopez, M. Carmen, La Estetica Ontologica de M Merleau-Ponty. *Pensamiento*, 189(48), 69–77, January–March 1992.

Low, Douglas, The Existential Dialectic of Marx and Merleau-Ponty. *Philosophical Research*, 11, 491–511, 1985.

—— The Continuity Between Merleau-Ponty's Early and Late Philosophy of Language. *Philosophical Research*, 17, 287–311, 1992.

—— Merleau-Ponty on Subjectivity and Intersubjectivity. *International Studies in Philosophy*, 24(3), 45–64, 1992.

—— Merleau-Ponty's Concept of Reason. *Philosophical Research*, 19, 109–125, 1994.

—— The Foundations of Merleau-Ponty's Ethical Theory. *Human Studies*, 17(2), 173–187, April 1994.

—— Merleau-Ponty and the Foundations of Multiculturalism. *Philosophical Research*, 21, 377–390, January 1996.

—— *The Existential Dialectic of Marx and Merleau-Ponty*, Beck, New York: Lang, 1987.

Lowry, Atherton C., Merleau-Ponty and Fundamental Ontology. *International Philosophical Quarterly*, 15, 397–409, December 1975.

—— Merleau-Ponty and the Absence of God. *Proceedings of the Catholic Philosophical Association*, 52, 150–158, 1978.

—— Merleau-Ponty and the Absence of God. *Philosophy Today*, 22, 119–126, Summer 1978.

—— The Invisible World of Merleau-Ponty. *Philosophy Today*, 23, 294–303, Winter 1979.

—— Condemned To Time: the Limits of Merleau-Ponty's Quest For Being. *International Philosophical Quarterly*, 319–327, September 1991.

Ludking, Karlheinz, Pictures and Gestures. *British Journal of Aesthetics*, 30(3), 218–232, July 1990.

Luijpen, William A., *Existential Phenomenology*, Pittsburgh: Duquesne University Press, 1960.

—— *Phenomenology and Atheism*, Pittsburgh: Duquesne University Press, 1965.

Macann, Christopher, Deux Concepts de Transcendance. *Revue de Métaphysique et de Morale*, 91, 24–46, January–March 1986.

Madison, G.B., Le Postulat d'objectivité dans La Science et La Philosophie du Sujet. *Philosophiques*, 1, 107–139, April 1974.

—— The Ambiguous Philosophy of Merleau-Ponty. *Philosophical Studies*, 22, 63–77, 1974.

—— Merleau-Ponty et La Contre-Tradition. *Dialogue*, 17, 456–479, 1978.

—— *The Phenomenology of Merleau-Ponty: A Search for the Limits of Consciousness*, Athens: Ohio University Press, 1981.

—— Merleau-Ponty et La Déconstruction du Logocentrisme. *Laval Theol. Phil.*, 46(1), 65–79, February 1990.

—— Merleau-Ponty's Destruction of Logocentrism in *Merleau-Ponty Vivant*, Dillon, M.C. (ed.), Albany: Suny Press, 1991.

—— Flesh As Otherness, in *Ontology and Alterity in Merleau-Ponty*, Evanston: Northwestern University Press, 1991.

—— Merleau-Ponty Alive. *Man and World*, 26(1), 19–44, January 1993.

Maesschalck, Marc, Questions sur Le Langage Poétique à partir de Roman Jakobson. *Revue Philosophique de Louvain*, 87, 470–503, August 1989.

—— Essai sur le Développement Historique de la Voie Phénoménologique. *Revue Philosophique de Louvain*, 185–210, May 1991.

Maiz Carro, Maria De Lourdes, Percepcion, Sentido y Perspectiva en Merleau-Ponty. *An. Seminar. Metaf.*, 17, 115–128, 1982.

Mallin, Samuel B., *Merleau-Ponty's Philosophy*, New Haven: Yale University Press, 1979.

—— Chiasm, Line and Art, in *Merleau-Ponty: Critical Essays*, Pietersma, Henry (ed.), Washington DC: The University Press of America, 1990.

Mancini, Sandro, Merleau-Ponty's Phenomenology as a Dialectical Philosophy of Expression. *International Philosophical Quarterly*, 36(4), 389–398, December 1996.

Margolis, Joseph, Phenomenology and Metaphysics: Husserl, Heidegger, and

Merleau-Ponty, in *Merleau-Ponty Vivant*, Dillon, M.C. (ed.), Albany: Suny Press, 1991.

Marsh, James L, The Triumph of Ambiguity: Merleau-Ponty and Wittgenstein. *Philosophy Today*, 19, 243–255, Fall 1975.

Martin, F. David, Sculpture and 'Truth To Things'. *Journal of Aesthetic Education*, 13, 11–32, April 1979.

Martinez Rodriguez, Fernando, Merleau-Ponty a La Luz del 'Avant-Propos' de 'Phénoménologie de la Perception'. *An. Seminar. Metaf.*, 17, 105–114, 1982.

Martino, Eutimio, El Pesimismo Relativo Del Ultimo Merleau-Ponty: A puntes de su Curso 1958–59 en el Collège de France. *Pensamiento*, 26, 73–88, January–March 1970.

Matera, Rocco, La Fenomenologia dell'esperienza. *Rivista di Filosofia Neoscolastica*, 69, 627–646, October–December 1977.

Matustik, Martin, Merleau-Ponty on Taking the Attitude of the Other. *Journal of the British Society for Phenomenology*, 44–52, January 1991.

—— Merleau-Ponty's Phenomenology of Sympathy. *Auslegung*, 41–65, Winter 1991.

Mazis, Glen A. Touch and Vision: Rethinking With Merleau-Ponty and Sartre On the Caress. *Philosophy Today*, 23, 321–328, Winter 1979.

—— *La chair et l'imaginaire*: the Developing Role of the Imagination in Merleau-Ponty's Philosophy. *Philosophy Today*, 32, 30–42, Spring 1988.

—— Merleau-Ponty: the Depth of Memory, in *The Horizons of Continental Philosophy*, Silverman, Hugh et al. (eds), 227–250. Dordrecht: Kluwer, 1988.

—— *Emotion and Embodiment: Fragile Ontology*, New York: Lang, 1993.

—— Matter, Dream, and the Murmurs Among Things, in *Merleau-Ponty: Difference, Materiality, Painting*, Foti, Véronique, M. (ed.), New Jersey: Humanities Press, 1996.

McBride, William L. and Schragg, Calvin O. (eds), *Phenomenology in a Pluralistic Context*, Albany: Suny Press, 1983.

McLane, Janice, The Voice On the Skin: Self-Mutilation and Merleau-Ponty's Theory of Language. *Hypatia*, 11(4), 107–118, Fall 1996.

McLure, Roger, Sartre and Merleau-Ponty, in *European Philosophy and the Human and Social Sciences*, Glynn, Simon (ed.), 170–211. Hampshire: Gower.

McMillan, Elizabeth, Female Difference in the Texts of Merleau-Ponty. *Philosophy Today*, 31, 359–366, Winter 1987.

Mcaddo, Nick, Hearing Musical Works in Their Entirety. *British Journal of Aesthetics*, 37(1), 66–74, January 1997.

Meier, Klaus V., Cartesian and Phenomenological Anthropology: the Radical Shift and Its Meaning For Sport. *Journal of the Philosophy of Sport*, 11, 51–73, September 1975.

Melendo Granados, Tomas, Sentido y Ser en Merleau-Ponty. *An. Seminar. Metaf.*, 17, 135–144, 1982.

Mestek, J., The Ontological Status of Communication in Merleau-Ponty (In Czech). *Filozof. Cas.*, 39(3), 489–493, 1991.

Meyer-Drawe, Kate, Merleau-Ponty's Opening of the Reason. *Filozof Istraz*, 15(3), 401–411, 1995.

Michaud, Thomas A., Schutz's Theory of Constitution: An Idealism of Meaning. *Philosophical Research*, 13, 63–71, 1987–88.

Mickunas, Algis, Perception in Husserl and Merleau-Ponty. *Philosophical Inquiry*, 2, 484–495, Spring–Summer 1980.

Miller, James, Merleau-Ponty's Marxism: Between Phenomenology and the Hegelian Absolute. *History and Theory*, 15, 109–132, 1976.

Mirvish, Adrian Michael, Merleau-Ponty and the Nature of Philosophy. *Philosophy and Phenomenological Research*, 43, 449–476, June 1983.

Monasterio, X.O., Paradoxes et Mythes de La Phénoménologie. *Revue de Métaphysique et de Morale*, 74, 268–280, July–September 1969.

Moran, Dermot, Heidegger's Phenomenology and the Destruction of Reason. *Irish Philosophy Journal*, 2, 15–35, Spring 1985.

Moreau, André, Merleau-Ponty et Berkeley. *Dialogue*, 5, 418–424, 1966.

Moreau, Joseph, *L'Horizon des Esprits: Essai Critique sur 'La Phénoménologie de la Perception'*. Paris: Presses Universitaires de France, 1960.

Moreland, John M., For-Itself and In-Itself in Sartre and Merleau-Ponty. *Philosophy Today*, 17, 311–318, Winter 1973.

Morita, Aki, La Situation de L'art en 'Endoontologie' de Merleau-Ponty (In Japanese). *Bigaku*, 40, 13–24, Summer 1989.

Morrison, James C., Merleau-Ponty and Literary Language. *International Studies in Philosophy*, 26(4), 69–83, 1994.

Morriston, Wesley, Perceptual Synthesis in the Philosophy of Merleau-Ponty. *Philosophical Research*, 3, no. 1129, 1977.

—— Experience and Causality in the Philosophy of Merleau-Ponty. *Philosophy and Phenomenological Research*, 39, 561–574, June 1979 and in *Phenomenology: Dialogues and Bridges*, Bruzina, Ronald (ed.), Albany: Suny Press, 1982.

Muldoon, Mark S., Time, Self, and Meaning in the Works of Henri Bergson, Maurice Merleau-Ponty, and Paul Ricœur. *Philosophy Today*, 254–268, Fall 1991.

Mullarkey, John C., Duplicity in the Flesh: Bergson and Current Philosophy of the Body. *Philosophy Today*, 38(4), 339–355, Winter 1994.

Munchow, Michael Hvid, Seeing Otherwise – Merleau-Ponty's Line. *Journal of the British Society for Phenomenology*, 25(1), 64–73, January 1994.

Munoz, Alberto Alonso, The Marxism and 'The Foundation of Human Sciences' (In Portuguese). *Discurso*, 21, 119–136, 1993.

Murphy, John W., Merleau-Ponty As Sociologist. *Philosophy Today*, 24, 104–113, Summer 1980.

Murphy, Richard T., A Metaphysical Critique of Method: Husserl and Merleau-Ponty. *Boston College Studies in Philosophy*, 1, 175–207, 1966.

Murungi, John, Merleau-Ponty's Perspective on Politics. *Man and World*, 14, 141–152, 1981.

Nagel, Chris, Sexualities: Merleau-Ponty and Foucault on the Meaning of Sex. *International Studies in Philosophy*, 27(1), 63–71, 1995.

Nebreda, Jesus Jose, Merleau-Ponty y La Fenomenologia del Lenguaje. *Pensamiento*, 38, 63–86, January–March 1982.

Nelson, Jenny L., Television and Its Audience as Dimensions of Being: Critical Theory and Phenomenology. *Human Studies*, 9, 55–69, 1986.

Nowaczyk, Jan, Das Gottesproblem bei Maurice Merleau-Ponty (In Polish). *Stud. Philosoph. Christ.*, 21, 79–110, 1985.

O'Connor, Dennis T., The Philosophy–Science Nexus in Early Merleau-Ponty, in *Continental Philosophy in America*, Silverman, Hugh et al. (eds), 189–207, Pittsburgh: Duquesne University Press, 1983.

O'Connor, Tony, Behaviour and Perception: a Discussion of Merleau-Ponty's Problem of Operative Intentionality. *Human Context*, 7, 39–48, Spring 1975.

—— Ambiguity and the Search for Origins. *Journal of the British Society for Phenomenology*, 9, 102–110, May 1978.

—— Merleau-Ponty and the Problem of the Unconscious, in *Merleau-Ponty: Perception, Structure, Language*, Sallis, John C. (ed.), 77–88, Atlantic Highlands: Humanities Press, 1981.

—— Categorizing the Body. *Journal of the British Society for Phenomenology*, 13, 226–236, October 1982.

—— Intentionality, Ontology, and Empirical Thought, in *Questioning Foundations*, Silverman, Hugh (ed.), New York: Routledge, 1993.

—— Foundations, Intentions and Competing Theories. *Journal of the British Society for Phenomenology*, 25(1), 14–26, January 1994.

Odin, Steve, *Process Metaphysics and Hua-Yen Buddhism: a Critical Study of Cumulative Penetration vs Interpenetration*. Albany: Suny Press, 1982.

Olafson, Frederick A., A Central Theme of Merleau-Ponty's Philosophy, in *Phenomenology and Existentialism*, E.N. Lee and M. Mandelbaum (eds), 179–205, London: Johns Hopkins Press, 1967.

—— Merleau-Ponty's 'Ontology of the Visible': Some Exegetical and Critical Comments. *Pacific Philosophical Quarterly*, 61, 167–176, January–April 1980.

Oliver, Kelly, The Gestation of the Other in Phenomenology. *Epoche*, 3(1 and 2), 79–116, 1995.

Olkowski, Dorothea, Merleau-Ponty's Freudianism: From the Body of Consciousness to the Body of Flesh. *Review of Existential Psychology and Psychiatry*, 18, 97–116, 1982–83.

—— Merleau-Ponty: the Demand for Mystery in Language. *Philosophy Today*, 31, 352–358, Winter 1987.

—— Merleau-Ponty and Bergson: the Character of the Phenomenal Field, in *Merleau-Ponty: Difference, Materiality, Painting*, Foti, Véronique, M. (ed.), New Jersey: Humanities Press, 1996.

O'Loughlin, Marjorie, Intelligent Bodies and Ecological Subjectivities: Merleau-Ponty's Corrective To Postmodernism's 'Subjects' of Education, in *Philosophy of Education*, Neiman, Alven (ed.), Urbana, 1995.

—— Ways of Thinking About Being: Explorations in Ontology. *Studies in Philosophy and Education*, 15(1–2), 139–145, January–April 1996.

Olson, Carl, The Human Body as a Boundary Symbol: a Comparison of Merleau-Ponty and Dōgen. *Philosophy East and West*, 36, 107–120, April 1986.

O'Neill, John, *Perception, Expression, and History: the Social Phenomenology of Maurice Merleau-Ponty*. Evanston: Northwestern University Press, 1970.

—— Can Phenomenology Be Critical? *Phil. of Sci.*, 2, 1–13, March 1972.

—— The Mother-Tongue: the Infant Search for Meaning. *Review of University Ottawa*, 55, 59–71, October–December 1985.

—— The Specular Body: Merleau-Ponty and Lacan on Infant Self and Other. *Synthèse*, 66, 201–217, February 1986.

—— *The Communicative Body*, Evanston: Northwestern University Press, 1989.

—— 'Merleau-Ponty's Critique of Marxist Scientism' in *Phenomenology and Marxism*, Waldenfels, Bernhard (ed.), London: Routledge and Kegan Paul.

Onyewuenyi, Innocent C., The Concept of God in Maurice Merleau-Ponty's Philosophy. *Second Order*, 5, 66–75, July 1976.

Ostrow, James, Habit and Inhabitance: An Analysis of Experience in the Classroom. *Human Studies*, 10, 213–224, 1987.

Palermo, James, Merleau-Ponty and Dewey On the 'Mind–Body' Question. *Proc. Philosoph. Educ.*, 34, 462–469, 1978.

Palmer, Michael D., On Language and Intersubjectivity. *Dialogue*, 24, 47–55, April 1982.

Panaccio, Claude, Structure et Signification dans L'œuvre de Merleau-Ponty. *Dialogue*, 9, 374–380, 1970.

Park, Ynhui, Merleau-Ponty et la Phénoménologie de Sens. *Revue de Métaphysique et de Morale*, 84, 343–365, July–September 1979.

—— Merleau-Ponty's Ontology of the Wild Being, in *Soul and Body in Phenomenology*, Tymieniecka, Anna-Teresa (ed.), 313–326, Dordrecht: Reidel, 1983.

Pax, Clyde, Merleau-Ponty and the Truth of History. *Man and World*, 6, 270–279, September 1973.

Penarando, Luz Pintos, Eidos-Factum: Lectura Merleau-Pontyana de un Fragmento de Husserl. *Revista de Filosofia* (Mexico), 28(84), 314–331, September–December 1995.

Peperzak, Adrian, Pointers Toward a Dialogic? *Man and World*, 9, 372–392, December 1976.

Perez Esteves, Antonio, *El Individuo y La Feminidad*. Zulia: University Zulia, 1989.

Pfeiffer, M.L., La Contingencia en Merleau-Ponty. *Stromata*, 29, 241–257, July–September 1973.

Phillips, James, Lacan and Merleau-Ponty: the Confrontation of Psychoanalysis and Phenomenology, in *Disseminating Lacan*, Pettigrew, David (ed.), Albany: Suny Press, 1996.

Pietersma, Henry, Merleau-Ponty and Spinoza. *International Studies in Philosophy*, 20, 89–93, 1988.

—— (ed.), *Merleau-Ponty: Critical Essays*, Washington DC: University Press of America, 1990.

—— Knowledge and Being in Merleau-Ponty. *Man and World*, 23(2), 205–223, April 1990.

—— Merleau-Ponty and the Problem of Knowledge, in *Critical and Dialectical Phenomenology*, Welton, Donn (ed.), 176–201, Albany: Suny Press.

Place, James Gordon, Merleau-Ponty and the Spirit of Painting. *Philosophy Today*, 17, 280–290, Winter 1973.

—— The Painting and the Natural Thing in the Philosophy of Merleau-Ponty. *Cultural Hermeneutics*, 4, 75–92, November 1976.

Plomer, Aurora, Merleau-Ponty on Sensations. *Journal of the British Society for Phenomenology*, 21(2), 153–163, May 1990.

Pochelu, Alicia G., El Caracter Viviente de la Relacion Yo-Tu, Segun Merleau-Ponty. *Logos* (Mexico), 20(59), 59–70, May–August 1992.

—— La Primacia de la Percepcion y del Mundo Vivido, in *Temas Actuales De Filosofia*, Palacios, Maria Julia (ed.), Buenos Aires: University Nacional Salta, 1993.

—— La Descentracion Vivida Como Instancia Decisiva en la Estructura de La Conciencia, Segun Maurice Merleau-Ponty. *Logos* (Mexico), 21(62), 109–121, May–August 1993.

—— El Origen de la Experiencia Humana. *Pensamiento*, 205(53), 113–125, January–April 1997.

Poole, Roger C., Indirect Communications: Merleau-Ponty and Lévis-Strauss. *New Blackfriars*, 47, no. 555, 504–604, 1966.

Popen, Shari, Merleau-Ponty Confronts Postmodernism: a Reply To O'Loughlin, in *Philosophy of Education*, Neiman, Alven (ed.), Urbana, 1995.

Preston, Beth, Merleau-Ponty and Feminine Embodied Existence. *Man and World*, 29(2), 167–186, April 1996.

Primozic, Daniel T., Merleau-Ponty's Ontology of the Lebenswelt. *Sw. Philosoph. Stud.*, 4, 47–50, April 1979.

Quinn, Andrew, Une Ethique du Regard: L'éthique Rationaliste du Structuralisme. *Laval. Theol. Phil.*, 49(3), 439–458, October 1993.

Rabil Jr, Albert, *Merleau-Ponty: Existentialist of the Social World*, New York: Columbia University Press, 1967.

Racette, Jean, Le Corps et L'Ame, La Chair et L'Esprit, selon Merleau-Ponty. *Dialogue*, 5, 346–359, 1966.

Ramirez, Mario Teodoro, La Fenomenologia de la Percepcion de Maurice Merleau-Ponty como Estetica. *Revista de Filosofia* (Mexico), 28(84), 332–362, September–December 1995.

Rauch, Leo, Sartre, Merleau-Ponty and the Hole in Being. *Philosophical Studies* (Ireland), 18, 119–132, 1969.

Raulet, Gérard, L'Equivoque de l'histoire: Ontologie ou Philosophie des Formes Symboliques – Bloch et Merleau-Ponty. *Man and World*, 28(1), 33–42, January 1995.

Regueira, Jose Blanco, Merleau-Ponty o La Agonia de La Subjetividad. *Revista de Filosofia* (Mexico), 28(84), 402–417, September–December 1995.

Reguera, Eduardo Bello, El Marxismo Heuristico de Merleau-Ponty. *Pensamiento*, 33, 269–296, July–September 1977.

Reineke, Martha J., Lacan, Merleau-Ponty, and Irigaray: Reflections on a Specular Drama. *Auslegung*, 14, 67–85, Winter 1987.

Rey, Dominique, L'Ontologie de Merleau-Ponty. *Review of Theol. Phil.*, 255–264, 1972.

—— Des Paroles inéditées 'Faisant Appel à des Zones Enfouies d'humanité Non-Dite'. *Frei Z. Philosoph. Theol.*, 31, 163–175, 1984.

—— La Phénoménologie Existentielle de Merleau-Ponty. *Frei Z. Philosoph. Theol.*, 35, 137–157, 1988.

Ricœur, Paul, Hommage à Merleau-Ponty. *Esprit*, no. 296, 1115–1120, 1961.

——, New Developments in Phenomenology, in *France: The Phenomenology of Language, Social Research*, 34, no. 1, 1–30, 1967.

Robinet, André, *Merleau-Ponty: sa vie, son œuvre, avec un éxposé de sa philosophie*. Paris: Presses Universitaires de France, 1963 (2nd edition 1970).

Rockmore, Tom, Merleau-Ponty, Marx, and Marxism: the Problem of History. *Studies in East European Thought*, 48(1), 63–81, March 1996.

Rohrbach, Augusta, Violence and the Visual: the Phenomenology of Vision and Racial Stereotyping. *International Studies in Philosophy*, 26(1), 71–82, 1994.

Rojo, Basilio, Palabra Sobre La Palabra. *Logos* (Mexico), 11, 95–114, January–April 1983.

Roman, Joel, Une Amitié Existentialiste: Sartre et Merleau-Ponty. *Review of Int. Phil.*, 39, 30–55, 1985.

—— Michelman, Stephen (trans.), Thinking Politics Without a Philosophy of History: Arendt and Merleau-Ponty. *Phil. of Crit.*, 15(4), 403–422, 1989.

Rosca, Ion, La Philosophie de l'histoire Chez Maurice Merleau-Ponty. *Phil. Log.*, 24, 433–443, October–December 1980.

Rosenthal, Abigail L., Getting Past Marx and Freud. *Clio*, 15, 61–82, Fall 1985.

Rosenthal, Sandra B., *Mead and Merleau-Ponty: Toward a Common Vision*, Albany: Suny Press, 1991.

Rosenthal, Sandra and Bourgeois, Patrick L., Mead, Merleau-Ponty and the Lived Perceptual World. *Philosophy Today*, 21, 56–61, Spring 1977.

—— Merleau-Ponty, Lewis and Ontological Presence. *Philosophical Topics*, 13, 239–246, Spring 1985.

—— Mead and Merleau-Ponty: Meaning, Perception, and Behavior, in *Analecta Husserliana*, XXXI, Tymieniecka, Anna-Teresa (ed.), Dordrecht: Kluwer, 1990.

—— The World of Truth: Merleau-Ponty and Mead. *Southwestern Philosophical Review*, 10(2), 49–58, July 1994.

—— Pragmatism and Phenomenology. *Southern Journal of Philosophy*, 18, 481–487, Winter 1980.

—— Peirce and Merleau-Ponty: Beyond the Noumenal–Phenomenal Break. *Proceedings of the Catholic Philosophical Association*, 59, 299–307, 1985.

—— Peirce, Merleau-Ponty, and Perceptual Experience: a Kantian Heritage. *International Studies in Philosophy*, 19, 33–42, Fall 1987.

—— Meaning and Human Behavior: Mead and Merleau-Ponty. *Southern Journal of Philosophy*, 26, 339–349, Fall 1988.

—— Sensation, Perception and Immediacy: Mead and Merleau-Ponty. *Southwestern Philosophical Review*, 6(1), 105–111, January 1990.

—— The Philosophy of the Act and the Phenomenology of Perception: Mead and Merleau-Ponty. *Southern Journal of Philosophy*, 28(1), 77–90, Spring 1990.

Ross, Howard, Merleau-Ponty and Jean-Paul Sartre on the Nature of Consciousness. *Cogit*, 3, 115–121, December 1985.

Rosthal, Robert B., France, in *Handbook of World Philosophy*, Burr, John R. (ed.), 33–97, Westport: Greenwood Press, 1980.

Rottgers, Kurt, The Surface of the Soul (In Czech). *Filozof. Cas.*, 41(4), 564–583, 1993.

Rouse, Joseph, Merleau-Ponty and the Existential Conception of Science. *Synthèse*, 66, 249–272, February 1986.

Russon, John, Embodiment and Responsibility: Merleau-Ponty and the Ontology of Nature. *Man and World*, 27(3), 291–308, July 1994.

Russow, Lilly-Marlene, Merleau-Ponty and the Myth of Bodily Intentionality. *Nous*, 22, 35–47, March 1988.

Rust, Holger, Methodologie und Geschichte: Ansatze Problemorientierter Gesellschaftsanalysen. *Arch. Rechts. Soz.*, 61, 305–324, 1975.

Said, Edward K., Labyrinth of Incarnation: The Essays of Merleau-Ponty. *Kenyon Review*, 29, no. 1, 54–68, January 1967.

Sallis, John, *Phenomenology and the Return To Beginnings*, New York: Duquesne University Press, 1973.

—— (ed.), *Merleau-Ponty: Perception, Structure, Language*, Atlantic Highlands: Humanities Press, 1981.

Salsa, Annibale, Life-World as a Moral Problem in Merleau-Ponty, in *Morality Within the Life and Social World*, Tymieniecka, Anna-Teresa (ed.), Dordrecht: Kluwer.

Sanabria, Jose Ruben, Maurice Merleau-Ponty Fenomenologo Existencial. *Revista de Filosofia* (Mexico), 21, 23–44, January–April 1988.

—— Fenomenologia de La Percepcion? Ontologia de La Percepcion? *Revista de Filosofia* (Mexico), 28(84), 363–401, September–December 1995.

Sanders, John T., Merleau-Ponty, Gibson, and the Materiality of Meaning. *Man and World*, 26(3), 287–302, July 1993.

—— Merleau-Ponty on Meaning, Materiality and Structure. *Journal of the British Society for Phenomenology*, 25(1), 96–100, January 1994.

Sapontzis, S.F., A Note on Merleau-Ponty's 'Ambiguity'. *Philosophy and Phenomenological Research*, 38, 538–543, June 1978.

—— Merleau-Ponty, Myth-Maker or Philosopher. *Philosophical Studies* (Ireland), 26, 41–55, 1979.

Sartre, Jean-Paul, Merleau-Ponty. *Journal of the British Society for Phenomenology*, 15, 128–154, May 1984.

—— Merleau-Ponty. *Review of Int. Phil.*, 39, 3–29, 1985.

Scharfstein, Ben-Ami, Bergson and Merleau-Ponty: a Preliminary Comparison. *Journal of Philosophy*, 52, 380–385, July 1955.

Schenck, David, Meaning and/or Materiality: Merleau-Ponty's Notions of Structure. *Journal of the British Society for Phenomenology*, 15, 34–50, January 1984.

—— Merleau-Ponty on Perspectivism, with References to Nietzsche. *Philosophy and Phenomenological Research*, 46, 307–314, December 1985.

Schmidt, James, Lordship and Bondage in Merleau-Ponty and Sartre. *Political Theory*, 7, 201–227, May 1979.

—— *Maurice Merleau-Ponty: Between Phenomenology and Structuralism*. New York: St Martin's Press, 1985.

Schmied-Kowarzik, Wolfdietrich, The Sketch of a Critical Philosophy of Social Praxis (In Yugoslavian). *Filozof. Istraz*, 22, 833–851, 1987.

Schmitt, Richard, Maurice Merleau-Ponty, I. *Review of Metaphysics*, 19, 728–741, June 1966.

—— Maurice Merleau-Ponty, II. *Review of Metaphysics*, 19, 493–516, March 1966.

Schrader, George Alfred (ed.), *Existential Philosophers: Kierkegaard to Merleau-Ponty*, New York: McGraw-Hill, 1967.

Schrag, Calvin O., The Phenomenon of Embodied Speech. *Philosophical Forum*, 7, 3–27, June 1969.

Schreiber, Alfred, Methodenkritische Uberlegungen Zu Merleau-Ponty Phänomenologie Der Raumerfahrung. *Philosophia Naturalis*, 18, 423–437, 1981.

Schroeder, Brian, *Altared Ground: Levinas, History, and Violence*, New York: Routledge, 1996.

Sebastian Garcia, Pablo, Percepcion y Corporalidad: Sobre una Lectura Posible de Merleau-Ponty. *Revista de Filosofia* (Argentina), 10(1–2), 67–73, November 1995.

Shapiro, Eleanor M., Perception and Dialectic. *Human Studies*, 1, 245–267, July 1978.

Shapiro, Kenneth Joel, *Bodily Reflective Modes: a Phenomenological Method For Psychology*, Durham: Duke University Press, 1985.

Sheets, Maxine, *The Phenomenology of Dance*, Madison: University of Wisconsin Press, 1966.

Sheets-Johnstone, Maxine, Existential Fit and Evolutionary Continuities. *Synthèse*, 66, 219–248, February 1986.

Sherburne, Donald W., Whitehead's Psychological Physiology. *Southern Journal of Philosophy*, 7, 401–407, Winter 1969–70.

Sheridan, James F., On Ontology and Politics, a Polemic. *Dialogue*, 7, 449–460, December 1968.

Siegel, Jerrold, A Unique Way of Existing: Merleau-Ponty and the Subject. *Journal of the History of Philosophy*, 455–480, July 1991.

Silverman, Hugh J., Re-Reading Merleau-Ponty. *Telos*, 29, 106–129, Fall 1976.

—— Heidegger and Merleau-Ponty: Interpreting Hegel. *Research in Phenomenology*, 7, 209–224, 1977.

—— Imagining, Perceiving, and Remembering. *Humanitas*, 14, 197–207, May 1978.

—— Merleau-Ponty on Language and Communication (1947–1948). *Research in Phenomenology*, 9, 168–181, 1979.

—— Merleau-Ponty and the Interrogation of Language, in *Merleau-Ponty: Perception, Structure, Language*, Sallis, John C. (ed.), Atlantic Highlands: Humanities Press, 1981.

—— Merleau-Ponty's New Beginning: Preface to the Experience of Others. *Review of Existential Psychology and Psychiatry*, 18, 25–31, 1982–83.

—— The Text of the Speaking Subject: From Merleau-Ponty To Kristeva, in *Merleau-Ponty Vivant*, Dillon, M.C. (ed.), Albany: Suny Press, 1991.

—— Merleau-Ponty and Derrida: Writing on Writing, in *Ontology and Alterity in Merleau-Ponty*. Johnson and Smith (eds), Evanston: Northwestern University Press, 1991.

—— Traces of the Sublime: Visibility, Expressivity, and the Unconscious, in *Merleau-Ponty: Difference, Materiality, Painting*, Foti, Véronique, M. (ed.), New Jersey: Humanities Press, 1996.

Silverman, Hugh J., *et al.* (eds), *The Horizons of Continental Philosophy: Essays On Husserl, Heidegger, and Merleau-Ponty*, Dordrecht: Kluwer, 1988.

Sinari, Ramakant, The Phenomenology of Maurice Merleau-Ponty. *Philosophical Quarterly* (India), 39, 129–140, July 1966.

Singer, Linda, Merleau-Ponty on the Concept of Style. *Man and World*, 14, 153–163, 1981.

Singh, Ravindra M. A Case For Phenomenological Realism. *Journal of the Indian Counc. Philosoph. Res.*, 12(3), 97–109, May–August 1995.

Sivak, Jozef, The Concept of Sense in Merleau-Ponty (In Czech). *Filozof. Cas.*, 772–787, 1990.

Slaughter Jr, Thomas F., Some Remarks on Merleau-Ponty's Essay 'Cézanne's Doubt'. *Man and World*, 12, 61–69, 1979.

Smith, Andrew R., Phrasing, Linking, Judging: Communication and Critical Phenomenology. *Human Studies*, 17(1), 139–161, January 1994.

Smith, Colin, The Notion of Object in the Phenomenology of Merleau-Ponty. *Philosophy*, 39, 110–119, April 1964.

—— *Contemporary French Philosophy, a Study in Norms and Values*. New York: Barnes and Noble, 1964.

—— Sartre and Merleau-Ponty: the Case for a Modified Essentialism. *Journal of the British Society for Phenomenology*, 1, 73–79, May 1970.

—— Merleau-Ponty and Structuralism. *Journal of the British Society for Phenomenology*, 2, 46–52, October 1971.

Smith, Dale E., Language and the Genesis of Meaning in Merleau-Ponty. *Kinesis*, 8, 44–58, Fall 1977.

—— Merleau-Ponty's Indirect Ontology. *Dialogue*, 27, 615–635, Winter 1988.

Smith, David Woodruff, Bodily Versus Cognitive Intentionality. *Nous*, 22, 51–52, March 1988.

Smith, Michael B., L'Esthetique de Merleau-Ponty. *Les Etudes Philosophiques*, 1, 73–98, 1988.

—— Two Texts On Merleau-Ponty By Emmanuel Levinas, in Johnson and Smith (eds), *Ontology and Alterity in Merleau-Ponty*, Evanston: Northwestern University Press, 1991.

Spicker, Stuart F., Inner Time and Lived-Through Time: Husserl and Merleau-

Ponty. *Journal of the British Society for Phenomenology*, 4, 235–247, October 1973.

Stack, George J., Sexuality and Bodily Subjectivity. *Dialogos*, 15, 139–153, April 1980.

Stapp, Henry Pierce, Quantum Mechanics, Local Causality, and Process Philosophy. *Process Studies*, 7, 173–182, Fall 1977.

Steinbock, Anthony J., Merleau-Ponty's Concept of Death. *Philosophy Today*, 31, 336–351, Winter 1987.

—— Reflections on Earth and World: Merleau-Ponty's Project of Transcendental History and Transcendental Geology, in *Merleau-Ponty: Difference, Materiality, Painting*, Foti, Véronique, M. (ed.), New Jersey: Humanities Press, 1996.

Stenstad, Gail, Merleau-Ponty's Logos: the Sens-Ing of Flesh. *Philosophy Today*, 37(1), 52–61, Spring 1993.

Stewart, Jon, Merleau-Ponty's Criticisms of Sartre's Theory of Freedom. *Philosophy Today*, 39(3–4), 311–324, Fall 1995.

Strasser, Stephen, Erotiek En Vruchtbaarheid in de Filosofie van Emmanuel Levinas. *Tijdschr Filosof*, 37, 3–51, March 1975.

—— *Understanding and Explanation: Basic Ideas Concerning the Humanity of the Human Sciences*, Pittsburgh: Duquesne University Press, 1985.

—— Réhabilitation de L'interiorité: Réflexions sur la Dernière Philosophie de Merleau-Ponty. *Revue Philosophique de Louvain*, 84, 502–520, November 1986.

Stroker, Elisabeth, *Phänomenologische Philosophie*. Germany: Alber, 1991.

Struyker Boudier, C.E.M., Genese, Struktuur en zin van het Verstaan (Zusammenfassung: Entstehen, Struktur Und Sinn Des Verstehens, P 109). *Tijdschr Filosof*, 40, 78–110, March 1978.

Sturani, E., Letture di Merleau-Ponty. *Rivista di Filosofia*, 58, 164–182, April–June 1967.

Sullivan, Shannon, Domination and Dialogue in Merleau-Ponty's 'Phenomenology of Perception'. *Hypatia*, 12(1), 1–19, Winter 1997.

Tagore, Saranindranath, The Echo of Silence: Toward a Reconstruction of Merleau-Ponty's Philosophy of History. *International Philosophical Quarterly*, 427–434, December 1991.

Taminiaux, J., Merleau-Ponty: De la dialectique à l'hyperdialectique. *Tijdschr Filosof*, 40, 34–55, March 1978. Published in translation as Merleau-Ponty: From Dialectic to Hyperdialectic, in *Merleau-Ponty: Perception, Structure, Language*, Sallis, John C. (ed.), Atlantic Highlands: Humanities Press, 1981.

—— The Thinker and the Painter in *Merleau-Ponty Vivant*, Dillon, M.C. (ed.), Albany: Suny Press, 1991.

Taylor, Charles, The Validity of Transcendental Arguments. *Proceedings of the Aristotelian Society*, 79, 151–165, 1978.

Theobald, D.W., Philosophy and Fiction: the Novel As Eloquent Philosophy. *British Journal of Aesthetics*, 14, 17–25, Winter 1974.

Tibbetts, Paul, Mead, Phenomenalism and Phenomenology. *Philosophy Today*, 17, 329–336, Winter 1973.

Tiemersma, Douwe, 'Body-Image' and 'Body-Schema' in the Existential Phenomenology of Merleau-Ponty. *Journal of the British Society for Phenomenology*, 13, 246–255, October 1982.

—— Phenomenology and the Foundation of Medicine: Structures of the Lived Body and Life-World and the Moral A Priori. *Man and World*, 16, 105–112, 1983.

—— Merleau-Ponty's Philosophy as a Field Theory: Its Origin, Categories and Relevance. *Man and World*, 20, 419–436, October 1987.

Tilliette, Xavier, *Merleau-Ponty ou la mesure de l'homme*, Paris: Seghers, 1970.

Toombs, S. Kay, Illness and the Paradigm of Lived Body. *Theoretical Medicine*, 9, 201–226, June 1988.

Townsley, A.L., Rosmini and Merleau-Ponty: Being, Perception and the World. *Rivista di Filosofia Neoscolastica*, 68, 75–84, January–March 1976.

Tuedio, James Alan, Merleau-Ponty's Rejection of the Husserlian Ideal of a Rigorous Science. *Philosophy Today*, 25, 204–209, Fall 1981.

—— Merleau-Ponty's Refinement of Husserl. *Philosophy Today*, 29, 99–109, Summer 1985.

Valdes, Mario, *Shadows in the Cave: a Phenomenological Approach to Literary Criticism Based on Hispanic Texts*, Toronto: University of Toronto Press, 1982.

Van Der Veken, J. Zien: Spreken: Denken. *Tijdschr Filosof*, 40, 3–33, March 1978.

—— Merleau-Ponty on Ultimate Problems of Rationality. *Ultimate Reality and Meaning*, 12, 202–209, September 1989.

Van Hooft, Stan, Merleau-Ponty and the Problem of Intentional Explanation. *Philosophy and Phenomenological Research*, 40, 33–52, September 1979.

Van Peursen, C.A., *Body, Soul, Spirit*. Oxford: Oxford University Press, 1966.

Vandenbussche, Frans, The Idea of God in Merleau-Ponty. *International Philosophical Quarterly*, 7, 45–67, March 1967.

Vangroenweghe, Daniel, M Merleau-Ponty En F de Saussure. *Tijdschr Filosof*, 35, 455–467, September 1973.

Varela, Charles R., Harre and Merleau-Ponty: Beyond the Absent Moving Body in Embodied Social Theory. *Journal of the Theor. S. of Behav.*, 24(2), 167–185, June 1994.

Vazquez Sanchez, J., La Semantica Fenomenologica de Merleau-Ponty. *An. Seminar. Metaf.*, 17, 61–84, 1982.

Ver Eecke, Wilfried, Interpretation and Perception. *International Philosophical Quarterly*, 11, 372–384, September 1971.

Virasoro, Manuel, Merleau-Ponty and the World of Perception. *Philosophy Today*, 3, 66–72, Spring 1959.

Waldenfels, Bernhard, Towards an Open Dialectic. *Dialogue and Humanism*, 3, 91–101, Winter 1976.

—— *Dialogue and Discourses in Writing the Politics of Difference*, Albany: Suny Press, 1991.

—— Vérité à Faire: Merleau-Ponty's Question Concerning Truth. *Philosophy Today*, 185–194, Summer 1991.

—— Respuesta a Lo Ajeno: Sobre La Relacion Entre La Cultura Propia y La Cultura Ajena. *Revista de Filosofia* (Costa Rica), 30(71), 1–6, 92.

—— Hearing Oneself Speak: Derrida's Recording of the Phenomenological Voice. *Southern Journal of Philosophy*, 32 (Supplement), 65–77, 1994.

Walsh, Robert D., An Organism of Words: Ruminations on the Philosophical-Poetics of Merleau-Ponty. *Kinesis*, 14, 13–41, Fall 1984.

Walton, Roberto J., El Sujeto Hablante y La Dominacion del Lenguaje. *Cuad. Filosof.*, 8, 81–89, January–June 1968.

—— Merleau-Ponty y El Problema del Tiempo. *Cuad. Filosof.*, 10, 77–98, January–June 1970.

Warren, Scott, *The Emergence of Dialectical Theory: Philosophy and Political Inquiry*, Chicago: University of Chicago Press, 1984.

Watson, Stephen, Language, Perception and the Cogito in Ponty's Thought, in *Merleau-Ponty: Perception, Structure, Language*, Sallis, John C. (ed.), Atlantic Highlands: Humanities Press, 1981.

—— Merleau-Ponty's Involvement with Saussure, in *Continental Philosophy in America*, Silverman, Hugh *et al.* (eds), 208–226, Pittsburgh: Duquesne University Press, 1983.

—— Merleau-Ponty and Foucault: De-aestheticization of the Work of Art. *Philosophy Today*, 28, 148–167, Summer 1984.

—— Cancellations: Notes On Merleau-Ponty's Standing Between Hegel and Husserl. *Research in Phenomenology*, 17, 191–209, 1987.

—— On How We Are and How We Are Not To Return To The Things Themselves, in *Ontology and Alterity in Merleau-Ponty*, Johnson and Smith (eds), Evanston: Northwestern University Press, 1991.

Weiner, Scott E., Inhabiting, in the Phenomenology of Perception. *Philosophy Today*, 342–353, Winter 1990.

Weiss, Allen S., Merleau-Ponty's Interpretation of Husserl's Phenomenological Reduction. *Philosophy Today*, 27, 342–351, Winter 1983.

Weiss, Gail, Ambiguity, Absurdity, and Reversibility: Responses to Indeterminacy. *Journal of the British Society for Phenomenology*, 26(1), 43–51, January 1995.

Welch, Cyril, A Preface To Reading. *Philosophy and Rhetoric*, 14, 31–50, Winter 1981.

Wertz, Frederick J., Merleau-Ponty and the Cognitive Psychology of Perception, in *Critical and Dialectical Phenomenology*, Welton, Donn (ed.), 265–284, Albany: Suny Press.

Westphal, Merold, Situation and Suspicion in the Thought of Merleau-Ponty, in *Ontology and Alterity in Merleau-Ponty*, Johnson and Smith (eds), Evanston: Northwestern University Press, 1991.

Whitehead, Margaret, Meaningful Existence, Embodiment and Physical Education. *Journal of the Philosophy of Education*, 3–13, Summer 1990.

Whiteside, Kerry, The Merleau-Ponty Bibliography: Additions and Corrections. *Journal of the History of Philosophy*, 21, 195–202, April 1983.

—— Perspectivism and Historical Objectivity: Maurice Merleau-Ponty's Covert Debate with Raymond Aron. *History and Theory*, 25, 132–151, May 1986.

—— Universality and Violence: Merleau-Ponty, Malraux, and the Moral Logic of Liberalism. *Philosophy Today*, 35(4), 372–389, Winter 1991.

Whitford, Margaret, Merleau-Ponty's Critique of Sartre's Philosophy. *Lexington French Forum*, 1982.

Wiggins, Osborne P., Merleau-Ponty and Piaget: An Essay in Philosophical Psychology. *Man and World*, 12, 21–34, 1979.

—— Merleau-Ponty's Phenomenological Ethics. *Graduate Faculty Philosophy Journal*, 10, 43–56, Winter 1985.

—— Political Responsibility in Merleau-Ponty's 'Humanism and Terror'. *Man and World*, 19, 275–291, 1986.

Williams, Linda L., Merleau-Ponty's Tacit Cogito. *Man and World*, 23(1), 101–111, January 1990.

Wilshire, Bruce, The Phenomenology of Language. *Journal of the British Society for Phenomenology*, 9, 130–133, May 1978.

Wing-Chchan, Wing-Cheuk, Phenomenology and Communicative Ethics, in *Morality Within the Life and Social World*, Tymieniecka, Anna-Teresa (ed.), Dordrecht: Kluwer.

Wirt, Cliff Engle, The Concept of Ecstasis. *Journal of the British Society for Phenomenology*, 14, 79–90, January 1983.

Wolin, Richard, Merleau-Ponty and the Birth of Weberian Marxism. *Praxis International*, 5, 115–130, July 1985.

Wylleman, A., La Philosophie et Les Expériences Naturelles (In Dutch). *Tijdschr Filosof*, 46, 5–18, March 1984.

Wyschogrod, Edith, Exemplary Individuals: Towards a Phenomenological Ethics. *Philosophy and Theology*, 1, 9–31, Fall 1986.

—— Does Continental Ethics Have a Future?, in *Ethics and Danger*, Dallery, Arleen B. (ed.), Albany: Suny Press, 1992.

Yamazak, Masakazui, Histrionics and Body (In Japanese). *Bigaku*, 27, 41, December 1976.

Yolton, John W., *Thinking and Perceiving: a Study in the Philosophy of Mind.* La Salle: Open Court, 1961.

—— Agent Causality. *American Philosophical Quarterly*, 3, 14–26, January 1966.

Young, Iris Marion, Throwing Like a Girl: a Phenomenology of Feminine Body Comportment Motility and Spatiality. *Human Studies*, 3, 137–156, April 1980.

Yount, Mark, Two Reversibilities: Merleau-Ponty and Derrida. *Philosophy Today*, 129–140, Summer 1990.

Zaner, R.M. *The Problem of Embodiment; Some Contributions to a Phenomenology of the Body*, The Hague: Nijhoff, 1964.

—— Merleau-Ponty's Theory of the Body-Proper as 'Etre-Au-Monde'. *Journal of Existentialism*, 6, 31–40, Fall 1965.

Zaytzeff, Véronique, Merleau-Ponty and Pseudo-Sartreanism. *International Studies in Philosophy*, 21(3), 3–47, 1989.

Zenzen, Michael J., The Suggestive Power of Color. *Journal of Aesthetics and Art Criticism*, 36, 185–190, Winter 1977.

Index